THE RELIGIOUS PROBLEM

IN ENGLISH EDUCATION

The Crucial Experiment

THE RELIGIOUS PROBLEM IN ENGLISH EDUCATION

The Crucial Experiment

by

JAMES MURPHY

Lecturer in Education
in the University of Liverpool

LIVERPOOL UNIVERSITY PRESS

1959

Published by

LIVERPOOL UNIVERSITY PRESS

123 Grove Street · Liverpool 7

© Copyright 1959 by
James Murphy

First published 1959

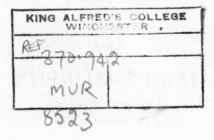
PRINTED AND BOUND IN ENGLAND BY
HAZELL WATSON AND VINEY LTD
AYLESBURY AND SLOUGH

ACKNOWLEDGMENTS

I WISH to acknowledge my indebtedness to Professor A. J. D. Porteous, who read the typescript with a scholarly care worthy of a better book; to Professor F. E. Hyde, Dr T. Kelly and Mr J. J. Bagley for friendly interest and encouragement; to the late Mrs Hugh Rathbone for permission to consult and quote from the *Rathbone Family Papers*; to Mr J. G. O'Kane, of Liverpool University Press, whose efficiency and advice proved so helpful; to the University of Liverpool for helping to make publication possible; and, above all, to my wife.

J. M.

CONTENTS

'THE United Kingdom is so much interested in Education that it is desirable that the proceedings at Liverpool should be diffused throughout the whole empire, especially as she is certainly taking the lead upon the great and important subject of national education.'

The Sun (London), 13 November 1837.

'. . . he trusted that the future historian would have to say that the Town Council of Liverpool had the honour of introducing this system of education into England, and that it rapidly spread throughout the empire, where it had scattered, and would scatter, innumerable blessings.'

THOMAS BLACKBURN, 23 November 1836.

'BUT it may be urged that this is a small matter, why ascribe so much importance to two schools in the town of Liverpool? . . . This is no local matter. It begins in Liverpool it is true. It must have a local commencement. But it cannot end where it begins. It is a feeler of the national pulse.'

REV. HUGH M'NEILE, 3 July 1836.

Chapter 1

THE LIVERPOOL CORPORATION SCHOOLS

I

THOSE who are familiar with the history of the long and bitter struggle to set up in England and Wales a system of elementary education financed and controlled by state or municipal authorities may be surprised to find that for more than forty years before the passing of the Education Act of 1870 two elementary schools in Liverpool were maintained from municipal funds and managed by an 'Education Committee' chosen by the local Council. S. E. Maltby has claimed, with justifiable civic pride, that during almost the whole of the period 1800–70 'no other single place was so much the focus of educational interest and the hotbed of educational proposals as Manchester and its neighbourhood'[1]; perhaps, however, it is worth remarking that Liverpool had quietly begun to provide municipal elementary schools before the agitation for the establishment of such schools had got well into its stride. Yet what is almost as remarkable as the founding and long continuance of the Liverpool Corporation Schools is the fact that historians of education seem to have been unaware of their existence; whilst even local historians appear to have considered the schools important only because differences of opinion concerning them had some influence on local politics,[2] especially during the years 1836–42. One of the schools—to this day known as the North Corporation School—is still in existence; but even those most closely associated with it are astonished to learn that it was once the cause of acrimonious disputes in places far beyond the boundaries of Liverpool, and even in Parliament itself.

The truth is that the schools were at one time the scene of an important educational experiment quite deliberately carried out by men anxious to demonstrate, in what was then claimed to be 'the second city of the Empire', that children of all sects might well be

---

[1] *Manchester and the Movement for National Elementary Education, 1800–1870*, Manchester, 1918, Preface, p. vi.

[2] T. Burke, in his *Catholic History of Liverpool*, Liverpool, 1910, p. 60, mentions that the schools were visited by 'the Bishop of Norwich, Mr Charles E. Trevelyan and Lord Russell'; but he gives no details. So far as the present writer is aware, this is the only indication given by any historian that the schools were ever considered of interest outside the town.

educated together in publicly owned elementary schools; and that therefore the 'Religious Problem', so often said to be insoluble, ought no longer to deter the government of the day from establishing a national system of elementary education. How close the experiment came to succeeding the reader may judge for himself. The purpose of this book is to show how the experiment came to be made, how it proceeded, what interest and excitement it aroused, and in what respects it influenced—and was influenced by—the opinions and the course of events of the period under review. It is hoped that the account will throw some light on the origins of the 'Religious Problem' as we know it in England today.

2

The circumstances which led to the decision that two elementary schools should be provided out of the town's revenues merit some attention. Liverpool's old Free Grammar School,[1] which had been maintained by the Common Council, ceased to exist in or about the year 1803, and from time to time thereafter proposals were made that the Council should provide a new grammar school for the sons of freemen. All these proposals came to nothing, and probably few people were impressed when, on 22 October 1824, the Select Finance Committee appointed a sub-committee, known as the Free Grammar School Committee,[2] to prepare yet another report on the possibility of building a grammar school. Suddenly, however, the atmosphere changed. On 3 November 1824 the newly elected Mayor, Mr J. B. Hollinshead, proposed, and the Council agreed, that the Free Grammar School Committee, which had been appointed barely a fortnight before, should be asked to consider 'the propriety of establishing one or more Schools for the purpose of educating the Children of indigent Parents according to the Faith and Practice of the Church of England in lieu of the re-establishment of the Free Grammar School.'[3] The *Liverpool Mercury*,[4] in its account of the proceedings, reported that the Mayor had advocated the setting up of 'one or more national schools, connected with the Establishment, at which the children of the indigent

---

[1] For a full account of the history of this school, see Henry A. Ormerod, *The Liverpool Free School (1515–1803)*, Liverpool, 1951.

[2] The members of the Committee were Alderman Thomas Case, Alderman Wright, Mr Peter Bourne and Mr W. W. Currie. It became the first Education Committee of the Liverpool Council; yet its early transactions were considered so unimportant that the minutes were found in an old MS. volume labelled *Committee Book on Town Dues, Leasing, Premises to Sell, Town Duties on Hides, etc., Threlfall's false entries, Free Schools*. This volume will be referred to henceforward as *'Minutes of Schools Committee'*.

[3] *Proceedings of Council*, Vol. XV, p. 472.

[4] 5 November 1824.

inhabitants might be instructed in more useful branches of learning than Latin and Greek'.

The Free Grammar School Committee resolved unanimously, and with alacrity, that no Free Grammar School should be built, and recommended instead that 'two Schools (one at the North, the other at the South end of the Town)' should be established in accordance with the suggestion of the Council and that 'provision should be made in each of these Schools for 400 Boys & 300 Girls'.[1] By March 1825 the Committee, now called the 'Sub-Committee on the Subject of the Free Schools', had recommended the purchase of one piece of land near Bevington Hill to form the site of the North School, and another, 'now occupied as a Timber Yard, opposite the end of Tabley Street, fronting Park Lane', on which to build the South School.[2] The Council, which had spent so long considering the possibility of building a grammar school, wasted no time in setting up its two elementary schools: the South Corporation School was opened on 22 January 1827,[3] and the North Corporation School on 23 April of the same year.[4]

It would appear that Liverpool founded its two Corporation Schools more or less as the result of a sudden impulse, and certainly without considering the difficulties which later prevented the general establishment of such schools elsewhere. That the members of the Council felt the step to be a wise one is obvious from the fact that they accepted the Mayor's proposal with such readiness and saw to it that there was no delay in building the schools. But it seems certain that the schools would never have come into existence had not one of the local clergy addressed a direct appeal to the Council to concern itself with the education of the poor in accordance with the principles of the Established Church. The circumstances were as follows. In June 1824 there took place the annual procession of the children attending the Church of England Sunday-schools, and the Rev. W. Hesketh, Minister of St Michael's, Toxteth, preached in the presence of 'the Mayor, Bailiffs and other Gentlemen'. The congregation was small, and Hesketh was shocked that so few adult members of the Church of England evinced any interest in the event: 'Scarcely could a Committee be brought together for its suitable arrangement; and when the day of celebration

---

[1] *Minutes of Schools Committee*, p. 40.

[2] *Ibid.*, pp. 43, 44.

[3] *Minutes of Schools Committee*, p. B5. (Some of the minutes are to be found at the *back* of the volume, and there is some repetition of page numbers. In order to avoid confusion the writer will refer to those pages at the *back* of the volume as if they were numbered B1, B2, etc.)

[4] Advertisement in *Liverpool Mercury*, 13 April 1827.

did arrive, there was not in this *"boasted* union of Church and State" a dozen persons to wait upon the Mayor. The procession through the public streets was a burlesque on the establishment; the want of courtesy towards the Chief Magistrate, who presided *ex officio*, a reflection on the town: the church itself was nearly empty; and the collection (on any other computation than that of the *few present*) a mere nothing.'[1]

Shortly afterwards Hesketh published a pamphlet in which he complained of the indifference made manifest on this occasion, and appealed to the clergy and laity of the town to be more active in setting up schools connected with the Church of England, pointing out that whilst the Dissenters had done much for the education of their children 'the means by which the children of the lower orders connected with the church are educated in Liverpool are undignified and totally inefficient'. He went on to declare that 'There are no Sunday-schools or day schools attached to either of the Parish Churches; there are none to St Paul's, St John's, St Thomas's, or St George's, though these churches have all been built by the Corporation.' Finally he made a direct proposal to the Council that they should provide an elementary school:

I confidently appeal to the 'Chartered Body of the Town' to assist us in this work; I look to them to lay the first stone and foundation of a building corresponding in munificence and superior in importance to those which now exist. In so laudable an undertaking, I am sure they would have the co-operation and the assistance of every individual well affected towards the church, and even were it deemed more worthy of their station to make such work exclusively their own, an institution thus endowed would serve as a rallying point and bulwark for the annual contribution of parishioners; and if the building were made capable of giving instruction to a thousand children, a thousand children might, I am sure, be found 'in the daily ministration of the clergy' thankful to receive such bounty.

There can be little doubt that the Mayor's unexpected proposal and the Council's ready assent to it constituted the prompt reply of the 'Chartered Body of the Town' to Hesketh's 'Appeal'.

3

On 27 December 1826 the 'Sub-committee on the subject of the Free Schools' met at the request of the Council and drafted 'Rules and Regulations for the general Management of the Schools'. It was

[1] Rev. W. Hesketh, *An Appeal to the Clergy and Laity of the Town of Liverpool, in Behalf of the National & Ancient Systems of Charity Connected with the Established Church,* Liverpool, MDCCCXXIV, pp. 12–13. The apathy displayed on this occasion was complained of also in *Gore's General Advertiser* of 24 June 1824.

decided that the schools, which would admit boys from the age of seven and girls from the age of six, should be conducted 'upon Dr Bell's System as detailed in his "Manual for conducting schools thro' the agency of the Scholars themselves".' The boys were to be taught 'reading, writing, English Grammar and Arithmetic—the girls the same, with the addition of sewing, Marking and Knitting'. The schools were 'to open and close with prayers', and the children were to assemble 'on Sunday and on Good Friday & Christmas Day at a quarter before ten in the morning and a quarter before two in the afternoon to proceed with the Master and Mistress to Church'. The 'Committee for the Superintendance of the Schools' was to consist of seven members of the Common Council, the two Rectors of Liverpool (the Rev. Jonathan Brooks and the Rev. Augustus Campbell), 'the Ministers of St George's Church for the time being and the Minister for the time being from each of the Churches at which the Children may attend'.

The schools were to be publicly examined by the Committee at least once in every half-year, and children were to be admitted 'by the Committee only'. It was considered 'essential for the well con-ducting of the Schools to have but one official Visitor, who should take upon himself this task with a view to secure uniformity in the Practical application of the System, and the instruction and discipline of the Schools'; although 'the assistance of Weekly Visitors would be highly advantageous, provided they direct their attention to the general state of the Schools only'. The Master and Mistress were 'to have the entire control of their respective Schools, as to the application of the System, and Correction of the Children, subject nevertheless to the suggestions of the Visitor'.[1] The 'Rules and Regulations' were duly approved by the Council on 3 January 1827, and the lay members of the 'Schools Committee' were at once chosen; to the four original members of what had begun as 'the Free Grammar School Committee' were added the Mayor and two Bailiffs.[2]

It was clearly not the intention of the Council simply to hand over the control of the schools to the local clergy of the Church of England, even though it was taken for granted by all that the schools should be closely 'connected with the Established Church'. From the first, how-ever, the Corporation Schools must have been scarcely distinguishable from what the Committee referred to as 'other Charity Schools under the Establishment of the Church of England'. One of the first steps of the new Committee was to call upon one of its members, the Rev.

[1] *Minutes of Schools Committee*, pp. B1–5.
[2] *Proceedings of Council*, Vol. XV, p. 616. William Ripley and Richard Houghton were appointed members of the Committee some months later (*ibid.*, Vol. XV, p. 651).

Jonathan Brooks, 'one of the Secretaries of the District Society for promoting Christian Knowledge . . . to supply in the first Instance the School Books on the Society's List'; it was also decided 'that no Books but those on the Society's List be admitted into the School without the special permission of the Committee'.[1] At a meeting of the Committee in June 1827 (the only members present being three laymen), it was resolved that 'The Anniversary Sermon for the Schools under the Established Church being to be preached on Tuesday 19th Inst. . . . the Children of both the Schools do attend, and walk in the procession under the Superintendance of the respective Masters and Mistresses'.[2] It would appear that the 'Official Visitor' to the schools was the Junior Rector, the Rev. Augustus Campbell, since it was on his recommendation that it was decided to appoint an assistant mistress to the South Corporation School; and reports that certain teachers were unsatisfactory or were about to resign came from him.[3] In 1832 he was even 'authorised to engage a new 2nd Mistress at the North School, subject to the approbation of the Committee'.[4] As time went on, the control of the schools seems to have passed more and more completely into the hands of the clergy, as more of them were appointed to serve on the Committee and the lay members became more slack in attendance; thus the only members present on 28 September 1835 were four ministers; whilst at the next meeting—the last recorded in the minutes before the decisive municipal elections of 1835—there were present the Mayor, one other layman, and no fewer than seven clergymen.[5]

In later years, when the controversy concerning the schools was at its height, it was sometimes denied that the 'Schools Committee' at this period refused to admit the children of Dissenters and Roman Catholics; it was agreed, however, that all the children admitted to the schools were instructed in the doctrines of the Church of England: they were taught the Church Catechism, made use of the Authorized Version of the Bible, and were obliged to attend on Sundays a place of worship connected with the Established Church.[6] No doubt some Dissenters sent their children to the schools, but their numbers were probably small. Very few Roman Catholic children attended.[7] In fairness to the

---

[1] *Minutes of Schools Committee*, p. B7.
[2] *Ibid.*, p. B14.
[3] *Ibid.*, pp. B24, 26, etc.
[4] *Ibid.*, p. B27.
[5] *Ibid.*, p. B40.
[6] *Proceedings of Education Committee*, Vol. I, p. 4.
[7] Burke, in his *Catholic History of Liverpool*, p. 44, quotes a Father Walker as stating on 20 May 1830 that 'nine thousand children were either not attending school or being educated in the Corporation and Hibernian schools'. The same historian, however, says a few pages later (p. 50) that the Corporation Schools 'were . . . only used by one section

Committee and to the Council, it ought perhaps to be said that until about 1833 most enlightened public opinion in Liverpool seems to have accepted the situation with little comment; it is significant that William Wallace Currie, the most liberal-minded man in the Council,[1] helped to draft the regulations governing the schools and was from the first a member of the 'Schools Committee'.

For the first eight or nine years of their existence, therefore, the history of the two Corporation Schools seems to have been quite un-eventful. From the beginning the monitorial system of education was adopted, and some of the teachers were recruited from the Liverpool Bluecoat Hospital, at this time one of the centres at which teachers were trained in the use of Bell's methods, and of which it had been said by the great Dr Bell himself that 'its state was most admirable, and that any one but himself would pronounce it to be a perfect specimen of the Madras system'.[2] Due economy was observed in the management of the schools: to each boys' or girls' school was attached one master or mistress with one assistant; each child was required to pay one penny (later three-halfpence) per week, and, of the money thus obtained, part was added to the teachers' salaries, part, at least for a time, went towards the cost of running the schools, part was expended on prizes, and part was spent on the purchase of materials to be made up by the girls into articles of clothing, which were sold at less than cost price.[3] Possibly the only noteworthy development during the years 1827-35 was the establishment of Infant Schools; none had been allowed for under the original plan, perhaps because the Rev. W. Hesketh had spoken of such schools with some disdain,[4] but on 28 December 1833, 'Upon the Motion of the Revd Aug^s Campbell it was resolved that it be recom-

of the community, though maintained entirely at the public expense'. Probably the most reliable evidence is that given by a Mr Johnson in 1837; at that time he was teaching in a Church of England School in Tabley Street, Liverpool, but he 'was formerly one of the teachers in the Corporation Schools, *before* their coming under the control of the re-formed Council'. When asked 'how many *Catholic* children had attended under the old system, his answer was that during a period of two years, to the best of his recollection, not more than *two* or *three* attended at any one given time, in a school consisting of about 350 boys'. (*Report of the Committee of the Reformers of Rodney Street Ward* . . ., Liverpool, 1837, p. 26). (Johnson had been appointed Master of the South Corporation School in May 1834.)

[1] He was elected to the reformed Council as a Reformer in 1835 and became its first Mayor (1835-6). As a member of the old Common Council, he had not agreed that its business should be conducted in secret and he surreptitiously sent reports of the proceed-ings to the (Whig) *Liverpool Mercury*. (See *Liverpool Mercury* of 19 November 1840.)

[2] Southey's *The Life of the Rev. Andrew Bell*, Vol. III, p. 293. See also the evidence of the Rev. J. C. Wigram, Secretary of the National Society, printed in the *Report of the Select Committee on the Education of the Poorer Classes in England and Wales*, 1838, p. 82.

[3] *Minutes of Schools Committee*, p. B23.

[4] *Op. cit.*, p. 26.

mended to the Council to grant the use of the South School Committee Room for the purposes of an Infant School'.[1] In the previous September it had been agreed, 'on the motion of the Mayor, to enlarge the North School, and appropriate a portion of it for the education of infants'[2]; and the new Infant School was in April 1834 reported to be 'ready for the reception of Children'.[3]

So it was that when, at the end of 1835, a new 'reformed' Town Council took over from the old self-elected body the direction of Liverpool's affairs, it found itself responsible for the maintenance and management of two large elementary schools, each having separate departments for the education of infants, girls and boys, and together providing accommodation for about 1,850 children; the children 'on the books' of the schools numbered about 1,543, and the average daily attendance was about 1,300.[4] In June 1836, just before this new Council assumed effective control of the schools, there took place the annual procession of children in attendance at Church of England elementary schools, and speaking of this event the Rev. Augustus Campbell said: 'We only returned at our last anniversary 7,611 as educated in the principles of that [the Established] church, and of that 7,611, 320 belonged to the workhouse, and 1,619 to the corporation schools, so that we only educated at our own expense 5,672.'[5] This statement shows clearly enough that, at this time, of all the Liverpool children being educated 'according to the Faith and Practice of the Church of England' in public elementary day-schools, more than 21 per cent were in the schools of the Corporation. A report made to the Education Committee of the new Council in March 1836 showed that about 6,154 children[6] were then being educated in public elementary day-schools *not* connected with the Established Church; so that altogether about 13,765 children

---

[1] *Minutes of Schools Committee*, pp. B33–4.

[2] *Liverpool Mercury*, 13 September 1833.

[3] *Minutes of Schools Committee*, p. B35.

[4] *Proceedings of Education Committee*, Vol. 1, pp. 4–5.

[5] *A Full Report of the Speeches Delivered at the Great Protestant Meeting at the Royal Amphitheatre, Liverpool, on Wednesday the 13th of July, 1836*, Liverpool [1836], p. 11. It would seem that not *all* of the 7,611 children were in day-schools, since Campbell said: 'The children are all, or almost all, really educated during the week as well as on the Sunday.' He hinted that the Dissenters were sometimes guilty of 'the pious fraud' of making returns which gave a false impression, and probably all of the religious bodies put forward the most favourable statistics available so that, if anything, the Corporation Schools were playing an even more important role than the figures given indicate.

[6] *Proceedings of Education Committee*, p. 7. The *Liverpool Courier* of 1 June 1836 claimed that this report under-estimated 'the number of children educated by the Church', and therefore Campbell's statement has been quoted as likely to be more authoritative on that subject. The figure here given allows for the inclusion of 80 of the 400 children at the workhouse, since Campbell claimed that only 320 were being educated by the Church of England.

in Liverpool were attending schools of the type indicated, and nearly 12 per cent of this total were to be found in the Corporation Schools.[1]

4

It is certain that the councillors who decided in 1824 to establish and maintain the two elementary schools out of the town's revenues did not do so in the spirit of adventurous pioneers: to them, as to the Rev. W. Hesketh, it seemed as reasonable to provide Corporation Schools 'connected with the Establishment' as it had been to erect Corporation Churches in the interests of the national religion. Indeed, the Mayor and Corporation were behind the times rather than ahead of them. Only a year after the schools opened their doors the Test and Corporation Acts were repealed; one year later still came 'Catholic Emancipation'; and when in 1833 the government offered its first small grant 'in aid of private subscriptions for the erection of school houses for the education of the poorer classes in Great Britain', it would have been politically impossible for it to have made the grant available only to organizations connected with the Established Church. In Liverpool it was not until 1829, apparently, that the suggestion was first publicly made that Dissenters and Roman Catholics should in fairness receive some part of the funds which the Council was prepared to spend on the provision of schools for the poor; even then it was not proposed that the same degree of assistance should be accorded to those outside the Church of England as had already been given to those within it. The suggestion referred to was made in a letter addressed to the Town Council,[2] urging it to build two free schools 'for the accommodation of the poor Dissenting and Catholic children of Liverpool'. The writer said:

> The Corporate body have already built, and munificently endowed, two splendid establishments . . . for the accommodation of the poor children connected with the Established Church; and my object is to remind them of the justice of building two more, to be called the East and West Free Schools, the latter for Catholics, and the former for Dissenters, or vice versa. This proposition appears . . . so just and equitable, in consequence of the large contributions which the Corporate funds derive from the commercial Catholics and Dissenters of the town, as well as the great number alluded to who are freemen, that it is only necessary to make the request in proper form

---

[1] B. D. White, giving a brief account of the Corporation Schools in his recently published *History of the Corporation of Liverpool (1835–1914)*, Liverpool, 1951, p. 12, makes the surprising statement that at the period immediately before the 'reformed' Council was elected in 1835 'the two Corporation schools, however good they may have been, catered for only 200 children'. As early as 1827 there had been at least twelve hundred children in attendance at the two schools (*Liverpool Mercury*, 22 June 1827).

[2] Printed in *Liverpool Mercury*, 2 January 1829.

to obtain the assent of our liberal Corporation. . . . I am aware that the parties in whose behalf I plead would not expect more than the schools rent-free.

After calling on his Catholic and Dissenting fellow-townsmen, if they approved of his plan, to 'memorialize the corporation', the writer made the interesting observation that 'if the Liverpool Corporation will set the generous example, they will have the honour of beginning a great and important work, which, in time, will become general in this kingdom'. It is noteworthy that the appeal seems to have aroused no interest, and there is no indication that steps were taken to 'memorialize the corporation'.

Yet only a few years later it became obvious that the feeling was gaining ground in Liverpool that it was urgently necessary to establish far more schools for poor children than could be provided by voluntary effort. In February 1833, William Ewart, one of the Members of Parliament for the town, was able to present in the House of Commons 'a petition in favour of a national system of education . . . from the Mayor and other principal inhabitants of Liverpool, including many distinguished literary characters, ministers of various denominations, merchants, bankers, tradesmen, and the head masters of ten public schools'.[1] Some months later William Wallace Currie, after giving evidence as a member of the committee which controlled the Corporation Schools, referred to the need to provide more schools in the town, and expressed the opinion that if the people of England were to be educated it would not be enough to rely on 'the benevolence of individuals or associated bodies'; it was essential that the government should introduce 'one general system of education', and that parochial schools should be established in every parish at the expense of 'the nation at large'. He was even in favour of making it 'compulsory on all persons unable to educate their children'[2] to send them to the schools thus set up.

In the same year it became obvious that the Roman Catholics of Liverpool, who, it was fairly generally agreed, formed about one-quarter of the population of the town,[3] were beginning to feel that

---

[1] *Ibid.*, 22 February 1833.

[2] *A Report of the Proceedings of a Court of Inquiry into the Existing State of the Corporation of Liverpool . . . Before . . . Two of His Majesty's Commissioners Appointed to Inquire into Municipal Corporations in England and Wales, in the month of November, 1833*, Liverpool, p. 448. (Henceforward this report will be referred to as *Report Liverpool Inquiry, 1833*.)

[3] Thus a Mr Rosson, a Roman Catholic barrister, basing his calculations on the proportion of Roman Catholic baptisms to all others in the town, sought to demonstrate in 1833 that Roman Catholics constituted 'considerably more than one-fourth of the whole population of Liverpool' (*Report Liverpool Inquiry, 1833*, p. 395). The Rev. Hugh M'Neile, a militant Protestant, claimed in 1836 that in Liverpool the population was 'three-fourths Protestant' (*Letters on National Education Addressed to the Town Council of Liverpool*, London, 1837, p. 54).

they might well expect to receive financial support for their schools from the Corporation funds. Only nine years earlier, in the year when the establishment of the Corporation Schools had been proposed, the Whigs had found it necessary to 'encourage' the Roman Catholics of the town to join in the struggle for their own political emancipation, the Roman Catholics having hitherto given the movement 'scanty support', seeming 'afraid of the great forces arrayed against them' and being 'influenced by the fear of provoking active Protestant hostility'.[1] Now in 1833, at a public inquiry, a Dr Collins, who claimed to speak after consulting some of the leading lay and clerical Roman Catholics of the town, pointed out that the schools for Roman Catholic children were carried on 'without any aid from the Corporation';[2] and he felt strong enough to add the somewhat broad hint that 'The £10,000 a year, given between the Corporation and the Parish, for the support of the clergy and churches of the establishment, . . . would educate nearly 20,000 children every year.'[3]

One Thomas Bolton complained that, although the Dissenters were more numerous in the town than were the members of the Church of England, 'the expenditure for religious purposes' of the Corporation had been exclusively for the benefit of the Established Church; apart from renewing the leases of Dissenting chapels or schools without the payment of the usual fine, the Corporation had done nothing 'for the maintenance of ministers, schools or places of worship, connected with the Dissenters'. It is interesting to note that at this time what was being asked of the Council was not detached neutrality but active benevolence towards all alike. But the Town Clerk's reply was unequivocal: he submitted that it would have been impossible for the Council 'consistently with the connexion they had with the established constitution of this country, to have given their funds, or expended their property for any ecclesiastical object distinct from the Church of England'.[4]

Probably not all of those in Liverpool who had petitioned Parliament in February 1833 for the establishment of a national system of education would have agreed with J. A. Roebuck when in his famous Commons speech a few months later,[5] he laid down the principle that

---

[1] T. Burke, *Catholic History of Liverpool*, p. 41.
[2] This statement was not strictly accurate, since the land on which the Roman Catholic schools in Seel Street were built had been leased from the Corporation on very generous terms. In the same tolerant spirit the Corporation had in 1821 and 1829 leased land to the Quakers at a nominal rent on the understanding that the school buildings erected on the land would be open to members of all denominations ('Indenture' and 'Declaration of Trust' in the possession of the Liverpool Meeting of the Society of Friends).
[3] *Report Liverpool Inquiry, 1833*, p. 462.
[4] *Ibid.*, pp. 233, 479–80.
[5] 30 July 1833 (Hansard, Third Series, Vol. XX, Cols. 154–5).

the 'universal and national education of the whole people' would have to be based upon the recognition of the rights of all denominations. But it is not surprising that some Liverpool men were coming to see more and more clearly that if a national system of education were ever to come into being in this country it would have to be founded upon some principle akin to that enunciated by Roebuck; it would not be possible to accord to the Established Church the position of authority in the schools of the nation which had up to this time been granted to it, almost without question, in the Liverpool Corporation Schools.

Chapter 2

'THE IRISH SYSTEM'

I

AT the time of the passing of the Municipal Corporations Act in 1835 Liverpool was governed by a self-elected Council consisting of forty-one members, all of whom belonged to the Church of England,[1] and all but five of whom were supporters of the Tory Party. The first municipal elections to be held in Liverpool in accordance with the Act took place on 26 December 1835, and the old Council passed out of existence when the results were declared two days later. The electors showed their gratitude to the party which had given them the vote; only three members of the old Council were chosen to serve on the new, and no fewer than forty-three Liberals were elected as against five Conservatives. At the subsequent election of aldermen fifteen Liberals were chosen and but one Conservative. The Liberals thus had an overwhelming majority in the new Town Council, and it must have seemed to them that a new era had begun.

The policy to be adopted in the Corporation Schools was not discussed, it would seem, during the municipal election campaign in 1835, although a few of the Liberal election addresses referred in general terms to the intention of candidates, if elected, to deal impartially with all sects; and the election manifesto signed by Hugh Hornby, William Rathbone and W. R. Preston stated that they were 'decided advocates of Civil and Religious Liberty', who considered that 'the Funds of the Corporation being raised from all should be expended for the benefit of all, without reference to Sect, Party, or Class in Society'. They went on to add that 'Education and innocent healthful Pleasures within the reach of all are objects which ought to be kept steadily in view'.[2] A letter addressed to the old Council in October 1835 by Thomas Bolton,[3] showed which way the new wind was blowing. He protested against the proposal of the Council before it left office 'to alienate a considerable

---

[1] *Report Liverpool Inquiry, 1833*, p. 234.
[2] Printed election address *To the Electors of Pitt Street Ward*, Liverpool, 1835 (among *Rathbone Family Papers*).
[3] *Liverpool Mercury*, 13 November 1835. Bolton, a Unitarian, was returned for Castle Street Ward as a Liberal in 1835, 1836 and 1839. He became Mayor in 1840.

amount of the Corporate funds[1] for the support of the Established Church'. He pointed out that 'as all sects contributed to the support of the Corporation funds' it appeared to him 'to be unjust that one sect in particular should have the whole of the pecuniary benefit'. He was 'not opposed to a public provision for the maintenance of religion', but only to 'the partial and sectarian application of such support'. He went on to suggest that such money as was to be expended should be divided so as to benefit members of the Established Church, Dissenters and Roman Catholics. But he made no direct reference to the Corporation Schools, and apparently it was not until some little time after they came to power that the Liberals decided what their policy in relation to the schools was to be.

A modern historian, writing of the new town councils set up at this time, remarks that 'few would have prophesied in 1835 that the education of the people would one day be carried on by these new bodies';[2] it is interesting, therefore, to note that the new Liverpool Town Council considered from the first that the education of the poor ought to be one of its chief concerns. On 8 January 1836, only eleven days after it came into existence, the Council agreed 'on the motion of Mr Rathbone, that a Committee of twelve persons be now appointed to promote the Improvement and Education of the Poorer Classes; to inquire into the means now in operation for these objects, and to report what farther may seem necessary and desirable'.[3] During the discussion on the motion, Rathbone stated that 'his object was that schools should be established in every district for boys, girls and especially infants; that there should be reading-rooms for the poorer classes in the evenings, furnished with works that might instruct and enlighten them. His object was not to promote any party purpose, either in religion or politics, but to educate the poor, and by finding them other sources of employment and amusement for their leisure hours to keep them out of the public houses'.

[1] The old Common Council had paid the stipends of a number of the Church of England clergy from the Corporation funds, and wished to ensure that, even after it had been superseded, permanent provision should be made for the payment of such stipends. An attempt to have inserted into the Municipal Reform Act a clause legalizing the payments was not successful; the Council thereupon raised a mortgage on the Corporation estates of £105,000, and invested the money so as to provide a permanent fund from which the payments could be made. The Liberal members of the 'reformed' Council disputed the legality of this step, and naturally their criticism of what some of them referred to as the 'Church Endowment Job' served to embitter the relations between them and many of the clergy of the Established Church. For a full account of the dispute, see J. A. Picton, *Memorials of Liverpool*, Second Edition, Vol. I, pp. 463–4.
[2] G. M. Trevelyan, *British History in the Nineteenth Century*, London, 1922, p. 245. Brougham's Bill of 1836 proposed to vest in the Town Councils of all Municipal Corporations the power to levy a school-rate for the establishment and support of schools.
[3] *Proceedings of Council*, Vol. XVII, p. 22.

When a member of the Council suggested that 'Normal Schools, for the education of the masters themselves' might be established,[1] Rathbone replied that his motion was so general as to provide for the possibility of establishing Normal Schools.[2] In view of later developments it is worth remarking that Rathbone's motion was agreed to unanimously, and that he 'had permission to state the Rev. Rector Campbell's concurrence in this project [of establishing municipal reading-rooms] provided that no political or controversial works were introduced'.[3]

The new Education Committee was made up of eleven Liberals and a single Conservative, Charles Horsfall; it included members of the Established Church, Dissenters and one Roman Catholic.[4] The Chairman was William Rathbone[5] (1787–1868), the fifth member of his family to bear that name, who had been brought up a Quaker but had formally withdrawn from the Society of Friends in 1829,[6] and had become a Unitarian. Probably no man in Liverpool was better fitted to act as Chairman of the town's Education Committee. His father before him (the fourth William Rathbone, 1757–1809) had helped to improve the 'Friends' day school' in Liverpool,[7] and the fifth William's mother and sister had both been members of the committee[8] which organized and managed the Friends' Infant School, one of the first infant schools to be established in Liverpool (1824). He himself, and his wife also, were interested in the latest trends in educational thought; their correspondence shows that they thought highly of Pestalozzi's ideas[9] and of

[1] *Liverpool Mercury*, 15 January 1836. Eight months earlier Brougham had suggested in the Lords that 'seminaries for training teachers' should be established 'in a few such places as London, York, Liverpool, Durham, and Exeter'. Hansard, Third Series, Vol. XXVII, Col. 1323. Parliament had promptly offered to make a grant of £10,000 for the erection of model or training schools in England.

[2] One Liberal member, Dr Carson, even gave notice of his intention to propose the foundation of a university, a project which he had first advocated in 1825. It was to be financed from the sale of shares to members of the middle-classes, but the 'controlling influence was to be that of the Corporation'. He was persuaded to withdraw his motion a few months later. See *Liverpool Mercury*, 15 January 1836, and, for a full account of the plan, *The Albion* (Liverpool), 25 April 1836.

[3] *Liverpool Journal*, 9 January 1836.

[4] The original members of the Committee were Dr Carson and Messrs. J. Cropper, Jnr., Walmsley, Thornley, E. Cropper, Alison, Hugh Hornby, Hope, Blackburn, Sheil, Rathbone and Horsfall. Wm. Lassell became a member in September 1836.

[5] Except where otherwise indicated, all references in this book to William Rathbone relate to this fifth William Rathbone.

[6] Entry in a MS. list of members of the Liverpool Preparative Meeting.

[7] From MS. *Minutes of the Men's Preparative Meeting of Liverpool from . . . 1782 to . . . 1811.*

[8] From MS. endorsed *Infant School Minute Book 1824–33* among records of the Liverpool Meeting.

[9] Letter of Mr Browne, schoolmaster in Cheam, to Mrs Rathbone, March 1829 (*Rathbone Family Papers*).

Robert Owen's[1] pioneer work in infant education; Owen and Lord Brougham were among the numerous distinguished visitors to their home; very soon after the foundation of the Central Society of Education William Rathbone became a member.[2] Thus the leading figure in the Education Committee of the new Town Council was well informed about current educational movements and policies; and what was potentially almost as important was the fact that he was well known to some of the most influential members of the government (particularly to Lord John Russell) chiefly because he had spent weary months in London, during 1833 and subsequent years, striving to have measures taken to put an end to the notorious corruption practised at Liverpool elections.

2

It was necessary to allow the newly formed Education Committee time to carry on its investigations and to prepare its report; on 20 January 1836, therefore, the Council agreed to Rathbone's proposal 'that the Rectors of Liverpool and the Ministers of Churches on the School Committees should continue their charge of the North and South Corporation Free Schools until further arrangements can be made; and that the Mayor be requested to express to those clergymen the desire of the Council that they should continue such charge'.[3] Thus set free, the Education Committee was able to undertake the task of trying to formulate such regulations for the Corporation Schools as would make it possible for parents of all denominations to send their children to them. From the first, most members of the Committee seem to have been particularly anxious to gather into the schools as many as possible of the large number of Roman Catholic children who were receiving no schooling whatever. The Committee's own survey[4] of 'the means now in operation for the education of the Poorer Classes' showed clearly enough not only that the general provision of elemen-

---

[1] Among the Rathbone family papers is an account, dated 'Lanark, 28th April 1818', of a careful inquiry into the methods employed at Owen's infant school. Evidently two or more members of the Rathbone family had visited the school, and before they left they wrote down a number of searching questions to which answers are written in another hand. When staying with William Rathbone in October 1836, Robert Owen attended a fancy-dress ball in Liverpool Town Hall dressed as 'The Schoolmaster Abroad'; with characteristic earnestness he distributed among the guests what the *Liverpool Standard* of 14 October 1836 described as 'dangerous and sophistical papers called "The Schoolmaster Abroad"', thus creeping into the paradise of innocent and happy hearts'.

[2] List of members appended to the *First and Second Publications of the Central Society of Education* (1837 and 1838).

[3] *Proceedings of Education Committee*, Vol. I, pp. 11–12.

[4] *Ibid.*, p. 7 (29 March 1836).

tary education in Liverpool was quite inadequate,[1] but that Roman Catholic children were even less well provided for than were children of Dissenters and of members of the Church of England. The same conclusion was emphasized a little later in the *Report of a Committee of the Manchester Statistical Society on the State of Education in the Borough of Liverpool, 1835–1836* (London, 1836); the investigators pointed out that there were 'only four Catholic Charity Schools in the Borough, and when the large number of Irish Roman Catholics resident in Liverpool is taken into consideration, it will be admitted that these four schools are by no means commensurate with their wants'.[2] A great part of the Roman Catholic population of the town consisted of wretchedly poor immigrants from Ireland; their priests had been unable to build schools upon anything like the scale required,[3] and of course they received no part of the government grants made available from 1833 onwards and distributed by the National and the British and Foreign School Societies.

In order to estimate correctly the importance of the experiment to be carried out in the Corporation Schools, one must take into account the fact that at this period the Roman Catholic authorities in England were not yet in a position to insist that the elementary education of the children of their persuasion should be carried on only in Roman Catholic schools; and it would seem that, generally speaking, although Roman Catholic parents were unwilling to send their children to the

---

[1] The investigations of the Manchester Statistical Society were at this time under way in Liverpool; they were completed in June 1836. The statistics ultimately published may not have been altogether reliable, owing to the failure to take into account the ever-changing nature of the population of the schools and also because of inaccurate estimates of the population of the town, the number of children aged five to fifteen, etc. But the comparison made with conditions in the Boroughs of Manchester and Salford is of some interest: in those boroughs 30·7 per cent of children aged five to fifteen were said to have been receiving no instruction in schools at the time of the Society's investigation, whereas the corresponding figure for Liverpool was 52·7 per cent. It should be noted, however, that the difference was largely caused by the greater number of Sunday-schools in Manchester and Salford, where far more children worked on week-days. It is possible to calculate from the returns that 77 per cent of the estimated number of children aged five to fifteen in those Boroughs were not attending *week-day* schools as against 59·2 per cent in Liverpool.

[2] P. 30.

[3] A Dr Collins, acting as spokesman for the Roman Catholics of Liverpool, stated in 1833 that a large school was being built at the north end of the town, but that 'for want of funds' it was 'not likely to come into operation for some time'. (The school, St Anthony's, was not opened until nine years later.) Another school, in Norfolk Street, had no accommodation for girls 'in consequence of the want of funds to procure the necessary departments—the present school being a large room or loft, over a cow-house, in a dirty, back, and ill-ventilated lane'. The witness stated that the annual expenditure on Roman Catholic schools was only £798, and that the number of children of his faith attending schools could have been doubled if funds had been available (*Report Liverpool Inquiry, 1833*, pp. 461, 462).

schools of the Church of England or of Dissenters, they were quite ready to send them to undenominational schools. The Roman Catholics were opposed to the reading of the Bible without note or comment, and could not conscientiously allow their children to read the Authorized Version, so that the priests discouraged the attendance of Roman Catholic children at schools in which all children were made to read (or to hear read) that version of the Bible, even if no other form of religious instruction were given.

Samuel Wilderspin, speaking of 'manufacturing districts of England where there are many Irish; in Lancashire for instance', testified that 'Catholics were willing to send their children' to his schools, but that the priests would not 'let them go'.[1] Henry Dunn, Secretary to the British and Foreign School Society, stated in 1838 that only 'a few Catholics' attended the schools of that Society; with reference to 'the poor districts, particularly with regard to the large towns of Lancashire', he said: 'We have in many of the schools a number of Catholics, but they bear a very small proportion to the whole number of the poor Catholics; we find that, generally speaking, the Catholics prefer educating their own children.' He added that since there were not enough schools for Roman Catholic children 'the great mass of them do not go anywhere'.[2] As might have been expected, few Roman Catholic children went to the National Schools connected with the Established Church; in a report published in *Minutes of the Committee of Council on Education* in 1841 on 'The State of Elementary Education in Birmingham, Manchester, Liverpool, and Several Other Towns in Lancashire' one observer wrote: 'Very few Protestant Dissenters and scarcely any Roman Catholics send their children to these [National] schools; which is little to be wondered at, since they conscientiously object to the repetition of the Church Catechism, which is usually enforced upon all scholars. Multitudes of Roman Catholic children, for whom some provision should be made, are consequently left in almost complete neglect, a prey to all the evils which follow profound ignorance and the want of early discipline.'[3] We have already seen that few Roman Catholic parents were willing to send their children to the Liverpool Corporation Schools.

On the other hand, there can be no doubt that many influential Roman Catholic priests and laymen were willing, and in some cases anxious, to have Roman Catholic and Protestant children educated in

[1] *Report from the Select Committee on Education in England and Wales*, 1835, p. 5.

[2] *Report from the Select Committee on Education of the Poorer Classes in England and Wales: together with the Minutes of Evidence*, 1838, pp. 51, 52.

[3] P. 176. See also *Central Society of Education, Second Publication*, 1838, pp. 355-6.

the same schools, provided that no attempt was made at proselytism. In 1830 Dr Doyle, Bishop of Kildare and Leighlin, had said:

I do not see how any man, wishing well to the public peace, and who looks to Ireland as his country, can think that peace can ever be permanently established, or the prosperity of the country well secured, if children are separated at the commencement of life on account of their religious opinions. . . . Children united know and love each other, as children brought up together always will; and to separate them is, I think, to destroy some of the finest feelings in the hearts of men.[1]

Similarly Dr (afterwards Cardinal) Wiseman, when asked whether he thought it 'desirable or not that the Catholics and Protestants should be educated in the same places of education', replied:

I think that in this country and in Ireland such an arrangement could be made, that both Protestants and Catholics could attend anything in the form of an University or Public School, without any harm ensuing, good might perhaps be done. I think also that in the lower branches of education it might easily be managed to give them a common education, reserving the religious education of their respective classes to their own pastors.[2]

In Liverpool numbers of Roman Catholic children attended the day schools run by the Unitarians, who earned the praise of the Roman Catholics because they made no attempt to proselytize.[3] One or two other undenominational schools[4] were attended by Roman Catholic children. But the most striking illustration of the readiness of the Roman Catholic clergy to sanction attendance at a non-Catholic school was afforded by the support given to the system in force at a school sometimes referred to as 'St Patrick's' and sometimes as the 'Hibernian' School, in Pleasant Street, Liverpool. This school had been founded in 1807 by an association called 'The Benevolent Society of St Patrick', the aims of which were to provide 'for the instructing in Reading, Writing and Arithmetic; the Cloathing and Apprenticing of Poor Children descended from Irish Parents'.[5] According to an account of the school given by a leading Roman Catholic of the town in 1833, it was then attended by between three and four hundred children, four-fifths of

---

[1] Quoted by Winifrede M. Wyse, *Notes on Education Reform in Ireland During the First Half of the 19th Century* . . . , Waterford, 1901, p. 10.

[2] *Report from the Select Committee on Education in Ireland*, Part II, 1836, p. 37.

[3] *Report Liverpool Inquiry, 1833*, p. 422.

[4] The twenty-fourth annual report of the Harrington Free School showed that of 2,003 children who had attended the school during the seven years preceding 1839, only 171 had been Roman Catholics (*The Albion* (Liverpool), 15 July 1839).

[5] *Gore's Directory*, 1807.

whom were Roman Catholics. The subscribers included members of all religious denominations, but most of them were Protestants. No religious instruction was given by the teachers, 'the children being left, in this respect, to the care of parents, guardians, and respective pastors'; all the children were allowed 'to go to their own proper worship without any interference with their religious tenets'; and 'the result was a full school, the absence of sectarian feelings, and the communication of a good commercial and moral education'. The Corporation had granted the reversion of the land on which the school was built, but had not given 'one penny towards its erection or support'. The speaker described the school as the best in Liverpool, and said that if all the other schools in the town were conducted 'with the same liberality, and the proselyting system were not pursued, the schools would be much better attended than they were'.[1] Among the 'distinguished friends of the institution' were William Rathbone[2] and the Earl Fitzwilliam.

The Hibernian School had one claim to fame which ought to be made known, especially as it is by no means irrelevant to our main theme: there is clear evidence that Thomas Wyse, when he was trying, about 1830, to formulate an educational policy likely to be acceptable to all denominations in Ireland, was encouraged by the success achieved by the Liverpool school in bringing children of different faiths together under one roof. In a speech delivered in the House of Commons on 9 September 1831, supporting the proposal that a national system of education should be established in Ireland, he showed that it had been found possible in other countries for children of different denominations to attend the same schools, receiving their secular education together and their religious instruction apart. He continued:

In almost every country on the continent where difference of religious creed exists, this system is pursued. But need we go so far? At Liverpool there exists a school and it has existed for twenty years. Catholic and Protestant have been there educated in perfect harmony together. Five thousand have issued from it; and I have been solemnly assured by the master, that he has narrowly watched them through their after-life, and always found them distinguished for the same kindly feelings and enlightened charity which they had imbibed in their youth. What was the secret of this? All provocation to religious dissension and rancour was sedulously kept away. Yet was their religious education neglected? Far from it; they were taught the Scriptures and catechism by their parents and pastors, and were not for that reason taught them less well. What prevents Ireland from having many schools like

---

[1] *Report Liverpool Inquiry, 1833*, pp. 422, 461.
[2] *Liverpool Mercury*, 23 March 1832.

this of Liverpool? Nothing but the strong will. It is our duty to rouse that will, to put it into action.'[1]

Two months later, commenting on Wyse's Bill proposing to set up a national system of education in Ireland, the *Liverpool Mercury* wrote:

We have . . . reason to know that if the wishes and intentions of the benevolent author of the bill be carried into effect, the system pursued at our Hibernian School will be adopted, and nothing will occur on this head to shock the prejudices of either Catholic, Protestant, or Dissenter. Mr Wyse has been for some time in correspondence with Mr Brennan (the Master of the Hibernian School), and has already, both in private communications and in his place in Parliament, spoken in the warmest terms of approbation of the system pursued at St Patrick's School, and of its effects. There is little doubt, therefore, that something similar will be adopted on a national scale in Ireland.[2]

It might have been expected that the Liverpool Education Committee, faced with the problem of making their Corporation Schools effectively available to children of all denominations, would simply have adopted the policy which had already been shown to be practicable in the Hibernian Schools. Instead they announced that they would take as their model the system of education which, largely owing to Thomas Wyse's efforts, had been established in Ireland about four years before. On 22 March 1836, barely two months after it had come into existence and before it had had time to prepare any detailed recommendations for submission to the Town Council, the Education Committee approved a suggestion made by one of its members, Thomas Blackburn,[3] and passed a resolution:

That in the first Report of this Committee to the Council it be recommended that the Irish National Education System be introduced into the Corporation Schools.[4]

Two weeks later the Committee's first report was presented to the Council (6 April 1836) and, although it did not contain the definite recommendation which the earlier resolution had foreshadowed, the report indicated that the 'Irish National Education System' was to receive the particular attention of the Committee, which proposed to

---

[1] Quoted in *Liverpool Mercury*, 23 September 1831, and referred to in *Gore's General Advertiser* (Liverpool), 22 September 1831. (The passage does not appear in the version of the speech given by Hansard or in *The Mirror of Parliament*.)

[2] *Liverpool Mercury*, 18 November 1831. (See also the same newspaper, 16 March 1832.)

[3] Blackburn, a Liverpool surgeon and a prominent Dissenter, was a member of the Council for Lime Street Ward.

[4] *Proceedings of Education Committee*, Vol. I, p. 3.

'enquire into what plans have been found most effectual for the Physical Intellectual Moral and Religious Improvement of the Pupils in similar Schools, particularly those adopted by the Irish Education Board; and cautiously to make trial of whatever shall appear most desirable, taking care to avoid any thing sectarian or exclusive in the regulations or in the Religious instructions imparted in order that the Schools may be open to and sought by all.'[1]

3

The policy which the Education Committee had referred to as the 'Irish National Education System' had, in effect, been inaugurated in September 1831. For a considerable time before that date it had been obvious to most impartial observers that little success had attended the government's policy in Ireland of making available to the Kildare Place Society funds with which to promote the establishment of elementary schools for children of all denominations. The Roman Catholic clergy accused the Society of engaging in proselytism, and in any case objected to those regulations of the Society which prevented the giving of denominational religious instruction and prescribed the reading of the Bible without note or comment; the result was that 'in Ireland, where five-sixths of the population were Roman Catholics, nearly two-thirds of the whole benefit of the Society went to Protestant Ulster; while the other three Catholic provinces had only one-third to their share.'[2]

A Select Committee of the House of Commons, after considering the reports of a number of Commissions which had been appointed at various dates to examine the state of education in Ireland, had proposed in 1828 that in that country schools for poor children of all denominations should be set up to provide what was described as 'combined literary and separate religious Education'. 'Moral and literary instruction' would be given on four fixed days in each week, and of the other two week-days one would be available for the religious instruction of the Protestant children and the other for that of the Roman Catholics. The clergy of the different denominations would superintend the religious instruction of the children of their own persuasions; copies of the New Testament would be provided in the Authorized Version and also in the version 'published with the approval of the Roman Catholic Bishops for the children of their Communion'. All children attending the schools assisted by government grants would be compelled to

[1] *Ibid.*, Vol. I, pp. 6–7.
[2] Speech of Edward Stanley, Chief Secretary for Ireland, 9 September 1831 (Hansard, Third Series, Vol. VI, Col. 1253).

attend their own places of worship on Sundays. Another Select Committee appointed to report on the State of the Poor in Ireland had urged the government in 1830 to act upon 'the practicable recommendations of the Select Committee of 1828'. But the government had shown an understandable reluctance to adopt a policy which was bound to lead to controversy and seemed unlikely, in any case, to prove acceptable to the leaders of the various denominations.

At this juncture no one did so much to persuade the government that it was both necessary and possible to establish a national system of elementary education in Ireland as did Thomas Wyse, who entered Parliament as member for Tipperary in 1830. Wyse devoted considerable attention to the problem of devising a system of education likely to be accepted by Protestants and Roman Catholics alike; he studied the workings of such systems abroad and, as we have seen, in the Liverpool Hibernian School; moreover, he made it his business to sound the opinions of many religious leaders in Ireland, and knew what difficulties were likely to be encountered. He had frequent interviews with Edward Stanley, then Chief Secretary for Ireland (later fourteenth Earl of Derby), and made available to him not only his detailed proposals for a suitable Parliamentary Bill but the 'full text' of the correspondence which Wyse had carried on 'with the Irish hierarchy and other distinguished leaders of public opinion'[1] on the subject of a national system of education. Since the government still did not seem disposed to act, Wyse planned to introduce a Bill in August 1831, but, because of a delay caused by faulty drafting,[2] he was not able to do so before Stanley unexpectedly announced on 9 September 1831 that the government intended to withdraw its support from the Kildare Place Society and to establish 'a system of national education' by placing government grants for that purpose at the disposal of the Lord-Lieutenant. The schools assisted by the government would be supervised by a Board made up of Catholics and Protestants, and provision would be made for the 'separate religious instruction' of the children of the various denominations.[3]

A month later Stanley formally set the new system in operation by issuing his Letter of the Rt. Hon. E. G. Stanley, Chief Secretary, to His

---

[1] J. J. Auchmuty, Sir Thomas Wyse, 1791–1862, London, 1939, p. 153.

[2] According to Wyse's niece, who adds that Stanley's speech of 9 September 1831 was taken 'verbatim from Mr Wyse's Bill without the slightest acknowledgment either then or at any subsequent period' (Winifrede M. Wyse, op. cit., p. 27). See also article on Wyse in D.N.B. On the other hand, it has been claimed that Stanley owed no debt to Wyse since 'all the Primary School Plans of both Stanley and Wyse' had their source in the 'labours and writings, based on personal experience and on years of steady work in official service' of Mr Anthony R. Blake, Treasury Remembrancer at Dublin Castle (Richard P. J. Batterberry, Sir Thomas Wyse, 1791–1862, Dublin, 1939, pp. 27, 28).

[3] Hansard, Third Series, Vol. VI, Col. 1258.

Excellency the Lord Lieutenant Addressed to his Grace the Duke of Leinster,
in which the general principles on which the new Board should act were
laid down. Wyse was anxious to have the new scheme embodied in an
Act of Parliament, since he feared that a change of administration might
mean the end of what was generally regarded as an experiment; he
therefore introduced his Bill on 29 September 1831, but failed to secure
its passage before he lost his seat in the general election of the following
year. He became member for Waterford in 1835, and thereupon made
renewed attempts to have the national system of education in Ireland
based upon a law of the realm; but he did not succeed. Nevertheless, it
could be said that the government in London had begun to establish in
Ireland what it had shown no disposition to set up in England—a system
of education for the children of the poor which was assisted from state
funds and was intended to benefit children of all denominations.

It was the provision made for the religious instruction of the children which most interested the Liverpool Education Committee in
1836, and which therefore most concerns us here. The 'Board of Commissioners of National Education in Ireland' consisted of seven men,
among them the Protestant and the Roman Catholic Archbishops of
Dublin, the Rev. James Carlile (a member of the Synod of Ulster), the
Duke of Leinster (Lord-Lieutenant of Ireland) and three other laymen,
one of whom happened to be a Unitarian.[1] Their regulations laid it
down that at least one day in each week, apart from Sunday, should be
made available for the religious instruction of the children, and that on
that day the clergy of the different persuasions should 'have access to'
the children of their own denominations. It was made clear that the
clergy could give religious instruction in the classrooms or elsewhere.[2]
Managers of schools were also required, if the parents of any of the
children so wished it, 'to afford convenient opportunity and facility' for
the giving of denominational religious instruction either before or after
the ordinary school business (as the managers might determine) on the
other days of the week.

The reading of the Authorized or Douay Versions of the Bible was
to be considered 'as a religious exercise, and, as such, to be confined to
those hours which are set apart for religious instruction'; the saying of
prayers was also to be regarded as denominational religious instruction.[3] In reply to a 'proposition' from the Synod of Ulster, it was
agreed in August 1833 that parents could demand that the Bible be

---

[1] Evidence of A. R. Blake before the Select Committee of the House of Commons on
Foundation Schools and Education in Ireland, 11 August 1835, Q. 3448.
[2] *First Report of the Commissioners of National Education in Ireland for the Year 1834,*
Preface.
[3] *Ibid.*

read during 'a convenient and sufficient portion of the stated School Hours' provided that no child was compelled to read it or to remain during the reading.[1] To sum up, then, denominational religious instruction, which could include the saying of prayers and the reading of whatever version of the Bible the parent might select, could be given at any time on at least one week-day, and also on every other week-day before or after 'the ordinary school business'; whilst, by special arrangement, the selected version of the Bible could even be read during the hours originally laid down for 'ordinary school business', provided that no child was compelled to be present against the wishes of the parents.

Since one of the principal aims of those who devised the 'Irish National System of Education' was to remove the barrier of animosity which separated Roman Catholics and Protestants, it was decided by the Board of Commissioners that some attempt should be made to bring children of all faiths together for undenominational religious instruction which should be based on selections from the Bible; the government agreed that 'Extracts from the Scriptures, if approved by the entire Board, might be read in the general course of Education by Protestants and Roman Catholics together.'[2] It must have seemed extremely unlikely that a Board so constituted would ever agree on a suitable set of extracts and, above all, on the wording of the translated passages; and yet unanimous agreement was reached without difficulty, and complete harmony reigned among the members of the Board whilst they were engaged upon their task.[3] In view of the controversy which later raged around these 'Irish Scripture Lessons' (as they were called) in Liverpool and elsewhere, it is necessary to consider what purpose they were intended to serve and how they were prepared. In the *First Report of the Commissioners of National Education in Ireland for the Year Ending March 1834*, the members of the Board said:

It having been imputed to us that we intended to substitute these extracts from the Scriptures for the Sacred Volume itself, we deemed it necessary to guard against such misrepresentation, by annexing to the first number of them the following preface: 'These selections are offered, not as a substitute

[1] *Four Propositions Submitted by the General Synod of Ulster to the Government, and to the Commissioners* (printed with *First Report of the Commissioners*).

[2] *Letter of T. F. Kelly, Secretary to Commissioners of Education in Ireland to Rt. Hon. Sir Henry Hardinge*, January 1835.

[3] Evidence of A. R. Blake before the Select Committee of the House of Commons on Foundation Schools and Education in Ireland, 11 August 1835, Questions 3365–8, 3449. See also the letter of Dr J. Carlile, one of the original members of the Board, printed by the Select Committee of the House of Lords which in 1854 inquired into 'the Practical Working of the System of National Education in Ireland' (*Evidence*, Vol. I, pp. 4–6).

for the Sacred Volume itself, but as an introduction to it, in the hope of their leading to a more general and more profitable perusal of the Word of God. The passages introduced have been chosen, not as being of more importance than the rest of Scripture, but merely as appearing to be most level to the understandings of children and youth at school, and also best fitted to be read under the direction of teachers not necessarily qualified, and certainly not recognized, as teachers of religion.'

The claim was made that no passage had 'either been introduced or omitted under the influence of any particular view of Christianity, doctrinal or practical'. In a later report it was explained that the extracts had not been taken 'either from the Protestant version or the Roman Catholic version exclusively, but are an original compilation avowedly made by ourselves upon a comparison of the Protestant and Douay versions with the original'.[1] The following passage taken from the report of the evidence given before the Select Committee of the House of Commons on Education by one of the Commissioners[2] on 4 August 1834 illustrates the surprising readiness to compromise which made it possible for the 'entire Board' to reach agreement on disputed points:

There are some words which create a difficulty in translation; for instance, the word rendered in the authorized version 'repentance', and in the Douay 'penance'. We got over that difficulty by appending a note, in which the Board unanimously concurred, explaining the meaning of the Greek word, and the view which the Roman Catholic Church takes of penance, and thus with the full consent of the Roman Catholic part of the Board we have uniformly used the word 'repentance'. In no part of the extracts we have used the word 'penance'; I think in one instance 'penitence'.

By 1836 the volumes of *Scripture Lessons* published comprised the *Book of Genesis*, the *Gospel of St Luke*, the *Acts of the Apostles* and the *Book of Exodus*; each was 'illustrated by copious appropriate selections from other books of Scripture',[3] and furnished with 'a few Notes,

---

[1] *Third Report of the Commissioners of National Education in Ireland* (dated 13 July 1836).
    The preface to the *Scripture Lessons* is a little more explicit: 'The translation has been made by a comparison of the Authorized and Douay Versions with the original; the language sometimes of the one and sometimes of the other has been adopted, and occasionally deviations have been made from both.' Richard Whately, the Protestant Archbishop of Dublin and one of the Commissioners, claimed that 'those few places in which there is a departure from the words of the authorized Translation of the Bible, such as at all to affect the sense, are those in which *that and the Douay Translation agree*; so that the departure is from both alike'. 'Replies to the Dean and Chapter and to the Clergy of the Diocese of Dublin, Relative to the System of National Education in Ireland,' printed in *Charges and Other Tracts*, London, MDCCCXXXVI, p. 131.)
    [2] Rev. J. Carlile (*Report from the Select Committee on the State of Education; with Minutes of Evidence*, 1834, Q. 2533).
    [3] R. Whately, *op. cit.*, p. 131.

chiefly explanatory and practical';[1] a few passages were omitted, these, it was explained, being 'merely such as no one would think suitable for the perusal of a child'.[2] The Commissioners 'earnestly and unanimously' recommended that the Lessons should be used in all schools receiving financial aid from the Board, but made it clear that there was no intention of adopting 'any rule for their use even bordering upon compulsion',[3] and gave instructions that the extracts were not to be employed for the purpose of giving denominational religious instruction during school hours.[4] In addition to the *Scripture Lessons* the Board of Commissioners published a volume of 'Sacred Poetry'[5] selected from 'works of different religious persuasions', the greater part of it being 'taken from Protestant writers'.

It is not necessary to recount in detail the events which followed the inauguration in Ireland of what came to be known as the 'Irish System of Education', but some reference must be made to the opposition which it aroused and to the state of affairs which obtained when the Education Committee of the Liverpool Town Council, four years after the System had been put into operation in Ireland, decided to recommend its adoption in the Corporation Schools. At first not even all of the Irish Board of Commissioners were very hopeful about the success of the new scheme, avowedly introduced as an experiment; Richard Whately, the Protestant Archbishop of Dublin, admitted that he 'was not sanguine as to the success of the measure', but thought that it ought to be given 'a fair trial'.[6] It was confidently forecast by others that 'no selection of Scripture will be agreed to by the Roman Catholic hierarchy which shall exhibit to the youthful mind a correct standard of faith and practice',[7] and Whately himself later confessed that he had not dared to hope 'that so large a portion of Scripture would have found admission into the system of daily *common* instruction in the schools.'[8]

The two criticisms most commonly made were firstly that the system would 'exclude' or 'virtually exclude' the Bible from the schools

[1] *Scripture Lessons for the Use of Schools*, published by Direction of the Commissioners of National Education, Preface.

[2] R. Whately, *op. cit.*, p. 131.

[3] *Scripture Lessons for the Use of Schools*, Preface.

[4] Evidence of the Rev. James Carlile before the Select Committee of the House of Commons on Education, 4 August 1834, Q. 2532.

[5] Evidence of A. R. Blake before the Select Committee of the House of Commons on Foundation Schools and Education in Ireland, 18 August 1835, Q. 4260.

[6] R. Whately, *op. cit.*, pp. 141, 142.

[7] 'Observations of the Archbishops and Bishops of the United Church of England and Ireland to the Clergy of Their Respective Dioceses,' printed in R.Whately, *op. cit.*, p. 214.

[8] R. Whately, *op. cit.*, p. 218.

assisted by the Board, and secondly that the selections from the Bible, often described as 'mutilated' versions of the Bible, were to be substituted for the Bible itself. Over and over again these charges were made in pamphlets, in newspapers, and at public meetings called to draw up petitions against the new system. The Earl of Roden spoke in the House of Lords of 'an infamous system of education from which the unmutilated Word of God was excluded',[1] and hoped that it would never be said that any Protestant Government—but above all, a British Government—united with Popish priests to withhold from the people the immutable word of God'.[2] The majority of the Prelates of the Church of Ireland instructed their clergy not to support a system which was 'rigidly excluding the Scriptures from the common schools';[3] the Commissioners, their agents and those who sent their children to the Board's schools were 'designated as infidels, apostates, everything opprobrious that language could supply'.[4] Repeatedly the defenders of the government's policy denied that the extracts from the Scriptures were intended to take the place of the whole Bible, and pointed out that every facility was offered for the reading of the complete Scriptures out of school hours;[5] unmoved by the arguments, the opponents of the new system persisted in making a distinction between 'National' schools and 'Scriptural' schools.

Naturally the debates were not confined to Ireland or to the Houses of Parliament; the suggestion that the government, in order to please the Roman Catholic hierarchy, was setting up schools from which the Bible was excluded, alarmed many sincere Protestants in all parts of the British Isles and, especially during the session of 1832, petitions poured into Westminster expressing disapproval of the 'Irish System'. In Liverpool the opposition to the new policy seems to have have been relatively mild: meetings of the 'friends of scriptural education in Ireland' were held and 'resolutions condemnatory of the Government plan' were passed with the support of some of the clergy;[6] but on the other hand 'petitions in favour of the Ministerial plan of Education' were 'agreed to by some of the Dissenting congregations in Liverpool.'[7] In Manchester the opposition seems to have been stronger, and on

---

[1] Hansard, Third Series, Vol. XIII, Col. 2.

[2] Ibid., Third Series, Vol. XVI, Col. 788.

[3] 'Observations of the Archbishops and Bishops . . .' (Whately, op. cit., p. 215).

[4] Speech of Archbishop of Dublin (Hansard, Third Series, Vol. XVI, Col. 794).

[5] 'The children read the Bible for one hour a day for five days in the week, and the other two days they read nothing but the Bible. He would ask how many of their Lordships' children, how many even of their Lordships themselves, read the Bible so much' (Archbishop of Dublin, in House of Lords, ibid., Col. 795).

[6] Liverpool Mercury, 17 March 1832.

[7] Ibid., 15 June 1832.

16 April 1832 Lord Kenyon in the House of Lords, and Sir Robert Inglis in the House of Commons, presented petitions 'against the new system of Education . . . signed by the borough reeve and municipal Magistrates, by all the clergymen of the town with only two or three exceptions, by all the Dissenting Ministers and . . . by 4,000 of the most respectable inhabitants';[1] as so often, the petitioners objected to 'a selection which was to exclude the use of the whole volume of the Scriptures'. Naturally enough, a good deal of the opposition to the government's scheme, both inside and outside Parliament, came from political opponents; and the Conservative newspapers in London, Liverpool and elsewhere eagerly seized the opportunity to accuse the Liberal Cabinet of truckling to the Roman Catholic priests, whilst the Liberal newspapers were not slow to charge the government's critics with intolerance and bigotry.

As time passed and the passions of all but the more extreme opponents of the new policy began to cool, it became obvious to many both that the system had in some quarters been 'grossly misrepresented and misunderstood',[2] and that it would be difficult to provide any national system of education in Ireland which did not follow the lines laid down in the regulations of the Board of Commissioners, especially if it were hoped to bring Roman Catholics and Protestants more closely together by educating them in the same schools. When the Education Committee of the Liverpool Town Council began, in the early months of 1836, to consider the possibility of adopting the 'Irish System of Education' in the schools under its control, that system seemed to have achieved a reasonably high degree of success in Ireland itself. *The Second Report of the Commissioners of National Education in Ireland for the Year Ending March 1835* had furnished statistics[3] which, it was claimed, showed that 'the new system of Education had proved generally beneficial and acceptable to Protestants and Roman Catholics alike, according to their respective wants'; the Commissioners believed that it would be possible to establish five thousand 'National Schools' during the following nine years if sufficient money were made available, and they declared that:

[1] Hansard, Third Series, Vol. XII, Cols. 496, 541. As illustrating the wide divergence of opinion concerning the 'Irish System' at this time, it is perhaps worth remarking that on the same day 'The Sheriffs of the City of London presented a petition from the Lord Mayor, Aldermen, and Common Council, approving of the new plan of Education proposed to be introduced into Ireland, and praying that the House would sanction the same' (*ibid.*, Col. 541).

[2] Marquess of Lansdowne (*ibid.*, Vol. XXVI, Col. 730).

[3] See the remarks on these figures in a speech of the Bishop of Exeter in the House of Lords (*ibid.*, Vol. XXXII, Cols. 283–91), and the reply given in the *Third Report of the Commissioners of Education in Ireland*, 1836.

although from a misapprehension of the rules which the National system enjoins respecting the use of the Scriptures, it originally met with much opposition, yet it has succeeded beyond our highest expectations, and reasonable men of all parties are daily manifesting more and more their approval of it.

The Protestant Archbishop of Dublin, in a book published in 1836, prefaced his remarks on the 'Irish System' with the statement that he thought 'it might be interesting to many persons to contrast [the system's] apparently unpromising beginnings, amidst so much disheartening opposition and censure, with its subsequent success, in a short space of time'.[1] In February 1836 the Marquess of Lansdowne felt able to claim that 'restricted and narrowed as the operation of the system was, not less than 200,000 children were in the course of receiving practical education under it';[2] and a month later Melbourne informed the House of Lords that 'the system had succeeded in a manner which was beyond all disputation'.[3] There can be no doubt that there still existed very considerable opposition to the system, and this was often forcibly expressed, especially by some of the Protestant clergy of Ulster, by Henry Phillpotts, Bishop of Exeter, who conducted a prolonged campaign in the House of Lords, and, later, by Dr MacHale, Roman Catholic Archbishop of Tuam in Ireland. Probably the clearest and most accurate account of the state of affairs at about this period is that given by the Rev. James Carlile (who, as we have seen, was one of the Commissioners), on 4 August 1834, before the Select Committee of the House of Commons on Education in Ireland:

We have a very large proportion of Roman Catholics with us, without any open opposition from that body.[4] We have also many Protestant Dissenters with us; but many are opposed to us. The proportion of the ministers of the Established Church who are with us is smaller than that of the others. I think the laity of the Established Church has as little objection as any others; but the ministers of the Established Church are more generally opposed to us than the ministers of other denominations.

The same speaker testified that considerable numbers of Roman Catholic children attended 'National' schools established by Presbyterians

---

[1] R. Whately, *op. cit.*, p. 127.

[2] Hansard, Third Series, Vol. XXXI, Col. 254.

[3] *Ibid.*, Vol. XXXII, Col. 311.

[4] Carlile later wrote of the agreed extracts from the Bible: 'When these extracts were first introduced, they were generally received by schools under Roman Catholic patronage. I made a tour of inspection of the schools in the South and West towards the end of 1836, and I found them in use in all the most respectable schools; in all the teachers of which had received any training in Dublin; and uniformly in the nuns' schools'. See letter referred to above, p. 25 n.

and by members of the Established Church, particularly in the north of Ireland; but that not many Protestant children attended schools established by Roman Catholics. Where schools were set up by clergymen 'that frequently formed a bar to the children of the opposite creed attending'; but when the schools were established by laymen and were not thought of as being under the control of clergymen, 'the Protestants and Roman Catholics appeared to attend without any difficulty'.

Thus, at the end of a very few years it was possible for those who had inaugurated and supported the new system of education in Ireland to claim that they had found the means of promoting the education of large numbers of children and had made some progress in persuading Protestant and Roman Catholic parents to allow their children to receive secular education, and sometimes even non-denominational religious instruction, together in the same schools. And what seemed to have set the seal on the success of the new policy was the declaration with regard to it which was made by Peel's short-lived administration of 1834-5. In spite of the fact that a great deal of the opposition to the 'Irish System' had come from Conservative politicians and the Conservative Press, Peel's Cabinet, on taking office, had had to admit that no better means of encouraging the spread of elementary education in Ireland was to be found; and on 2 March 1835 Sir Henry Hardinge, the new Chief Secretary for Ireland, announced in Parliament, that there was 'no intention on the part of Government to alter the system of education in Ireland as settled by the late Administration'.[1] Thus it was that when Thomas Wyse moved in the Commons on 24 March 1836 for leave to bring in a Bill designed to 'give legislative sanction . . . permanence and certainty' to the 'Irish System', he was able to claim that 'in the late change of parties the system had had the good fortune to win . . . at last, though late, the protecting smiles of the very men who hitherto had been active in their vituperation.'[2] He might have added that the very man, now Lord Stanley, who, as Chief Secretary for Ireland, had officially introduced the 'Irish System' and defended it ably against a host of critics, had resigned from the Liberal Party in 1834, and was now well on the way towards becoming one of the most trusted members of the Conservative Party.

By the beginning of 1836, therefore, it must certainly have appeared that the 'Irish System' of education was so well established in Ireland as to make the provision of elementary education on a nation-wide scale in that country merely a matter of time. It is not surprising that some

[1] Hansard, Third Series, Vol. XXXI, Col. 479.
[2] Ibid., Vol. XXXII, Col. 585.

men were encouraged to hope that England would bestir herself and take steps towards providing her own people with some such national system. In this same year (1836) in which the Liverpool Council's Education Committee was called upon to formulate the policy which it would recommend the Council to adopt in the Corporation Schools, Wyse described the situation as he saw it, and expressed his hopes almost in the form of a challenge:

No measure, with the exception of Lord Stanley's 'Instructions to the Duke of Leinster' for establishing the present Irish Board, has been attempted, for . . . organising on a broad, efficient, and permanent scale, a National System of Education. . . . The minister waits for the country and the country waits for the minister, each fearing to go first, both, it seems, have come to a sort of tacit agreement to stand still. This is the more remarkable, as in the interval no other nation has followed the same ignoble course. Since 1833, the few countries who, like England, were unprovided with a National System of Education, have had the wisdom and the courage to adopt one. In England only, a National System is still wanting.[1]

As we shall see, William Rathbone and some of the members of his committee were determined that one part at least of 'the country' should no longer 'wait for the minister . . . fearing to go first', but would show that the 'Irish System' could overcome the same obstacles in England as had once seemed so formidable in Ireland.

[1] *Education Reform: or the Necessity of a National System of Education*, London, 1836, pp. iii–iv.

Chapter 3

THE EXPERIMENT BEGINS

I

O N 23 May 1836 the Liverpool Town Council had to consider two
quite different proposals concerning the policy to be adopted in
the Corporation Schools. One of these proposals had been put forward
in a letter from the Rev. Augustus Campbell, who asked that the Church
of England clergymen on the Committee which up till now had managed and supervised the schools should be allowed 'to retain the management of the Schools so long as they undertake to pay the ordinary
expenses (not including the repairs and maintenance of the building)'.[1]
Henry Lawrence, a Conservative, suggested that no action should be
taken with regard to the schools until Campbell's letter had been given
more careful consideration than he felt it had received, and his suggestion was supported by two Liberals, William Rushton and James Lawrence. The Town Clerk, aware that the new Education Committee had
no desire to hand over control of the schools to some outside body,
thought it necessary to point out that in his opinion the Council had no
legal power to spend money on the schools 'excepting out of the surplus,
and anything the Council did in this way, however laudable its object,
must be in anticipation of a surplus'.[2]

The majority of the members of the Council ignored the Town
Clerk's opinion, probably agreeing with Councillors Hope and
Robinson 'that as the schools had been erected by the old Corporation
. . . outlay might be considered as necessary expenditure'. Thomas
Bolton, who was a member of the Finance Committee, boldly
announced that 'there would be no surplus', but that the Corporation
Schools 'were public schools, and recognized no distinction of church,
chapel or Dissenters, and that the Council had no more power to
dedicate their management to Mr Campbell than to a Catholic Priest
or Unitarian Minister'. Councillor Sheil, a Roman Catholic, pointed

[1] *Proceedings of Council*, Vol. XVII, p. 51.
[2] John Cropper, Jnr., a Liberal, had resigned from the newly appointed Education
Committee some weeks earlier 'as I see I cannot be of any use on this Committee, and as
I differ on so many grounds with almost all on the Committee and as I consider the
appropriation of the Corporate Funds to these purposes until there is a surplus is illegal'
(*Proceedings of Education Committee*, Vol. I, p. 8).

out that 'the Town had sent into that room men of all classes, and if they took the proposal of Mr Campbell into consideration for a single moment, they would commit a direct insult on the persons whom they pretended to represent'.[1]

That the climate of opinion had changed since the schools were opened only nine years earlier was tacitly acknowledged by Campbell and his fellow clergymen when they offered to pay the running costs of the schools; even more remarkable was the fact that of the five Conservative councillors present four were not in favour of giving further consideration to Campbell's letter—including the only two Tory members[2] of the old Council who had been elected to sit on the new. Rathbone was therefore able to inform Campbell that the Council had itself decided 'to defray the Expence of the Schools'. He went on:

> As respects the management of the Schools, there is no doubt some difficulty in arranging plans for their future conduct so as to change them from their former exclusive character, and make them accessible to and desirable for the instruction of all classes of Christians. This change is imperative on a body representing all the different Religious Sects of Christians all of whom contribute to the maintenance of the Schools. The Committee feel no doubt of being able to arrange Plans for the conduct of the Schools which by the exercise of a little mutual concession, and liberal, they may say Christian, feeling will prove generally satisfactory and promote the general object of a useful moral and religious Education of the Poor. The Committee feel they have undertaken a very serious duty, and that they could not therefore without a violation of that trust for which they are responsible delegate the management of the Schools to other hands, however respectable, and especially to the Clergy of one particular persuasion.[3]

The Council then considered the Education Committee's declaration concerning the policy it proposed to adopt in the schools. It will be remembered that the Committee had at first agreed to recommend quite bluntly 'that the Irish National Education System be introduced into the Corporation Schools', but had later decided to make the less definite announcement that it would 'immediately proceed to enquire into what plans have been found most effectual for the Physical Intellectual Moral and Religious Improvement of the Pupils in similar Schools particularly those adopted by the Irish Education Board'; it would 'cautiously . . . make trial of whatever shall appear most desirable'; but the governing principle of its policy was to be quite clear—it would take care 'to avoid anything sectarian or exclusive in the

---

[1] *Liverpool Mercury*, 27 May 1836.

[2] Charles Horsfall and John Shaw Leigh. One Tory member was not present. The voting against giving further consideration to Campbell's proposal was 42–3.

[3] *Proceedings of Education Committee*, Vol. I, pp. 11–12.

regulations or in the religious instructions imparted', so that the schools might 'be open to all and be sought by all'.[1] Apart from the fact that, as we have said, one Conservative member and two Liberal members were in favour of giving further consideration to Campbell's offer to take over the schools, the Education Committee's announcement of its intentions was surprisingly well received. One member inquired whether the 'sacred scriptures' would be 'prohibited in the schools'; but apparently was satisfied when Rathbone assured him that such would not be the case, and asked in his turn whether the gentlemen who formed the Education Committee, including Mr Horsfall (a Conservative), were 'men likely to get rid of the Bible'.[2] Indeed, so calm was the reception accorded to the Education Committee's declaration that the Mayor 'was happy to state that there was no material difference of opinion, and that he had not the least doubt that the Committee would take such steps as would render the working of the school system satisfactory to all parties, and obtain the object in view'.[3]

The absence of serious criticism within the Council is all the more interesting since the members of the Council, and particularly the Conservative members, must have been aware that some opposition to the Education Committee's policy was already being voiced in the Conservative Press. Thus the *Liverpool Courier* had stated some weeks earlier:

> We believe the Town Council are to decide today whether or no they will put the Corporation schools upon the Irish system; and we advise them maturely to consider the question, lest, being deceived by false analogies, they should come to false and dangerous conclusions . . . the Council may rely upon it, that the exclusion of the Bible, and the substitution of the Irish Scripture lessons will not promote union, and (what perhaps is more likely to be influential) will not gain popularity in Liverpool.[4]

It was in the face of such criticism that almost all of the members of the Council had accepted the principle that the Corporation Schools should be made available to children of all denominations, and that the 'Irish System' should receive the particular attention of those whose duty it was to put that principle into effect.

Probably the uncritical attitude of most of the members of the Council on this occasion surprised the Education Committee much less than we might imagine, and that not merely because the 'Irish System' had achieved some success in Ireland and had recently received the blessing of a Conservative government. After all, some, at least, of those

[1] *Ibid.*, Vol. I, pp. 6–7.   [2] *Liverpool Mercury*, 27 May 1836.
[3] *Ibid.*   [4] *Liverpool Courier*, 4 May 1836.

'principal inhabitants' of the town who, only three years earlier, had signed the petition in favour of the establishment of a national system of education, might have been expected to recognize that such a system would have to provide for the children of all sects;[1] and, as it happened, the chief signatory of that petition, Charles Horsfall, the then Mayor of the old Common Council, who was a Conservative and a member of the Established Church, was now serving on the new Education Committee. Many Dissenters, in Liverpool[2] as elsewhere, had helped the Roman Catholics to obtain political emancipation, and felt that Roman Catholic children would have to be provided for under any national system of elementary education.[3]

It is true that many members of the Church of England were, quite naturally, becoming uneasily aware that the Established Church was losing its privileged position, and some, including those who came under the very different influences of the Oxford Movement or of the militant Protestantism of some Irish clergymen, were reluctant to make further concessions to those whom they were coming to regard as powerful enemies of the Church. At a time when attitudes were quickly changing, it was not easy to know where support might or might not be found, and sometimes the bitterest opposition, as we shall see, came from moderate-minded men who felt that they were being called upon to make one concession too many. Yet the first moves of the Committee seemed to have met with marked success, and its members had every reason to persevere hopefully with their plans.

2

The records of the proceedings of the Education Committee[4] contain an entry under the date 7 April 1836 which is of some interest. It reads as follows:

[1] On presenting the petition, William Ewart, one of the M.P.s for Liverpool, had expressed the hope 'that it would not be long before a system of education for England, as general as that for Ireland, would be adopted' (*Liverpool Mercury*, 22 February 1833).

[2] See *Liverpool Mercury*, 16 January 1829, for some account of their petitions to Parliament.

[3] When Henry Dunn, giving evidence in 1838 as Secretary of the British and Foreign School Society, was asked whether 'any extension, by means of either a rate or grant, made to schools on the principles of the British and Foreign School Society, would be met with approbation by the great body of dissenters throughout the country', he replied that he did not think that 'the Protestant dissenters generally would approve of any national grant which, directly or indirectly, excluded from its benefit Catholics or Jews, or any who differed from them; they would hold that all ought to be educated, that none ought to be left in ignorance' (*Report from the Select Committee on the Education of the Poorer Classes in England and Wales*, 1838, Q. 404).

[4] Vol. I, p. 10.

A letter from Mr Simpson of Edinburgh proposing to give Lectures on Education in Liverpool having been read
Resolved
That Mr Simpson be invited to come over to Liverpool.

James Simpson (1781–1853) was a Scottish advocate whose work as one of the legal assessors in Edinburgh had enabled him to obtain first-hand information about the 'condition of the great body of the lower classes' in that city. This had led him to appreciate how necessary it was to provide many more schools for the poor and to improve the education generally given in such schools. He had become 'a member of the direction of some of the principal schools . . . for the lower classes' in Edinburgh, and was particularly interested in the work of the Lancastrian and Infant School Societies. He claimed to have been 'rather active in the first establishment of the Model Infant School'[1] in Edinburgh in 1830, and had then found himself faced with the difficulty which now had to be overcome by the Liverpool Education Committee: that of satisfying the claims of those who differed in their religious beliefs so as to make it possible for children of all sects to attend the same school. Simpson's own solution was to leave denominational religious instruction to the clergy of the various denominations, whilst in the school the 'plan of communicating religious truths' was by means of the 'narratives, the precepts, and plainest announcements of Scripture'; but such a solution[2] was not one to appeal to many of those who customarily made donations to schools for the poor, and, as we shall see, his endeavours did not meet with the success he hoped for.

In 1834 he published his *Necessity of Popular Education as a National Object . . .*[3] in which he stressed the importance of education, showed that it was the duty of the government to provide a national system of public instruction and asked that

---

[1] The quotations are taken from Simpson's evidence as printed in *Reports from the Select Committees on Foundation Schools and Education in Ireland; together with the Minutes of Evidence*, Part 1, 1835.

[2] It is perhaps worth noting that in Scotland as elsewhere there was some difference of opinion at this time among the Roman Catholic clergy as to the attitude to be adopted towards such compromise solutions as Simpson favoured. Thus Simpson found that Roman Catholic children were withdrawn from the Glasgow Model Infant School; but he 'was assured by the Catholic Bishop of Edinburgh and some of his clergy that they would have no scruple in advising their people to send their children to the Edinburgh Model School, which they visited', although the system of religious teaching was 'precisely' the same in both schools (*Philosophy of Education . . .* , p. 196).

[3] A revised edition appeared in 1836 with the title *The Philosophy of Education with its Practical Application to a System and Plan of Popular Education as a National Object*, Edinburgh. Internal evidence indicates that the revision took place after Simpson's visit to Liverpool.

the example of Prussia should be followed; and in order that the schools to be provided *by* the nation shall be beneficial *to* the nation . . . all direction of the schools of secular instruction shall be denied to sects, as such, dominating and dissenting; and . . . all schools shall be constituted on the principle adopted by the Model Infant Schools of Edinburgh and Glasgow.[1]

He summed up his views on the situation in the declaration:

Nothing more is wanted than the degree of liberality now advocated to obtain for Britain at large the invaluable boon of popular education . . . for it has come to this issue—EDUCATION TO EMBRACE ALL SECTS, OR NO EDUCATION.[2]

As might have been expected, Simpson was an enthusiastic supporter of the 'Irish System'; and in the book referred to he not only praised the system but defended it spiritedly and at some length against most of the charges commonly made against it, particularly against what he described as the 'insensate' and 'unfair' cry that it countenanced the 'mutilation' of the Scriptures.[3] It was, no doubt, because of his interest in plans for providing elementary education, and especially because of his interest in the 'Irish System', that he was invited to give evidence before the Select Committee on Foundation Schools and Education in Ireland, the chairman of which was Thomas Wyse; he was questioned over a period of seven days,[4] and his evidence was considered so important that it was not only published with the report of the committee concerned with education in Ireland, but was reprinted as an appendix to the *Report from the Select Committee on Education in England and Wales* of 1835. He made it clear that he was in favour of the provision of a system of education which should be free to all classes, financed by government grants and local assessments, and supervised by state-appointed inspectors; he wished to have made 'a most perfect provision for education in revealed religion . . . by allotting to every elementary school both secular and religious instruction, but under different teachers and at separate hours'; and he thought it 'would be better' to prohibit the teacher (as distinct from the appropriate clergyman) from making 'any reference in the course of his lessons to Christian doctrines or Christian history as such'.[5]

The presence in Liverpool of such a man as Simpson at a time when

---

[1] P. 259. In the revised edition the reference is to 'the Model Infant Schools of Wilderspin' (p. 196).

[2] *Necessity of Popular Education* . . . , p. 260.

[3] *Ibid.*, p. 257.

[4] July and August 1835. In the brief article on Simpson in the *Dictionary of National Biography* it is stated that the evidence was given in 1837: this is obviously an error.

[5] *Reports from the Select Committees on Foundation Schools and Education in Ireland; together with the Minutes of Evidence* . . . , Part 1 (1835), p. 185.

the Reformed Council was being called upon to decide what its educational policy was to be could hardly have been without influence; and even more important was the fact that as a direct result of Simpson's visit William Rathbone found himself associated with the movement for the provision of a national system of elementary education in England. This came about in the following way. The *Manchester Guardian* of 30 April 1836 carried an advertisement in which it was stated that:

A number of Gentlemen, friends of enlightened Education, residing in Manchester, having observed with admiration, that a large proportion of the friends of intellectual improvement in Liverpool, including the Mayor and Educational Committee of the Town Council, have invited James Simpson, Esq., advocate, of Edinburgh, . . . to deliver a course of Lectures on Moral and Educational Philosophy, and being desirous that he should have an opportunity of delivering a similar course in Manchester, resolved that a Committee should be formed . . . for the purpose of inviting Mr Simpson to this town.

One of the members of the Committee, according to the advertisement, was Richard Cobden.[1] Simpson accepted the invitation and delivered a course of lectures, which began on 2 May[2] and ended on 20 May 1836.[3]

At the end of Simpson's ninth lecture on 18 May,

Mr Cobden announced the intention of many gentlemen to testify their respect for Mr Simpson, and their estimation of the service he had rendered to the cause of education, by giving him a public dinner.[4]

Cobden became the Chairman of the committee elected to make arrangements for the dinner, and advertisements signed by him appeared,[5] inviting to it all who wished to pay tribute to 'the able and enlightened Advocate of National Education'. But the committee wished to do much more than pay their respects to Simpson; they organized the public dinner

in the hope and belief that from such a meeting of persons, actuated as they might be expected to be by one enlightened impulse, an ulterior object—the formation of an education association—would be gained.[6]

[1] The others were G. W. Wood, Thomas Potter, John Brooks, W. R. Callender, Peter Ewart, Charles Cumber, J. N. Rawson.
[2] *Manchester Guardian*, 30 April 1836.
[3] *Ibid.*, 21 May 1836.
[4] *Ibid.*
[5] *Ibid.*
[6] *National Education. Report of the Speeches Delivered at a Dinner Given to James Simpson, Esq., by the Friends of Education in Manchester; Thomas Wyse, Esq., M.P., in the Chair*, Manchester, 1836, p. iii.

The public dinner took place on 25 May 1836, and there were present 'about a hundred gentlemen'.[1] Thomas Wyse came from London 'specially to do honour to Mr Simpson, his friend and coadjutor in the great work of national education'.[2] Richard Cobden was to have presided, but was unable to attend because of the death of his sister on the previous evening;[3] the chair was therefore taken by Wyse, with James Simpson on his right and William Rathbone on his left.[4]

Simpson's speech was on the lines of his evidence before the Select Committee in the previous year.[5] Wyse described the meeting as being

in an especial degree remarkable as having been, as I am informed, the first which has met within your town, and I may say, the first in any part of England, for the promotion of the great and general object of a national system of education.

He went on to propose the toast of 'A national system of education, more especially the infant system, and that it may speedily become, as it should be, the paramount object of a wise and constitutional government'. He suggested that the government should provide schools, train teachers and supply inspectors, whilst local committees should be empowered to levy rates for repairs to school buildings and for the payment of teachers. He continued:

. . . where the community is of one sect, let the teacher be of that sect also, and let him teach his religion. If they happen to be of mixed sects, why not give them religious instruction out of the schools? . . . Will any one tell me that religious instruction is not better attended to, if given out of school hours with the additional sanction of the pastor of the place?

He went on to give the very definite warning: 'You must not attempt to give religious instruction of any one sect in your schools.'

Cobden, as we have seen, was not present, but it is clear that he had been the prime mover in organizing the meeting, and it is worthy of note that at this period he began to give his attention to the same task as that which had for some time been occupying the attention of William Rathbone and his Education Committee; the task, that is, of trying to persuade the clergy of the different denominations to accept some compromise which would make it possible to establish schools available to

[1] *Manchester Guardian*, 28 May 1836.
[2] *Report of the Speeches* . . . , p. 3.
[3] *Manchester Guardian*, 28 May 1836.
[4] *Ibid.*
[5] He claimed that besides addressing other audiences he had explained 'his views of a system of national instruction . . . to the working classes, 2,000 of whom at Liverpool, and many last night in the Manchester Mechanics' Institution, had listened to him with a deep and undivided attention' (*Report of the Speeches* . . . , p. 5).

children of all sects.[1] Years later he stated that 'could he have at all seen his way to the attainment of so desirable an object, he would have devoted himself to it, and postponed the repeal of the Corn Laws as a matter of secondary importance'.[2] In January 1851 he said: '. . . so long ago as 1836, when Mr Wyse, himself a Roman Catholic, and Mr Simpson, of Edinburgh, and others, came down here to enlighten us on the subject of education—I remember having in my counting-house in Mosley Street the ministers of religion of every denomination, and trying to bring them to some sort of agreement on the system of education we were then anxious to advocate.'[3]

Whether any public references were made at the meeting to Rathbone's work as Chairman of the Education Committee in Liverpool is not stated in the *Report*; probably such references were made when his health was proposed 'in just and complimentary terms'.[4] But the fact that he was invited on such an occasion and treated as a guest of honour showed clearly that the policy which he was advocating with regard to the Corporation Schools was already attracting attention outside the town; and it is important that such men as Wyse, Cobden and 'the friends of education in Manchester' should thus early have had their attention drawn to the important experiment which it was proposed to carry out in Liverpool, with, as it must have seemed after the Liverpool Council meeting of two days earlier, good prospects of success. Moreover, Rathbone could hardly have failed to have derived encourage-

[1] It may be said that the opinions and efforts of both Wyse and Cobden in this connection seem to have been heartily approved of by Roman Catholics in Manchester. See *Report of the Proceedings of the Meeting Held in St. Augustin's School, Manchester*, . . . *October 27th* [1837] *on the Occasion of Presenting an Address from the Catholic Sunday School Teachers to Thomas Wyse, M.P.*, Manchester [?1837].

[2] Rev. William Harness, *Letter to James Phillips Kay-Shuttleworth, Esq., Considering Dr. Hook's Plan for Educating the People, and Suggesting Another*, 'Not Published', Westminster, 1846, p. 5.

[3] *Speeches on Questions of Public Policy by Richard Cobden, M.P.*, ed. John Bright and J. E. T. Rogers, 2 vols., London, 1870, Vol. II, p. 573. In spite of the reference made by Cobden to the visit of Wyse and Simpson at this time, Maltby seems not to have known of the important meeting of May 1836 but, evidently basing his remarks only on a report of the speech of January 1851, speaks merely of Cobden and other Manchester merchants and manufacturers having 'opened communications' with Thomas Wyse (*op. cit.*, p. 48), and of Simpson having 'visited Cobden in 1836' (p. 75). He is surely in error in stating, as he does, that 'the first public action of Cobden and his friends seems to have been not in Manchester, but in Salford, where a town's meeting was held in the Town Hall on 23rd September 1837' (p. 49).

[4] *Report of the Speeches Delivered at the Dinner to James Simpson* . . . , p. 25. Rathbone himself proposed a toast to George Combe, the celebrated phrenologist and educationist, who was a friend of Simpson's and shared many of his views on education; Combe and Simpson became the proprietors in 1848 of the Williams Secular School in Edinburgh. Combe lectured on education in Liverpool on 29 April 1837 (advertisement in *Liverpool Chronicle* of that date).

ment from the meeting with two of the most important educationists of the time or to have been confirmed in his belief that the system of instruction to be adopted in the Liverpool Corporation Schools could well become a matter of more than local importance.

3

The Liverpool Education Committee had now to draw up and submit to the Council detailed regulations for the schools. It might have been expected that, before formulating the rules relating to the giving of religious instruction, the Committee would have sought the advice and co-operation of the clergy of the different denominations; but there is no record of any consultation with the Nonconformist ministers, and Rathbone later stated 'decidedly and unreservedly that the Catholic clergy had never been consulted respecting the regulations of the Corporation Free Schools. Mr Horsfall was requested to ask Mr Wilcock a simple question, as to one of the regulations of his church. This was the only instance in which the committee had any communication with the Catholic clergy. It was a simple inquiry as to a matter of fact— not a consultation'.[1] The 'simple question' asked of Mr Wilcock (the Roman Catholic priest in charge of St Anthony's Church) was whether the Roman Catholic clergy would permit the children of their persuasion to join in prayer with children of other denominations, since it was hoped that each school day would begin with prayer.

The discussions which took place on this point between Charles Horsfall and Mr Sheil (a Roman Catholic member of the Education Committee) show that the former was genuinely anxious to obtain the support of the Roman Catholic clergy and not seeking to emphasize a difference of belief: he 'thought the objections were not insuperable and . . . he hoped the catholic clergy would be of his opinion.'[2] The Rev. P. Wilcock, after consulting other Roman Catholic clergy in the town, stated that it would not be possible to allow the Roman Catholic children to join in prayer with other children,[3] but that no objection would be raised to their joining in the singing of certain hymns. The Education Committee thereupon decided (15 June 1836) that the school

---

[1] Letter from William Rathbone to the Rev. Augustus Campbell published in *The Albion* (Liverpool), 18 July 1836. In a letter published in the same newspaper on 25 July 1836, Charles Horsfall wrote to Rathbone: 'I may observe that what you stated with regard to my communication with Mr Wilcox [*sic*] is precisely what took place.'

[2] *Liverpool Journal*, 30 July 1836.

[3] There is, however, clear evidence, as will be shown later, that at this or some subsequent time the Roman Catholic clergy agreed to allow all the children in the Infants' Departments to pray together.

day should begin not with a prayer but with a hymn, to be sung by all the children together. It is worth remarking, as an indication of the willingness of some of the Conservatives at this stage to seek an agreed solution of the 'Religious Problem', that it was one of the few Conservative members of the Council who had thus actively sought to have Protestant and Roman Catholic children praying together, and that when his attempt failed Horsfall not only continued to be a member of the Education Committee but agreed to serve on one of the sub-committees[1] elected to supervise the day-to-day working of each of the Corporation Schools.

The members of the Education Committee, and William Rathbone in particular, recognized the importance of obtaining the co-operation of the Rev. Augustus Campbell, not merely because he was the spokesman of the clergy who had served on the earlier 'Schools Committee', but because he was by far the more active of the two Rectors of Liverpool and a man whose example was bound to affect the attitudes of numbers of his fellow-clergymen, especially those who, like Campbell himself, were not illiberal or extreme in their views. He seems to have been a kindly, able and conscientious clergyman, who was far more interested in charitable works than in religious or political controversies; he and Rathbone, in spite of the great difference in their religious views, had often worked amicably together on charitable projects, and on one occasion when Campbell's character was being maligned Rathbone had gone out of his way to 'bear . . . testimony to Mr Campbell's high character and attention to all the charities in Liverpool, whether Protestant or Dissenting, and to the confidence that persons of all religions feel in his upright principles and Christian feeling'.[2]

Nor was the Junior Rector without courage. In 1829, at the time of the movement for Roman Catholic Emancipation, the then Senior Rector moved the adoption of a petition 'against all further concession' to the Roman Catholics, and thirty-two Church of England clergymen signed the petition; thereupon a second petition was prepared expressing 'the acquiescence of the subscribers in a measure for relieving the Catholics from civil disabilities, provided that care is taken to guard effectively the Protestant establishment',[3] and this petition was signed by sixteen clergymen of the Established Church, one of them being Campbell. What was even more encouraging to the Education Committee was the fact that the Junior Rector had approved of the introduction of the 'Irish System of Education' into Ireland. Could he now

[1] *Proceedings of Education Committee*, Vol. I, p. 14.
[2] *Report Liverpool Inquiry, 1833*, p. 536.
[3] *Liverpool Mercury*, 20 March 1829.

be persuaded to play a somewhat similar role in Liverpool to that which the Protestant Archbishop of Dublin had played in Ireland as a supporter of the 'Irish System'?

It would seem that he came very near to doing so. Rathbone quite definitely stated that Campbell was at first prepared to accept the new policy but changed his mind later;[1] Rathbone's son, the sixth William Rathbone, was certainly expressing his father's opinion when he wrote, many years afterwards, that 'Mr Campbell was at first cordially with my father and the Corporation in this matter, but he could not withstand the outcry that was raised, and left them in the lurch'.[2] This statement is perhaps not just to Campbell, whose reactions to the new proposals may well have been more complex than the remark implies. But there can be no doubt whatever that he came very close to agreeing to co-operate with the Education Committee even if, in the end, he did not undertake to do so. According to his own account of his opinions at this time, he was no longer an admirer of the 'Irish System'.[3] However, he 'knew, from the different constitution of the local government, that things could not go on under the old system'. He 'was prepared to submit to change'. He was 'no bigot' and did not claim to belong to an infallible Church. He said:

I declare that I do not wish, and never did wish, to force my method of teaching on any man, woman, or child, against his will. Of course I think my own right ... But I do not say that it is infallible; therefore I leave others to choose what methods they please. For these reasons I was determined to stay in the schools, if I might have been allowed to teach, not Roman Catholics or Dissenters, but my own communion in my own way. This was all I asked: I might have been wrong; but this was my determination, and for this purpose I had many communications with those who had taken the matter in hand; and I besought and implored them not to lay down such written laws as would oblige us, as ministers of the Established Church, to retire.[4]

On a later occasion he explained that he had sought to co-operate with the Education Committee because he wished to avoid discord, and he added:

[1] See letters published in *Liverpool Courier*, 10 July 1839.
[2] W. Rathbone (6th), *A Sketch of Family History During Four Generations* ..., p. 91.
[3] 'As for the Irish system, I honestly confess I do not know how it is working at present. When first proposed I was rather captivated by its seeming beauty. I thought it practicable for Ireland. My opinion, however, on this subject has changed. But had it been ever so practicable for Ireland, why ... should it be forced upon England?' (*A Full Report of the Speeches and Proceedings at the Meeting Held at the Amphitheatre on Wednesday July 13, 1836, for the Promotion of Scriptural Education in Liverpool*, Liverpool, 1836, p. 11.)
[4] *Ibid.*, p. 10.

fearing . . . that I might be excluded from the old schools, and have no others where I might continue to teach my Protestant children, I reserved to myself (under this apprehension) the discretion of continuing to teach my Protestant children without interfering with any others, if the Council would leave the management of the schools discretionary with the sub-committees, and not publish any code of laws compromising any religious principle, or plainly injurious to the Established Church, or contrary to my duty as one of its ministers.[1]

The qualifications here stated are somewhat vaguely worded, but read in the light of what follows the passage evidently means that Campbell was prepared to accept an arrangement which made it possible for him to teach what he called his Protestant children 'without interfering with any others' so long as the Council drew up no regulations preventing the giving of religious instruction in general or harmful to the interests of the Established Church in particular. He was clearly prepared to accept the principle that the schools should be made available to children not of his own faith.

From the correspondence between Campbell and Rathbone[2] we learn that the Education Committee first drew up a plan which, in Campbell's words, 'did not exclude the Bible in school hours. It allowed three-quarters of an hour for religious instruction *every morning*, from a quarter past nine to ten, and additional hours on such afternoons as might be appointed'. Apparently Campbell declined to give any opinion concerning this arrangement, but protested against the introduction of the 'Irish Scripture Lessons'; according to his own account, he stated that if the 'Irish System' were to be adopted he would 'withdraw'. Since he admitted that he had not seen the 'Irish Selections' from the Bible, a copy of them was sent to him with, according to Rathbone, a request that Campbell would state any objections which he had to them so that his opinions 'might be laid before the Education Committee, previous to its being settled what books were to be used in the schools'. No answer was received, and Rathbone 'felt justified in assuming' that Campbell had no strong objections to the selections which had been sent to him. Shortly afterwards, on 15 June 1836, the Education Committee decided that denominational religious instruction should be given not during the first period of each school day but on the two half-days normally regarded as holidays;[3] but when

---

[1] *Address of the Rev. A. Campbell at the Opening of the South Church of England School, Cornwallis-Street, December 5th, 1837*, Liverpool [n.d.], pp. 7–8.

[2] Printed in *The Albion* (Liverpool), 18 July 1836.

[3] 'Resolved . . . That a portion of each Thursday and Saturday afternoon be a Holy day as to the ordinary Duties of the School, and be appropriated to the formation of Bible classes for the Children whose Parents have no objection thereto and to other Religious instruction' (*Proceedings of Education Committee*, Vol. I, p. 14).

Campbell expressed his 'disappointment' with this arrangement Rathbone requested him to meet the sub-committee which had been set up to supervise the work of the South School 'to state [his] wishes, and to consult how, without any compromise of principle, they could be met'.

Campbell met the sub-committee and was understood to have said that the 'former plan' (that is, of giving denominational religious instruction during the first period of the school day) 'would be satisfactory',[1] so that, to quote Rathbone, 'at the next meeting of the Education Committee [on 5 July 1836] it was proposed as such; and the committee, in order to secure the co-operation of the clergy, rescinded their former resolution'. What he meant by these words was that the proposal to give denominational religious instruction on half-day 'holidays' was abandoned, and the original plan of giving such instruction daily was accepted instead, with what Rathbone evidently considered to be the minor modification that the religious instruction should be given not during the first period of the day, but during the last. The amended regulation then read:

> That one hour of each day be devoted to the Religious instruction of those Children whose Parents do not object and that such hour be in the Afternoon after the School has closed.
> That the School shall be considered as closed at 3 o'clock in Winter and at 4 in Summer.[2]

Conscious of their own good intentions, almost all of the members of the Committee failed to recognize that, since the first period of the school day would have fallen within school hours, whereas the hour now to be devoted to denominational religious instruction was described as falling outside them, the change appeared to involve an important question of principle. Not appreciating this, men like Rathbone were puzzled and indignant at Campbell's resuming his opposition after they had, in their own view, gone out of their way to accommodate him.

If Campbell had broken off negotiations with the Education Committee as a protest against the use of the words 'after the School has closed', it would not have been surprising; but he did not do so. He spoke of the offending regulation later as one which excluded 'all peculiar religious instruction from the schools' and only permitted it

---

[1] Campbell later claimed that he had been misunderstood and that he had not described this proposal as 'satisfactory'; but at any rate in his own letter to Rathbone he described it as a plan which 'did not exclude the Bible in school hours' (*The Albion*, 18 July 1836).

[2] *Proceedings of Education Committee*, Vol. I, p. 16.

'in the school-room for one hour, "when the school was closed" and then only to those "whose parents did not object"'. But he went on:

Surely, never was a conciliatory spirit so thwarted and baffled before. But, still, as I was led to believe this system would not be strictly enforced, as every inducement of personal favour was shown to me, individually, and peculiar privileges conceded to me, personally, as a visiter; I reserved to myself the discretionary power to teach the Protestant children, if I could not provide them with accommodation elsewhere; and thus, as the least of evils, to mitigate the injury of the new system by giving them all the religious instruction that the new laws allowed.

Why, then, was he unable, in the end, to co-operate with the Education Committee? He himself explains:

... when I found (what I did not know at first, though I might have known it) that prayer was prohibited because the Roman Catholic clergy would not permit any form of prayer to be used at all; when I found that the simple expedient of a Bible class for Protestants during morning school hours had been abandoned, upon the principle, as I believed, that the Protestant Bible might not be read at all, even by Protestants during the ordinary business of the school; when the old masters and mistresses resigned, and I should have had to act with strangers, at least, if not with enemies, I then conceived that I had made every concession that Christian charity required, and more than Christian prudence could justify.[1]

The last part of the Rector's explanation shows quite clearly that he had sought a compromise until the control of events was taken out of his hands. There can be little doubt that if the Education Committee had not attempted to bring Protestants and Roman Catholics together for the singing of hymns and reading selections from the Scriptures,[2] and had made it more clear that the giving of denominational religious instruction was to be (as they wished it to be) a recognized part of the school day, then the motives and actions of the Committee would have been much less open to misrepresentation; and there is every indication that men of moderate opinions, including Campbell and a number of other Church of England clergymen, would have found it not too difficult to accept the new policy.

It was particularly unfortunate that the regulation relating to the time when denominational religious instruction could be given was so worded as genuinely to convince numbers of honest men like Campbell

[1] *Address . . . at the Opening of the South Church of England School*, pp. 7–8.
[2] It will be remembered that the reading of these *Scripture Lessons* was not made compulsory in the schools assisted by the Irish Board of Commissioners.

that the new Education Committee wished to exclude the Bible from the Corporation Schools. It is perfectly clear from the statements of the members of the Committee at the time and from their subsequent practice that the phrase 'after the School has closed' was intended to convey no more than that the religious and secular instruction would be given separately. As soon as the phrase was objected to, Rathbone explained that the new system could operate only if 'the first or last of the school hours' was set aside for the religious instruction, and 'the latter was chosen as likely to be most convenient to the teachers'. The schools were to be 'considered as closed' *an hour before the time at which such schools were usually closed*, specifically so that the denominational religious instruction should be given:

> As to the Bible being read only out of school hours,—every one knows the usual school hours are till five in the summer and four in winter, and therefore that the hour fixed, being within these, would be regarded as regular school hours by both teachers and children, though not so called in the resolution of the committee.[1]

It may be said at once that not only was denominational religious instruction given on each school day from the very inauguration of the new system (Protestant children having the Authorized Version and Roman Catholic children the Douay Version of the Bible), but it was given to all of the children in attendance, since in practice it was found that no parent objected to the giving of such instruction to his child.[2] The claim that the Bible was excluded from the schools was based, as even the arguments of the critics of the new scheme showed, on the fact that the phrase 'after the School has closed' appeared in the regulation of the Education Committee. Less than six months later, to meet what Rathbone and many members of the Committee considered to be 'a paltry quibble',[3] the phraseology of the regulation was changed so as to make it quite clear that the school day did not in fact end until the denominational religious instruction had been given; but by that time, a good deal of opposition had been unnecessarily aroused.

4

Whilst the Rev. A. Campbell had been giving careful consideration to the plans of the Education Committee and hesitating to take definite

---

[1] *Liverpool Mercury*, 22 July 1836.
[2] Letter of William Rathbone to J. C. Symons, printed in *Cheltenham Free Press*, 23 February 1839.
[3] Letter to C. Otway dated 17 May 1838.

steps to reject them, in the hope that some agreement would eventually be arrived at, a clergyman of very different calibre had been setting to work in the town to arouse quite uncompromising opposition to the new system. The Rev. Hugh M'Neile had arrived in Liverpool only two years before to become perpetual curate at the Church of St Jude. He was an Ulsterman, having been born at Ballycastle in Co. Antrim in 1795. After graduating at Trinity College, Dublin, he had studied at King's Inn, Dublin, and at Lincoln's Inn, London, with the intention of being called to the Irish Bar; but later he changed his mind and became a minister of the Established Church. He first served the parish of Stranorlar in Co. Donegal, where, according to the writer of a memoir[1] published in the *Church Magazine* for July 1839, he found even the Kildare Place system of education which had preceded the 'Irish System' too much inclined towards compromise. He

resisted all the compromising schemes of education propounded by the Kildare-place and Hibernian Societies, and others who disclaimed what they called proselytism as uncharitable, and omitted Scripture *instruction* (beyond the bare reading) in order, as they unwisely thought, to conciliate all classes and bring all to school. Mr M'Neile had a strictly *Church* and Bible school, filled with children, all learning the Catechism and the Liturgy.

In 1822 he was presented to the rectory of Albury in Surrey, and thereafter he was frequently invited to preach in London, where his powers as a speaker made him well known. In the memoir already referred to, he is described as 'one of the first orators of the age', and it is asserted that 'whenever it is known that he is to preach or speak anywhere in London or the vicinity, crowds assemble to listen to his sound and admirable sermons and his brilliant speeches'. Another contemporary writer says of him:

In personal appearance, in action, in voice, in all the exterior attainments of an orator we know none that come up to M'Neile. His acting is truly dramatic. . . . He is the O'Connell of Protestantism, as far as grossness and perjury can be dissociated from that name, and activity or agitation only

[1] The same writer makes known the curious fact that M'Neile 'while on a tour of Switzerland, in the summer of 1816, . . . was taken suddenly and dangerously ill at a country inn, and, humanly speaking, had his life saved by Henry Brougham, Esq., now Lord Brougham, who happened to be in the house at the time, and hearing a young man was unwell, benevolently volunteered his medical skill, and prescribed successfully'. Few men did more to arouse opposition to Brougham's plans to set up a national system of education than did M'Neile in later years; and certainly the Liverpool Liberals must sometimes have been tempted to wish that Brougham had been a little less ready to 'strive, officiously to keep alive'. The story was not denied by M'Neile (so far as the writer is aware), and it is repeated in the *D.N.B.*, where it is also stated that it was the saving of his life which led M'Neile to take Orders.

represented by it. M'Neile is not a mere enthusiastic declaimer; he works and perseveres until he gains the mastery.[1]

It need hardly be said that his opponents in political and religious controversies spoke of him in less laudatory terms, but of his skill in debate, his energy, sincerity and power to sway many of his hearers there can be no doubt.[2] He was proud to describe himself as a religious agitator, since religious agitation, he felt, was to be approved, although political agitation was not;[3] and he spent a great deal of time denouncing the Roman Catholic Church from platforms in many English towns and cities, always with a fervour and conviction which arose quite evidently from an honest belief that any form of compromise with the enemy was to be condemned.

Such was the man who became incumbent of St Jude's in 1834. He soon became known as an eloquent platform speaker, his first appearance in the town in that capacity being in November 1834 at a public meeting to receive a deputation from the Orange Societies in Ireland.[4] His fiery addresses to the newly formed Protestant Associations in Liverpool, Warrington and other towns in the area soon made him in effect the chosen leader of those whose favourite slogan was 'No Popery'. Few of the Church of England clergy wished to have any connection with the local Protestant Association which he helped to found in Liverpool in October 1835, at a meeting which did much to stir up religious dissension in the town,[5] but M'Neile was not easily

[1] *Fraser's Magazine for Town and Country*, January 1839, p. 31. See also J. Evans, *Lancashire Authors and Orators*, London, 1850, pp. 187, 189.

[2] It was probably M'Neile of whom Sydney Smith wrote: 'If he will limit himself to thirty minutes, and carry up a book into the pulpit in conformity with our well-known habits, he would beat all the popular preachers in London. My clerk said to me, "Your honour is not fit to light a candle to his honour!" He is a handsome man also, and has a kind of Ten Commandments look about him, which is very suitable to a preacher.' See Nowell C. Smith (ed.), *The Letters of Sydney Smith*, Oxford, 1953, Vol. II, p. 673 n. See also the reference to M'Neile's 'plaintive twaddle' in *Further Letters of Gerard Manley Hopkins* . . . , ed. C. A. Abbott, London, 1938, p. 8.

[3] *Liverpool Mercury*, 24 June 1836. M'Neile believed that: 'It is only through the stirring that controversy occasions that truth can be kept clear. Without it the church becomes a stagnant pool, the stillness of whose surface serves but to hide a deep bed of corruption.' (Quoted from one of his sermons in *A Letter to the Rev. Hugh M'Neile* . . . by 'A Lean Unwashed Artificer', Liverpool, 1835.)

[4] J. A. Picton, *Memorials of Liverpool*, Second Edition, Vol. I, p. 458.

[5] Representatives of the Manchester Statistical Society, when reporting on the state of education in Liverpool in 1836, stated that 'at the outset of the inquiry, and amongst the inferior schools, party spirit, evidently excited by a large meeting held 29 October, 1835, followed by other proceedings, was found to rage with considerable virulence. In one of the dame schools the mistress stated the feeling between Protestant and Catholic to be so violent, that, on the admission of a new scholar, she frequently received injunctions from the parents not to allow the child, if a Catholic, to sit on the same form with Protestant children, or if a Protestant to sit with a Catholic' (*Report of a Committee of the Manchester Statistical Society on the State of Education in the Borough of Liverpool*, p. 5 n.).

discouraged. Anxious that the 'voice saying "No Popery" shall be responded to from city to city and town after town, each and all answering "No Popery" ',[1] he addressed Protestant Associations in many parts of the country, usually in the company of one Dr Sullivan (a former Roman Catholic priest) and a Dr M'Ghee, and sometimes supported by the Rev. Hugh Stowell of Manchester.

The Liverpool Education Committee found themselves opposed by a man who was probably the most eloquent, the most able and the most consistent religious agitator of his day, and one who had platforms available to him in many places outside the town. Moreover, there is no doubt that when he began to speak and write against the introduction of the 'Irish System of Education' into the Corporation Schools, some part of what he said expressed the opinions of many clergymen of a more liberal and flexible turn of mind than himself, clergymen who were feeling a growing and not unnatural resentment that the Church of England was so frequently being called upon to make concessions to meet the new conditions of the nineteenth century. It says a great deal for the fair-mindedness of the Rev. Mr Campbell that he should honestly have sought a compromise with men (many of them Dissenters) who were determined that the Established Church should have no special privileges and should no longer receive endowments from the Corporation. And it is remarkable that the alliance between M'Neile and most of the other Church of England clergymen in the town was so much lacking in cordiality and so comparatively short-lived.

Although M'Neile became the most determined and the most implacable opponent of the proposal to adopt the 'Irish System' in the Corporation Schools, it would seem that a large majority of the clergy of the Established Church in the town decided to demonstrate their opposition to the Education Committee's plans without receiving any lead from him. On 22 June 1836, whilst the negotiations with the Junior Rector were still proceeding, the *Liverpool Courier* announced that it had been learned

with extreme satisfaction that the cause of Scriptural education in our local schools has been warmly taken up by the clergy of the Established Church. A public movement is intended to be made in a few days, preparatory to founding schools independently of the Corporation, in which *the whole Bible* shall be taught.

A week later the same newspaper announced that 'the intended

[1] *Authentic Report of the Great Protestant Meeting Held at the Amphitheatre, Liverpool on Thursday the 29th of October 1835 for the Purpose of Communicating Important Documents and of Forming a Protestant Association*, Liverpool [1835].

meeting of the clergy is postponed, to await the determination of the Council'. There was still hope that Campbell would persuade the Education Committee to modify its policy, and, moreover, there was still the possibility that the Council would refuse to approve the detailed regulations which the Committee was preparing to lay before it at its next meeting. The delay gave M'Neile his opportunity to make himself, in the eyes of the public at least, the leader of the opposition to the new policy. On the evening of Sunday, 3 July 1836, he preached a sermon in the course of which he forcefully denounced the Education Committee's proposals, claimed that the 'Irish Scripture Lessons' perverted Protestant teaching, and declared that it was the intention of the Committee 'to take away the Bible from the schools'. He warned the Council that Protestant children could not be sent to schools where the Bible was not read, and also warned his congregation that they should 'beware of compromise', since the Council might attempt to devise 'some more moderate scheme', which might have the effect of 'dividing the friends of Scriptural education'. But if the recommendations of the Education Committee were to be adopted by the Council then, he said, 'when they take away the Bible from the schools, we must ask you for help to enable us to take away the children also. We shall ask you, then, to build other school-rooms'.

He exhorted those present to explain the situation to other Protestant parents and to ask them to 'withhold their children' from the Corporation Schools. He wanted the subject to become 'the topic of conversation through the town' so that when a public meeting was held 'thousands of Englishmen [would] come where we invite you with minds prepared to appreciate our arguments, and hands prepared to meet the call on you for help'. But undoubtedly the most interesting part of M'Neile's sermon is that in which he made it clear that he appreciated the importance of the experiment which it was proposed to carry out in Liverpool:

But it may be urged that this is a small matter, why ascribe so much importance to two schools in the town of Liverpool? . . . This is no local matter. It begins in Liverpool it is true. It must have a local commencement. But it cannot end where it begins. It is a feeler of the national pulse. . . . It will be pleaded as a precedent. The time is well-chosen. The opportunity is shrewdly seized. Why? Because just at this time, there exist a number of town councils in England composed during a violent reaction of men's minds last winter, who it is to be feared are ready and willing to follow this precedent.[1]

[1] The sermon was published in the *Liverpool Courier* on 6 July 1836, with the explanation that 'The cause of its being taken down [by newspaper reporters] was the previous intimation of the subject, and its likelihood, at the present moment, to be of service'.

It is obvious that the Rev. Hugh M'Neile saw, just as clearly as did William Rathbone, the significance of the struggle which was about to begin.

5

Three days after M'Neile had delivered his outspoken warning, the Liverpool Town Council met to consider the detailed regulations which the Education Committee proposed to prescribe for the Corporation Schools. But before the Council began to examine the recommendations a discussion took place which is of some interest as illustrating the determination of most of the members that the Council should not favour or assist any particular 'denomination of Christians'. As far back as 1789 the Common Council had granted to the Roman Catholic clergy on very favourable terms leases of land in Seel Street on which a chapel, house and schools had been built. It was now proposed by the Finance Committee that the lease of the land under the schools should be renewed, again on generous terms. Mr Blackburn, one of the most enthusiastic supporters of the policy of the new Education Committee, of which he was a member, introduced a modern note into the discussion, arguing that

the only course by which they could avoid dissensions and contentions in their future proceedings was to show no favour to any class, to place all on a footing of perfect equality, and to require the full payment for any property that might be leased or re-leased. . . . They would thus prevent the possibility of its being said that one denomination had been treated with more favour than another. He moved that the grant be suspended for a month, and he assured the Council that had it been made to his own denomination he should have pursued exactly the same course.[1]

Blackburn's motion was successful, and later it was 'laid down as a fixed principle that no grant shall be made in aid of any Schools except those which are the property of the Corporation and under the immediate management and control of the Council.'[2]

The regulations proposed by the Education Committee for adoption in the Corporation Schools were then considered; those relating to the provision of religious instruction in the schools read as follows:

That the Schools shall be open at Nine o'Clock each Morning and commence by the Children singing a Hymn from the selections of the Commissioners of National Education in Ireland and by the Master or Mistress reading a portion of the Scriptures from the same Selections.

[1] *Liverpool Courier*, 13 July 1836.
[2] *Proceedings of Council*, Vol. XVII, p. 201.

That one hour of each day be devoted to the Religious instruction of those Children whose Parents do not object and that such hour be in the Afternoon after the School has closed.

That the School shall be considered as closed at 3 o'Clock in Winter and at 4 in Summer.

That the Clergy of the different denominations be solicited to attend for these purposes and that every practicable accommodation be afforded to them.

That the Children be required to attend the Schools at a quarter before Ten o'clock on Sunday Morning and that the same religious instruction be given as on the other Mornings and that the Children be expected regularly to attend their respective places of Worship.[1]

The Committee recommended also that the text-books used in the schools should be those which had been prepared for use in Irish schools at the request of the 'Commissioners of Education in Ireland'; these books were 'to have a fair Trial previous to the introduction of any other'.[2]

The first member of the Council to express disapproval of the proposed regulations was Mr E. Cropper, a Liberal, who was supported, as on a former occasion, by another Liberal, Mr Rushton. Cropper stated that he was 'opposed to the introduction of the Irish selections from the Scriptures', not 'on account of the selections themselves, but because they were accompanied by notes calculated to confirm error rather than elucidate the passages to which they referred'. He moved an amendment to the proposal that the Education Committee's report should be accepted, suggesting instead that the report should be 'referred back to the committee with a view to the substitution of the Bible for the selections'. William Rathbone replied to the attack made on the Committee in the Rev. Mr M'Neile's sermon, and did not mince his words when denying that it was proposed to exclude the Authorized Version of the Bible from the schools:

. . . when a clergyman prostituted—he used the term advisedly—when a clergyman prostituted the pulpit for the base purposes of faction and sectarian zeal—to cast every species of odium on the honest intentions of the committee of the Corporation schools, he would tell that clergyman . . . that the statements he had made in the pulpit were false and unchristian.

Rathbone pointed out that even under the former régime selections from the Bible had been used by all except 'the elder classes', whilst catechisms had merely been learnt by heart; there had been no scriptural lessons and no explanations of the Collects or the Liturgy. He went on:

[1] *Proceedings of Education Committee*, Vol. 1, pp. 14–16.
[2] *Ibid.*, p. 15.

It was said that they wanted to exclude the Bible:—no such thing. The Rev. Hugh M'Neile might have heard, might have known that it was false. . . . The Committee wished the Bible and Collects to be read, and the Liturgy explained to those who belonged to the Church, and this was what was called excluding the Bible . . . he believed that the system would do more for the religious education of the poor than any thing that had ever been attempted before.

Rathbone's angry reply to M'Neile was followed by an eloquent speech from Thomas Blackburn in which he replied point by point to criticisms which M'Neile had made of the 'Irish Scripture Lessons', and showed that the extracts from the Bible had received the approval of several members of the Irish Board of Commissioners who could scarcely be suspected of countenancing the substitution of Roman Catholic doctrines for Protestant teachings.

The most striking feature of the debate, and the most significant from the point of view of those interested in the shifts of opinion which were taking place at this time, was the moderate and sometimes even hesitant tone of those who opposed the adoption of the Committee's recommendations. When Rathbone hinted that E. Cropper had proposed his amendment and criticized the *Scripture Lessons* under the influence of M'Neile, Cropper not only denied this, but made the frank admission that he had not made up his mind when he entered the Council Chamber whether or not to put forward any amendment.[1] Of the other two speakers against the proposals, both of them Conservatives, one was Charles Horsfall, who had remained a member of the Education Committee long after the decision to recommend the adoption of the 'Irish System' had first been arrived at,[2] and who now, it would seem, was a prey to doubts because of the use of the phrase 'after the school had closed'. He deemed it '. . . as the question had been raised . . . quite right to say that he felt some difficulty with regard to the introduction of this Irish system of education . . . if they looked to the resolution they would find that the Bible was never used till the school was closed. . . . He thought that as the compilers of the selection never intended it to supersede the Bible in any respect, but rather to lead to a better understanding of it, there was no reason whatever why it should have been excluded during school hours.' He went out of his

---

[1] This admission was omitted from the *Liverpool Courier's* account of the proceedings.

[2] Horsfall (as we have seen) had even consented to become a member of the sub-committee set up to supervise the affairs of the North Corporation School, and had done so at the very meeting of the Education Committee at which all the recommendations now laid before the Council had been decided upon, except for that change in the times at which denominational religious instruction should be given which had been made in the hope of satisfying the Rev. A. Campbell.

way to praise 'the most anxious attention' which the Committee had devoted to their recommendations, and regretted that 'he could not entirely agree'. Mr Henry Lawrence, the other Conservative speaker, made observations which were even more mild; he said simply that 'he had been very much struck with some of the very sensible observations of Mr Blackburn, but on the whole, as the system came before him as something new, and he really did wish to understand it, he felt bound to support the amendment. He did so with considerable hesitation, because he had been very much struck with the reasoning of Mr Blackburn'.

So that, of the three speakers who could not give their support to the Education Committee, one had done so until almost the last moment, one had not yet decided to propose an amendment on entering the Council Chamber and the third supported this amendment only 'with considerable hesitation'. The amendment was rejected by forty-five votes to six,[1] four Conservatives and two Liberals voting in favour of it. The Council then formally accepted the recommendations of the Education Committee, and so authorized it to inaugurate the new system in the Corporation Schools.[2]

[1] Twelve members of the Council were absent.
[2] *Liverpool Mercury*, 8 July 1836.

Chapter 4

THE CHURCH AND THE PRESS

I

IT was one thing for the Education Committee to defend its proposals and explain its motives in the Council Chamber; it was quite another thing to make itself heard elsewhere, above the clamour of those who believed, or affected to believe, that the Committee intended to exclude the Bible from the Corporation Schools and to substitute for it untrustworthy selections. The public meeting which a number of the clergy of the Established Church had proposed to hold earlier had, as we have seen, been postponed 'to await the determination of the Council'; now that the Council's decision was known there was no reason for delay. On the day following the Council meeting a number of the Church of England clergy 'and of the friends of a sound scriptural education for the poor' met together and decided to call 'a general meeting of the inhabitants of Liverpool' in the following terms:

We, the undersigned, Clergy of the Parish and Municipal Borough of Liverpool, impressed with the necessity of making the Authorised Version of the Bible the basis of Religious Education, and deeply regretting that we are compelled to withdraw our co-operation from the Corporation Schools, by rules, the effect of which, in our apprehension, will be virtually to exclude the Bible from any practical use in the Schools, and the Clergy from any effective superintendence there, earnestly call upon all persons who are members or friends of the Established Church, and advocates for the fundamental principle of Protestantism, '*the free use of the unmutilated word of God*', to assist us in building and supporting Schools where that Word may be freely taught, under our own direction and superintendence. And for the furtherance of this important purpose we invite them to meet us in the Amphitheatre . . . when and where a Meeting will be held to solicit subscriptions, and determine upon the measures which it may be expedient to adopt.

This announcement was signed by the Rev. Jonathan Brooks, as Senior Rector, the Rev. A. Campbell, as Junior Rector, and twenty-nine other clergymen of Liverpool.[1]

[1] The appeal and an account of the proceedings at the subsequent public meeting are to be found in a pamphlet entitled *A Full Report of the Speeches Delivered At The Great Protestant Meeting at the Royal Amphitheatre Liverpool on Wednesday, the 13th of July, 1836*, Liverpool [1836]. Another account with a somewhat similar title (for which

The public meeting took place on 13 July 1836, and it is doubtful whether any similar gathering in the history of the town had ever aroused so much interest.[1] Yet almost all of the speakers criticized the Education Committee's proposals in a restrained and responsible manner, as if anxious rather to make clear the reasons for their opposition than to arouse ill-feeling against the Council. The Rev. A. Campbell even went out of his way to pay a tribute to William Rathbone:

. . . honour and conscience oblige me to say a few words in respect of one who is an object, I know, of general political enmity, I mean Mr William Rathbone. . . . In all the transactions connected with this troublesome affair I have not only been indebted to him for personal kindness, courtesy and friendship, but I have not detected in him one act of enmity to the church. I do not believe that he wished to exclude the clergy from the schools.

He went on to account for Rathbone's actions in words whose meaning is not altogether clear:

I believe, in my conscience, that in this matter he has been over-ruled—that some witchcraft prevails in higher quarters and throws a spell over the executive government and impedes the progress of rational amendment and religious peace which prevailed here.

Speaking for 'the clergy whose mind has been moved in this case almost as the mind of one man', he informed the meeting that they were present not for purposes of political or religious agitation, to stimulate excitement or 'accelerate that movement, which seems, I fear, unhappily, and most sorely, against our disposition, to be hurrying us into the troubled ocean of civil and religious discord'. He evidently felt that the true purpose of the meeting was not to arouse opposition to the Council but to call for funds with which to build new schools; the general principle which he believed to be at stake he was reluctant to discuss:

We are here to contend for the liberty wherewith the reformation set us free, the unfettered use of the unmutilated word of God. But I waive this topic, because I do not want it. I will waive it, moreover, because I wish to avoid excitement.

see Bibliography) is extant. The two accounts are by no means identical, and where this second report is quoted the source will be indicated as *Report of Speeches . . .* , *13 July 1836* (2).

[1] According to the *Liverpool Standard* (19 July 1836) the meeting was attended by five thousand people, including seventy clergymen. One speaker expressed his pride at seeing 'before him so numerous a meeting; a more respectable assembly he had not witnessed in the town, although he had been forty years a resident' (*Report of Speeches . . .* , *13 July 1836*, p. 9).

Nevertheless the Junior Rector did much to arouse hostility to the Council by alleging, or seeming to allege, that, whilst the Roman Catholic clergy had been consulted as to their attitude to the proposed new system, the Church of England clergy had not been so consulted. According to one widely published version of his speech the Junior Rector expressed his deep regret that 'the rectors were not officially consulted by the education committee. ... The Roman catholic clergy were consulted; the rectors and acting committee might, as an act of policy have been consulted too'. In another, almost certainly more accurate, version of the speech, Campbell is said to have made very different remarks: 'I lament, sir, that the education committee, before they decided upon the rules, had not been so kind as to consult more our wishes upon the subject. The Roman Catholic clergy's wishes were consulted, I believe. ... It would certainly have been discreet and wise to have gained our concurrence.'[1]

Whatever the Junior Rector's exact words may have been, a good deal of ill-feeling was aroused both among those who believed that the Church of England clergy had been slighted and those who, knowing the facts, felt that Campbell was making a monstrously false statement for his own purposes. Nothing did more than did this incident to convince some influential Dissenters in Liverpool that the Church of England clergy were not to be trusted; and the distrust engendered at this period lasted for many years after the events here described.

The Senior Rector, the Rev. J. Brooks, claimed that if the 'Irish System' were to be introduced into the Corporation Schools, selections from the Scriptures would replace the complete Bible, which would become 'a sealed book'; he alleged that 'the new system placed the Bible out of the reach of the schools altogether', and pointed out to his audience that 'the free, unmutilated, unshackled use of the Bible was the true principle on which they founded their faith'. Nevertheless, he indicated that it was not his wish or that of his colleagues to 'cast any reflections on the corporate body'; he and they were willing to concede to the Council 'the right of conducting their schools in such manner as they deemed expedient and consistent with their own convictions. It was not for him to call in question, nor did he dispute, the purity of their motives; but still they [the clergy] had the right of approving or rejecting the principles they might wish to maintain or inculcate, in the minds of others.'[2]

Similar sentiments were expressed by Adam Hodgson as a representative of the laity. 'Nothing', he said, 'was further from his intentions

[1] *Report of Speeches ... , 13 July 1836* (2), p. 11.
[2] *Report of Speeches ... , 13 July 1836*, pp. 2–6.

than to speak disrespectfully of those gentlemen of the corporation to whom they had referred, as introducers of this new system of education. He conceded to them that right of private judgment which he claimed for himself and exercised.' He hoped that his hearers would 'all feel superior to any party feeling'. But if it was considered that it was 'necessary to secure the unrestricted and unmutilated scriptures for the use of the rising generation, and that the plan now proposed was dangerous and fallacious, he thought there was an insuperable objection to the system'. Charles Horsfall also addressed the meeting, and expressed the hope that in the new schools which it was proposed to build 'the Bible should not be excluded as the Irish system of education evidently aimed at'. The Rev. Dr Ralph spoke as a representative of the Scotch Church in Liverpool and emphasized the value of the Scriptures; while the Rev. Mr Dixon, a Wesleyan minister, maintained that if it was a hardship 'that the Roman catholic population of the town should be obliged to send their children where the Bible was not prohibited', it was 'a greater hardship to oblige the protestants to send their children where there was no Bible at all'. Mr Dixon 'concluded a speech of great force by calling upon all protestants to defend the citadel of their God'.

But undoubtedly for the greater part of the audience the chief event of the day was the speech of the Rev. Hugh M'Neile,[1] described by the Rev. Dr Ralph as 'that most lion-hearted of churchmen since the days of Luther'. In the course of a long and eloquent speech M'Neile assured his hearers that if 'they permitted such a system as that now proposed in the borough schools to be carried on they would be sanctioning that which would end in atheism'. He claimed that it was intended to 'establish a system of education for the children which would effectually exclude religious instruction'. He drew a ludicrous picture of the situation which would arise when clergymen of different persuasions were imparting denominational religious instruction in different parts of the school building at the same time, and asked, 'When the four corners of the building were thus occupied who . . . would be Tom in the middle?' He suggested that the children would be in no mood for Bible-reading during the hour 'after the school has closed', and went on to allege that when the then Mr Stanley had introduced the 'Irish System' into Ireland it was because, without knowing it, he had been 'fixed upon as an instrument wherewith to effect the object of the

---

[1] 'It would be difficult to describe the effect produced by some of the passages of Mr M'Neile's speech. His commanding and varied powers of persuasion and expression, his brilliant flights of fancy, rich humour and cutting, though playful sarcasms, will long be remembered as one of the most powerful and finest specimens of popular oratory that has ever been heard in Liverpool' (*ibid.*, pp. 29–30).

priests'. M'Neile dealt at some length with the comments made at the recent Council meeting by Rathbone and Blackburn on the criticisms of the 'Irish Selections' which he had made in his sermon. And he concluded as follows:

> The question was this, is England so infatuated with the passion of liberal philosophy as to be prepared to adopt such a system as a substitute for the sound principles she now enjoys? If that meeting had no other good effect, it would at least show what was the popular feeling. Liverpool had been selected as the arena for trying this question, and what does Liverpool answer? The masters' and mistresses' answer was their resignation—the clergy of the establishment answer with a protest—the laity have nobly rallied round the standard of scriptural education, and here, in 5,000 voices, and twice 5,000 hands, reiterated the cry of 'No Popery!'

The first resolution passed at the meeting was one expressing regret that rules had recently been introduced 'for the government of the corporation schools, which exclude the scriptures from general practical use in school hours'; the second resolution went on to state that it was 'expedient to build and maintain schools . . . in which the scriptures shall be freely taught, under the direction and superintendence of the clergy of the established church'. Finally a committee was to be formed 'for the furtherance of this important purpose, and to solicit subscriptions, and adopt such measures as may be deemed expedient to effect it in the best and speediest way'. Before the audience dispersed the sum of £3,000 had been subscribed; soon the subscriptions totalled over £11,000. The various speeches had shown that some doubt existed about the precise policy which the Council intended to pursue in the Corporation Schools—whether the Authorized Version of the Bible was to be 'excluded', for instance, or would be 'virtually excluded', or would be used in a 'restricted' fashion; and M'Neile's speech had differed markedly in tone from those of most of the other speakers. But during the course of the meeting it had been made quite clear that almost all of the Church of England clergy in the town would refuse to co-operate with the Education Committee by giving religious instruction in the Corporation Schools.

Moreover, the magnitude of the demonstration against the new policy naturally gave new hope to those political opponents whom the Liberals had so overwhelmingly defeated at the last municipal elections; the Conservative journals saw their opportunity and seized it, as will be seen. That some of the comment in those journals was inspired by religious zeal it would be unjust to deny; but there can be little doubt that a good deal of misrepresentation originated from political hostility. It is difficult, for example, to believe that the *Liverpool Standard* was genuinely of the opinion that the Council wished to 'O'Connelize and Socinianize the children of the poor',[1] or that the *Liverpool Courier* sincerely feared that the Education Committee's recommendations were the fruits of 'a deep-laid scheme for uprooting the principles of the Reformation'[2] and were part of 'a Popish plot'.[3] Until this time most of the comments on the proposal to introduce the 'Irish System' into the schools had come from sincere and responsible men, almost all of whom were anxious to avoid strife. Henceforward these were joined, and sometimes influenced, by many who may have had strong religious convictions, but who also had a not unnatural desire to assure the supremacy of their own political parties and who were prepared for that reason to indulge in personal abuse, gross exaggeration and distortion of facts.

2

It was, of course, to be expected that such a meeting of protest on such a subject would attract attention outside the town: the Conservative *Liverpool Standard* boasted that 'In London, Edinburgh, Dublin, Bristol, etc., the decision of the meeting was hailed with expressions of satisfaction', and the journal was able to support the claim with quotations[4] from the *Morning Herald* (London), the *Edinburgh Evening Post* ('a journal which is the principal organ of the Church of Scotland'), the *Dublin Record* ('which speaks the sentiments of a large portion of the protestant clergy and laity of Ireland'), *The Watchman* ('the leading popular organ of the Wesleyan Methodists') and the *Scottish Guardian*. The Liverpool newspaper might have added that a full report of the proceedings at the Amphitheatre meeting appeared also in *The Standard*[5] (London), which had long been critical of the working of the 'Irish System' in Ireland. Moreover, the *Morning Post*[6] (London) declared that the clergy and laity of Liverpool were 'entitled to the warmest gratitude and admiration of their fellow-Protestants' for having 'signally defeated', so far as Liverpool was concerned, a 'covert attack upon our Protestant institutions'.

On the other hand, the *Manchester Guardian* published[7] a leading article on 'The Clergy of Liverpool and the Irish System of Education' in which a full and sympathetic account was given of the aims and policy of the Liverpool Education Committee; the 'Irish System' of Education was defended, and the claim was made that 'nothing

[1] 19 July 1836.
[3] 20 July 1836.
[5] 15 July 1836.
[7] 23 July 1836.

[2] 13 July 1836.
[4] 22 and 26 July 1836.
[6] 16 July 1836.

better than a spirit of sectarian bigotry and faction is at the bottom of the opposition which has been made in Liverpool to the corporation system of education'. The *Guardian's* comment on the proposal of the Church of England clergy in Liverpool to build new schools for the children withdrawn from the Corporation Schools was somewhat tart:

> Most heartily do we wish them 'God speed'. The habit of putting their hands into their own pockets, instead of continuing to be, as they have too long and too often been heretofore, generous on *exclusive* principles but *with the money of the whole community*, will do them good.

It may be added that the *British and Foreign Review* subsequently criticized in the severest terms the speech which the Rev. Hugh M'Neile had made at the Amphitheatre meeting, and remarked that it was 'indescribably painful to witness such attempts made by fiery partisans to disseminate hatred and malice and all uncharitableness between the members of the two most numerous classes of religionists in the British Empire.'[1]

But what did more even than 'the Great Protestant Meeting at the . . . Amphitheatre' to draw the attention of many outside the town to the events taking place in Liverpool was a step taken by one of the speakers at the meeting, Adam Hodgson, who had become a member of the committee appointed to collect money wherewith to establish the new Church of England schools which it had been decided to set up. One of the arguments most frequently put forward[2] by those who supported the 'Irish System' was that it had been introduced into Ireland and defended by no less a person than Mr (by this time Lord) Stanley, who could scarcely be accused of indifference or hostility to the Established Church, especially since he had resigned from the Liberal Party to show his abhorrence of a proposal to alienate part of the revenues of the Church of Ireland, and had formally joined the Conservative ranks in 1835. Hodgson sent to Lord Stanley an account of the proceedings at the Amphitheatre meeting, and invited him to state whether or not he approved of the attempt of the Liverpool Town Council to introduce the 'Irish System' into England.

Stanley replied on 6 August 1836, and stated that:

> the system, which I did recommend as adapted to the peculiar state of Ireland, I never should have thought of recommending as in the least applicable to the very different state of England.[3]

[1] Vol. V, No. IX (1837), p. 237.
[2] E.g., in the *Manchester Guardian* article to which reference has just been made.
[3] *Liverpool Courier*, 10 August 1836.

He claimed that the system had been introduced into Ireland with two purposes in view. The first of these was 'to diminish the Violence of religious animosity' by making it possible for Protestant and Roman Catholic children to associate 'in a system of education in which both might join, and in which the large majority, who were opposed to the religion of the state, might practically see how much there was in that religion, common to their own'. The second aim had been to give the great majority of the Roman Catholic population 'as extensive a knowledge of Scripture truth as they could be induced to receive'. One detects a hint of weariness in his reference to the oft-repeated arguments which he had formerly been called upon to rebut:

I will not now discuss the questions which I have so often had to discuss in Parliament, of the 'mutilation of Scripture', nor the various criticisms which have been made on certain passages of the published extracts; nor the exclusion of the Bible itself 'during school hours'.

He thus, perhaps somewhat disingenuously, avoided having to discuss once again those very arguments against the 'System' which were now being put forward by men who were asking for his support. Instead, he was able to declare in general terms that the 'Irish System'

never was supported as the *best possible* education for Protestants taken separately; but as the *most Protestant*, because the most Scriptural education which could be given to Protestants and Roman Catholics jointly. . . . I will only say that in my humble judgement, all the circumstances which justified and rendered necessary the Irish arrangements for Ireland, are wholly wanting, when the parallel is attempted to be established in England. We do not want to establish schools for a large majority of Roman Catholics, and it is the Roman Catholics only who object to the unrestricted use of the Scriptures in schools. On this point the Church of England and the *Protestant* Dissenters are agreed; and the regulation is not, therefore, called for, to meet the scruples of the great body of Dissent in *this* country. *Here*, therefore, the modification which, though liable to grave objections, was indispensably necessary in Ireland, if you meant the bulk of the population to benefit by your system, is called for by no necessity; and if not called for, is, as I think, indefensible.

He went on to give the assurance which it had been the purpose of his correspondent to obtain from him:

I regret therefore extremely that the Corporation should have withdrawn their schools from their former management, for the purpose of introducing a system never intended, except for the peculiar case of Ireland; and I should be very sorry that my opinion, however unimportant, should be liable to be quoted in favour of the transfer.

Lord Stanley gave added strength to his assurance by enclosing with his letter a donation of £20 to the fund for the erection of Church of England schools to cater for the children withdrawn from the Corporation Schools.

Stanley's letter was printed in *The Times* (London) on 12 August 1836,[1] with a brief explanation that it referred to the action of 'the new Radical corporation who are about introducing into the corporation schools' what was described as 'the system of Irish education'. Less than a month later *The Times* found it necessary to discuss at greater length the decision of the Liverpool Town Council to introduce the 'Irish System' into its schools; but before considering what that newspaper had to say in 1836 we may find it of interest to glance for a moment at the opinions it had expressed only a few years earlier. In December 1831 *The Times* had praised the proposals outlined in Stanley's letter to the Lord-Lieutenant of Ireland, and had felt that what later became known as the 'Irish System' was 'a solid and useful system of practical policy, for working by unexceptionable means, and through wholesome channels, upon the heart of a kindly and susceptible body of men'. The hope was even expressed that 'neither from the pulpit nor the altar, nor at meetings, nor through newspapers, shall we hear of the beneficent designs of the Legislature being perverted to the bad uses of irreligious strife, or made handles by the needy demagogue for his own base and heartless machinations'.[2] As late as 1 October 1834 *The Times* was referring sarcastically to those who fought against 'the sinful efforts of the reforming ministry in Ireland, and especially against the impious and d-mn-ble efforts of theirs to introduce Christian benevolence into the practice of education in Ireland'.

But two months later, in December 1834, came the 'Tamworth Manifesto' and with it the decision of Thomas Barnes not merely to withdraw from the Liberals the support of *The Times* but to make of that journal a stern and often abusive critic of Liberal policies.[3] In a leading article published on 8 September 1836 the readers of *The Times* were informed that:

Some of the Ministerial prints[4] are endeavouring to throw discredit on the noble and Christian conduct of the members of the established church in

[1] It appeared also in *The Standard* (London) of the same date.
[2] 15 December 1831.
[3] For an account of the negotiations between Thomas Barnes, the Editor of *The Times*, and the leading Conservatives before the terms of the 'Tamworth Manifesto' were decided upon, see *The History of the Times (1785–1841)*, London, 1935, Chapters XIX, XX.
[4] The reference is to articles published in *The Globe* and *The Courier* on 7 September 1836.

Liverpool, who, in the short space of a few weeks, have subscribed no less a sum than 12,000 *l.* in order to establish schools in which the Holy Scriptures may be read *unmutilated.* The reason of this demonstration of the pure spirit of the Reformation is to be found in the fact, that the town council of Liverpool have rejected the Bible from the schools under their control, and substituted in its stead a version of the Holy Scriptures, modelled, we suppose, after their own fanatic or free-thinking form. These 'liberals' in religion appear to think that their spiritual radicalism will not stand the test of the Bible, and therefore they garble that sacred volume. They are in effect—that is to say, in cowardice of conscience, and in the tyrannous use of power—utter Papists; and although they cunningly supposed they might shield themselves from censure by means of the example and authority of the Board of Education in Ireland, yet Lord Stanley has taken very good care to expose that contemptible pretence.

One would scarcely imagine, when reading this attack on 'the town council of Liverpool', that the 'version of the Holy Scriptures' which it was suggested that the 'liberals in religion' had found to be 'modelled ... after their own fanatic or free-thinking form' had been described by Stanley himself as 'an excellent preparation for a course of religious instruction to be separately pursued.'[1]

On the following day, in the course of a leading article on the subject of the 'Charitable Trustees Bill', *The Times* expressed the hope and belief that 'the example of Liverpool' would be 'productive of substantial benefit in exciting all parties in and out of Parliament to guard effectively against the rejection of the Scriptures by other town councils'. *The Standard* was another London newspaper which criticized the policy of the Liverpool Town Council; on 15 July 1836, as has been pointed out above, it had published a lengthy report of the protest meeting which had been held in the Liverpool Amphitheatre two days earlier, and it now (8 September 1836) joined *The Times* in praising Lord Stanley's letter. The *Morning Post* (8 September 1836) joined in the fray and praised the members of the Established Church in Liverpool who, it said, 'entertained a violent prejudice in favour of the unmutilated and ungarbled Scripture'. Among the Liberal newspapers in London which took the side of the Liverpool Council at this time were *The Globe* (7 September 1836) and the *Morning Chronicle*, in the latter of which there appeared on 9 September 1836 a leading article giving an account of what the Liverpool Education Committee was attempting to do and endeavouring to show that the sentiments expressed in Lord Stanley's letter were not consistent with remarks he had made when defending the 'Irish System' in the Commons some years before. *The*

---

[1] Hansard, Third Series, Vol. X, Col. 1172.

Spectator also published articles commenting on Stanley's letter and praising the line taken by the Liverpool Council,[1] whilst *The Courier* of 7 September 1836 sarcastically praised those members of the Church of England in Liverpool who had collected money wherewith to build their own schools instead of adopting the policy of 'their brethren in Ireland', who 'instead of nobly subscribing their own funds to support their own religion . . . obstinately persist in taxing the unwilling Catholics to support it'.

3

The members of the Liverpool Education Committee were surprised that their plans should have met with such definite and almost unanimous opposition from the Church of England clergy in the town; they were particularly angry and disappointed that the Rev. A. Campbell and Charles Horsfall should have joined the critics of the new policy after having, as it seemed, indicated a readiness to accept it. On the day after the 'Great Protestant Meeting' it must have seemed to most people that it would now scarcely be possible for the Committee to act upon the recommendations which it had laid before the Council. The schools which some had hoped might become models for the rest of the country to copy were now quite without teachers and almost without pupils, for all the teachers had resigned and the clergy of the Established Church began to have 'the walls of the town placarded with great posters, signed by clergymen. These exhorted parents not to send their children to the Corporation schools, promising them the speedy opening of others, where the unmutilated Word of God should be taught'.[2] Temporary schools, said to be capable of accommodating 1,800 children, were hastily established in rooms of various kinds in different parts of the town, and most of the children who had formerly attended the Corporation Schools followed their teachers to them. On 14 July 1836, the day after the meeting at the Amphitheatre, only thirty-one boys and thirteen girls were in attendance at the North Corporation Schools.[3] Feeling ran so high that 'some of the lower classes maltreated

---

[1] 10 September 1836, pp. 863, 866. *The Spectator* seems neither to have been very well informed about the schools nor very much inclined to be fair to Lord Stanley, since it wrote: '. . . because the Liverpool Town Council, rather than drive the poor Catholic children from their schools, order extracts from the Bible instead of the Bible itself to be read there, Lord Stanley helps to swell the cry of the political hypocrites against "the mutilation of the Word of God."'

[2] H. M. Walmsley, *The Life of Sir Joshua Walmsley*, London, 1879, pp. 88–9.

[3] *Liverpool Standard*, 15 July 1836.

children on their way to the schools, pelted and hooted members of the committee as they passed'.[1]

Nevertheless, the Committee concealed the misgivings which they must have felt, and set about coping with the new situation in an astonishingly resolute fashion. At least one of the members, Mr Hope, was himself obliged to become a temporary schoolmaster. Within a week, however, a new master had been found for the North School and a number of temporary teachers had been appointed; in a very short time both of the schools were adequately staffed according to the standards of the day. Placards were posted about the town to announce that the Corporation Schools were now 'open for the instruction of children of all religious denominations', and numbers of Roman Catholic children at once began to attend. For a time the opponents of the Committee were able to make use of the taunt that the schools had in effect become Roman Catholic establishments, and to claim that the attempt to draw into them the children of all sects had failed. Thus on 14 September 1836 the *Liverpool Courier* stated that 'out of 320 children in the North Corporation School we are credibly informed that not much above twenty are Protestants'. In the same month the Senior Rector, the Rev. J. Brooks, spoke of 'the general expression of feeling' which had responded to the call of the Church of England clergy of the town—'a feeling not confined to the town of Liverpool, but extended to every remote corner of the island'; and he went on: 'I conceive it to be the glorious distinction of the town of Liverpool that that system [i.e. 'the Irish System'] has received its death-blow here.'[2]

Before long, however, numbers of parents who were members of the Church of England or Dissenters were sending their children to the Corporation Schools, knowing that, whatever might be said outside the schools, denominational religious instruction was, in fact, given within them at stated times. In view of the opposition of almost all of the Church of England clergy of the town to the policy adopted in the Corporation Schools, it is not to be wondered at that Roman Catholic children for some time predominated in both of the schools; this was the less surprising since there were so few schools open to such children and since the Corporation Schools were situated in districts

---

[1] Walmsley, *op. cit.*, p. 89. The *Liverpool Times* of 20 September 1836 reported that a man had been sent to prison 'for throwing stones at the children attending the North Corporation School'.

[2] *Liverpool Courier*, 7 September 1836. The Rector was speaking at the ceremony of laying the foundation-stone on a site in Bond Street of the first of the schools to be provided for the Church of England children withdrawn from the Corporation Schools. The ceremony had been preceded by a procession through the town of children, clergymen, members of the Conservative Operatives' and Conservative Tradesmen's Associations, and others.

largely inhabited by poor Irish Roman Catholics. Even so, to antici-
pate a little, it may be said that by September 1837 of 260 boys in
attendance at the South Corporation School 131 were Protestants.[1]

According to Joshua Walmsley, a member of the Education Committee who belonged to the Established Church, 'Dissenting and Roman
Catholic clergymen came eagerly to teach the children of their respective flocks during the hour appointed for religious instruction',[2] but
this statement needs to be qualified. The Rev. A. Campbell claimed in
October 1837 that none of 'the leading dissenting ministers' had 'con-
formed to the Irish system' and mentioned, as having refused to co-
operate with the Council, Dr Raffles, 'minister of the independents';
Mr Lister, 'minister of the baptists'; Dr Ralph, 'of the Scotch established
kirk'; and all the Wesleyan ministers. He went on to state that the
system, as far as he could learn, was sanctioned only by men whose
names he had never heard before.[3] Nothing in Campbell's statement,
of course, conflicts with the statement of Walmsley that some Dissenting clergymen did, in fact, attend the schools.

The Roman Catholic clergy, according to the headmaster of the
North Corporation School at the time, at first sent catechists to instruct
the Roman Catholic children on three afternoons each week, and
attended in person during the other two periods when denominational
religious instruction could be given in the schools. It soon became
obvious, however, that 'the management of more than 300 boys was
a task quite beyond the capabilities of the catechists—confusion prevailed and nothing could be accomplished'. It was therefore agreed
that the catechists should no longer visit the schools and that in their
stead suitably trained monitors should give instruction in the Roman
Catholic catechism.[4] It would seem that some of the Roman Catholic
priests ceased to consider it necessary to make personal visits to the
schools after the new system had been in operation for about twelve
months.[5] Rathbone later stated that 'The Catholic clergy have acted

[1] Letter of Mr Buchanan, headmaster of the South School, in *The Albion* (Liverpool),
16 October 1837.

[2] Walmsley, *op. cit.*, p. 89.

[3] *Conservative Triumph, or the Three Glorious Days! A Full and Corrected Report of the
Speeches Delivered at the Meetings Held in the Amphitheatre on the 16th, 18th and 20th
October, 1837, to Celebrate the Return of Lord Sandon and Cresswell Cresswell, Esq., as the
Representatives of the Borough of Liverpool in Parliament*, Liverpool [? 1837], p. 27.

[4] A. Farrill, *The Schoolmaster's Appeal to Public Candour: Being a Statement of Facts
Explanatory of the Reasons Which Have Occasioned the Removal of the Author from the
Corporation Schools. With Observations on the General Management of these Institutions, as
Conducted under the Direction of the Present Town Council of Liverpool*, Liverpool, 1837,
pp. 5–6.

[5] In *The Albion*, 24 April 1839, it was stated that no Roman Catholic priest had
visited the South Corporation School since the summer of 1837.

with great liberality, and with a most gratifying confidence in us, allowing and encouraging the children to come to schools under the direction of a committee at one time[1] wholly Protestant, and the teachers also.'[2]

At first only one clergyman of the Established Church was willing to attend the schools: he was the Rev. James Aspinall of St Luke's Church, who gave instruction in the doctrines of the Church of England at the South Corporation School. Nothing daunted by the refusal of most of the Established Clergy to visit the schools, members of the Education Committee, their wives and others undertook to teach the Church of England children; William Rathbone himself, although a Unitarian, 'often attended the schools when those who ought to do so purposely absented themselves (he meant the Clergy of the Church of England) and on these occasions he had taught the catechism of the Church of England, and given, as far as he could, an exposition of it to the children.'[3] The clearest account of the arrangements made for the giving of religious instruction in the schools is given in a speech addressed to the Town Council by Joshua Walmsley on 12 October 1836; he was speaking only of the 'daily system of instruction observed at the North School', but this seems not to have differed materially from that in force at the South School:[4]

On the assembly of the children, at nine o'clock in the morning, a portion of the Scripture from the selections is read by the visitor, the teacher, or one of the monitors, so as to be heard by all present; a hymn is then sung, and the usual course of instruction proceeds until twelve. At four o'clock, until a few minutes before five in the afternoon, the children are again occupied with religious instruction. While the Roman Catholic Priests and visitors attend to their own flocks, the Protestant classes, so far conducted by the visitors only, proceed as follows:

Monday.—The collects and a portion of Scripture, committed to memory

---

[1] This refers, it appears, to the period November 1836 to November 1838.

[2] See p. 191.

[3] Speech at a meeting of the Town Council, 9 November 1836, quoted in Rev. H. M'Neile, *Letters on National Education Addressed to the Town Council of Liverpool . . .*, London, 1837, Letter I, p. 12. Rathbone later explained that he had 'heard the children their catechisms, simply requiring the words of the book where he did not agree with it, and endeavouring to enforce and illustrate it where he did' (*Liverpool Courier*, 30 November 1836).

[4] There, as Rathbone explained to the Council, 'The Bible was read by all Protestants who could read, every day, in the authorised version, either to the Rev. Mr Aspinall or to a teacher. Mr Aspinall devoted the first half hour to the girls, and the second to the boys, every day. The other half hour was devoted to the Catechism, explanation of the Collects, Scripture lessons, instruction in the eastern manners and customs, &c.' (*Liverpool Courier*, 30 November 1836).

on Sunday, are repeated. The younger children say the Lord's Prayer and the Apostles' Creed.

Tuesday.—They read the Bible, and receive other religious instruction.

Wednesday.—The elder children are taught the Church Catechism; the younger children Watts's Catechism.

Thursday.—The elder again read the Bible, and are examined upon it, and the younger repeat hymns or a portion of the Bible.

Friday.—The collect for Sunday is explained to the elder children, and the Bible read by them, and the younger children repeat and are instructed upon a verse from the Bible.

Rules, prescribing this course of religious education, are affixed in a conspicuous part of the school, and the observance of them is strictly enforced.[1]

The teachers were not allowed to inculcate 'doctrinal points'[2] during the periods set aside for the reading of the much-discussed 'Irish Scripture Lessons'; only 'the historical and moral parts of Scripture' were studied at such times,[3] 'all points of Doctrine' being 'left to the hour for [denominational] religious instruction'[2] when Protestant children were taught from the Authorized Version and Roman Catholic children from the Douay version of the Bible.

When the Rev. Hugh M'Neile (accompanied by the Rev. Mr Lyon) visited the North Corporation School in November 1836, some four months after the new system had been inaugurated, he found, according to his own account, 'the Protestant children, both boys and girls, in one corner of the room, and two ladies teaching them the Church collect for the following Sunday. The remainder of the room was occupied by classes of girls saying the Douay Catechism.' In a room below he found Roman Catholic boys awaiting the arrival of their priest, who was late in coming.[4] On 29 March 1837 Samuel Wilderspin wrote: 'I heard the Catholic clergyman, this very day, . . . read a chapter from Luke to the whole of the Catholic children, and afterwards address them upon it, in a manner which surprised me and excited my admiration.'[5] 'So particular was the Educational Committee', said Walmsley, 'that each child should be taught the creed of

---

[1] *Liverpool Mercury*, 14 October 1836.

[2] Declaration of Education Committee published in *Liverpool Mercury*, 20 November 1837.

[3] Letter of Master of South Corporation Boys' School (*Albion*, 16 October 1837).

[4] Rev. H. M'Neile, *Letters on National Education Addressed to the Town Council of Liverpool*, Letter II, p. 31. M'Neile asked the Council with some asperity 'by what authority the master, as in the case above stated, keeps the boys in school after three o'clock', claiming that it was the teacher's duty to dismiss them at that hour if the religious instructor had not arrived!

[5] *Liverpool Chronicle*, 8 April 1837.

its parents, that every sect seemed represented. I remember one child, on being asked the invariable question on entering the schools, to what persuasion her parents belonged, answered, to the "New Church". We were puzzled to know what the "New Church" was; it proved to be Swedenborgian. She was the single lamb belonging to this flock, yet a teacher of her creed was found ready to undertake her education.'[1]

It might have been expected that the accusation levelled against the Education Committee that it wished to 'exclude the Bible from the schools' would no longer have been made once it became obvious that the complete Authorized Version was in fact made available to all Protestant children during the time set apart for denominational religious instruction; but the charge continued to be made year after year, and it undoubtedly influenced the attitude towards the new system of large numbers of people who, if they had not been misinformed, might have been much less hostile to it. Most of the clergymen of the Church of England refused to enter the schools, in spite of the repeated requests of the members of the Education Committee that they should go to see for themselves how the religious instruction of the children was conducted; some of those who did so were, as we shall see, agreeably surprised. The Rev. Hugh M'Neile, to whom many people looked for information and guidance, could not deny that when, on the occasion referred to above, he visited one of the schools, he found that 'the Protestant children were assembled in a class under the tuition of some pious ladies, learning their collects, and they had Bibles, *genuine orthodox Bibles*, upon all their knees'.[2] But he could still maintain that 'the Bible was excluded', and continue to convince many who were not capable of appreciating the special sense in which he employed the word 'excluded' that the Authorized Version of the Bible was never used in the schools.

One such special sense of the term is indicated in the following argument:

If clergymen can be found willing to go, then the Bible, after three o'clock, may be read. But if the system be such in other respects as to deprive clergymen, on conscientious grounds, of the power of availing themselves of the one hour, then, as far as they are concerned, the Bible cannot be read at all. This is precisely our position. The system excludes the Bible, except for one hour. We cannot, by attending during that hour, give our sanction to this system; so that, as far as we are concerned, the system excludes the Bible altogether.[3]

[1] Walmsley, *op. cit.*, p. 90.
[2] See letter in *Liverpool Telegraph* of 23 November 1836.
[3] *Letters on National Education Addressed to the Town Council of Liverpool*, Letter II, p. 32.

Another example of the special sense in which M'Neile interpreted the expression 'excluding the Bible' was provided when, having explained that only the Authorized Version could be accepted as being 'the Bible,' he went on:

It is not enough to say that you or I may go at a certain hour of the day— even a school hour—and teach *some* of the children out of the Bible. Can we bind ourselves not to teach *all* the children, even the Roman Catholic children? We never can. And, therefore, though we concede the statement, that a visit to the school daily may be made, and the authorised Bible read in a corner of the schoolroom, still we maintain the system is against the Word of God. For mark the circumstances. During that hour when the Protestant clergyman is permitted to teach the Protestant children, the Roman Catholic children have been withdrawn by the Roman Catholic clergyman, and he can only teach those of his own creed. This is of some consequence; this should not be overlooked, because, on the ground of the possibility of a visit to *some* of the children, it is boldly and repeatedly declared that the Bible is not excluded from the schools, and we are called insane for persevering in saying that it is. What is 'the school'? Does it consist of some or all the children? Undoubtedly of all. Now there is not one moment of the day when the Bible may be put into the hands of *all* the children. There is a certain portion of the children by whom the Bible may not be and cannot be read.[1]

Thus the Bible could be described as being 'excluded from the schools' because, although the Protestant children admittedly read the Authorized Version, the Roman Catholic children did not. It was perhaps not to be wondered at that many understood the word 'excluded' to mean something else, or that numbers of those who knew what went on in the schools were inclined to make disparaging remarks about M'Neile's regard for the truth.

4

Before the storm of protest burst about their heads, the members of the Liverpool Education Committee, anxious to do all in their power to improve the Corporation Schools, had invited Samuel Wilderspin to reorganize the infant departments of the two schools, and William Rathbone was authorized[2] at the beginning of July 1836 to offer 'the sum of Forty Pounds' to Wilderspin in order to obtain his services. Wilderspin, undoubtedly 'one of the great educational influences of the day',[3] was no stranger to Liverpool, and, moreover, he was well aware

---

[1] *Speech of the Rev. Hugh M'Neile, at the Church of England School Meeting Held in the Amphitheatre, Liverpool on . . . 11th July 1837*, Liverpool [1837], p. 10.

[2] *Proceedings of Education Committee*, Vol. I, p. 17.

[3] C. Birchenough, *History of Elementary Education in England and Wales from 1800 to the Present Day*, London, 1920, p. 236.

of the difficulties likely to be encountered by those who wished to set up schools for children of all denominations.[1] On 12 July 1836 it was recorded that

> A letter from Mr Wilderspin having been read [it was] Resolved That the Committee agree not to interfere with Mr Wilderspin for one Month as required in his Letter; and that the apparatus recommended by Mr Wilderspin be ordered for both Schools the cost for each school being Fifteen Pounds. That Mr Wilderspin be requested to engage a Master or Mistress for the North Infant School.[2]

Eventually it was decided that Wilderspin should continue to be engaged until the end of October and should be 'paid One hundred Pounds including the amount already agreed to be paid to him'.[3] He was therefore actively at work in the Corporation Schools during the first three months of the stormy period which followed the introduction of the 'Irish System' into the schools. On one occasion he was 'very much hurt' when attempting to turn out of the playground of one of the Corporation Schools men who had entered it to show their disapproval of the new system by 'using the most improper language'.[4]

Yet in spite of the difficult conditions in which he had to work he not only reorganized the Corporation Infant Schools, but found the time to engage in missionary work in support of his ideas on infant education. In September 1836 he delivered at the Royal Institution a course of four lectures on his 'method of developing and training the Infant Faculties in the nursery or school-room from twelve months old to seven years', the lectures being 'illustrated with suitable apparatus, and enlivened with amusing dialogues'.[5] Towards the end of Wilderspin's stay, William Rathbone sought and obtained the permission of the Town Council[6] for Wilderspin to make use of the ballroom at the

---

[1] See his reference to Liverpool in *Early Discipline Illustrated; or the Infant System Progressing and Successful*, London, 1832, p. 58: 'On leaving Manchester I went to Liverpool, where three schools were commenced.' In 1835 he stated that Liverpool, with eleven infant schools, was 'the place with the greatest number, with reference to the population'. As we have seen, he had found that Roman Catholic priests did not in general approve of the system of religious instruction which he wished to see adopted in infant schools, and he said of them: 'They are now having Infant Schools of their own. We have a large Infant School in Seal-street [*sic*], Liverpool, where there are 200 children, and the priest superintends it principally himself. I went to see it, and found the children exceedingly well trained.' (*Report from the Select Committee on Education in England and Wales, together with the Minutes of Evidence*, 1835, pp. 13, 24–5.)

[2] *Proceedings of Education Committee*, Vol. I, p. 19.

[3] *Ibid.*, Vol. I, p. 26.

[4] *Liverpool Mercury*, 23 September 1836.

[5] *Liverpool Journal*, 27 August 1836. The advertisement described Wilderspin as 'the originator of the Infant System'.

[6] *Proceedings of Council*, Vol. XVII, p. 276.

Town Hall on 13 October 1836 in order to demonstrate publicly the results of his work in the infant departments of the Corporation Schools; when objections were raised by some members of the Council, Rathbone undertook to be personally responsible for any injury done to the rooms.[1] The demonstration, which took the form of a public examination of the children, was attended by the Mayor, by many councillors and by so many members of the public that a second display had to be arranged for those who were turned away. For those who could not afford to pay the entrance fee of one shilling charged on these occasions another exhibition was held in the police-station in Seel Street 'to which the lower classes were . . . admitted gratuitously'.[2]

As might, perhaps, have been expected, Wilderspin's methods and ideas were praised enthusiastically in the newspapers which supported the policy of the Education Committee and abused with even greater enthusiasm in those journals which opposed that policy. Probably the most unrestrained criticism came from the *Liverpool Mail*, in which articles and letters appeared denouncing what was called 'The Wilderspinian Humbug'.[3] In one article, headed 'Infant Education Quackery', Wilderspin was referred to as a 'cockney lecturer on education'; in the course of the article it was suggested that arguments put forward in favour of infant education would cause children to have less respect for their parents, and that 'mathematical knowledge' was not 'calculated to improve the usefulness, the happiness, or the respectability of the future domestic servant or poor man's wife'. It was pointed out that 'fatuity and insanity' had been increasing, and 'the philanthropists who are so forward to carry education to its greatest possible extent' were asked to consider whether 'the infant mind' might be 'destroyed or impaired . . . if forced to exertions beyond its strength'.[4] It was claimed on other occasions that 'it was the disease of the sect to which Mr Rathbone belongs to take too many liberties with the infant mind',[5] and insinuated that Wilderspin devoted insufficient attention to religious instruction.[6] Wilderspin thus found himself involved in the controversy concerning the Corporation Schools, and he engaged in lively disputes with his opponents and critics, replying to their attacks in letters printed in the Liberal newspapers of the town.[7] It is not surprising that

[1] *Liverpool Courier*, 5 October 1836. [2] *Ibid.*
[3] *Liverpool Mail*, 18 October 1836. [4] *Ibid.*, 11 October 1836.
[5] *Ibid.*, 4 October 1836. [6] *Ibid.*, 15 October 1836.
[7] E.g., *Liverpool Telegraph*, 12 October 1836; *The Albion* (Liverpool), 17 October 1836. In the course of a letter printed in the *Liverpool Times* on 19 October 1836 he defended himself against the charge that he was 'inattentive to the all-important subject of religion', and added, 'I have seen most of the infant schools in Liverpool at several different periods, and know well what is taught in them and can assert that in the first school in London as much religion was taught 17 years before as was taught in any of them'.

he became, as we shall see, a fervent supporter of the system inaugurated in the Corporation Schools by those who had invited him to the town and who treated his ideas with respect.

5

In numerous pamphlets, newspaper articles and speeches the policy of the Council was attacked or defended. Some of the pamphlets were little more than prolonged diatribes against the Roman Catholic Church, conventionally described as the whore of Babylon, the mother of harlots, etc.[1] 'A Bible Christian' somewhat unnecessarily sprang to the defence of the Rev. Hugh M'Neile; he reproached Mr Blackburn for 'the tortuous course' which he claimed that the latter was pursuing in his union with Papists and Socinians, for the purpose of pulling down the Established Church, and taking the Bible from the schools';[2] and he supported 'the claim of our children to their undoubted birthright, the entire unmutilated word of God'.[3] The charge that 'certain *extracts* from the Bible' were to be used by the children in the schools, not in addition to, but 'in lieu of, the *entire* Word of God which they had before possessed'[4] was the accusation most commonly made. Only rarely was the claim explicitly made that those who were not Protestants were not entitled to the same treatment as those who were, but probably many in fact agreed with the Rev. John Lyons of All Saints Church, Liverpool, when he put forward that claim in no uncertain terms:

It is this latitudinarianism that constitutes the deadly evil of the Irish system. Whether the extracts be excellent or objectionable is a matter of second-rate importance in the scale of enquiry. This system teaches the infidel principle that Protestantism and Popery, Judaism and Socinianism, may be taught, without guilt, in a professedly christian land—ought to be treated with on equal terms, and each have the facilities granted to them of teaching doctrines that stand to each other as Christ to Belial, righteousness to unrighteousness, light to darkness.[5]

[1] *Auxiliary 'Explanatory Notes' for the Use of the 'Children of All Sects', 'Who are to be Instructed at the Two Corporation Schools, Liverpool, from the Irish Bible Selections, with Notes'!!* [Anon.], Liverpool, 1836. A similar production was *The Happy Effects of Reading the New Scripture Lessons in the National Schools of Ireland*, by Thady Brady [pseud.], Liverpool [n.d.].

[2] *A Letter to Mr Councillor Blackburn, Containing a Few Friendly Observations on His Speech at the Meeting of the Municipal Council on the 6th July, 1836 on the Subject of the Corporation Schools.* By a Bible Christian. Liverpool, MDCCCXXXVI, p. 7.

[3] *A Second Letter to Mr Councillor Blackburn Containing a Scriptural Refutation of His Defence of the System Adopted in the Corporation Schools of Liverpool.* By a Bible Christian. Liverpool, 1836, Dedication.

[4] *Ibid.*, pp. 6–7.

[5] *Ibid.*, Appendix.

Of all the reasons put forward to justify the opposition to the Education Committee's proposals none was so naïve and so engaging as that advanced by the *Liverpool Courier*,[1] which felt that the new system would

tie the hands of the ministers of the Gospel from preaching the Gospel honestly and boldly: for it is not to be supposed that men, who are in the habit of meeting together on terms of friendly intercourse in a schoolroom or at a committee can stand up in the pulpit and preach against one another's doctrines with the same freedom and force as if they were perfect strangers, or that the softening recollections of personal kindness and attention should not mitigate the proper severity of professional conflict.

The Conservative newspapers, chief among them the *Liverpool Standard*, the *Liverpool Courier* and the *Liverpool Mail*, were vehement in their attacks on the Council, but the Liberal newspapers, and especially the *Liverpool Mercury*,[2] the *Liverpool Telegraph*, the *Liverpool Times*, the *Liverpool Journal* and *The Albion*, were as eloquent in defence. During the first months of the experiment bitter controversies were carried on in leading articles and in letters to the editors; every important speech on the subject, and especially those of the Rev. Hugh M'Neile, was reported and commented upon in terms laudatory or contemptuous.

Thomas Blackburn (whose speech in the Council Chamber supporting the Education Committee's proposals had, as we have seen, impressed even Conservative members of the Council) published about September 1836 what he called *A Defence of the System Adopted in the Corporation Schools of Liverpool*; this, however, was not only 'a defence' but an onslaught on those who had attacked 'the System'. He set out to show:

that Schools supported by public property should be open to all classes without exception; that the Irish National System is well adapted to effect this object; that the Scripture lessons of that system are unobjectionable; that the introduction of it in the Corporation Schools is perfectly compatible with the communication of as large a measure of religious instruction to *Protestant* children as can be given in any other day schools, and that the Bible in the authorised version not only *may consistently*, but is *actually* used in giving that instruction.

He claimed also that it was wrong 'to force religious instruction on those who did not wish their children to receive it, and that to exclude from public schools on that account is neither more nor less than

[1] 20 July 1836.
[2] The proprietor and editor of the *Liverpool Mercury* was Egerton Smith, a Liberal member of the Town Council.

persecution for conscience sake, and therefore at variance with the true genius and spirit of Christianity.' But he went further, and expressed the opinion that some of those who accused the Council of being enemies to all religion, mutilators of the Bible, secret promoters of heresy and so on were actuated by political motives since 'men who are well-known as political partizans, but who have not hitherto displayed much concern about either education or religion, have all at once become interested in both, and have joined the outcry in favour of scriptural education with most astonishing earnestness'. Even less propitiatory were his statement that no conscientious Dissenter could agree to make all the children repeat the Church Catechism, 'as that compound is full of Popery from beginning to end', and his claim that 'the exaltation of one denomination in the high places of the earth, in alliance with the state—whose pretended rights and prerogatives are secured by law, while all others are barely tolerated . . . is the very essence of Popery, in its worst and most injurious form, though under another name'.

This was the voice of the earnest Dissenter rather than of the spokes-man of a Committee that included some staunch Churchmen, and his remarks naturally did little to make the Established clergy more kindly disposed towards the Education Committee. A number of Churchmen sprang to the defence of the Church, among them, once again, 'A Bible Christian'[1] and also one Alexander Watson[2] who wrote an *Examination of and Observations upon Mr Blackburn's Defence of the Conduct of the New Town Council of Liverpool in Connexion with Their Recent Efforts to Deprive the Children of the Poor of Instruction from the Unmutilated Bible*, Liverpool, 1836. With a fervour not inferior to that of Blackburn, Watson proclaimed that:

A vast majority of the new Councillors are seceders from the doctrines and faith, as well as the discipline of the Church. Their conduct, from the moment that they came into office, does not allow the belief that their hostility to the Church is confined to dissent from her religious tenets. Their rallying shout has been 'Down with her'; and to consummate her overthrow has been their chief endeavour.

The Town Council had, therefore, according to Watson, done all in its power to 'unchristianize education' so as to 'weaken the attach-ment of the poor man to the church of his fathers'; it encouraged the reading of selections from the Bible which had been 'framed, clearly and demonstrably, with a view to encourage loose Protestantism,

[1] *A Second Letter to Mr Councillor Blackburn* . . . , Liverpool, 1836.
[2] His 'Advertisement to the Second Edition' is dated from 'Corpus Christi College, Cambridge, 31st Dec. 1836'. Parts of the book had already been printed in the *Liverpool Mail*.

Popery, and indifference to all religion alike'; and these were selections, moreover, which, in a metaphor not unmixed, Watson described as containing 'jesuitical mummeries by which the poison of Popery and irreligious apathy is concealed beneath a flimsy guise of shallow and lukewarm Protestantism'.

6

Yet in justice to some of those who opposed the Town Council's policy—including a number who did so most vehemently—it must be pointed out that it might have been possible to arrive at a compromise reasonably satisfactory to all the parties concerned if the Liberal members of the Council had been willing to consider an alternative solution to the problem which they felt called upon to solve. In the course of the parliamentary debates which followed the adoption of the 'Irish System' in Ireland it had been stated by some Conservative critics[1] of 'the System' that they would raise no objection if Roman Catholics and Protestants were to receive financial assistance from the government to enable them to build their own *separate* schools. We have seen that in Liverpool it would probably not have been difficult to have persuaded such men as the Junior Rector and some of the Conservative members of the Council to accept such a policy as this, which would have circumvented most of the difficulties caused by the proposal to educate children of all denominations in the *same* schools. It is still more remarkable that for a brief period in Liverpool even much less tolerant men professed themselves ready to accept the principle that the municipal or central government might make grants for the provision of Roman Catholic schools. The Rev. Hugh M'Neile himself, in the course of the very sermon in which he first announced his bitter opposition to the Education Committee's recommendations, had said:

If the Corporation has so much money and so much liberality, let them set up Popish schools. I say not that it would be well done, it can never be well to teach men what is opposed to the Word of God. But if they talk of justice to numbers let them be just to both sides. To plead tenderness of conscience on one part as a pretext for forcing conscience on the other, this, under the sheep's clothing of liberality is to be most illiberal, most bigoted, most exclusive and unjust.[2]

Here M'Neile's point was that if the Council were to set up separate schools for Roman Catholic children Protestants would be able to

---

[1] See, e.g., speech of Earl of Wicklow in House of Lords, 19 March 1833. Hansard, Third Series, Vol. XVI, Col. 820.

[2] *Liverpool Courier*, 6 July 1836.

send their children to the existing Corporation Schools without having to do violence to their consciences. The *Liverpool Courier*, one of the journals most hostile to the Liberal Town Council, took the same line and expressed the opinion that:

> If the Roman Catholics are so unsocial that they will not join in prayer with any sect, or go where the Protestant Bible is read in school-hours, why they must have schools of their own, and the Corporation may subscribe to those schools.[1]

A few months later the same newspaper made its proposal still more clear:

> If they [the Liberal councillors] wish, as they pretend, to be impartial, and will interfere with education, then let them act upon the principle that government has set them an example of. Government gives £20,000 for education—£10,000 to the Church, and £10,000 to Dissenters. Let the Town Council act on a similar principle—let them quit the trade of schoolmaster—give up the schools to their proper owners, the Protestants, and then make grants, if they please, to Roman Catholic schools.[2]

Later still the *Liverpool Courier* proposed that if the Town Council wished 'to conform in any degree to the ministerial pattern for England' they might 'keep up one of the schools (the north for instance) for the Irish system' and allow the 'Church School Committee' to have the use rent-free of the 'South Schoolrooms, for the education of any children that choose to conform to the Church system'.[3] Even when the attacks made on the new policy had become most severe the Rev. Hugh M'Neile could still say in an open letter to the Council:

> . . . Had you retained the former schools exclusively Protestant for the Protestant population, and established additional schools exclusively Roman Catholic for the Roman Catholic population, this would have been, on your own principles, impartial. And, however we might have mourned over your indiscriminate patronage of truth and error, we would not have practically interfered.[4]

Three years earlier, as we have seen, the Town Clerk of Liverpool had roundly declared that it was impossible for the Council, 'consistently with the connexion they had with the established constitution of this country, to have given their funds, or expended their property, for

---

[1] *Ibid.*, 20 July 1836.
[2] *Ibid.*, 7 September 1836. It was, of course, untrue that the government grant was divided equally between 'the Church' and 'Dissenters'.
[3] *Ibid.*, 23 November 1836.
[4] Rev. H. M'Neile, *Letters on National Education: Addressed to the Town Council of Liverpool*, p. 53.

any ecclesiastical object distinct from the Church of England'. Yet in 1836 even a man so extreme in his views as M'Neile (who was still campaigning for the repeal of 'Catholic Emancipation') was beginning to believe that some concessions to the spirit of the times would have to be made and was prepared, even if reluctantly and with bad grace, to allow public funds to be spent on Roman Catholic schools.[1] But the most influential members of the Town Council were in no mood for compromise, and moreover they felt that much good would come from bringing up children of all denominations to work and play together and to think of each other as friends. The contest, therefore, went on.

7

In August 1836 the British Association for the Advancement of Science held its annual meeting in Bristol, and on the 21st of that month a group of members of the Association met under the chairmanship of Thomas Wyse to consider the possibility of acting together in order to further the progress of education in England. It was resolved 'that an Educational Committee should be formed, independent of the British Association but holding its meetings at the same time; that whereas the Statistical Section [of the Association] confined itself to the collection of facts, this new Society should concern itself with the examination of results and measures'.[2] No doubt those present would have preferred to have set up an Education Section within the Association itself, but wished to forestall the objection that discussions of educational policy were bound to give rise to controversy and political dispute. That they had judged wisely was shown a few days later when a paper was read before the Statistical Section giving the results of inquiries carried out by the Manchester Statistical Society into the state of education in Liverpool. On that occasion 'Mr Wyse, the Rev. E. G. Stanley, and several other gentlemen deprecated in strong terms the continuance of the present chaos of education in England, and recommended the adoption of

---

[1] This was all the more striking since only four years earlier M'Neile, at a meeting called to protest against the introduction of the 'Irish System of Education' into Ireland itself, had spoken in support of a petition to the Lords which expressed 'equal regret surprise and alarm' at 'that regulation in the new system which provides for the inculcation of the peculiar doctrines of the Church of Rome at the expense of Parliamentary grants' and asked that 'in the application of such money no unholy compromise be made with the Church of Rome'. (*Scriptural Education in Ireland. A Full Report of the Great Protestant Meeting Held in Exeter Hall, Strand, February 8, 1832.* London, 1832, p. 44.)

[2] *The Athenæum*, 10 September 1836. (The proceedings of this 'unofficial' group of members were not widely reported and the writer is indebted for knowledge of the accounts given in *The Athenæum* to I. D. Harry, *Sir Thomas Wyse and the Central Society of Education*, Unpublished Dissertation, University of Wales, 1932.)

Normal Schools'. The discussion was thereupon described as having become 'economic rather than statistical, a departure from the strict rule which Lord Sandon condemned'.[1]

Commenting on the formation of the 'new Society' a contemporary journal said:

> The whole proceeding . . . seems to have originated in the impulse of the moment; but we fancy we see in this association of Catholics, Protestants, and Dissenters (for it was observed that each of these classes had more than one representative present)—of gentlemen from north, south, east, and west, the germ of many Local Committees, all we trust to be found hereafter co-operating with a Central Committee, whose office it shall be to bring all the moral energy of this great country to bear upon Parliament, and force upon its consideration, as its great duty, the education of the people.[2]

Since it had been decided that the British Association would hold its next series of meeting in Liverpool, this newly formed group of members interested in education agreed that 'a further meeting should be held in the year 1837, at Liverpool, on the Saturday preceding the week appointed for the assembling of the British Association'.[3] That meeting was duly held, and must be referred to later; but in the meantime it may be noted that among those chosen at Bristol to constitute the committee of the group were the three men who, as we have seen, had been the guests of honour of a comparable group at Manchester four months earlier: they were Thomas Wyse, James Simpson and William Rathbone of Liverpool.[4]

---

[1] *The Athenæum*, 3 September 1836. Lord Sandon was one of the two representatives of Liverpool in the House of Commons.

[2] *Ibid.*, 10 September 1836.

[3] *Ibid.*

[4] *Ibid.* Another member of the committee was William Rathbone Greg of Manchester, a brother of William Rathbone's wife.

Chapter 5

COMPROMISE REJECTED

I

No doubt the Liberals in the Liverpool Town Council prepared for the municipal elections of November 1836 with some trepidation. Even under the most favourable conditions it was to be expected that the Conservatives would improve their representation in the Council, since it was not likely that the Liberal landslide of the previous year would be repeated in traditionally Conservative Liverpool; moreover, the Liberals who had to defend their seats on this occasion would be those in each ward who had obtained the smallest majorities—some of them very small indeed[1]—at the elections of 1835. During their first year in control of the Council the Liberals had aroused the opposition of almost all of the Established clergy in the town and that of some of the Nonconformist ministers as well; whilst it was true that they had won the support of nearly all of the Roman Catholics, it had to be remembered that many of these were too poor to be qualified to vote.[2] Undoubtedly the Liberals would have to rely for their chief support on those Protestants who approved of the policy which the Council had adopted in the Corporation Schools—for the Conservatives made it clear that the 'Schools Question' was to be the main, indeed almost the only, issue on which the elections would be fought. Although there was much less heat engendered than during some subsequent elections, the criticism of the policy pursued in the schools was by no means lacking in vigour, and of course the most damning cry of some of the Conservatives was the quite unjust accusation that the Liberals had 'excluded the Bible from the schools'. Typical of many election speeches was that delivered by a Mr Holme to the Liverpool Operative Conservative Association, during the course of which he asked:

Did they wish that the children of their poorer neighbours should be educated upon strict scriptural principle, or did they wish that the Word of

[1] Two seats had been won with majorities of four votes each and one with a majority of two.

[2] At a public meeting in Liverpool in 1839 it was stated that 'only about a thousand' Roman Catholics were 'registered electors'. In that year the number of voters on the municipal electoral register was 9,056 (*Liverpool Mercury*, 7 July 1839).

the eternal God should be expelled from their schools? He would call upon them to be united at the next election, not to be led away by fanciful theories, and then he doubted not but they would return men who were not mere party men, but who would most zealously maintain those institutions which it was their duty to hand down unimpaired to the latest posterity.[1]

In the elections of the previous year there had been forty-eight seats at stake, and of these the Liberals had obtained forty-three; in the elections which now took place seventeen seats were contested, and of these the Liberals retained nine whilst the Conservatives retained three and gained five seats previously held by Liberals. The system of voting somewhat exaggerated the shift in opinion which had taken place, as it had exaggerated the strength of the Liberals' support in the previous year; about 59 per cent of those who voted had supported the Liberals in the municipal elections of 1835, whereas now, at the end of their first year of office, they received the votes of about 51 per cent of those who went to the polls.[2] It is clear that the Liberals had lost some support among the voters but, surprisingly, in spite of the very outspoken opposition of almost all of the Church of England clergy, they were still able to claim that most of those able and willing to vote were prepared to support the Liberal policy. As a result of the elections, the new Council contained 53 Liberals (including 15 aldermen) and 11 Conservatives (including 1 alderman).

The Conservatives, naturally, claimed to have won an important victory; the *Liverpool Courier*[3] announced that Liverpool had shown her distrust of a Council 'composed of such heterogeneous materials that it can express no opinion on religious matters at all except that of indifference or infidelity'. The Liberal newspapers had to admit that, as *The Albion*[4] put it, the Liberals were 'not, of course, pleased at the result'; the *Liverpool Times*[5] conceded that 'the school question' had 'told much against the Council and driven from them many friends'. But probably most of the Liberals would have agreed with *The Albion*[6] when it summed up the position as follows:

It was clear to all reflecting men that in a community like that of Liverpool, in which the Tories form a numerous, a rich, and an influential class, the members of that party never could be so few in number as they were in the first reformed Council. At every subsequent election, it was evident, the Tories would recruit their forces, until, in process of time, they would

---

[1] *Liverpool Courier*, 26 October 1836.
[2] The figures here given are calculated from the returns printed in *A Record of Elections Parliamentary and Municipal for Liverpool* [etc.], compiled by Richard Bennett, Liverpool, 1878.
[3] 2 November 1836.   [4] 7 November 1836.
[5] 8 November 1836.   [6] 14 November 1836.

approach to something like an equality, in point of numbers, with the Reformers . . . But to argue, that, because some two, or at the very utmost some three, Tories more than the number calculated upon have slipped into the Council-room, public opinion is decidedly against the system of education introduced into the Corporation schools, is to attempt to build an important conclusion upon very untenable ground. Public opinion, fairly and honestly collected, has never yet been expressed on the school question. And why? Because owing to the calumnies and slanders which have been industriously circulated respecting that question, the public mind has not been in any fit state to form any opinion worthy of the consideration of a deliberative body like the Town Council. . . . A clamour, and nothing beyond a clamour, has the outcry against the schools been up to this time. Like all clamour it will gradually die away.

2

Nevertheless, the loss of five seats to the Conservatives caused a few of the Liberals some concern; not so much, it would seem, because they thought it represented a serious political defeat, as because they had scruples about continuing to pursue a policy of which many of the electors manifestly disapproved. The result was that men like William Rathbone and Thomas Blackburn suddenly found it necessary to defend that policy against attacks from members of their own party; and the discussions which thereupon took place were of importance since they made clear what the opponents of the Liberals had hitherto merely suspected—that the leaders of the Liberal Party in Liverpool were playing for far higher stakes than success in municipal elections, and were, in fact, hoping to demonstrate in their two Corporation Schools that the 'Religious Problem' need no longer present an obstacle to the setting up in England of a national system of elementary education.

At the Council meeting of 9 November 1836 the Liberal Charles Birch claimed that the members of the Council as 'the representatives of the whole community . . . were bound to concede everything to the feelings of the public, when their feelings had been decidedly expressed. They had been decidedly expressed and he need only point to the results of the late elections as proof'. He agreed that the Council would not have been justified in spending public money for the benefit of any one denomination, and even admitted that this opinion was shared by 'the calm, judging part of the community of whatever party or sect'. Nevertheless, 'whether the mode of education which had been pursued were proper or not', he doubted whether it was 'politic to go against the feelings of the public'; and he went on: 'To combine religious with secular instruction seemed the only way; the experiment had been fairly tried and had proved a failure.' He claimed that the Corporation Schools were at this period, as they had been when the Conservatives controlled them, 'little better than places of sectarian education'—an allusion to the fact that they were now attended mainly by Roman Catholic children. He felt that 'the safest course was to abandon the schools altogether', and therefore put forward the motion:

That it be an instruction to the Finance Committee to sell the schools in two lots, for seventy-five years, with the stipulation that they shall be used as schools for the future.[1]

He was supported by two Liberals: John Cropper, who complained that people who disapproved of the policy pursued in the schools were compelled to support them financially; and Lawrence Heyworth, who, while admitting that 'no schools could have been established on greater principles of justice than these', yet felt that Birch's proposal was 'a most righteous one, and one which they were compelled by the existing state of society to accept'. After some discussion it was agreed that the motion should receive further consideration at a later meeting of the Council.

Before that meeting took place William Rathbone wrote to all of the Liberal members of the Council, urging them to remain resolute in support of the policy which they had inaugurated in the Corporation Schools. In his letter (of which no other copy seems to exist than that found among the *Rathbone Family Papers*) Rathbone roundly declared:

Our plan was, as soon as our arrangements were carried well into effect and the Schools in order, to make them Model Schools for the training of Masters and Mistresses. Everyone acknowledges how much such are needed; and thus the benefit would extend over the country, and we may prove the practicability of a National System which should include a religious education *for all*.

If you give up the schools on the ground of their unpopularity, how can you expect Government to risk what our Reform Corporation feel they have not the strength to stand against; and when our unfortunate failure will have added greatly to their discouragement?

The *Liverpool Times* issued a similar warning a week later, when it declared that

. . . the Council have . . . to decide on a matter of no small importance, not only to the people of Liverpool, but to the whole kingdom; for there is no reason to believe that, if the attempt to devise a system of education acceptable to all parties should fail here, . . . it will succeed anywhere else. The

[1] *Liverpool Courier*, 16 November 1836.

abandonment of the present system will, in fact, be a confession that the divisions among the different sections of the Christian world are so deep and so irreconcileable [sic], that no common ground can be discovered on which they can meet, and that education must either exclude religion altogether, or be purely sectarian in its character.[1]

On 23 November the Council met to discuss Birch's proposal that the schools should be sold. Before the debate began there was laid before the Council a memorial, 'professing to come from a large majority of the reform burgesses of North Toxteth Ward', protesting against Birch's proposal; indeed, the petitioners 'were in hopes that the surplus funds of the borough would be sufficient not only to support those schools, but also to establish other schools on the same principle in every ward of the town.' And even the originator of the suggestion that the Council should sell its schools had by this time changed his mind; he now put forward the very different motion:

That it is just and proper that the benefits of religious instruction should be open to the children of the poor of every denomination, and that, in order effectually to promote this object, it is expedient to erect additional schools to be conducted on the plan formerly pursued in the Corporate schools of this borough.[2]

He explained that if the motion were accepted the two Corporation Schools then in existence would continue 'on their present footing', and that two or three other schools, 'without stating any precise number', would be erected as soon as possible by the Corporation, it being implied by the terms of the motion that these would be, in effect, schools conducted 'according to the faith and practice of the Church of England'. Birch hoped 'that by this very simple arrangement they might set at rest for ever this extremely vexatious question'. It may be said at once—and the fact surely merits attention—that the Conservative members of the Council seem to have been quite ready to accept the compromise which Birch proposed: one of them, Henry Lawrence, stated that 'he and the gentlemen with whom he acted thought that Mr Birch's plan, if adopted, might give general satisfaction to the town, and he thought it should be tried'; whilst another, James Heyworth, 'strongly approved of Mr Birch's proposition, which he described as a healing measure, in which the public would at once coalesce and agree'.

Indeed, so anxious were the Conservatives to support Birch's motion that when two Liberals, John and Edward Cropper, proposed and seconded an amendment urging that the Corporation Schools

[1] 22 November 1836.
[2] The account of the proceedings here given is based on the report published in the *Liverpool Mercury*, 25 November 1836.

should be sold, Henry Lawrence begged them to withdraw their amendment temporarily, since if the amendment were taken first the Conservatives 'by voting for Mr Cropper's motion to dispose of the schools . . . might preclude themselves from an opportunity which they would otherwise have, of sanctioning Mr Birch's proposition'. So that in spite of the great outcry against the 'Irish System' and the regulations adopted in the Corporation Schools, the most responsible members of the Conservative Party in Liverpool were at this time quite prepared, and even eager, to support the policy of providing Corporation Schools in which children of all denominations would be educated together, if only the Liberals would agree to the provision of denominational Corporation Schools for the use of those Church of England children whose parents wished them to attend such schools. The Liberals, however, refused to accept this proposal, and an amendment in favour of continuing the existing system without modification was carried by forty-five votes to ten, the seven Conservatives present and three Liberals, Charles Birch, J. Cropper and E. Cropper, voting against the amendment.

Some of the statements made during the course of the debate were at least as interesting as the final decision. In reply to the suggestion that public opinion was opposed to the policy pursued in the Corporation Schools, several of the Liberals claimed that this was by no means the case. Egerton Smith (proprietor and editor of the *Liverpool Mercury*) felt quite sure that if the public were given an opportunity of expressing their opinion on the subject the Council 'would have a most sufficient and satisfying proof that the opinions expressed at the Amphitheatre by political parsons were not the opinions of the sound portion of the community'. Thomas Blackburn, after remarking that the 'Irish System' came to them 'with the sanction and approbation of some of the best and wisest men that ever adorned the Church', maintained that in Liverpool 'a great number of the Church of England approved of the system and supported the schools', whilst 'a great majority of the Protestant Dissenters cordially approved of the system they had adopted in the schools; and as to the Roman Catholics, no inconsiderable proportion of the population, they were with the Council as one man. They hailed the establishment of these institutions as of immense benefit to them'.

Blackburn replied to the criticism that the schools had become, in effect, Roman Catholic institutions, by pointing out that, in spite of the opposition of almost all of the Church of England clergy, and the placards which they had caused to be posted about the town urging Protestant parents not to send their children to the Corporation

Schools, there were at that time in attendance at the schools 250 Protestant children along with 1,050 Roman Catholic children. Dealing with the same charge, William Rathbone stated that at the South Corporation School, of 221 children in the Boys' Department 63 were Protestants and 158 Roman Catholics, whilst, in the Girls' Department, of the 214 children attending 70 were Protestants and 144 Roman Catholics; he added that all the members of the Committee[1] which controlled the schools, and all the masters and mistresses in them, were Protestants.

In view of what happened later it is worthy of note that Blackburn confirmed what Rathbone had said in his letter to the Liberal councillors as to its being the intention of those most closely connected with the schools to turn them eventually into training schools for teachers; he asked why there should not be Normal Schools for the education of teachers at Liverpool, as well as at London, Edinburgh and Dublin— 'were they not as competent to provide instruction in Liverpool instead of sending elsewhere for teachers?' But the most important declaration of the day was Blackburn's defiant reply to the accusation which the Rev. Hugh M'Neile had made some months earlier—that the leaders of the Liberal Party in Liverpool had introduced the 'Irish System' into the Corporation Schools as a 'feeler of the pulse of England'. Blackburn said that:

Popular education had now excited such a degree of public attention that it well became them to make these schools an object of example to the country at large in every possible direction. They had been taunted with the introduction of this system as a feeler,—a *feeler* in order to ascertain whether the people of this country would adopt a system so favourable, as they were told, to Popery. He himself had had the honour to introduce this subject to the notice of the Education Committee; he had been the first to propose the adoption of the Irish system, and he was proud of it. He gloried in it, and he was frank to own that it *was* a feeler on his part, and it was done with the hope and belief that if that system was once fairly tried in any part of England, the result would be a conviction that what was morally right in one part of the country, could not be morally wrong in another. It could not be right on the other side of the water and wrong on this. Wherever there was a mixed population of Protestants and Roman Catholics, he contended that it was highly advisable that this system should be introduced without loss of time in every part of the empire, and he trusted that the future historian would have to say that the Town Council of Liverpool had the honour of introducing this system of education into England and that it rapidly spread throughout the empire.

---

[1] Richard Sheil, the one Roman Catholic who had hitherto served on the Education Committee, had lost his seat in the recent municipal elections.

Blackburn hoped that the Reformers in the Council 'would not be influenced by the malignant howl of a disappointed faction', or 'consent to withdraw from the admiring view of the united empire the noble example they had set of a policy liberal and truly Christian'.

The statement of policy thus made by Blackburn and that of Rathbone in his letter to the Liberal councillors left no further room for doubt about the ultimate purpose of those who had most strongly advocated the introduction of the 'Irish System' into the Corporation Schools; and now that they had nailed their colours to the mast the Education Committee thought it advisable to deprive their critics of the tactical advantage afforded to them by the use of the phrase 'after the school has closed' to indicate the period at which the complete Authorized Version of the Bible might be read in the schools by Protestant children. As we have seen, secular instruction in the Corporation Schools ended an hour earlier than was customary in similar schools, in order that denominational religious instruction could be given; but, as Blackburn not very graciously admitted, the regulation was so worded as to give rise to some misunderstanding and to make misrepresentation easy. He remarked that:

Great stress had been laid . . . on the use of the term 'school-hours'. They were told that the Bible was not read in school-hours, and taking the resolution of the Council for their guide, there certainly was some plausibility in this. It would have been very wise if, instead of using the simple term 'school-hours', they had said 'hours for secular instruction'; but they had not sufficient perspicacity to foresee the objection that would be taken by those subtle and eloquent dialecticians, and therefore they used plain and simple language. They saw the effect produced in the public mind by the ingenious use of the term 'school-hours'. By the cautious and skilful management of that phrase, it passed for an assertion that the Bible was not used at all in these schools.

Accordingly, at a meeting of the Education Committee held on 20 December 1836, it was decided to extend the 'official' school day by one hour, and to describe the hour during which denominational religious instruction could be given not as the hour after the school had closed but as the 'last hour' of the school day. The regulation governing the giving of religious instruction in the schools then read:

The School to commence each Morning by the Children singing a Hymn: after which a Scripture Lesson[1] to be read to them. The last hour each Afternoon to be appropriated to reading the Bible, and other Religious Instruction under the Ministers of their respective Churches.[2]

[1] Taken, of course, from the volumes of *Scripture Lessons* prepared and recommended for use in the Irish National Schools.

[2] *Proceedings of Education Committee*, Vol. I, p. 31.

But the Committee were to be disappointed if they imagined that the most bitter of their opponents would henceforward cease to make use of the damaging cry that 'the Bible was excluded from the Corporation Schools'; and, as we have seen, so long as they had the Rev. Hugh M'Neile at their head, such opponents were not likely to be without ingenious arguments with which to support the charge.

3

It was not be expected that the critics of the Education Committee would ignore the declarations of Rathbone and Blackburn that the Corporation Schools were intended to serve as models for the rest of England to copy. The *Liverpool Standard* gloomily commented that 'England perhaps is doomed to run the same revolutionary course as France—appearances seem to justify the conclusion. The very first step taken in France was to relax the bonds of religion—and this step is just taken in England'.[1] The *Liverpool Mail* was rather more hopeful:

We beg to remind protestants in other parts of England that this town has been first selected by the agents of the government, and by the advisers of the popish rebels of Ireland, to try the experiment of undermining religious belief in the young, the fatherless, and the unprotected, by means of an unchristian education, the most execrable merit of which is, that it excludes the Bible from the schools. The plan has been tried and it has failed. . . . The consequence has been that the mutilated Bible is almost wholly in the hands of Roman Catholic children, who are under the tuition of popish priests.[2]

But the most forceful criticism of the Education Committee at this juncture came from the Rev. Hugh M'Neile, who addressed to the members of the Town Council, and subsequently published, a series of letters[3] in which he attacked the system in force in the Corporation Schools. Much of what he had to say about the 'Irish System' had been said many times before, not only by M'Neile himself but by others. (The *Letters* showed that M'Neile had carefully studied H. Newland's *An Examination of the Scripture Lessons as Translated and Published by His Majesty's Commissioners of Education in Ireland, Addressed to the Right Hon. Lord Stanley*, Dublin, 1836.) What makes M'Neile's *Letters* worthy of notice is the fact that they obtained such a wide circulation. M'Neile said of them a year later (November 1837):

[1] 25 December 1836.
[2] 29 December 1836.
[3] *Letters on National Education Addressed to the Town Council of Liverpool. To which are Added a Correspondence Hitherto Unpublished with Two Members of the Council*, London, 1837.

These letters appeared first in the newspapers of Liverpool. The friends of Scripture Education caused them to be struck off in large numbers, for circulation among the poorer inhabitants, and they afterwards caused them to be struck off on letter paper, that they might be sent to different individuals and to Members of both Houses of Parliament; and the Committee of the Liverpool Protestant Association voted, unanimously, to me a request that they should be published in the present shape; thus they went through four successive stages, and a number of copies, to the amount of twenty or twenty-five thousand, have been circulated through the country.[1]

From the point of view of the Liverpool Education Committee it was unfortunate that the most widely published account of the experiment being conducted in the Corporation Schools came not from the Committee itself or even from one of its more moderate critics, but from a man of such extreme views that almost all of his fellow clergymen had hitherto found it impossible to associate themselves with the branch of the Protestant Association of which he was the ruling spirit in Liverpool and which now begged him to make public his *Letters*.

In these somewhat lengthy epistles M'Neile's chief purpose was to show that the *Scripture Lessons* originally prepared for the use of children of all denominations in Irish schools, and now so used in the Corporation Schools, were objectionable: because they contained notes, in accordance with 'Romish practice'; because they 'elevated the Douay and Rhemish versions into a position of parallel authority with our authorised version'; because they 'inculcated Roman Catholic doctrines'; and because they constituted a new translation of the Bible, and thus furthered the aims of the Roman Catholic Church, which ever wished 'to produce uncertainty as to the Word of God'. He proclaimed that 'a system of National Education, whether in School or College, in which the Bible is only tolerated, while it is provided that Romish Catechisms, which contradict the Bible, shall be taught, is a system in open defiance of the revealed will of God'. The duty of the Council, of the government and of the Church of England clergy was plain: the two former should 'Legislate for God and let all his Majesty's subjects, who are of God's mind in this matter, receive a willing benefit; and all those who are opposed to God's mind, receive an unwilling benefit, conferred upon them by rulers wiser and holier than themselves'; whilst the clergy, he suggested, could not sanction a system which did not '*ensure* and *enforce* the Word of God', and could not undertake 'to refrain from the Scriptural instruction' of even the Roman Catholic children, whose own pastors, he said, would not 'teach them the pure

[1] *The Rev. Hugh M'Neile On The Irish System of Education, More Particularly As Regards The System Now In Operation In Liverpool: Being A Speech Delivered By Him At The Assembly Rooms, Cheltenham, November 10th, 1837*, Cheltenham [?1837], p. 11.

Word of God'. It was in this publication that he made the observation, referred to earlier, that so far as the Church of England clergy were concerned the Bible was excluded from the schools, since they could not conscientiously attend during the hour when the Bible was studied.

Yet of all the statements made by M'Neile in his *Letters* probably those most likely to convince an unbiased reader (and especially one living outside the town) that the policy of the Liverpool Education Committee was unsound and doomed to fail were to the effect that the Corporation Schools were at this time 'as exclusively Roman Catholic as they were formerly exclusively Protestant', whilst the Church of England clergy in the town were *above fifty to one* against the new system'. The first of these two contentions was, as we have seen, not strictly accurate; but the determination of almost all of the Church of England clergy to refuse to co-operate with the Liverpool Education Committee was made more obvious than ever when in January 1837 the Church of England School Society, which had been founded at the great protest meeting at the Amphitheatre six months earlier, opened its 'North Church of England School' in Bond Street, Liverpool, to provide for Church of England children withdrawn from the North Corporation School. (A 'South Church of England School' to cater for children formerly taught in the South Corporation School was erected in Cornwallis Street and opened in December 1837.) It may be added that, in order to demonstrate their support for the policy adopted by their clergy, the masters of the Church of England schools in the town went so far as to 'secede from the general body of the public teachers'[1] who had been 'accustomed to meet monthly for educational purposes' and had formed The Liverpool Teachers' Society,[2] 'a reading society for circulating among the teachers, male and female, works on instruction'. A 'Church of England Schoolmasters' Reading Society', it was decided, should be founded without delay.

4

Nevertheless, the Liverpool Education Committee were not deterred. By the end of the year 1836 some, at least, of the Liberals were beginning to feel that 'the current was now running as strongly in favour of the system of education adopted by the Council as for a season bigotry and prejudice forced it to run against them'.[3] They were glad

---

[1] *The Albion* (Liverpool), 24 October 1836.

[2] When the society had been formed, about 1823, Dr Bell had declined an invitation to become a patron on discovering that it 'consisted of men of various religious denominations' (Rev. C. C. Southey, *The Life of the Rev. Andrew Bell*, Vol. III, p. 293).

[3] *Liverpool Telegraph*, 21 December 1836.

to announce that a Church of England clergyman[1] had agreed to instruct the children of his faith at the North Corporation School, as the Rev. James Aspinall had for some months been doing at the South Corporation School.[2] In January 1837, the Committee, anxious to make the schools as efficient as possible, again invited Samuel Wilderspin 'to undertake the arrangement' of the schools—chiefly, it would appear, of the girls' schools—for a period of three months 'at a remuneration of One Hundred and fifty Pounds';[3] and in April 1837 Wilderspin was requested 'to continue his services for Three Months from the Seventh day of May on the same terms as before'.[4] One disgruntled master in the schools, who had been trained at the Liverpool Blue Coat Hospital to employ the monitorial system in accordance with the precepts of Dr Bell, gave what purported to be an account of the situation in the schools at this time:

> What occasioned the dislike to the Dr [i.e. Bell] I am not quite prepared to say. But it was evident that to supersede, or rather, to exclude his name and system altogether from the schools was considered exceedingly desirable. For a while we had daily and weekly novelties. There were Systems from Ireland, Models from London, and Methods from Edinburgh. Our Councillors were industrious. Some of them hunted theories from morning till night. Every pretender to some new discovery in the *art* and *mystery* of School Teaching was sure of being entertained, if not well paid, by the Corporation School Committee. . . . Any thing and every thing but Dr Bell . . . appeared welcome.[5]

According to this master's calculations, which allowed for payment of interest at 5 per cent on capital invested in the schools, the cost of educating each child under the new régime had risen to the shocking sum of £2 15s. 6½d. per annum, whereas in the Liverpool Wesleyan Schools in 1835 'the total expense of giving daily instruction to 1,594 children, and sabbath tuition to 1,792' had amounted only to £1,028 18s. 5d.[6]

---

[1] Apparently this was the Rev. Mr Stokes, who was reported in the *Liverpool Journal* of 9 September 1837 to have been occupied for months past at the North School 'in the same pious office' as the Rev. Mr Aspinall performed at the South School.

[2] *Ibid.*

[3] *Proceedings of Education Committee*, Vol. I, p. 34.

[4] *Ibid.*, Vol. I, p. 39.

[5] A. Farrill, *The Schoolmaster's Appeal to Public Candour* . . . , pp. 14–15. Wilderspin resented Farrill's description of his 'System' (as applied in the Corporation Girls' Schools) as 'ridiculous mummery'; he challenged Farrill to appear with him 'in public debate', and undertook to prove 'that Mr F. is unacquainted both with the man and the system which he condemns; and that he is both a partial and unjust judge' (*The Albion*, 27 March 1837). Wilderspin's challenge was not accepted.

[6] Farrill, *op. cit.*, p. 19.

During the early months of 1837 it seemed likely that the Education Committee would be allowed a period of comparative calm—disturbed only by the regular outbursts of the Rev. Hugh M'Neile[1]—in which to improve its schools and to attempt to convince the more open-minded of its critics that the policy which had been adopted in order to make the schools available to children of all denominations had not only succeeded in its purpose but was, in spite of the misrepresentation of intolerant men, such as reasonable people of all sects might conscientiously support. But if the members of the Committee hoped that peace would reign until the next municipal elections were about to take place they were in fact disappointed: William IV died on 20 June 1837, Victoria ascended the throne, and it at once became obvious that a General Election would not be long delayed. The Tory election campaign began quietly enough with a meeting at the Liverpool Amphitheatre on 5 July 1837, and the corresponding Liberal meeting took place two days later; by the time that voting took place, on 25 July, the election campaign had become one of the most bitter in the history of the town.

In 1832, during the first flush of enthusiasm over the passage of the Reform Bill, the Liverpool voters had, to most people's surprise, returned a Liberal, William Ewart, at the top of the poll; but the second of the representatives chosen for the two-seat constituency was a Conservative, Viscount Sandon. The 1835 elections provided very clear evidence that enthusiasm for Liberal policies had much diminished among the Liverpool parliamentary electors. Nor was this surprising, since a number of the local Liberals, headed by William Rathbone, had expended a great deal of time and energy between the two elections in the unsuccessful attempt to have Parliament disfranchise the Liverpool freemen on the ground that as voters they were notoriously corrupt. Although the Liberal Ewart was once again returned to Parliament, it was Viscount Sandon who topped the poll in 1835, and Ewart's majority over the unsuccessful Conservative candidate was only 176. Of the total votes cast in January 1835 only about 48·1 per cent went to the two Liberal candidates, a considerable fall from the 54·6 per cent which they had obtained in 1832. It should be noted that this sharp drop in the Liberal parliamentary vote took place before the Liverpool Liberals gained control of the local Town Council, and was therefore in no way connected with the policies which they

---

[1] In May 1837 he informed a London audience that the enemies of the Church, after having introduced the 'Irish System' into Ireland, had 'endeavoured to import the plague into Lancashire'. He added: 'But we put their ship into quarantine' (*Liverpool Courier*, 17 May 1837). M'Neile was speaking at the Second Annual Meeting of the Protestant Association in Exeter Hall.

subsequently pursued in municipal affairs. In the parliamentary election of 1837 the leaders of the Liverpool Conservatives could reasonably hope to win some consolation for the loss of the control of the Council, especially since in a parliamentary election they could rely on the support of many[1] disgruntled freemen who were unable to make their influence felt at municipal elections because they lacked the appropriate household qualification which would have entitled them to vote.

The Conservatives, naturally, strained every nerve to wipe out Ewart's slender majority, and of course the controversy over the Corporation Schools provided them with an opportunity too good to be missed. Viscount Sandon, in his published appeal to the electors, made the usual allegation that the Authorized Version of the Bible had been excluded from the schools and replaced by extracts—although he framed the charge in language less direct than was customarily employed:

I believe that I shall find you more deeply than ever impressed with the conviction, that Education, to be wholesome and efficient, must not only be based on Religion generally, but also be interwoven with some recognised and defined form; and that it is not right to limit those who are desirous of receiving the whole Scriptures as the basis of Instruction, to such portions only of the Bible as another part of the population are permitted by their Religious Teachers to receive.[2]

Rather less dignified was the language employed in the Conservative and Liberal newspapers as the campaign progressed and tempers rose. Less dignified still were the means sometimes employed to drive home what was considered to be an effective argument: thus Wilderspin reported that

. . . the Bible was made into a political stalking-horse, one party had a large wooden one made and carried in front of their candidates with flags and banners, on which were inscribed 'the whole Bible and nothing but the Bible'. All this was done amidst the *hootings* and *howlings* of a *drunken mob*. I saw it and heard it, and I was grieved at the prostitution and profanation of the Holy Volume.[3]

---

[1] According to a speaker at a meeting of the Tradesmen's Reform Association in August 1837, 'only 600 out of 3,100 freemen had a householder's qualification and consequently a vote for the members of the Town Council' (*Liverpool Mercury*, 18 August 1837).

[2] *Liverpool Courier*, 19 July 1837.

[3] S. Wilderspin, *A Reply to the Various Speeches Delivered at a Meeting Held at the Assembly Rooms, Cheltenham, on Friday October 27th, on the Subject of National Education*, London, Cheltenham, 1837, p. 16. See also E. A. Rathbone, *Records of the Rathbone Family*, p. 211.

Another observer wrote:

> The Tories ... have adopted 'The Bible' as their war-cry in the impending contest. They have, accordingly, printed thousands of slips of red paper, with the inscription, 'The Bible, and nothing but the Bible'. These slips they have mounted on little bits of stick, like the flags which pedlars sell to children; and they were, on Saturday evening, busily engaged in throwing them, from the windows of their committee-rooms in the different wards, among the children in the streets.[1]

The Conservatives, for their part, complained that the 'inflammatory placards' of their opponents were calculated to 'call together a mob of the most ruffianly desperadoes in Christendom'. Some Conservatives, it was said, were attacked by 'the rankest scum of Irish Popery, being *non-electors*'.[2] The Liberal *Liverpool Mercury* complained bitterly of the tactics employed by its political opponents in the course of what it called 'the Bible election', but admitted that some supporters of the Liberals had not limited themselves to verbal combat:

> Outrages of the most violent and disgraceful kind occurred in various parts of the town, more violent and more disgraceful indeed than ever occurred at any previous contested election within our memory . . . we are obliged to admit that those who called themselves friends of the Liberal candidates were the original aggressors.[3]

William Rathbone himself sadly remarked:

> To our friends the Roman Catholics, and to Irishmen, I would say one word;—I have fought for them, but I do say that some of the tumults which have occurred at this election have done much to take several votes from us.[4]

When the election results were made known it was found that the Conservatives had succeeded in defeating William Ewart; the two successful candidates were Viscount Sandon and Cresswell Cresswell, both Conservatives. The Liberal newspaper *The Albion*, after pointing out that Conservative candidates had been defeated in many of the larger towns, commented:

> Amongst the leading cities in the land, Liverpool is alone a political plague-spot on the face of liberty. But . . . let it be known to every one, that the battle has not been fought here merely on political grounds. . . . The struggle here has not been a national, but a local conflict; it has been fought altogether by the Tories on the School Question; and they have only been

[1] *The Albion*, 24 July 1837. This report is confirmed by Wilderspin, *A Reply to the Various Speeches* . . . , p. 16.
[2] *Liverpool Courier*, 26 July 1837.
[3] *Liverpool Mercury*, 28 July 1837.
[4] *Ibid.*

too successful in imposing the often exploded untruth about the exclusion of the Bible upon the credulity of the multitude.[1]

All of the Liberal journals echoed this opinion, although some also pointed out that the hostility of the freemen had influenced the results.[2] The Conservatives were equally convinced that their success was very largely due to the stand which they had taken on the 'Schools Question'. The Liberals lamented their defeat; the Conservatives celebrated their triumph: neither side seems to have noticed the surely interesting and significant fact that in spite of the fierce opposition, wild accusations and crude misrepresentation of some of their political opponents, and in spite also of the denunciation of many respected clergymen, the Liberals had lost very little support as a result of their schools policy. In 1835, before the controversy over the schools had begun, the percentage of the votes cast in the Liverpool parliamentary election which had gone to Liberal candidates had been, as we have seen, about 48·1; in this hotly contested parliamentary election of 1837 that percentage fell by less than 0·5 to about 47·64. The contest over the Corporation Schools was clearly far from being ended, and there was still reason to hope for the eventual success of the 'first experiment' alluded to by Viscount Sandon, at a meeting held to celebrate the Conservative success, when he said:

I know that the first experiment has been tried within the walls of Liverpool—I know that the experiment which has been so tried here is but a sample of that system which her majesty's government will be anxious to introduce into every town and hamlet of the empire. Now, gentlemen, this is the object which we must keep constantly in view; we must keep a watchful eye on all the plausibilities of the manner by which they will try to introduce it.[3]

5

Probably the most important result of the parliamentary election of July 1837 was that it led to a worsening of the relations between those in favour of the Education Committee's policy and the many Church of England clergy who opposed it. Very few indeed of these latter would at any time have endorsed the more extreme opinions of the Rev. H. M'Neile, but as time went on even moderate-minded men like the Rev. A. Campbell gradually became more and more outspoken

[1] 31 July 1837.
[2] See, for example, *Liverpool Times*, 1 August 1837.
[3] *Conservative Triumph or The Three Glorious Days!* . . . , p. 6.

in their condemnation of the Liberal Council. It ought to have been obvious to those who were conducting the important experiment in the Corporation Schools that they could scarcely hope to persuade others to repeat that experiment elsewhere so long as they themselves had to admit their failure to win the support of at least a fair number of the Church of England clergy in the town; but some of the Liberal spokesmen, angered by what they considered to be unreasonable opposition, unfounded accusations and politically-inspired animosity, gave up the attempt to win over the clergy of the Established Church, and, indeed, helped to confirm the worst fears of some of the clergy by indulging in insults and abuse. Many of the Liberals had been shocked, as we have said, when the Junior Rector had seemed to claim that the Church of England clergy had not been consulted about the system of religious instruction which had been introduced into the Corporation Schools; and relations between the two sides had not been helped when Thomas Blackburn in his published defence of the Liberal policy had expressed the opinion that Church of England doctrines were 'full of Popery'. Equally provocative and undiplomatic had been the language of the Liberal Mayor, William Earle, when, in the course of a Council discussion on the Corporation Schools, he had remarked that it was not to be wondered at if the Church of England clergy were lacking in tolerance since 'they were brought up at Oxford and Cambridge, where the light of reason was scarcely ever allowed to enter'.[1]

To make matters worse, the first anniversary meeting of the Liverpool Church of England School Society—another great protest meeting like that called by the clergy in the previous year—happened to take place when the parliamentary election campaign of 1837 was at its height, when tempers were already running high, and contemptuous allusions to 'political parsons' were frequently to be found in the Liberal newspapers.[2] At the meeting, the two Rectors of Liverpool spoke from the same platform as Mr T. B. Horsfall, who proclaimed that 'the Papist, the Socinian, the rebel, and the revolutionist, combined to exclude the Scriptures from the schools';[3] and the Rev. H. M'Neile announced that 'the old Vatican has proved too wily for the

---

[1] *Liverpool Mercury*, 25 November 1836.

[2] 'For weeks and months past the pulpits of this town have been desecrated by political parsons, for the purpose of rousing one portion of the community against the other' (*ibid.*, 28 July 1837). The *Liverpool Mercury* printed a squib entitled 'The Liverpool Election or The Political Parsons', in which it was said of the Church of England clergy that it was a

'Shame that they should their heavenly cause abandon,
To *plead* the *cause* of Cresswell and of Sandon.'

[3] *Ibid.*, 14 July 1837.

young unfledged liberal, and while he thinks himself an ally the liberal is indeed a dupe'.[1]

But what did most to embitter the relations between the leading Liberals and the Church of England clergy was a report that the Junior Rector had criticized the policy of the Liverpool Town Council at a political meeting held at Newton on 28 July 1837 as part of the election campaign of the Conservative candidate for the South Lancashire constituency; according to the account of the meeting given in the *Liverpool Mercury* the Rev. A. Campbell had 'repeated the proved falsehood about the expulsion of the Bible and the clergy from the Corporation Schools. "The Reformers of Liverpool", he said, "succeeded in getting into the Corporation, and these persons, some of the party who denounced against [sic] the connexion of politics and religion, soon managed matters in such a way, that the clergy and the Bible were turned out of the Corporation schools."' The newspaper added the extremely pointed comment: 'Mr Campbell *knows* that neither the Bible nor the clergy have been "turned out of the Corporation schools"; and if he looks into the Bible, he will find there something addressed to those who bear false witness against their neighbours.'[2]

This, clearly, was no small matter; here, according to the view one took of the matter, one had a fair-minded, kindly and responsible leader of the Church of England clergy in the town—no firebrand like M'Neile—being unjustly accused, in a newspaper owned and edited by a Liberal member of the Town Council, of deliberate lying, or else one had a man, to some extent the spokesman of the clergy of the Established Church, who had been so carried away by political and religious prejudice that he had been prepared to attend a political meeting, and there lie most irresponsibly to men who knew nothing of the true state of affairs in the Corporation Schools. William Rathbone was deeply shocked. He at once wrote a letter to the Press, in which he reminded the Junior Rector of the efforts which had been made and which Campbell 'more than any other person in Liverpool ought to recollect', to persuade the Church of England clergy to give religious instruction in the schools; he felt 'compelled to give a direct contradiction' to the statement that the Bible was excluded from the Corporation Schools, and considered that some attempt to find out the truth before such an assertion was repeated was 'essential to the character of a gentleman, and especially a Christian minister'. Rathbone went on to express the opinion that the Established Church was truly

[1] *Speech of the Rev. Hugh M'Neile at the Church of England School Meeting Held in the Amphitheatre, Liverpool, on Tuesday, the 11th July, 1837*, Liverpool [n.d.], p. 14.
[2] 4 August 1837.

in danger if it could be supported only by 'unchristian denunciation and misrepresentation of others'. He concluded by saying: 'You have, indeed, Reverend Sir, drawn the sword and thrown away the scabbard.'[1]

The scholarly, aged and much-respected Unitarian minister, Dr Shepherd[2] of Gateacre, intervened in the dispute by visiting the schools and reporting that the Authorized Version of the Bible *was* read in them;[3] during the arguments which ensued he likened the Junior Rector to a jackdaw[4] and was in return described by Campbell as 'an old political servant' who had been 'summoned . . . to do the work of his employers by bearing false witness against his neighbour'.[5] The Liberals of Rodney Street Ward appointed a committee to examine the working of the Corporation Schools and to investigate the truth of Campbell's statements: the committee duly published a lengthy report in which they declared it to be one of their findings that 'all the reports advanced by the opponents of the Town Council, with reference to the exclusion of the Bible and Clergy from their schools, turn out to be a tissue of misrepresentations, evidently propagated for electioneering purposes; a fact not the less true on account of the sacred office of some of the propagators of such misstatements'.[6]

There is ample authority for the statement that Campbell was an honest, well-meaning and charitable man, but one who should never have engaged in controversial discussion since he frequently failed to say precisely what he meant, and so misled his hearers. When challenged he was apt to reply somewhat angrily or to shun further discussion, evidently feeling that his honesty of purpose ought never to be called in question, whatever views might be held about the matter in dispute. No man did more to stimulate and increase the suspicion and mistrust which many Liverpool Nonconformists felt towards the clergy of the Church of England during the latter half of the nineteenth century, and yet few men could have had more willingness to seek the honest course and pursue it. When challenged to give some explanation of his speech at Newton, Campbell at first characteristically indicated that

[1] *Liverpool Mercury*, 11 August 1837.

[2] See *D.N.B.*

[3] *Liverpool Journal*, 26 August, 9 September, 21 October 1837.

[4] *Liverpool Mercury*, 6 October 1837.

[5] *Conservative Triumph, or The Three Glorious Days!...*, p. 27. Campbell was speaking at a meeting held to celebrate the Conservative victory in the parliamentary election of 1837.

[6] *Report of the Committee of the Reformers of Rodney Street Ward Appointed at a Public Meeting Held the 14th August, 1837, to Enquire into the Truth of Certain Statements Made Relative to the System of Religious Instruction in the Corporation Schools*, Liverpool, 1837, p. 22.

he 'must decline entering into any discussion of it'[1]; but later made it clear[2] that he had intended merely to indicate that the clergy of the Established Church had felt obliged to withdraw from the Corporation Schools at the time when a 'law' had been passed prohibiting the reading of the Authorized Version of the Bible during school hours.[3] When it was pointed out to him that the 'law' to which he objected had not in fact prevented the reading of the Authorized Version within the accepted school hours, and that in any case the hour during which it might be read was now called 'the last hour' of the school day, Campbell replied that 'he knew nothing officially and said nothing at Newton' about the *actual* working of the new system in the schools, making the somewhat odd observation that whether or not the 'law' complained of had been acted upon or had later been repealed did not 'alter the question'.

There can be little doubt that most of those ignorant of the facts who heard Campbell speak at Newton or read reports of his speech were led by it to believe that the policy adopted in the Corporation Schools had involved the deliberate exclusion of the Bible (at least during school hours) and of the Church of England clergy, both having been 'turned out of the schools'. It is also true, perhaps, that Campbell might have taken greater care not to give a false impression of the system actually in force in the schools: even if 'officially', as he said, he knew nothing of it, he had had every opportunity to learn the facts, and in any case he might have made it more clear than he did that he was not speaking of the state of affairs which obtained in the schools at the time of his speech. The anger which his words aroused in those who knew that the Authorized Version was read regularly in the schools to and by Church of England clergymen can easily be imagined and, indeed, understood. Yet it seems certain that the Junior Rector had spoken in good faith, had had not the least intention to deceive, and was puzzled and hurt when his opponents accused him of 'bearing false witness'.

His critics, even the most forbearing and charitable of them, felt

[1] In a letter to the Committee of the Reformers of Rodney Street Ward. Campbell simply forwarded a copy of the old regulation which had stated that denominational religious instruction was to take place 'after the school had closed' (*Report of the Committee of Reformers of Rodney Street Ward*, p. 15).

[2] In a letter to Alderman Evans, published in the *Liverpool Chronicle*, 14 October 1837.

[3] Both the Liberal *Liverpool Mercury* (see above) and the Conservative *Liverpool Standard* (1 August 1837) had reported Campbell as stating simply that the Bible and the clergy had been 'turned out of the Corporation Schools'; the Conservative *Liverpool Courier* quoted him as saying that the Bible and the clergy had been 'excluded from the corporation schools: the first during school hours, the second altogether' (2 August 1837).

that the Rev. Augustus Campbell had, in Rathbone's words, 'drawn the sword and thrown away the scabbard'; Campbell, indignant at receiving what he considered unmerited abuse, began to draw somewhat closer to those who held extreme views in religion and politics; and the possibility that the main body of the Church of England clergy in the town would give their support to the system in force in the Corporation Schools began to seem more remote than ever. Such was the unfortunate consequence of remarks which Campbell claimed to have made 'good-humouredly, and solely to prove the necessary connexion between religion and politics, not to cast an unjust reflexion on the council, still less to calumniate any particular individuals of it'.[1]

[1] *Liverpool Chronicle*, 14 October 1837.

Chapter 6

THE CONFLICT SPREADS

I

IN September 1837 the British Association for the Advancement of Science held its annual meetings in Liverpool. It will be remembered that some of the members of the Association who were interested in the spread of education had agreed in the previous year to confer together at Liverpool during the visit of the Association, and that a committee, which included among its members Thomas Wyse, James Simpson and William Rathbone, had been set up to make the necessary arrangements. No doubt Rathbone had hoped that at the proposed meeting he would be able to present an impressively favourable report on what had been accomplished during the first year of the experiment which was being conducted in the Corporation Schools; but when the meeting took place he was scarcely in a position to do so. It was true that the policy adopted in the schools had won some support from men of all denominations, and that the new system was still in being in spite of the very determined opposition which it had encountered. It could even be said that that opposition was beginning to fail in its effect, since with each week that passed more and more Protestant parents were showing their willingness to allow their children to be taught with Roman Catholic children in the Corporation Schools. At this period (September 1837) the position in the schools was as follows:

	South Corporation School			North Corporation School		
	Protestants	Roman Catholics	Total	Protestants	Roman Catholics	Total
Boys	136	127	263	80	298	378
Girls	100	98	198	40	220	260
Infants	101	80	181	about 75	125	about 200
	337	305	642	about 195	643	about 838

Of the total of about 1,480 children in attendance at the two schools, therefore, about 532 were Protestants.[1] A good deal had been achieved

[1] *Report of the Committee of the Reformers of Rodney Street Ward* . . . , p. 26. The report was based on inquiries made at the schools; although the inquirers were not impartial there is no reason to doubt their honesty of purpose, and in any case the figures could easily have been checked by their political opponents, who were constantly being invited to examine for themselves the working of the schools.

in little more than a year, probably very much more than ought to have been expected. On the other hand the Rev. H. M'Neile was able to encourage his followers with the remark: 'It is certainly gratifying to find that it is now a year since it [the 'Irish System'] was imported and that, with the exception of the private use of the corporation, it is still in bond. Neither canal, nor coach, nor railway, has carried the slightest participation of it to any town in England. The worshipful the corporation of Liverpool have the exclusive credit of the patriotism manifested in its importation, and the hospitality exhibited in keeping it so long and so entirely to themselves.'[1] And it had to be admitted that, as we have seen, the opposition of the Church of England clergy in the town, so far from diminishing, was at this period becoming daily more bitter; the conclusions drawn by any visiting educationists were likely to be that the outcome of the Liverpool Education Committee's experiment was still in doubt and that to repeat the experiment else-where might well be to stir up a hornets' nest.

The Rev. H. M'Neile, at any rate, was anxious to impress these conclusions upon any of the visiting educationists who might have failed to arrive at them unaided. A study of the newspapers and pam-phlets of the period has revealed the interesting fact that an endeavour was made in Liverpool at this time to establish an Education Section of the British Association, an endeavour which was nipped in the bud by the ever-vigilant M'Neile. At Bristol, a year earlier, all that had been hoped for was some arrangement by which certain members of the British Association who were interested in education might take advan-tage of their coming together for the annual meetings of the Associa-tion to assemble, independently of the Association, for discussions on education. Now, something much more ambitious and potentially influential was to be attempted. The facts are given in M'Neile's words, since, although he somewhat lacked the detachment desirable in a wit-ness, he is in this matter the only source of information available; and, moreover, as he himself said, his statement was never contradicted by his opponents:

Upon the occasion of the late meeting of the British Association in Liverpool, there was a preliminary meeting to arrange for the Monday a public meeting on the subject of that [i.e. a national] system of education . . . Mr Wyse made a speech on the importance of having an additional section in aid of the statistical section, which should enter into important principles . . . Mr Simpson, of Edinburgh, stood up, eulogized the plan of the chair-man's speech, and declared that the grand object was to give their *scheme the weight of the British Association, in order he said to strengthen the hands of Govern-*

[1] *Speech of the Rev. Hugh M'Neile . . . 11 July 1837*, p. 10.

ment in establishing a national system of education.[1] This had gone on so far when I thought it my duty to rise and address the chairman. I said I got up to ask a question: under what designation was the meeting on Monday to be convened; was it to be the friends of some special educational movement, or was it to be as members of the British Association? This led to a considerable disagreement among themselves; in the course of the debate, Mr Simpson argued that the whole weight and importance of the meeting depended on giving it the sanction of the Scientific Association; on which I stood up and said that if the meeting on this subject was to consist of the members of the British Association, it would bring together elements amongst which harmony could not be expected: that I for one should feel myself called upon to attend such a meeting, to declare my conviction that any system not based on the Word of God would prove a curse and not a blessing to the nation. That as a consequence of such a meeting being convened they must be prepared for interminable discussion. This led to another debate among themselves, for there was no objector present except myself. My friends in Liverpool knew not of it.[2] . . . Upon this Mr Wyse spoke with very great tact and talent. . . . He said there was much common ground we might work upon, in which we were all agreed: we were all of one mind about communicating scientific knowledge and the cultivation of the human intellect. There was a large common ground which we might occupy in harmony before we reached the point in which religion was inculcated, in which, unfortunately, differences existed. This seemed to meet the approbation of the meeting; but I stood up again and said I was forced to disagree with them, for as we were divided with respect to the materials on which science was to be conducted, we could not agree at all on the mode of conducting it. . . . And I suggested that it would be better to call together the friends of their system, if they thought some plan necessary; but I protested against inviting members of the Association: this led to further discussion, and at last my plan was honoured by their adoption, and they put out a placard, inviting the friends of the Central Society for Education—the Central Society was not known in Liverpool, and in consequence they had not 100 persons at the meeting.[3]

M'Neile added:

This statement found its way into the Liverpool papers, and it was not controverted or commented upon by any of the opposition papers. Mr

[1] An account in the *Liverpool Courier*, based on M'Neile's information, quoted Simpson as saying 'that it were a light thing for some friends of education to have a meeting of their own at Bristol or Liverpool,—the main point was connexion with the British Association' (20 September 1837).

[2] Elsewhere in M'Neile's account he states that this preliminary meeting was held in a private house. The *Liverpool Courier* (20 September 1837) stated that the meeting took place at the Royal Institution, but this seems to have been an error.

[3] *The Athenæum* of 7 October 1837 reported that 'originating out of, though in no way connected with the British Association . . . an Educational meeting was held . . . at the Mechanics' Institute, Mr Wyse, M.P., in the chair, and Dr Jerrard acting as Secretary'. Among the papers read was one by Wyse on the Lyccum system in the United States.

Porter then wrote a letter to the *Liverpool Courier*, with his name to it, in which he gave this account: neither was his letter noticed in any of the opposition papers.[1]

As M'Neile said, no reference was made in the Liberal newspapers to the discussions of which he spoke; but the Conservative *Liverpool Courier* proclaimed that M'Neile was entitled to the lasting gratitude of the enlightened Protestant community of Liverpool, since he had 'crushed a project in the egg which might have grown into a viper of very dangerous dimensions'—a project which, had it succeeded, would have enabled Ministers of the government to stand 'upon higher ground in their endeavours to palm upon the people of England' a national system of education.[2]

2

When Thomas Wyse and James Simpson set out upon their famous 'education tour' of 1837, they did so immediately after the events here recorded, so that it was with the protests of the Rev. Hugh M'Neile (and of his supporters in the Liverpool Press) ringing in their ears that they left Liverpool to begin their campaign at Salford. If one studies the detailed reports of the proceedings at the various meetings addressed by Wyse and Simpson, once can now see that over the whole tour hung the shadow cast by the controversy over the Liverpool Corporation Schools. At the meeting held at Salford on 23 September 1837 references to those schools were in a very real sense conspicuous by their absence. Wyse sought examples from far and near to illustrate his contention that it was possible to have children of different denominations taught within some comprehensive system of education—but he carefully avoided all mention of the Liverpool schools. He suggested that the 'religious difficulty' could be surmounted if in areas in which the greater part of the population was of one religion that form of religious instruction were given in the schools 'which was most agreeable to the general wish',[3] whilst in places 'where two denominations existed in any numbers' there could be 'a school for each, or, if they were desirous to join in the same school, as in Ireland—why should they not meet together in school, and receive religious instruction apart, when their intellectual instruction was over?' Here, if anywhere, a reference to the

---

[1] *The Rev. Hugh M'Neile On The Irish System of Education* . . . , pp. 17–19.

[2] 20 September 1837. The Education Section of the British Association was not founded until 1901.

[3] This account of parts of the proceedings at the Salford meeting is taken from the *Manchester Guardian*, 27 September 1837.

Corporation Schools might have been expected, but (so far as one can gather from the newspaper reports) none was forthcoming. Nor did James Simpson or Richard Cobden, who also spoke, mention the schools.

One resolution passed at the meeting declared that it was the duty of the government to provide for the mental improvement and moral training of all the population subject to its control; another, which was seconded by Cobden, stated that the meeting regretted the failure of 'rich corporations, lay and clerical' to make good use of 'those ample means for educating the people' which they possessed; the resolution went on to claim that the cause of this failure on the part of the corporations referred to was to be found 'in the exclusive spirit which has distinguished their administration, and in the misapplication of the funds placed at their disposal'. Finally the fervent hope was expressed that 'in the event of the government resolving to adopt the principle and practice of a national system of education', such a system might be 'based on liberal principles, and afford to every subject of the state a medium for obtaining sound and useful knowledge, untinged by sectarian prejudices'. It was agreed that petitions based upon the resolutions passed at the meeting should be submitted to Parliament: in view of the interest later taken in the Liverpool Corporation Schools by Edward Stanley, Bishop of Norwich, it is of some interest that to him was entrusted the task of presenting one of the petitions to the House of Lords.

Wyse and Simpson then proceeded to Cheltenham (possibly at the suggestion of Samuel Wilderspin who resided in the town) and there addressed a meeting held on 18 October 1837 to advocate the establishment of a national system of education. The speeches of Wyse and Simpson were very much on the same lines as those which they had made at Salford, but Wilderspin, who also spoke, lacked the good sense and discretion of his companions; although he later tried to make it clear that it was the intention of those who had arranged the meeting 'to propose no system at all' but merely to call upon the government 'to appoint a board, to examine the merits of the various systems and to choose the best',[1] he made the mistake which Wyse and Simpson had very carefully avoided: he supported his arguments with laudatory references to the Liverpool Corporation Schools. The report of his speech published in the *Cheltenham Chronicle* of 26 October 1837 seems to be a very garbled one, although it must be said that he was content

---

[1] S. Wilderspin, *A Reply to the Various Speeches Delivered at a Meeting Held at the Assembly Rooms Cheltenham on Friday October 27th on the Subject of National Education*, p. 7.

to reprint it later, without comment, in a pamphlet. It is at least clear from the report that he spoke in favour of the system adopted in the Corporation Schools and expressed some contempt for those in Liverpool who opposed that system. The result, as might have been expected, was that attention was to a great extent diverted from the important general principles under discussion and concentrated upon the heated disputes which at once broke out concerning the system in force in the Liverpool Corporation Schools—and this at a time when even the most determined supporters of the policy adopted in those schools were more conscious of the hostility which it had aroused than confident of its ultimate success. But before describing the storm which burst about Wilderspin's head in Cheltenham, it will be convenient to say something of events in Manchester, the next stopping-place in the 'tour' of Simpson and Wyse.

3

It is, of course, unnecessary to give here a detailed account of the proceedings at the great meeting held in Manchester on 26 October 1837: all that is intended is to show that the experiment taking place in the Liverpool Corporation Schools and the controversy to which it had given rise were never far from the minds of those who took part in the important discussions on education which were carried on in Manchester at the time. In the *Manchester Guardian* of 14 October 1837 there appeared an advertisement which announced that the 'Friends of National Education' in the locality had arranged to hold a public meeting, to be addressed by Thomas Wyse, Samuel Wilderspin and others, at the Theatre Royal, Manchester, on 26 October. The meeting had been arranged a few days after the Salford meeting, and those who publicly promised support included thirty-eight members of the Established Church, thirty-eight Unitarians, twenty-three Independents, fifteen Methodists, eleven Quakers, nine Baptists and a small number of members of other Churches, including two Roman Catholics.[1]

It was obviously important to avoid as far as possible topics likely to give rise to controversy among supporters of so many different beliefs, and the handbills[2] calling the meeting carefully stated that it was not the purpose of the organizers to move resolutions or approve petitions; the meeting would be held only with the philanthropic object of 'offering a demonstration in favour of some comprehensive

[1] According to figures furnished in a letter written by Richard Cobden to the *Manchester Guardian*, 25 October 1837.
[2] *Ibid.*

system of education', and there was no intention of propounding 'the details of any particular plan'. In the advertisement of 14 October the committee went out of their way to make it clear 'in explanation of their object and plan' that whilst they desired 'to awaken the public mind to a knowledge of the abandoned condition of the younger portions of this great and rapidly augmenting population, and also to arouse the legislature to a commensurate effort for remedying the evil', they did not seek at the proposed meeting 'to commit the judgments of those who attend upon the details of any particular system of education for the nation at large'. This of course meant that the meeting would be very different from that which had been held in Salford, at which resolutions and petitions had certainly been adopted, and Wyse had even ventured to say a few tentative words in favour of the 'Irish System'. It was made abundantly clear that at the Manchester meeting there would be no advocacy of the system which was on trial in Liverpool: every effort was made to show that there was to be, so to speak, 'no connection with the establishment next door'.

But it was scarcely to be expected that the declarations of the committee would lull the suspicions of those well acquainted with, and strongly opposed to, the opinions so frequently expressed by Thomas Wyse and James Simpson, who were to be among the principal speakers at the meeting. The Rev. Hugh Stowell,[1] who may be described as having been in many respects the 'opposite number' in Manchester of the Rev. Hugh M'Neile[2] in Liverpool, and who was, like M'Neile, a very active member of the militant Protestant Association, felt that he, at any rate, was not to be taken in. He determined to get in his blow before the Theatre Royal meeting took place, and in a pamphlet addressed to the inhabitants of Manchester 'on the proposed system of national education' he confidently maintained that those who were organizing the meeting had in view a very clear-cut plan of action and that 'the intended plan' was to be essentially the same as that which had been 'inflicted upon Ireland, and more recently attempted in Liverpool'.[3] Richard Cobden replied to Stowell in a letter published in the *Manchester Guardian* on 25 October. He denied that the forthcoming meeting was being held in order to advocate the acceptance of some particular

[1] The Rev. Hugh Stowell (1799–1865) was incumbent of Christ Church, Salford; he became honorary canon of Chester Cathedral in 1845.

[2] The two men spoke from the same platform on a number of occasions to protest against concessions to Roman Catholics: e.g. at Manchester in September 1838 (*Manchester Guardian*, 29 September 1838) and at Lancaster in April 1840 (*Liverpool Standard*, 21 April 1840).

[3] Quoted by Cobden in his letter to the *Manchester Guardian* of 25 October 1837. (It would appear that no copy of Stowell's pamphlet is now in existence.)

plan of education, but it is interesting to find that in the course of his letter Cobden not only revealed that he had visited the Liverpool Corporation Schools but showed that he was prepared to defend and even to praise the system which had been adopted in them. These are his words:

> Your attack upon the Liverpool Corporation Schools, for excluding the Bible from their classes, leads me to infer that you have not visited those excellent establishments; in one of which I spent an hour very lately, and there found a clergyman of the Church of England in the centre of a circle of 20 boys, each holding a perfect copy of the scriptures in his hand, from which they were reading.

When the great meeting of 26 October took place, one of the speakers, G. M. Wood, referred to Stowell's allegations concerning the 'system of national education' said to be favoured by those who had organized the meeting:

> What system of national education had been proposed to them? He knew of none; and most assuredly with regard to the object of this assembly no system of education was to be offered to their consideration. They were asked whether they should be willing to permit the mutilation of the Scriptures. He trusted that it was not necessary, in order to procure the blessing of education for their fellow-countrymen, that any mutilation of the sacred volume should take place.[1]

Stowell at once replied with *A Second Letter to the Inhabitants of Manchester on the Proposed System of National Education, Containing Strictures on Mr. Cobden's Letter and on the Recent Meeting in the Theatre Royal*, Manchester [? 1837]; in the course of his letter he said:

> ... it is argued, that I had no grounds for inferring that any such system as the Irish one, or indeed that any system at all was contemplated by the requisitionists. They disavow all plan, Mr Cobden assures us. ... Is there not reason to conclude that there *had* been a plan kept prudently in the background, and that the Manchester muster, like its fraternity in Sheffield,[2] Salford and Cheltenham, would have been crowned with resolutions and petitions, but that the tide of popular feeling set in so strongly against the idea of an unscriptural education that the whole projected machinery was swamped, and a set of *toasts* appeared instead?[3]

Stowell remained on guard against any attempt to introduce into Manchester a system of education similar to that which had been

---

[1] *Manchester Guardian*, 28 October 1837.
[2] An allusion to a stormy meeting on the subject of national education which had recently been held in Sheffield.
[3] Pp. 5–6.

adopted in Liverpool: at a meeting held in Manchester a year later to call for the extension of scriptural education in Ireland he said:

We are probably about to have a corporation for Manchester; I neither meddle with it, nor care about it: but I fear that if we get one at all akin to that of Liverpool, we shall be assessed and amerced for a system of education akin to that of the Liverpool Corporation; and I do trust, if any such attempt should be made, that Manchester will not be second to Liverpool; but will act with the same noble, unanimous feeling, and that all classes will conspire together to protect, to foster, to shelter, and to shield Scriptural education, with the Bible, the whole Bible, and nothing but the Bible, the foundation of the protestant faith.[1]

Thus men like Wyse, Simpson and Cobden were more than once given notice that any attempt to repeat in Manchester the experiment which was in progress in Liverpool would at once give rise to controversy at least as bitter as that which had been aroused in the neighbouring town. It was therefore not surprising that when, a few weeks after the great meeting in the Theatre Royal, 'the Manchester Society for Promoting National Education' was formed 'to obtain from Parliament a legislative provision for securing to all classes of the community an improved and permanent system of education', no mention was made of the 'Irish System' of education with its provision for the separate religious instruction of children of all denominations, use of agreed extracts from the Bible, and so on; instead, 'the practice of the British and Foreign School Society of prescribing Bible classes for every school and placing the entire volume of Holy Scripture, without note or comment, in the hands of every child (excepting from this rule only Catholics and Jews)' was declared, perhaps rather pointedly, to be 'the best system hitherto devised for meeting the difficulties arising from the varieties of religious sects in this country'.[2]

4

Samuel Wilderspin seems not to have mentioned the Liverpool Corporation Schools when he addressed the Manchester meeting of 26 October 1837; some notion of what would probably have happened if he had done so can be gathered from a consideration of the extremely lively disputes which broke out as a consequence of his references to the schools in the course of his speech at Cheltenham eight days earlier. On 27 October a meeting was held in the Assembly Rooms,

---

[1] *Manchester Guardian*, 10 November 1838.
[2] Quoted in Maltby, *op. cit.*, p. 52. In spite of its caution in 'refraining from suggesting any particular plan' in the petition which it addressed to the government at this time, the Society, according to Maltby, probably went out of existence about 1842.

Cheltenham, at which a number of the clergy of the town, led by the Vicar, the Rev. Francis Close,[1] sought to reply to the speeches advocating the establishment of a national system of education which had been delivered by Wyse, Simpson and Wilderspin at the meeting of 18 October. Wilderspin's enthusiastic praise of the system in force in the Corporation Schools had immediately aroused the suspicions of some of the Cheltenham clergy, and during most of the discussions which subsequently took place it was taken for granted by them that Wyse and his companions had come to Cheltenham to advocate the adoption on a national scale of the policy favoured by the Liverpool Town Council. At the protest meeting of 27 October the Rev. F. Close claimed that a system had been recommended to Cheltenham which was 'unscriptural, tyrannical, oppressive and Utopian.' He said:

The fact is this, the Town Council of Liverpool have perverted the Sums entrusted to them for the Education of the Children of the Poor, to introduce the Irish system of Education into the Corporation Schools—the introduction of it in all its parts, with all its deformities; they have caused the Children of the Town and Port of Liverpool, three-fourths of whose Inhabitants are Protestants—they have endeavoured to compel them to read in these Schools the Bible mutilated and unfaithfully translated, with Popish notes and references!![2]

The Rev. J. Browne exhorted his hearers to 'petition against the Papists, Socinians, and Infidels, who would mutilate the Bible, and withhold some portions of it from our Infant and National Schools', and he invited them to take as their watchword 'The Bible! the whole Bible!! and nothing but the Bible!!!' The Rev. Charles G. Davies spoke of the system in force in the Liverpool Corporation Schools as one which excluded from the schools 'as a book to be used in the schools, the Bible as a whole,' and which substituted for it 'garbled extracts, and extracts, let it be remembered, so altered and perverted, as, if not positively to support, at least not to be repugnant to, popish errors and superstitions'.

Wilderspin replied to these assertions in a striking and somewhat unusual way: he had placards printed and posted about the town in which he accused some of the leading clergymen of the town of making false statements. The placards[3] began as follows:

[1] Close (1797–1882) was a popular and influential evangelical preacher, well known outside Cheltenham. Palmerston nominated him Dean of Carlisle in 1856. See *D.N.B.*

[2] This account of some of the speeches made at the meeting is based on reports in the *Cheltenham Chronicle* of 2 November 1837 and on the now very rare pamphlet *A Reply to the Various Speeches Delivered at a Meeting Held at the Assembly Rooms Cheltenham . . . on the Subject of National Education*, by Samuel Wilderspin.

[3] S. Wilderspin, *A Reply to the Various Speeches . . .*, pp. 40–1.

To The Lovers of Bible Truth

Inhabitants of Cheltenham,

Having taken part at the great Meeting on the subject of *National Education*, held at Manchester last week, I did not see a Report of the Meeting at the Assembly Rooms, Cheltenham, until my return to Liverpool. Astonished at the extraordinary *mis-statements* made by the Reverend Gentlemen on that occasion, I felt it to be my imperative duty to take immediate steps to counteract the impression, which such *false statements* were calculated to produce on the minds of those present, respecting the Liverpool Corporation Schools; for I assert that every Protestant Child in those schools who can read, has an unmutilated Copy of the Authorized Version of the Bible for his or her use.

This announcement of Wilderspin's was followed, on each placard, by a copy of what he called 'a memorial', signed by the teachers of the Liverpool Corporation North and South Schools, in which the following declaration was made:

We, the teachers of the North and South Corporation Schools, whose names are hereunto subscribed, having heard that the Rev. F. Close and the Rev. C. Davies have asserted, at a Public Meeting held in Cheltenham, that the authorized version of the Bible was excluded from the Liverpool Corporation Schools; do assert that this is not the fact, but that it is read every day; and such false statements are calculated to impede the cause of truth, and greatly injure those who profess to be such friends to the Established Church.[1]

This statement of the Liverpool teachers was also published as an advertisement in a Cheltenham newspaper[2] under the heading 'CLERICAL CALUMNY REFUTED', and with the explanation that it was a direct contradiction of 'the falsehoods uttered at the Meeting for the professed purpose of promoting SCRIPTURAL EDUCATION'.

The Rev. F. Close replied by denying that he had made 'false statements' and explained that he had not spoken of the 'exclusion of the Bible from the Liverpool Corporation Schools', but *had* spoken of 'the garbled extracts ... substituted for the Bible during school hours';[3] nor had he understood his fellow-speakers to say 'that the Bible was excluded', but only that it was 'excluded *as a lesson book* and *during school hours*'. By this time little more was needed than the presence in the town of the Rev. Hugh M'Neile to give to an observer the illusion

---

[1] Wilderspin added a note: 'The original Memorial, with the Signatures attached, may be seen at my Residence, 9 Portland Street.'

[2] *Cheltenham Free Press* ... , 4 November 1837.

[3] He was evidently unaware of the change which had been made ten months earlier in the wording of the school rules so that the period set aside for denominational religious instruction was described as 'the last hour' of the school day.

that he was living in the stormy atmosphere of Liverpool rather than in peaceful Cheltenham; and the Rev. Hugh M'Neile duly arrived! During the course of his speech of 27 October the Rev. F. Close had supported his criticisms of the system adopted in the Liverpool Corporation Schools by quoting from a pamphlet of M'Neile's to which reference has already been made: his *Letters on National Education: Addressed to the Town Council of Liverpool*. In a placard,[1] of which almost all trace seems to have been lost, Wilderspin described this pamphlet as being 'obscure' and a mere 'fourpenny affair'; presumably he indicated, not too gently, that his opponents were obtaining their information about the Liverpool Schools from an extremely untrustworthy source.

A further meeting was therefore held on 10 November 1837, 'principally to give the Rev. H. M'Neile, of Liverpool, an opportunity to establish the truth of his charges against the System of Education adopted by the Corporation of Liverpool in their public schools'. It was explained that 'The truth of these charges had been warmly denied by several advocates of National Education . . . and handbills, by no means complimentary to the Reverend Gentleman's character for veracity, had recently been plentifully circulated'[2] in the town. M'Neile's speech was in his usual vein, being remarkable only because he contrived to maintain both that, by his letters[3] to the Liverpool Town Council, he had obliged the Liverpool Education Committee to permit the study of the Authorized Version of the Bible during school hours, and also that the Bible was in some sense excluded from the course of instruction provided in the Committee's schools:

Is England so fallen as to admit a National system of Education which leaves the whole revealed will of God out as one of the elements of instruction? If the answer is no, bestir yourselves, for your opponents are awake, they are stirring, they are gaining ground, they are deceiving the unwary, and they will deceive you into it, if you are silent.[4]

Wilderspin attempted to interrupt M'Neile's speech, and claimed the right to be heard, but M'Neile's reply was harsh:

. . . if any clergyman of the Church to which I belong, feels it his duty to defend this system, I am ready to meet him . . . ; but I will not consent to

[1] The quotations from it here given are those furnished by Wilderspin himself in his *A Reply to the Various Speeches* . . . , pp. 43, 44.

[2] *The Rev. Hugh M'Neile on the Irish System of Education, More Particularly as Regards the System Now in Operation at Liverpool: Being a Speech Delivered by Him at the Assembly Rooms, Cheltenham, November 10th, 1837*, p. 5.

[3] 'In November, these obscure letters were published, and in December a change was made in one of the rules' (*ibid.*, p. 11).

[4] *Ibid.*, p. 20.

be called in question by any obscure individual—neither will I consent, though it is said the schoolmaster is abroad, that a clergyman of the Church of England should stand to compete with a schoolmaster.[1]

In the pamphlet which Wilderspin thereupon published in order to reply to his clerical opponent, he did not mince his words. After remarking that 'When anything is proposed for the benefit of the human race, the alarm bell is sure to be sounded by the clergy',[2] Wilderspin went on to claim that, having spent nine months in the Liverpool Corporation Schools, he was in a position to speak of them with more authority than could 'one of the most violent political agitators in Liverpool'. He described M'Neile also as 'a fanatic', an 'arch-agitator', a 'master of sophistry', and a 'political preacher', who had not attempted to controvert the evidence adduced in Wilderspin's placards or dared to hear the truth—'and yet', Wilderspin continued, 'this incumbrance of St Jude's calls himself a *Clergyman*, and would have the world believe that he is a Christian and a Gentleman!' He declared that the Liverpool Corporation Schools were 'conducted in the best and most efficient manner' of any he had yet seen in the United Kingdom, and added:

I believe they are the only schools in this kingdom for poor children in which are to be found a system of religious—moral—intellectual—and physical education united; and in which, the children of every *sect* may be found learning in harmony—playing in harmony—and above all living in Heavenly love and charity amongst each other. Oh! how I do lament, that Christian men should throw an apple of discord amongst them, and that many of the Clergy should shew the first example.

The full flavour of the controversy raging in Liverpool was brought to Cheltenham by Wilderspin's quotations from the comments made by William Rathbone and Dr Shepherd on the Rev. A. Campbell's speech at Newton, and by his citing in support of his statements letters written by Liverpool clergymen who had inspected the work of the Corporation Schools. Wilderspin ended with a warning and a prophecy:

The public voice declares that the mind of the rising generation shall not any longer be neglected—the signs of the times demand of the Government a speedy attention to this great matter, unanswerable proof is given that our educational system is sadly defective. All practical men lament the fact, and have determined that this national stain on our character shall exist no longer. We bid defiance to the ignorant, narrow-minded bigots of the age, and tell

---

[1] *Ibid.*, p. 15; *Cheltenham Free Press*, 11 November 1837.
[2] *A Reply to the Various Speeches . . .*, p. 5.

them plainly that they cannot and they shall not prevent it. The vituperation of such men may retard it for a time, but in the end they will be vanquished.

It may be added that, as a result of Wilderspin's spirited and by no means ineffective defence of the system adopted in the Liverpool Corporation Schools, the Cheltenham Liberals began to take a considerable interest in the schools; numbers of the letters published in the Liverpool newspapers in support of the Education Committee's policy were reprinted without delay in the *Cheltenham Free Press*;[1] the same journal copied from the *Liverpool Telegraph* a very full account of the 'Public Examination of the Children Belonging to the Corporation Schools',[2] and later devoted four and a half columns to a report[3] of the proceedings in the Liverpool Town Council when a new Education Committee was elected in November 1837. In the following year the Rev. F. Close made an outspoken attack on the schools in his *National Education and Lord Brougham's Bill Considered: in a Series of Nine Letters* . . ., Cheltenham, 1838; and on 23 February 1839 the *Cheltenham Free Press* published a letter from William Rathbone intended to settle a dispute between those in the town who opposed and those who supported the policy adopted in the Corporation Schools. Moreover, the controversy in Cheltenham did not pass without notice outside the town: the *Manchester Guardian*[4] and the (London) *Examiner*[5] quoted approvingly from one of Wilderspin's placards, and naturally the Liverpool Liberals followed the course of the dispute in Cheltenham with considerable interest.[6]

As what one might now call a 'publicity agent', Samuel Wilderspin had certainly made his mark. But since, as the immediate result of his rushing in where Wyse and Simpson had feared to tread, 13,050 signatures were attached to petitions from Cheltenham protesting against 'the introduction into this country of any system of education similar to that . . . in operation in Ireland' (as against 348 in favour of proposals put forward by Wyse and Simpson),[7] it is scarcely surprising that Wilderspin's example was not at once followed by his more discreet companions.

5

Meanwhile the members of the Liverpool Education Committee were beginning to realize that unless vigorous efforts were made to

---

[1] See, for example, *Cheltenham Free Press*, 4 November 1837.
[2] *Ibid.*, 11 November 1837.   [3] *Ibid.*, 18 November 1837.
[4] 18 November 1837.   [5] 12 November 1837.
[6] See, for example, *Liverpool Telegraph*, 9 December 1837.
[7] Rev. F. Close, *op. cit.*

counter the attacks of their critics, the important experiment being conducted in the Corporation Schools could not be carried on much longer. The municipal elections were once more drawing near, and the Conservatives had been convinced by their success in the parliamentary election of July 1837 that they had only to continue their campaign against the system in force in the schools to win a resounding victory in the local elections. Obviously such a Conservative victory would have persuaded most of the Liberals, in spite of their comfortable majority in the Council, that the policy hitherto pursued in the schools would have to be abandoned; even such enthusiastic supporters of that policy as William Rathbone and Thomas Blackburn would have had to admit defeat, since it would have been scarcely reasonable to persist in advocating measures which could only have the effect of handing over to the Conservatives the control of the Council—and of the Corporation Schools.

Up to this time the Liberals had shown little skill in their handling of 'public relations'; the violence of the opposition which their policy in the schools had aroused, and some of the methods used to give expression to that opposition, had clearly astounded them; and although, as we have seen, they from time to time denied the truth of the inaccurate statements frequently made by their opponents, they were often so conscious of the goodness of their own intentions and the purity of their motives that they found it difficult to realize that the allegations of some of their critics could be sincerely believed even by those who made them. Almost all of the Liberal councillors, it must be remembered, were quite unaccustomed to the rough-and-tumble of political life. Moreover, it was admittedly difficult for them to deal with those of their adversaries who were content to repeat on all occasions simple slogans embodying statements which had been shown over and over again to be false; it was not easy to reply effectively to processionists carrying wooden 'Bibles' on poles. But even so, much more might have been done during the first year of the experiment to make known what went on in the schools, especially among those who could not afford to buy newspapers.

One striking instance of the Education Committee's failure to ensure that its actions received adequate publicity had occurred when the wording of the rule relating to the giving of denominational instruction had been altered in December 1836. Having decided to correct the original tactical error, so eagerly seized upon by their critics, of describing the hour devoted to such instruction as the hour after the school had closed, and to describe it instead as the last hour of the school day, the Committee did little or nothing to make known the important change in the wording of the rule, apart from hanging up the amended regulations in the schools; conscious that the alterations, as Rathbone put it, were 'only verbal, to meet a quibble on that subject',[1] and that no real change of policy was involved, the Committee failed for months to reap whatever advantage was to be gained from the adoption of the new wording, which, after all, made it more difficult for honest critics who knew little of the schools to believe that 'the Bible was excluded' from them.

That such men as M'Neile and Campbell were aware of the altered wording is not, of course, to be doubted, since they were scarcely likely to ignore the newspaper reports of the Council's discussions on matters relating to the schools; and indeed, as we have seen, M'Neile claimed that the rule in question had been changed because of remarks he had made in his *Letters on National Education*. Yet months after the regulation had been re-worded even supporters of the Education Committee's policy were in a state of confusion about the change,[2] and it was possible for the Conservative *Liverpool Courier*[3] to complain that the clergy of the Established Church had received no official notification of the alteration—even though that alteration had been made to meet the objections of the clergy and with the purpose of gaining their co-operation, or at least of depriving them of an excuse for withholding it.

But by August 1837 the Education Committee seems to have learned its lesson; much more vigorous efforts were made by it to expound and justify its policy and to cause the results of that policy to be made as widely known as possible. It did so, moreover, with an air of confidence, fortified with the knowledge, derived from the newly-published poll book, that the Liberal defeat in the recent parliamentary election had been caused chiefly by the opposition of the freemen; a majority of the all-important household voters had continued faithful to the Liberals[4] and might presumably be persuaded to remain so. The first step in the campaign to make the schools better known was the holding of a public examination of the pupils towards the end of August 1837,

---

[1] Quoted from a letter of Rathbone's in a report of 'The Church of England School Society' contained in a single printed sheet obviously published in Liverpool in 1837.

[2] Thus Dr Shepherd believed that the new rule had been made almost immediately after the Education Committee had taken over control of the schools (*Liverpool Journal*, 21 October 1837); whilst another supporter of the Committee wrote to the *Liverpool Mercury* (13 October 1837) advocating the alteration which had in fact been made ten months before.

[3] 25 October 1837.

[4] According to figures published in the *Liverpool Mercury* of 18 August 1837, 6,100 householders had voted Liberal and 5,811 Conservative, whereas 1,487 freemen had voted Liberal and 3,627 Conservative. It will be remembered that only a small proportion of the freemen were qualified to vote in municipal elections.

to mark the end of Wilderspin's engagement as supervisor. Two days were allotted for the examination of each school, and considerable interest seems to have been aroused, especially, of course, by the arrangements made for the giving of religious instruction. On the last day of the examinations, according to *The Albion* (admittedly a biased source), 'about two hundred strangers were present, some from a considerable distance';[1] but of more immediate importance was the fact that a number of Liverpool clergymen attended, several of whom took an active part in the examination. Those present included the Rev. J. Aspinall and the Rev. J. Stokes, who taught the Church of England children in the schools; the Rev. J. Kelly and the Rev. J. Carruthers (Independents); and the Rev. S. Spence of the Secession Church of Scotland.[2] The Education Committee 'requested any gentleman present either to ask the children questions, or to name any which they wished to be put to them, and several gentlemen availed themselves of the opportunity'.[3]

The Committee had every reason to be pleased with the result of its decision to hold public examinations. On one occasion 'so pleased were the audience with the examination, and more especially the religious part of it, that Mr Ledger . . . a member of the Rev. F. Ould's congregation and one of his school committee, moved that the thanks of the audience should be given to the Corporation committee for the great pains they had taken in managing the schools. The motion was seconded and carried unanimously.' This indeed was a triumph, since the Rev. Fielding Ould referred to, the Minister of Christ Church, Liverpool, was second only to the Rev. Hugh M'Neile (a fellow-countryman) in the bitterness of his opposition to the Education Committee's policy—although, since he apparently had little of M'Neile's intelligence and debating skill, his hostility was much less effective.

Apart from a correspondent in the Conservative *Liverpool Standard* who complained that the children had not been sufficiently examined 'upon Doctrinal points', and that their answers to questions on such points had been unsatisfactory, almost all who witnessed the religious examinations of the children seem to have been very deeply impressed. Several of the Dissenting clergymen present, who were visiting the schools for the first time, wrote to the Education Committee and

---

[1] 28 August 1837.

[2] Presumably the Roman Catholic children were also examined in religious knowledge by their own clergy, but the newspaper reporters concerned themselves solely with the examination of the Protestant children.

[3] *Liverpool Mercury*, 25 August 1837.

expressed their satisfaction; the letters were gratefully received[1] and were promptly published in some of the Liberal newspapers. The Rev. S. Spence expressed the wish that 'the Bible were just as faithfully taught and as completely understood in every school in Liverpool'; the Rev. J. Carruthers said: 'The Amount and accuracy of the Biblical knowledge possessed by the Children is astonishing,—in this respect they will bear comparison with the Children of any Sabbath School with which I am acquainted.'

Soon after the examinations had been held, the Rev. Dr Buck, a Church of England clergyman, who had recently been appointed 'Minister-in-charge of the district of St Matthew's Key-Street', within which district the North Corporation School was situated, visited that school 'to enquire minutely into its plans and to examine the different classes, both in their secular studies and Religious reading' so that he 'might be enabled without partiality or prejudice, to make known to the Inhabitants of the District' his opinion 'as to the propriety of their encouraging or discouraging this School'. As a result of his visit, he felt impelled to write to the Education Committee offering his services as a teacher of religion in the schools and promising to make 'every Christian exertion . . . to induce the Poor of the extensive Population of St Matthew's District to send their Children, where an excellent and Scriptural Education is freely provided for them'. William Rathbone, in his letter of thanks, expressed his satisfaction that another clergyman of the Church of England had had the moral courage, after having examined the system adopted in the schools, to give the Committee and the public 'the benefit of his countenance and assistance'.[2]

As part of the same policy of making known what went on in the schools, distinguished visitors present in Liverpool for the meeting of the British Association were invited to inspect the schools; the *Liverpool Mercury* of 22 September 1837 was able to report that the Countess of Burlington (whose husband was President of the Association) had 'visited the South Corporation schools, and witnessed the course of education there practised in the girls' school. She particularly witnessed the valuable instruction bestowed upon the pupils in interpretation of their Bible reading by the Rev. Mr Aspinall, and expressed herself highly gratified with what she had observed, of which she took copious notes'. According to the same report 'upwards of thirty gentlemen eminent in science and members of the Association also visited the schools and expressed themselves in warm terms of approbation as to the system of instruction there adopted'. It may have been on this

---

[1] *Proceedings of Education Committee*, Vol. I, pp. 46 ff., 57-9.
[2] *Proceedings of Education Committee*, Vol. I, p. 60.

occasion that Leonard Horner made the visit to the schools[1] to which William Rathbone alluded some time later.[2]

Those closely connected with the schools and able to speak with first-hand knowledge of their day-to-day working were evidently encouraged to reply to false statements concerning the schools. Thus when Lord Sandon was reported in the Conservative newspapers[3] as having said that there was hardly a Protestant child left in the Corporation Schools, the Rev. J. Aspinall at once published the following terse statement, to prove to him that he had 'been grossly imposed upon':

There are 191 infants in the South Corporation Schools, of whom 100 are Protestants; 219 girls of a more advanced age, of whom 103 are Protestants; and 255 boys, of whom 130 are Protestants; total 665, of whom 333 are Protestants.

Aspinall added:

Your Lordship, then, will see the necessity of being more careful in future as to the statements which you may make upon this subject.[4]

We have noted that all the teachers in the Corporation Schools had signed the 'memorial' which Samuel Wilderspin had made public as part of a placard in Cheltenham; a little earlier the masters of the two schools had written to Liverpool newspapers[5] to defend the system in force in their schools against the attacks of the Rev. Fielding Ould. One of the masters, Robert J. Nelson of the North School, gave up-to-date figures showing the number of children 'exclusive of Infants' in his school to be as follows (October 1837):

	Catholics	Protestants	Total
Boys	299	79	378
Girls	242	50	292
	541	129	670

[1] Horner was certainly in Liverpool at this time; he was present at the opening of the rebuilt Mechanics' Institution on 15 September (*Liverpool Mercury*, 22 September 1837). It would appear, however, that Horner was impressed less by the success claimed for the Corporation Schools than by the opposition which they had aroused, since when he added some 'Preliminary Observations' to his translation of Cousin's account of the *State of Education in Holland, as Regards the Working Classes*, Horner remarked that it would not be possible to introduce the 'Irish System' as 'any part of a legislative measure for Great Britain'; and he went on: 'The great objection urged against that system is the exclusion of what is termed "the entire Bible"; or as it is sometimes expressed, "the mutilation of the Scriptures". How far that last term is fair, or consistent with Christian charity, we shall not stop to enquire. But the objection is urged not only by members of the Established Church, but by persons among the Protestant Dissenters of every denomination' (p. xxxvi).

[2] In a letter to C. Otway dated 17 May 1838.

[3] See *Conservative Triumph or The Three Glorious Days!* . . . , p. 6.

[4] *Liverpool Mercury*, 20 October 1837.

[5] *The Albion*, 16 October 1837.

He was also able to announce that there were now *two* Church of England clergymen giving denominational religious instruction at the North School, the Rev. Dr Buck, in accordance with his promise to Rathbone, having recently begun to assist the Rev. Mr Stokes.

6

In the face of such unimpeachable testimony, and especially of the evidence of well-respected clergymen, it was scarcely possible for anyone interested in the Corporation Schools to remain ignorant or doubtful about the arrangements made in them for the provision of denominational religious instruction; objections could no longer be based on honest misconceptions, on the misleading wording of rules or on anything other than the facts so authoritatively made known. It seemed impossible that anyone could now seriously maintain that 'the Bible was excluded from the schools' either completely or 'during school hours'; nor could it now be said that the schools were 'exclusively Roman Catholic institutions'. It remained to be seen what the reply of the more responsible Church of England clergy in the town would be to the clear challenge of the Liverpool Education Committee.

The Committee of the Church of England Schools Society, which spoke for almost all of the Church of England clergy in the town, and the chairman of which was the Rev. A. Campbell, first demanded from William Rathbone, as chairman of the Education Committee, official information about the change of rule relating to the hour during which denominational religious instruction was given in the schools; Rathbone sent a copy of the school regulations together with an assurance that the change of rule had in fact involved no change in practice, which had been the same 'from the time the schools passed into the hands of the Town Council'.[1] The Church of England committee nevertheless decided that 'its conduct . . . in protesting against those Schools should remain unchanged', and gave its reasons. It first objected to the fact that the schools were carried on without prayer; it could not accept the singing of a hymn each day as 'an adequate substitute for so plain and imperative a Christian duty as Prayer'. The committee complained also that the 'Irish extracts' from the Bible were used by all the children; some of the notes given in the 'extracts' were 'unscriptural', and in any case the provision of notes involved the

---

[1] Rathbone's reply was published with the report of the Committee of the Church of England School Society (quotations from which are here given) which appeared as a single printed sheet with the heading 'The Corporation Schools'.

'sacrifice of a great Protestant principle',[1] and the sanctioning of 'an essentially Roman Catholic practice'. The third reason given by the committee for continuing to oppose the system in force in the schools was simply that it could not conscientiously 'sanction, by co-operation' any policy which led to the inculcation of 'the peculiar doctrines of the Romish Church'. It is interesting to note that once again the suggestion was made to the Council that *separate* schools might be provided from its revenues for the children of different faiths:

The Committee are aware of the argument used in defence of the Council, that being Trustees of a Fund to be managed for the benefit of all, they are bound to respect equally the religious peculiarities and conscientious scruples of all. But whatever ground this argument may afford for the establishment and support of separate schools, by the Council, or for not interfering with School Education at all, it affords none for their attempt to compel us to join a system of which we disapprove. . . . On the contrary, by the whole force of this *their* own argument, we claim to have *our* own conscientious scruples respected.

Lastly the committee pointed out that, according to its intepretation of the word, the Bible was still 'excluded' from the Corporation Schools. It now justified this claim in the following way: the teachers in the schools, it claimed, were not permitted to instruct the children from the Authorized Version of the Bible—such instruction, according to the school rules, was to be given 'under the Ministers of the respective Churches'. All that the Town Council did, the committee suggested, was to lend their rooms for an hour every afternoon whilst the children were assembled 'to any irresponsible catechists, whether clergymen or sent by clergymen', who might 'choose to volunteer their services'. The committee's statement went on:

This Committee are aware that PERMISSION is given to any Protestant Clergyman, who has no scruples about joining himself to the system; and who, in other respects, finds it convenient to go and teach the Protestant children, during the last hour of each day. They are aware also, that on the ground of this PERMISSION to persons in no way connected with the general Superintendence of the Schools, it is alleged, with confidence, that the Bible is not excluded.

But they cannot consider such *permission* (*and it can be nothing more than mere permission*) as an adequate substitute for Scriptural instruction in the Schools; and therefore they are compelled, as the result of careful and candid investigation and discrimination, to reiterate, and to call the attention of the town to the fact, that (so far as any authoritative and certain *provision* by the

[1] It should be noted that the Archbishop of Canterbury was of a different opinion; see p. 162 n.

Council for religious instruction in the Schools is concerned) the Bible is excluded.

Some notion of how exasperating the Rev. A. Campbell could be as an opponent, and why many came to mistrust him, may be gained if one considers that two months later he was indignantly protesting that the Church of England clergy had been 'shamefully slandered by party writers and speakers, and wrongfully accused of falsehood, as if they had said that the Bible was never read within the walls of the Corporation schools';[1] it really seems not to have occurred to him that both his supporters and his critics might easily misunderstand the meaning which he attached to his claim that the Bible was 'excluded' from those schools.

Very soon after the report of the Church of England School Society was published, the Rev. A. Campbell put forward another important claim on behalf of the Church of England clergy of the town: speaking at the opening of the second school to be erected for the accommodation of Church of England children withdrawn from the Corporation Schools, he maintained that the clergy of the Established Church had to 'assert their privileges' as the 'legal religious teachers of the Protestant poor'; if the clergy accepted the position of being 'mere catechists' and did not have 'some influence at least in the committees and the appointment of schoolmasters, and a due share also in the secular education of our own Protestant children', but had to leave those children in the hands of teachers in whose appointment they had 'no voice', and who were 'indifferent perhaps, perhaps decidedly hostile' to the Church and its doctrines, then this must eventually degrade and destroy the influence of the Church of England clergy with the labouring classes and 'break off that connexion which on every ground, religious and political, ought to subsist' between them.[2]

As the municipal elections of November 1837 drew near, all of these objections were repeated over and over again at ward meetings,[3] in newspaper articles and in sermons. Some critics went even further. Thus the *Liverpool Standard*[4] maintained that it was a dishonour to the Established Church that the clergy of that Church were not permitted

---

[1] *Address of the Rev. A. Campbell at the Opening of the South Church of England School, Cornwallis Street, December 5th, 1837*, Liverpool [n.d.], p. 2.

[2] *Ibid.*, p. 5.

[3] At a meeting of the Conservative electors of the Everton and Kirkdale Wards the report of the Committee of the Church of England School Society was read in full, and a resolution was passed unanimously 'that a memorial be submitted to the Council expressing concurrence in the protest' of the Committee (*Liverpool Standard*, 24 October 1837).

[4] 17 October 1837.

to enter the schools and 'examine the children in the Holy Scriptures' at any hour they pleased or might find convenient. The *Liverpool Courier*[1] felt that 'a Protestant clergyman' should be allowed not only to give religious instruction at any hour he pleased but also to instruct 'any portion of the children he may think proper' (including, of course, Roman Catholics) 'out of what Protestants have been taught to consider the Bible'; indeed, more and more was now heard of the claim orginally put forward by M'Neile that the Authorized Version was still excluded from the schools since the Roman Catholic children, who formed part of 'the schools', were not allowed to read it. M'Neile himself published a further three letters to the members of the Town Council a few days before the elections, in which he warned voters that 'the propagation of popery' was 'more disastrous . . . than the propagation of cholera or plague', and that to vote in parliamentary or municipal elections for 'supporters of this Popery propaganda' system would be to share the guilt of those supporters.[2] Petitions against the Education Committee's policy were addressed to the Council by the Conservative voters of Lime Street, St Anne's, and Rodney Street Wards; resolutions expressing disapproval of that policy were passed at almost all Conservative meetings.

The Liberals replied with vigour to the attacks made upon them; the Education Committee published as an advertisement in the newspapers a forceful reply to the Committee of the Church of England School Society, pointing out that it was simply not true that the teachers were forbidden to give doctrinal religious instruction:

. . . from the commencement, the masters and mistresses have been, and continue daily, teaching the Bible and conveying other Religious instruction to the Protestant children, during the period allotted for that purpose, and under the guidance of those Ministers of the Established Church whose conscientious scruples do not prevent their attendance.[3]

They took care to rub in once again the fact that the much-criticized 'Irish extracts' from the Bible had 'received the sanction of an eminent prelate of the Established Church' and had been 'confirmed by the Legislature under different Administrations'. And they made the interesting observation that 'the utmost harmony' prevailed in the schools among the children of the different denominations; the Committee was not 'aware of a single instance of dissension or disagreement having occurred' because of the children's 'respective modes of belief'. If

[1] 6 September 1837.
[2] *Liverpool Standard*, 27 October 1837.
[3] *Liverpool Mercury*, 20 October 1837.

Conservatives could send petitions concerning the Corporation Schools to the Council, so also could the Liberals: among the 'memorials' supporting the Education Committee's policy were those of the Liberals of Rodney Street Ward and of Exchange Ward, who had set up committees to report on the working of the schools. With respect to the petition from Exchange Ward it was explained that 'the gentlemen who presented this memorial were . . . all of them members of the Established Church, who spoke to facts, having personally examined these schools'.[1]

Both of the political parties in Liverpool seem to have made up their minds to fight the municipal elections of 1837 on the single issue of the policy to be followed in the Corporation Schools: the Liberals, in effect, sought from the electors a vote of confidence, and the Conservatives strained every nerve to ensure that no such encouraging vote should be given. Both sides knew that important consequences would almost certainly follow a victory for either party, consequences that would be felt far outside the range of local politics; and, although exaggerated claims and wild accusations were very much the order of the day, most of the electors must by this time have become fairly well informed about what, in fact, went on in the schools. And perhaps it would be true to say that the more responsible Conservatives and critics of the Education Committee were a little ashamed of some of the methods which certain of their followers had employed at the 'wooden-Bible' parliamentary election a few months earlier. At any rate, on this occasion, in spite of the intense bitterness of the electoral campaign and the great importance attached by both sides to the result of the elections, 'there was no music, no colours, no processions, no drunkenness, not a single breach of the peace. The householders went to record their votes in a peaceable orderly manner. . . . A stranger would hardly have been aware that anything extraordinary was going on.'[2]

[1] Report of Proceedings of Town Council Meeting held 30 October 1837 (*Liverpool Mercury*, 3 November 1837).
[2] *Liverpool Mercury*, 3 November 1837.

Chapter 7

'THE DAY IS WON'

I

IN the municipal elections of 1837 the Liberals were surprisingly successful; they received what they considered to be a most impressive assurance that the policy which they were pursuing in the Corporation Schools was winning increasing support among the electors. A year earlier, as we have seen, the Conservatives had obtained eight out of the seventeen seats available; on this occasion they headed the poll in only four of the sixteen wards. Five of the wards which had gone over to the Conservatives in 1836 now elected Liberals,[1] one of them being William Rathbone; since Thomas Blackburn was also re-elected, with a much-increased majority, the two men who had done most to initiate and to defend the policy followed in the schools, and who had openly declared that it was their desire to see that policy adopted on a national scale, could claim to have won important and significant victories.

Once again the returns considerably exaggerated the movement of opinion which had taken place: of the votes cast in the municipal elections which had first brought them to power in 1835 the Liberals had received nearly 59 per cent; in the following year, after the agitation concerning the Corporation Schools had begun, they had obtained nearly 51 per cent of the votes cast; and on this occasion[2] about 52 per cent. Moreover, all of the retiring councillors in 1837 were Liberals, so that the four Conservative victories meant that four additional Conservative members entered the Council. Nevertheless, it was a source of great encouragement to the Liberals that all of the strenuous exertions made by their lay and clerical opponents to bring about a decisive Conservative victory over 'the Schools Question' had been made in vain; instead of falling, the Liberal vote had increased.

The Liberals, naturally, were jubilant. *The Albion* wrote of their opponents:

[1] The Conservatives were successful in Exchange Ward, which had returned a Liberal in 1836; but since the Liberal had on that occasion been elected only by the casting vote of the Mayor, the Conservative victory in 1837 was not considered important.

[2] In Castle Street Ward, a Liberal stronghold, there was no contest. The figure given has been arrived at on the assumption that the votes cast in this ward would have been the same as those cast in the previous year.

The generality of them candidly confess, what is the very truth, that they have been beaten on the School Question. . . . They have been blown up by the mine which they dug for others . . . ; with daring and unblushing audacity, they repeated falsehood upon falsehood on the subject of the Schools, until they awakened a spirit of examination, which led to the reaction which has proved fatal to their cause. . . . They must now, however, look out for another war-cry. *Io Triumphe !* The day is won.[1]

All of the Liberal newspapers expressed the confident opinion that, as the *Liverpool Journal* put it, 'the school lie [had] served its turn . . . though ripe in July, it was rotten in November. Thanks to indefatigable discussion, a few weeks thoroughly instructed all who really looked at it with a view to truth. The delusion failed to delude twice.'[2] William Rathbone suggested that those who had not hesitated 'to peril the education of . . . children for party purposes' might have 'learnt an important lesson, that although *for a time* the people may be misled, yet in the end Truth will ever be triumphant.'[3]

Rathbone's personal success was particularly welcome to the Manchester Liberals; the *Manchester Guardian* described him as 'the zealous and consistent reformer, the able and philanthropic chairman of the education committee, and the champion of the corporation schools. Against his re-election all the malice and rancour of party,—all the bitterness of fanaticism, were arrayed. . . . We are convinced that very many [of the Conservatives], the clergy included, would rather have lost fifteen of the wards and succeeded in this, than lost four and gained four out of the sixteen. We rejoice to say that they were most completely disappointed.'[4] A fortnight later,[5] evidently encouraged by the success of the Liberals in the Liverpool elections, the *Manchester Guardian* defended the Corporation Schools vigorously against the attacks which had been made upon them earlier by the Rev. Hugh Stowell in the letters 'to the inhabitants of Manchester' already referred to.

Meanwhile the Liverpool Conservatives were unable to hide their disappointment and despondency. The *Liverpool Courier* came dangerously near to making a rueful admission that the less scrupulous Conservatives had been hoist with their own petard:

Among the prominent causes of the comparative success of the Liberal party has been the false but specious colouring given to the school question. The Liberals, feeling the force of this weapon in the hands of the Conserva-

[1] 6 November 1837.
[2] *Liverpool Journal*, 8 November 1837.
[3] Printed address, *To the Electors of Pitt-Street Ward*, dated 6 November 1837 (*Rathbone Family Papers*).
[4] *Manchester Guardian*, 4 November 1837.
[5] *Ibid.*, 18 November 1837.

tives, at the municipal election of 1836, and the parliamentary election of 1837, set all their engines to work to create a counter-impression. . . . False-hood, boldly and pertinaciously reiterated, has been at last taken for truth: the reformed Corporation has appeared a much calumniated body.[1]

But perhaps most interesting of all were the comments of the *Liverpool Standard*, which, after describing the 'temporary triumph' of what it called 'the radicals' as 'this unexpected issue, which we have now reason to lament', went on to ask with bitter anger:

But how have our radical friends obtained the majority? Has it been by the aid of the Papists, the Socinians, the political Dissenters, or the infidels of the town? No, to their shame and confusion be it told, by a preponderating number of men who *call* themselves *churchmen*. . . . It is to them—the pseudo, self-degraded, hypocritical churchmen of Liverpool, that we owe the slights and indignities offered to the clergy—the contemptuous rejection of the sacred scriptures from the prescribed system of instruction introduced into the public seminaries of the town. . . .[2]

Shortly afterwards the same newspaper felt it necessary to assure its readers that the government, then anxious to set up a national system of education, would not take as its model the Corporation Schools. With an appearance of confidence which may well have been assumed the *Liverpool Standard* observed:

Whether any measure which may be submitted to either house may pass into law or not, of this we feel persuaded, that the experiment which has been tried in Liverpool will not be followed up in any general system of education. We are sure that no plan, which is at all assimilated in character to that pursued in the corporation schools, will obtain the sanction of the legislature.[3]

When the Council met, soon after the elections, to choose its various committees, the proposal was made as a matter of form by Mr C. Lawrence, one of the Conservative councillors, that the Corporation Schools should be sold: a long debate ensued but no new arguments emerged, and of course there was never any doubt about the outcome. Thomas Blackburn 'referred to the municipal elections, in which the school question had been made the sole test of fitness for office, and the public had pronounced its decision by returning a majority of three-fourths friendly to the system pursued'.[4] The proposal was rejected by forty-three votes to thirteen, three Liberals, Charles Birch,

[1] *Liverpool Courier*, 8 November 1837.
[2] *Liverpool Standard*, 3 November 1837.
[3] *Ibid.*, 5 December 1837.
[4] *Liverpool Journal*, 11 November 1837.

John Cropper and James Lawrence, voting against their party's policy.[1]
A new Education Committee was thereupon appointed, Thomas
Blackburn becoming its chairman in place of William Rathbone, who
had been elected mayor. More interesting than the discussions themselves was the fact that they were commented upon in the editorial
columns of the *Manchester Guardian*,[2] and reported at length in the
Cheltenham Free Press[3] and *The Sun*[4] (London); the latter journal added
to its report a remark which must have gratified the Liberal Council as
seeming to set a seal upon the efforts so far made:

> The United Kingdom is so much interested in education that it is desirable
> that the proceedings at Liverpool should be diffused throughout the whole
> empire, especially as she is certainly taking the lead upon the great and
> important subject of national education.

2

It seems safe to assume that the success of the Liverpool Liberals in
the municipal elections of November 1837 did not go unnoticed in
government circles. True, even the most optimistic members of the
Liverpool Education Committee must have realized that the government could hardly be expected to decide overnight to establish a
national system of education modelled upon the system adopted in the
Corporation Schools; yet at least it could be said that the Liverpool
experiment appeared to have been crowned with success at the very
time when the government were seeking most anxiously some solution to the 'Religious Problem'. A few weeks after the elections had
been held, R. A. Slaney proposed in the Commons the establishment
of a Select Committee 'to inquire into the condition of the labouring
classes, with a view to devising some means of national education';[5]
and Lord John Russell, replying as Home Secretary, agreed that 'a
lamentable degree of ignorance' existed in the country, but added that

> . . . it would require the utmost skill and discretion to discover the means
> whereby the various obstacles in the way of any general plan of education
> could be surmounted. He was certain that, if any plan were attempted in
> which the religious feelings of the country were not consulted, it would be a
> signal failure. . . . But, admitting that the religious feelings of the country

[1] *Liverpool Mercury*, 10 November 1837. Birch resigned his seat in 1838 and Cropper
in 1839; when Lawrence defended his seat in Great George Ward in 1838 he did so as a
Conservative.
[2] 18 November 1837.
[3] 18 November 1837.
[4] 13 November 1837.
[5] 30 November 1837. Hansard, Third Series, Vol. XXXIX, Col. 381.

were, as they ought to be, consulted, then came the consideration how they were to reconcile the differences existing between the Established Church and the Dissenters. . . . He wished, likewise, as another motive for delay, to see the effect of those discussions on the subject which had already taken place in the country, and which, he expected, would soon be renewed in Parliament. . . . He could not but expect that from the various meetings[1] which had already been held, and which he was sure would soon be held again, some valuable light would be thrown upon the plan hereafter to be adopted, and upon the system to be acted upon for the purpose of reconciling the differences of various sects.

Lord John felt that it would be proper for Parliament 'to take, ere long, decisive measures for the promotion of education', but pointed out, in a passage which was curiously prophetic, that

. . . if they unhappily introduced a plan which excited either resentment or repugnance on account of religious feelings, or which gave additional motives for dissension between the Established Church and the great body of Dissenters, they would not be furthering, they would only be obstructing, the great cause which they had at heart.[2]

It is interesting to note in passing that these remarks of Lord John Russell were approved of in the pro-Catholic *Liverpool Journal*, and that, in spite of the Liberal success in the recent municipal elections, the same newspaper advised the government not to attempt to set up a national system of education based upon the 'Irish System': after praising that system wholeheartedly, the *Liverpool Journal* said:

But even in Liverpool, where the standard of public intelligence must be taken to be much higher than in the average of the country generally, when we see the excitement and dissension which its very partial introduction, even under the most powerful auspices, has occasioned, we scarcely think that any ministry would be warranted in perilling its existence, even if it thought it right to do so, by so difficult and dangerous an attempt as that of extending it throughout the kingdom.[3]

3

All but the most sanguine and confident of the Liverpool Liberals must have been astonished to find that very soon after the results of the municipal elections of 1837 were declared the agitation concerning the Corporation Schools died away almost to nothing. For months past

---

[1] A reference to the meetings in Liverpool, Salford, Manchester, Cheltenham, etc., to which reference has already been made.
[2] *Ibid.*, Cols. 394–5.
[3] 2 December 1837.

scarcely any issue of the town's newspapers had failed to make its contribution to the dispute; now it was possible to be a regular reader of a Liverpool newspaper for months without finding in it a single reference to the schools. There can be no doubt that the results of the elections persuaded many who had seen in 'the Schools Question' an opportunity to break the power of the Liberals that they had put their trust in a weapon which had come to pieces in their hands. Even when the Bishop of Exeter condemned the 'Irish National School System' in the House of Lords in May 1838, the opponents of that system in Liverpool were slow to take their cue from him, and *The Albion* was able to comment on the failure of the Bishop's attack as follows:

> We, in Liverpool, have especial cause to rejoice in the Bishop of Exeter's motion, followed, as it has been, by such results. Had it been successful, the old School Question here, often as it has been laid, would have been brought out again fresh from the mint of Tory agitation. . . . As it is we have been saved from much, if not from all, of such infliction.[1]

Two weeks later the same journal reported that there had been a public examination of the children attending the Corporation Schools: among the clergy who had attended were the Rev. Messrs Aspinall, Stokes, Kelly, 'Birrall',[2] with Mr Otway from Dublin 'and several other clergymen of the Church of England from various parts of the country'. A comment was added: 'As for the turn of the tide in public opinion on the subject of the schools, it was sure to come.'[3]

In the years 1836 and 1837 the high point of the agitation against the Liberal policy in the Corporation Schools had come at the annual public meeting in the Amphitheatre of the Church of England School Society, a meeting which was particularly important since it provided the Rev. H. M'Neile with an opportunity to speak from the same platform as clergymen, among them the two Rectors of the town, who normally did little to give countenance to his extreme opinions. The speeches delivered at these meetings had naturally been made much of by the Conservative Press. But now in 1838 it was announced that the annual meeting would take place quietly in one of the Society's schools; the Rev. A. Campbell explained that it was not thought necessary to

---

[1] 4 June 1838.

[2] Presumably Charles Morton Birrell, the Minister of Byrom Street Baptist Chapel, father of Augustine Birrell. As an old man Augustine Birrell recalled that the name of the Rev. Hugh M'Neile was often on his father's lips, 'and usually by way of disparagement, though only on account of the clergyman's opposition to any scheme of public education' (*Some Early Recollections of Liverpool in a Letter Addressed to the Lord Mayor of that City from Augustine Birrell, P.C., K.C.*, Liverpool, 1924, p. 7).

[3] *The Albion*, 18 June 1838.

have the usual great public meeting, 'as the society, by the blessing of God, seemed to be now so firmly established that it was not necessary to stimulate the sympathy of the public this year by any public appeal'. It was true that the Junior Rector added that it would be necessary, in his opinion, to have a public meeting before the next parliamentary session opened 'in order that the sense of the public might be taken, and embodied in a petition to the legislature upon the most important subject of national education, based upon the doctrines as well as precepts of the Bible, and in which the established clergy should have their legitimate influence and share'.[1] But not to hold the great meeting which all had come to expect, not to allow the Rev. H. M'Neile to make his most important annual speech against the Liberal Council— this was indeed surprising to Liberals and Conservatives alike, or at least to such of them as had not yet come to believe that the campaign against the schools was now virtually at an end. A writer in *The Albion* quietly remarked: 'We may now . . . assume that they [the Church of England clergy] have ceased to agitate the question because they are convinced, that they were in error in the accusations which they brought against the Corporation Schools.'[2]

A correspondent in the *Liverpool Standard* revealed that the more extreme opponents of the Council were uneasy at being forced to draw the same conclusion: he wrote regretting that there would be 'no public protest against the anti-bible system of education, introduced into this town by our liberal, popish, and dissenting Town Council'. He added: 'Surely our clergy are not becoming lukewarm in the cause? . . . Our clergy in general are too lukewarm, too modest, too retiring. This will not do in these times. But, thank God, there are a few honourable exceptions—the Irish clergy are bold and determined soldiers. Oh that we had more M'Neiles, more M'Ghees, more Greggs.'[3] M'Neile was obliged to celebrate the anniversary of the founding of the Church of England School Society in his own church, where he introduced into his sermon 'a forcible and pointed attack upon the new-fangled system of education'.[4] But even he seems to have preserved silence on the 'Schools Question' for months on end; discouraged, as we learn elsewhere,[5] by the lack of support he had received in his campaign against the Liberal Council, he occupied himself largely with the preparation of a pamphlet[6] in which he sought to establish that support for slavery

[1] *Liverpool Standard*, 13 July 1838.
[2] 30 July 1838.
[3] 13 July 1838.
[4] *Liverpool Standard*, 10 July 1838.
[5] See p. 143.
[6] Rev. H. M'Neile, *Anti-Slavery and Anti-Popery*, Second Edition, Liverpool, 1838.

and a belief in 'Popery' went hand in hand. The long-drawn-out controversy which followed the publication of this work must have left him little time for attacks on other fronts; and it ought to be added that at this time he was devoting a good deal of energy, and applying his considerable gifts as a speaker, to the task of gathering funds wherewith to relieve the sufferings of the poor of Liverpool in a period of great economic depression.

In short it began to appear that the pattern of events which had followed the inauguration of the 'Irish System' in Ireland had been repeated on its being introduced into England; the widespread misunderstanding, misrepresentation and vehement opposition which had at first prevailed had in a relatively short time very much diminished, so that now the more optimistic supporters of the system could begin to hope for a fairly general acceptance and extension of it in both countries, with most of its critics refusing to co-operate rather than seeking to obstruct and destroy.

4

But quite suddenly the success of the 'Irish National System' of education in Ireland and that of the experiment being conducted in Liverpool were imperilled by onslaughts from an unexpected quarter: John MacHale, the Roman Catholic Archbishop of Tuam, began to denounce the system, and to win some support for his view that it was, or ought to be considered, unacceptable to Roman Catholics. MacHale had been appointed Bishop of Maronia and Coadjutor, with right of succession, to the Bishop of Killala in 1825; he became Archbishop of Tuam in 1834. According to a modern biographer, MacHale 'looked on the [Irish] System with mistrust and dislike' from its very inception, and 'regarded the whole organisation as an insidious method of proselytism'. The same writer remarks:

In the first years of the National Education system, Dr MacHale was not in a position to do more than protest formally against the scheme. Daniel O'Connell's support of the plan kept his expressions of mistrust in check for a few years. While he was coadjutor-bishop, he could do nothing more than observe and disapprove.[1]

The reasons given are not entirely convincing, especially to anyone acquainted with the character of the blunt and uncompromising 'John

[1] N. Costello, *John MacHale, Archbishop of Tuam*, Dublin, 1939, pp. 64–5. For a markedly less enthusiastic account of MacHale's activities than is given by this author, see the unpublished dissertation of the (presumably) non-Catholic writer, W. Bradley: *Sir Thomas Wyse, Irish Pioneer in Education Reform*, University of Dublin, 1945.

of Tuam'. The truth seems to be that at first MacHale on the whole approved of the 'Irish System'. In 1835, it is true, he pointed out in a letter to Wyse that the composition of the Irish Board of Commissioners was not 'fair or equitable according to the rules of Arithmetic', there being only one 'Catholic Ecclesiastic' to watch over the interests of nearly seven million Catholics, whereas there were two Protestant clergymen to represent about one million Protestants: he asked that every precaution should be taken to make Wyse's plan 'a source of unmixed blessing to the people', and pointed out that safeguards were important since the liberality and tolerance then being shown by the government might not last. But the letter as a whole is scarcely that of one who 'could do nothing more than observe and disapprove'; after referring to Wyse's 'admirable speech on education'[1] and his 'no less admirable plans' for extending the benefits of education to what he described as 'our unhappy country', MacHale continued:

We are all much indebted to you for the persevering spirit with which you have pursued your original laudable intention of opening to the poor of this country, and I may add to the rich who have been often so badly reared the long locked treasures of a useful and practical education. To give you however a sincere proof of my estimation . . . of your labours I have directed petitions to be forwarded from all the parishes of this district praying for the benefits of an enlarged system of Education such as you Contemplate. I take the liberty of enclosing to you the copies of those petitions which I believe have been already forwarded. I think it is the duty of all who appreciate the blessings of knowledge to aid you in your noble exertions to impart it and if the people petition for this as strenuously as for other objects there can be no doubt of the final triumph of your efforts in their Cause.[2]

Within a short time after this, however, the Archbishop of Tuam had become a most determined opponent of the Irish National System of Education, and in 1838 he wrote and published a number of open letters addressed to Lord John Russell in which the system was criticized most severely. MacHale objected every bit as strongly as did the Rev. Hugh M'Neile to the use of the *Scripture Lessons*[3] in the 'National' schools, disapproved of the method of nominating members of the Board of Commissioners, protested that the Board, because of its constitution, was bound to favour Protestantism, and claimed that schools

[1] A reference to Wyse's speech in the House of Commons on 19 May 1835 asking permission to introduce a Bill intended to give statutory authority to the Board of Commissioners of National Education in Ireland.

[2] Letter to Thomas Wyse, 9 July 1835. From the *Wyse MSS.* in the National Library of Ireland (uncatalogued). This letter is quoted also in W. Wyse, *op. cit.*

[3] He described them as being 'pernicious', likely to spread 'pestilent contagion', and 'covered over with the leprosy of unsound and suspicious doctrine'.

whose patrons were supporters of the government were given greater financial support than others. He particularly resented the provision by which any member of the Board of Commissioners could veto the employment of books proposed or adopted for use in the schools, a provision which had been made with a view to achieving harmony between the adherents of the various faiths; the Archbishop wrote to Russell:

Over the books used for the religious instruction of my flock, I have stated that I shall exercise, without regard to any Board, exclusive and absolute control.

This constituted a direct challenge not only to Lord John Russell but to the Roman Catholic Archbishop of Dublin, Dr Murray, who, as we have seen, was a firm supporter of the Irish National System and a member of the Board of Commissioners.

So as to throw light on the background to subsequent events in Liverpool, it will be convenient here to give some account of the later history of the dispute to which Archbishop MacHale's actions gave rise, even though in order to do so it will be necessary to pass beyond the chronological limits set for this and some succeeding chapters. What happened next is best told in the words of one of the Archbishop's biographers:

The breach between the two Archbishops widened appreciably during the year [1838], news of it eventually reaching Rome. Early in January, 1839, Cardinal Fransoni wrote privately to Archbishop Murray, warning him that Propaganda regarded the system of National Education with disfavour, and hinting that it might be as well if Dr Murray were to resign his seat on the Board. In his reply, Dr Murray set forth the comparative advantages of the scheme, and added that if the Sacred Congregation condemned it 'no other alternative will be left for me than to relinquish into the hands of the Protestants, as heretofore, the public aids bestowed for the education of the poor— leaving them to be expended, as I fear they will be, on attempts to weaken the faith of our young people—I shall likewise recede from the Board of Trustees, prepared to deplore, with my latest breath, the calamities which, I foresee, will result to religion from such a course'.[1]

Gradually MacHale began to win the support of some of his fellow-bishops; at a meeting held early in 1840 eighteen of the Irish Roman Catholic prelates declared themselves to be in favour of the Irish National System of Education, but ten were opposed to it. In an attempt to heal the breach, it was agreed that the government should be asked

[1] N. Costello, op. cit., p. 68.

to modify the system by making concessions to the Roman Catholics: when the government refused to do so, MacHale gave orders that all of the 'National' schools in his diocese should be closed. In the meantime representatives of the Archbishop of Dublin and of the Archbishop of Tuam had proceeded to Rome to state and defend the views of those who had sent them. The dispute placed the authorities in Rome in something of a quandary, as one biographer of MacHale, himself a Roman Catholic clergyman, has explained:

As the system of mixed or secularized education was patronized by nearly all the governments of Europe, even by those who were nominally Catholic, a public and solemn doctrinal sentence on so momentous a question was, under the circumstances, one which might lead the Holy See into very serious embarrassments and international complications. The question was submitted *as one of discipline and government*, to the Congregation of Propaganda, rather than to the Congregation of the Inquisition, which is in the Church the supreme doctrinal tribunal, presided over by the Pope himself.[1]

It was not until January 1841 that the Holy See delivered its verdict in the form of a *Rescript of His Holiness Pope Gregory XVI, to the Four Archbishops of Ireland, in Reply to the Appeal to the Holy See on the Subject of the National System of Education in Ireland*.[2] This document appears to be little known, although it is obviously of importance since it constitutes an official statement of the views of the highest authorities in the Roman Catholic Church on what at that time they considered to be an acceptable plan for the education of Roman Catholic children in Ireland and, by inference, in Great Britain. The *Rescript* emphasized that the matter in dispute had called for very careful consideration since

. . . the protection of the Catholic Religion—the facility afforded for the instruction of youth—the gratitude due to the British parliament for having granted a large sum of money for the support of the schools of the people of Ireland—the necessity of preserving concord among Catholic Bishops—the duty of fostering the public tranquillity—the apprehension, in fine, lest the entire funds, together with the authority, should be transferred to masters not being Catholics,—could not but have filled the Sacred Congregation with the greatest solicitude.

The result of the prolonged examination of the subject was that the

[1] Rt Rev. B. O'Reilly, *John MacHale, Archbishop of Tuam. His Life, Times, and Correspondence*, 2 vols., New York and Cincinnati, 1890, Vol. I, p. 421.
[2] The quotations here given are from the translation published in Dublin in 1841, a copy of which is in the National Library of Ireland.

individual bishops were empowered to decide for themselves whether or not to support the 'Irish System':

Having . . . accurately weighed all the dangers, and all the advantages of the system—having heard the reasoning of the contending parties—and having, above all, received the gratifying intelligence that, for ten years since the introduction of this system of education, the Catholic religion does not appear to have sustained any injury—the Sacred Congregation has, with the approbation of our Most Holy Father, Pope Gregory the XVI, resolved that no judgment should be definitely pronounced in this matter; and that this kind of education should be left to the prudent discretion and religious conscience of each individual bishop, whereas its success must depend on the vigilant care of the pastors, on the various cautions to be adopted, and the future experience which time will supply.

The Sacred Congregation recommended that all books which contained 'any noxious matter either against the canon or the purity of the Sacred Scriptures or against the doctrine of the Catholic Church or morality' should be removed from the National Schools, pointing out that this could easily be effected since there was 'no law of the said system opposed to it'. The Irish prelates were urged to make 'every effort' to ensure that those training to become Catholic schoolmasters should receive their 'religious, moral, or historical lectures' from Catholic instructors. In view of the opposition aroused in other quarters by the (optional) use in the Irish National Schools of the selections from the Bible known as the *Scripture Lessons* it is interesting to note the opinion expressed in the *Rescript*:

. . . it is much safer that literary instruction only should be given in mixed schools, than that the fundamental articles, as they are called, and the articles in which all Christians agree, should alone be taught there in common, reserving for separate instruction the tenets peculiar to each sect; for this manner of acting, in regard to children, appears very dangerous.

It was pointed out that it was the duty of the clergy to see that Catholic children contracted 'no taint' from this 'system of national instruction', and also 'strenuously to endeavour to obtain from the government, by degrees, a better order of things, and more equitable conditions'. Finally the 'Sacred Congregation' asked 'that henceforward the Bishops and other Ecclesiastics should refrain from contending on this controversy in the newspapers, or other such publications, lest the honour of religion, their own characters, or Christian charity, should be injured, to the disedification of the people'.

Fortunately for the Liverpool Education Committee, and for the Liberal Town Council as a whole, those Roman Catholic authorities ultimately responsible for advising the Liverpool priests[1] seem to have remained firm in their support of the 'Irish System' as adopted in the Corporation Schools. As we have seen, after insisting that Roman Catholic children should not join with other children in prayer (except in the Infants' Schools)[2] or be obliged to read the Authorized Version of the Bible, the Roman Catholic clergy in the town had readily co-operated with the Education Committee, not even requiring that some of the teachers in the Corporation Schools should be Roman Catholics. In December 1837 the *Liverpool Journal*, which seems to have voiced the opinions of the Roman Catholic Liberals of the town—and by this time, of course, there could have been few Roman Catholics in Liverpool who supported the Conservatives—made the unequivocal declaration:

> We ourselves can see no solid objection to the system introduced by Lord Stanley into Ireland, and regard it as a close approximation to a nearly perfect Adaptation to all the prevalent forms of religious faith.[3]

This was before Archbishop MacHale had made widely known his opposition to the 'Irish System'; but even after he had done so the attitude of the Roman Catholics of Liverpool, as we shall see, remained unchanged.

5

Naturally, those observers living outside the town who were supporters of the policy adopted in the Liverpool Corporation Schools were delighted when the agitation concerning the schools died down during the year 1838, though some were more anxious than others not to claim too soon that victory had been won; and, just as naturally, some of those who had ignored or made little of the Liverpool experiment began to show some signs of apprehension.

On 25 May 1838 Henry Phillpotts, Bishop of Exeter, made a speech in the House of Lords attacking once again the working of the 'Irish System' in Ireland. During the course of the debate which followed, the Marquess of Lansdowne confidently stated that between

---

[1] It can scarcely be supposed that the Roman Catholic clergy in Liverpool were merely acting on their own initiative when they agreed to support the 'Irish System'. William Rathbone's wife welcomed the restoration of the Roman Catholic hierarchy in 1851 because, as she said in a letter to Lady Noel Byron, 'we should have been very thankful to have had a Liverpool Bishop to negociate & reason with, who knew the state of the town instead of always being answered "I do not see any objection to it, *but our orders are—*" &c., so he and we were helpless' (*Rathbone Family Papers*).

[2] See p. 212.

[3] 2 December 1837. Of the two joint proprietors of the *Liverpool Journal* at least one, Robert Rockliff, was a prominent Roman Catholic.

160,000 and 170,000 children were at this time attending the 'National'
schools in Ireland;[1] whilst the Duke of Wellington felt obliged to
intimate that, although he admitted the force of the Bishop of Exeter's
criticisms, he considered that the members of the House of Lords ought
to 'give their assistance and support to the Government in making the
system, now that it was established, as complete as possible'.[2]

At the beginning of his speech the Bishop of Exeter pointed out
that the subject on which he was to speak was 'of great importance, not
only as concerned England and Ireland, for a similar system had been
attempted to be introduced in England and even in our colonies';[3]
but he made no further reference to what had been happening in Liverpool. One of the most important speeches made in reply was that of
Edward Stanley, Bishop of Norwich, a Liberal who was keenly interested in the 'Irish System' and had published a pamphlet in support of
it in 1835 after a visit to Ireland.[4] In his speech he ignored the Bishop of
Exeter's reference to the attempt to introduce the system into England;
but when he published the speech later he included in the same volume[5]
copies of letters which had passed between William Rathbone as Mayor
of Liverpool, one Cæsar George Otway of Dublin, who described
himself as 'one of the Assistant Commissioners of the Hand-loom
Inquiry Commission', and an Irish clergyman, the Rev. Fielding Ould,
already referred to as being Minister of Christ Church, Liverpool, and
a supporter of the Rev. Hugh M'Neile.

The correspondence had been initiated by Otway who, hearing
Ould criticize the policy of the Liverpool Education Committee, wrote
to Rathbone asking for information concerning the Corporation
Schools, which, he said, he had been led to believe were *eminently*

[1] Hansard, Third Series, Vol. XLIII, Col. 249. Compare the figure given earlier (p. 30).

[2] *Ibid.*, Col. 261.

[3] *Ibid.*, Col. 221. See the Rev. F. Close, *National Education and Lord Brougham's Bill
Considered: in a Series of Nine Letters . . .* , Cheltenham, 1838, p. 14: 'By a singular
coincidence we found that about the same time the Irish system was introduced at
Liverpool, and recommended by the Government to the inhabitants of the remote
colony of New South Wales.'

[4] *A Few Observations on Religion and Education in Ireland*, Second Edition, London,
1835. It may be noted that he complained in this work of the harsh words which he had
heard employed in Liverpool, at a meeting of the 'Protestant Society', to describe the
conduct of the Protestant Archbishop of Dublin, who was said to have sat down with
the Roman Catholic Archbishop of Dublin 'to the great dishonour of the Protestant
Church, to mutilate the word of the holy God' (p. 31). The Liverpool meeting referred
to was evidently that held on 29 October 1835. See p. 50 n.

[5] *Speech of the Lord Bishop of Norwich, Delivered in the House of Lords, May 21st* [sic]
*1838, on the National System of Education in Ireland: with an Appendix of Letters on the
Causes of the Opposition Made to the System in Ireland and on the State of the National
Schools in Liverpool*, London, MDCCCXXXVIII. (The speech was in fact delivered on
25 May 1838.)

successful'. Rathbone wrote in reply an account of what had been achieved in the schools and Otway accepted an invitation to inspect them; he was so satisfied with the information he thus obtained that he sent copies of the whole correspondence, including the Rev. F. Ould's letters, to the 'Irish National Board of Education' and to the 'Liverpool Corporation School Committee', with permission to make such use of it as might be thought fit. From what source the Bishop of Norwich received copies of the letters is not clear, but at any rate William Rathbone had the satisfaction of seeing his defence of the Education Committee's policy and his account of the success which had been achieved published in most exalted company and assured of far more publicity[1] than he could have hoped for. It must have been particularly encouraging for him, as for the Liberal Council as a whole, to read the words (not written by the Bishop himself) with which the correspondence was introduced:

All evidence from Ireland may be laid aside, but the correspondence respecting the operation of the system in Liverpool, which is subjoined to this letter, must convince every unprejudiced man that it is perfectly adequate to give such an education as will best prepare the young for the performance of all their secular duties, and fit them for the reception of religious instruction.

The somewhat odd description of the Liverpool Corporation Schools in this pamphlet as 'the National Schools in Liverpool' must also have given some little satisfaction to all who hoped eventually to see similar schools established throughout the kingdom.

It may be said in passing that the correspondence thus made public under the auspices of the Bishop of Norwich, especially when read together with the annotated edition of the correspondence[2] published by the Rev. Fielding Ould, makes interesting reading. Otway had little difficulty in showing both that a considerable number of Protestant children were now attending the Corporation Schools and that in any case it was scarcely just of those who had done everything possible to dissuade Protestant parents from sending their children to the schools to complain that the schools were attended chiefly by Roman Catholic children. Ould's chief contentions were that it was wrong to encourage the spread of false religion, and that teachers who were responsible for preserving order whilst the Roman Catholic monitors were giving

[1] See the Rev. J. Hayden, *Observations Addressed to the Lord Bishop of Norwich on His Lordship's Speech and Pamphlet on the National System of Education in Ireland*, Dublin, 1838.
[2] *An Exposure of the Means Employed to Prop Up the Modern Scheme of Liberal Education at present in Operation in Ireland, and in the Schools of the Liverpool Corporation, in a Correspondence between the Author and the Son of an old Friend; with Notes, Explanatory and Reprobatory*. Liverpool, 1838.

religious instruction were themselves, in effect, being called upon to propagate false doctrines and to support 'the Priest of Antichrist'.[1] The letters of William Rathbone are full of the confidence which at this time he seemed justified in feeling:

> I can only say that we are not aware of a single person who has warmly adopted the plan who does not steadily continue to support it. On the contrary what was in the first instance looked upon by some as an experiment is now considered by these parties as an ascertained fact.[2]

Perhaps feeling that he had not made the best of his brief, Ould challenged Otway to call upon the Rev. H. M'Neile, whom he described as the person best calculated to provide information on the subject, he having 'fought and won the battle against the Corporation Schools' before Ould himself had 'come into the field'; Otway was even informed that failure to visit M'Neile would be taken to indicate fear of encountering 'the distinguished opponent of modern Popery'. Otway duly sought out M'Neile, explained why he had been referred to him, and asked for some comment on the different views held by Ould and Rathbone as to whether or not the Corporation Schools had succeeded. M'Neile's reply was evidently given in pique; but it was nevertheless significant, and must have pleased the numerous supporters of the 'Irish System' who later were able to read Otway's report: the chief antagonist of the Liverpool Education Committee answered

> that he thought the schools had succeeded, and would succeed, for there was not sufficient vital religion in the country to stop them, and that they would overthrow Protestantism and piety, and be supported by infidels, Romanists, and Liberals.[3]

The satisfaction of M'Neile's opponents was probably not greatly diminished when Ould explained that when M'Neile had said that 'he thought the "*Schools had succeeded*"' he had used the term 'relatively to the objects which the propounders of the new system had in view'; Ould suggested that those objects had been 'the giving of a severe blow and heavy discouragement to the Church and the gratification of the prejudices of political partisans at the expense of the best interests of the children, of Protestantism, and of true religion'.[4] Such remarks could scarcely conceal the fact that the triumph of the Liverpool Education Committee was almost complete and the discomfiture of its adversaries profound.

[1] Rev. F. Ould, *op. cit.*, p. 11.
[3] *Ibid.*, pp. 25–6.
[2] *Ibid.*, p. 11.
[4] *Ibid.*, p. 6.

6

In one of his 'Notes Explanatory and Reprobatory', the Rev. Fielding Ould, after speaking of the system in force in the Corporation Schools, had expressed the fear that it was 'seriously contemplated in high places to apply the principle of this system generally to the National schools of England as soon as matters are sufficiently ripe, and they can venture with safety on the perilous course recommended so plausibly by Mr Wyse, of Waterford, and with such indefatigable activity by Mr Simpson, of Edinburgh, and his colleagues of the Central Education Society'.[1] Mr Simpson, as we shall see later, not only considered that matters were 'sufficiently ripe' to warrant the establishment of a national system of education based on principles similar to those adopted in the Liverpool Corporation Schools, but was prepared to point to the success achieved in those schools as giving support to his arguments. Thomas Wyse, however, was rather more cautious, although he evidently noted with great interest all that happened to the schools, and steps were taken to keep him well informed about them. The writer has come across the following entries in Wyse's diary:

March 3, 1838. Corporation schools various details of high interest for which see Note Book.[2]

June 2, 1838. Dr Shepherd[3] said man chosen to be opponent of Corp. schools an adulterer and yet McNeil [sic] stands godfather.

But it is not surprising that Wyse still hesitated to claim that the success achieved by the Liverpool Education Committee had made it clear that it was possible everywhere in England to educate children of different faiths in the same schools; after all, by June 1838 only eight months had elapsed since those schools had been the cause of considerable controversy in Manchester and Cheltenham, not to speak of Liverpool itself. On the other hand, some of those who opposed the policies favoured by Wyse and the Liverpool Education Committee appear to have become by this time not at all sure that the Liverpool experiment had failed. Thus there was an interesting passage of arms in the House of Commons on 14 June 1838, when an opponent who preferred not to refer to the Liverpool schools in support of his own case almost defied

---

[1] *Ibid.*, p. 9.

[2] *Wyse MSS.*, National Library of Ireland (uncatalogued). Unfortunately the notebook into which the 'various details of high interest' were copied seems to be no longer extant.

[3] The well-known Unitarian minister whose dispute with the Rev. A. Campbell has already been referred to.

Thomas Wyse to allude to them as justifying the holding of different views.

On that day Wyse presented several petitions, including one from Liverpool,[1] in favour of the establishment of a national system of education, and later proposed that an address be presented to the Queen asking for the appointment of a Board of Commissioners of Education in England, 'with the view of especially providing for the wise, equitable, and efficient application of sums granted, or to be granted, for the advancement of education, by Parliament, and for the immediate establishment of schools for the education of teachers.'[2] He pointed out that such a Board as he proposed had been established in Ireland, and went on:

I would wish the Government to take the subject early into consideration, and appoint a board on the principles which I have suggested; that they should set to the work heartily, and not tremble in hesitation and the wish to know what this party or the other would think of their proceedings. There is no fear of collision; but if there be, it must be risked in such a case. In fact the country cannot stand as it is.[3]

The first speaker to oppose Wyse's motion was Mr J. C. Colquhoun, member for Kilmarnock, who, as a determined opponent of the 'Irish System' of education and one of the most prominent supporters of the Protestant Association, could scarcely have been unaware of the existence of the Liverpool Corporation Schools.[4] Part of his speech is of some importance, not only in the context in which we are now considering it, but also as indicating the claims which such men felt strong enough to make concerning privately-conducted experiments comparable with that being made by the Liverpool Town Council. Colquhoun said:

What favour do the schools founded on the liberal system meet with? There are indeed but few specimens of these. One, however, is to be found in Edinburgh, under the auspices of Mr Simpson,[5] who accompanied the Honourable Member [Thomas Wyse] in his educational tour; the other is in

---

[1] *Mirror of Parliament*, Second Series, Vol. VI, 1838, p. 4751.

[2] *Ibid.*, p. 4761.

[3] *Ibid.*, p. 4764.

[4] It seems most unlikely, for instance, that he had heard nothing of the proceedings at the meeting of the Liverpool branch of the Protestant Association held on 4 October 1837, when the Rev. H. M'Neile made one of his many speeches against the Corporation Schools: Colquhoun was to have presided at this meeting but was unable to be present (*Liverpool Courier*, 11 October 1837). In 1838 he made a bitter attack on the 'Irish System' in a pamphlet entitled *The System of National Education in Ireland: its Principle and Practice* (Cheltenham).

[5] See p. 37.

Bath. Now, what acceptance do these schools meet with? Mr Simpson tells you, it is hardly possible to keep his liberal school in Edinburgh alive; the subscriptions are languishing; and as for establishing a second school, it is out of the question: that is in a population of 160,000. While numerous schools on the sectarian system are established, and flourish, it is hardly possible to keep alive this dwarfish and dwindling specimen of a liberal school. . . . In Bath, the liberal school was established under favourable auspices, as I believe it has the patronage of Mr Roebuck.[1] . . . Ushered in with great pomp, with the parade of a numerous committee, with assurances of high success, it has fallen from one degree of weakness to another, until disappearing from a principal street into an obscure lane in an obscure quarter of Bath, its committee have dissolved, its funds are withdrawn, its benches empty, and master reduced to the starvation point, it offers a memorable proof of the degree of favour with which the people of England regard liberal schools [*sic*].

Colquhoun issued a direct challenge:

I call on the Honourable Member to exhibit some specimens of this liberal system of education which is to unite all sects.[2]

But 'the Honourable Member' was not to be drawn; neither Wyse nor any of the subsequent speakers judged that the moment had yet come to put forward any claims concerning the 'liberal schools' in Liverpool.

---

[1] 'The exclusion from the model school he [Roebuck] founded in Bath of all religious instruction beyond a reading from the Bible by the Master, proved a not inconsiderable factor in his defeat at Bath in 1837' (R. E. Leader (ed.), *Life and Letters of John Arthur Roebuck, with Chapters of Autobiography*, London, 1897, p. 342). Roebuck visited Liverpool in 1840 and delayed his departure 'in order to see some of the leading Liberals' (*ibid.*, p. 56).

[2] *Mirror of Parliament*, Second Series, Vol. VI, 1838, pp. 4766–7.

Chapter 8

LORD JOHN RUSSELL DECIDES

I

IN the course of the House of Commons debate of 14 June 1838, to which reference has just been made, Lord John Russell explained in some detail why the government felt unable to support the proposals put forward by Thomas Wyse that a Board of Commissioners of Education should be appointed and that schools for the training of teachers should be established by the state. Since Russell himself was to be found making very similar proposals before many months had passed, it seems reasonable to ask why a course of action which in June 1838 he considered doomed to failure seemed to him very soon afterwards to be such as he could recommend to the Cabinet.

There is, of course, no doubt whatever that when Russell spoke on Wyse's proposals he was, as he said, 'fully convinced that it was the duty of Parliament and of the state to further and encourage education in this country'. But, he explained, he had to take into account the great conflict of opinion which existed concerning the giving of religious instruction in schools. He himself, he said, favoured the policy of the British and Foreign School Society, which had adopted 'a system, in his opinion, best adapted for this country—namely, that the education should be a religious education, but that no catechism of any sort should be introduced into the schools, and that the children should not be confined to any place of worship, but might go where their parents liked'. On the other hand, he pointed out, if this practice were to be adopted in government schools 'a great many of the National Society and a great many churchmen would object to it, because the catechism was not taught in the school'.

To overcome this difficulty a third system had been suggested as suitable for adoption in state schools: 'that the education given in the schools should be entirely of a secular nature, and that the clergymen of the church, and the ministers of each particular sect, should give religious instruction separately to the children at different times and places from the education given in the schools'. It is important to note that Russell was convinced that this policy of completely separating secular education from religious instruction 'would not meet with the general assent of the people of this country'; what is more, he personally was opposed to it on the ground 'that it would fail to implant in the minds of the children that religious and moral culture which was necessary, in order to enable them to become good members of society'. The upshot of all this was that Russell considered that the government could not attempt 'to establish a commission or a board of education' until 'there was more likelihood of agreement among the leading persons who were in favour of general education in this country.'[1]

Russell might, of course, have added that a further difficulty arose from the fact that the Roman Catholics, in general, refused to send their children even to the schools of the British and Foreign School Society, because in them only the Authorized Version was read: yet a place for such children would have had to be found in a national system of education, especially since the existing provision for their education was even less satisfactory than that available for poor children of other denominations. Even if the government had tried to make easier the task of arriving at some agreement by consenting to exclude the Roman Catholics from some projected state system of education, it appeared doubtful whether very much would in fact have been gained. It was true that many would have wished to see the Roman Catholics so excluded. At about this time R. A. Slaney, acting as chairman of a select committee on education, failed to carry a motion that 'where there is any large number of poor Roman Catholics, or other persons, who, from religious scruples, are unwilling to send their children to either of those Schools [i.e. of the National or British and Foreign Societies], it is desirable that Government should afford assistance to them, on satisfactory proof that the Holy Scriptures (in any version) are used and taught in their schools'. A similar proposal made by G. W. Wood also failed to win the approval of the select committee, which, indeed, eventually reported that 'under existing circumstances, and under the difficulties which beset the question,' it was not prepared 'to propose any means for meeting the deficiency [of schools] beyond the continuance and extension of the grants which are at present made by the Treasury for the promotion of education, through the medium of the National and British and Foreign Societies'.[2]

On the other hand many, even among those who were not Roman Catholics—and especially many Protestant Dissenters—felt that no

---

[1] Hansard, Third Series, Vol. XLIII, Cols. 731-2.

[2] *Report from the Select Committee on Education of the Poorer Classes in England and Wales: together with the Minutes of Evidence. Ordered, by the House of Commons, to be Printed, 13 July 1838*, pp. XIII, XI. Wood's motion was opposed by Sir S. Canning, Mr Pusey, Mr Scrope, Mr Acland, Lord Ashley and Lord Sandon (one of the parliamentary representatives for Liverpool).

state system of education could be considered acceptable if it failed to provide for the education of Roman Catholics. It was at this time that Henry Dunn himself, the Secretary of the British and Foreign School Society, declared that 'he did not think that the Protestant dissenters generally would approve of any national grant which, directly or indirectly, excluded from its benefits Catholics or Jews, or any who differed from them; they would hold that all ought to be educated, that none ought to be left in ignorance'.[1] And meanwhile, as if to demonstrate the impossibility of bringing the Protestants and Roman Catholics of these islands within the same state system of education, John MacHale, Archbishop of Tuam, was now informing Russell that the Irish National System of Education could not satisfy Roman Catholic wishes; whilst Henry Phillpotts, Bishop of Exeter, supported by (among others) the Archbishop of Canterbury and the Bishops of London and Chichester, was declaring that system to be unacceptable to Protestants.[2] In the face of all this, Russell must have been tempted to smile somewhat wryly when Thomas Wyse, urging him to take action, added the assurance that 'there was no fear of collision'.[3]

Yet there was truth in the remark with which Wyse accompanied this observation: that even if 'collision' were to be the result of government action, such action would have to be taken, since the country could not 'stand' as it was. With each day that passed it was becoming more obvious that the existing provision for education was quite inadequate; yet the repeated efforts of Lord Brougham in the Lords, and of Wyse and others in the Commons, to stir the government to action had been without effect. Disappointment and discontent were increasing among the many Liberals who had expected to see a Liberal Cabinet taking decisive action in this field, but who were now asked to believe that it was impossible for the government to take even a small step on the way towards providing a national system of education.

Many petitions on the subject were addressed to Parliament, and Lord John Russell, as an active supporter and a Vice-President of the British and Foreign School Society, must have found it particularly difficult not to be swayed by the petition which the Committee of that Society had submitted to him by deputation in April 1838. The Committee wished to see established a national system of education 'based on the Scriptures, but positively excluding from all schools aided by Parliament the formularies of any particular church'; it acknowledged,

---

[1] See p. 36 n.
[2] See report (Hansard, Third Series, Vol. XLIII) of the debate in the House of Lords, 25 May 1838.
[3] *Mirror of Parliament*, Second Series, Vol. VI, 1838, p. 4764.

however, that no such system was likely to be set up for some time to come. In the meantime it asked that a Board of Education should be established which should enjoy 'the confidence of the various religious denominations'. In schools assisted by the state there should be periods devoted to Bible-reading, Jews and Catholics being excused from attendance at such times; where instruction in the doctrines of the Established Church was given, the children of all Dissenters should similarly be excused. The petitioners felt that the Board 'should not interfere in religious instruction' and ought not to 'undertake the training of teachers'.[1] Even these modest proposals Russell had found it impossible to support.

But as the pressure on the government increased, it became more and more clear that whatever misgivings the Cabinet might have, and whatever justification there was for Russell's fear that to take a wrong step at this time would be to increase the hostility between the various religious groups, the government could not afford to remain much longer in the possibly prudent but certainly unheroic attitude of men who seemed, in Wyse's words, to 'tremble in hesitation and the wish to know what this party or the other would think of their proceedings'.[2]

2

Among those who at this time looked to the government for some definite action in the sphere of education were the Liberals of Liverpool, a group of men less likely than any others to listen indulgently to governmental protestations about the impossibility of devising a system of education acceptable to members of all denominations. During the difficult days when the opposition aroused by the Liverpool experiment had been at its height and had seemed impressively strong, men like William Rathbone, as we have seen, had argued that to admit defeat would be to discourage the government from following the example which the Liverpool Council had set, and that those who wished to see a Liberal administration embarking upon the admittedly dangerous policy of providing a national system of education ought themselves to be prepared to encounter risk and opposition. Now that such risk and opposition appeared to have been triumphantly overcome, the Liverpool Liberals must have felt entitled to ask that the government should show a determination and courage equal to their own.

They were, moreover, in a position to point out that the system

---

[1] This account of the petition is taken from H. B. Binns's history of the British and Foreign School Society: *A Century of Education, 1808–1908*, London, 1908, pp. 128–9.

[2] *Mirror of Parliament*, Second Series, Vol. VI, 1838, p. 4764.

which they had fought to establish seemed to solve all of the problems which Lord John Russell considered so discouraging. In the Corporation Schools there *was* provision for doctrinal teaching such as the National Society demanded; there *was* undenominational religious instruction such as would give no offence to Dissenters; the Authorized Version *was* available to all who wished to read it; there *was* no sharp cleavage between secular and religious instruction, since both denominational and undenominational religious instruction were given within school hours; in addition to all this, there *was* provision for the education of Roman Catholic children, and that such as the Roman Catholic clergy had demonstrably approved. It was true that most of the Church of England clergy in the town still refused to support the policy adopted in the schools, but they now offered little active opposition; and criticism was rarely voiced nowadays even by political opponents. In short, very considerable success, it seemed, had been won, in spite of strong initial opposition, within the space of little more than two years.

There was one further important point. When Wyse had last proposed the establishment of a Board of Education (14 June 1838) he had envisaged 'a central board . . . to be composed of fair proportions of the representatives of the different parties and feelings prevalent in the country.'[1] It would appear that Wyse had had in mind a board similar to that established in Ireland, on which the chief religious groups were represented. Lord John Russell had pointed to the difficulty of setting up such a board in England 'because in whatever way it might be constituted, it would create jealousy on all hands on this subject';[2] and certainly he could be forgiven if he quailed at the prospect of inviting, say, the Archbishop of Canterbury to sit on the same board as some leading Roman Catholic cleric. In the previous December Lord Brougham had tried to meet objections to the setting up of a state-controlled board by proposing that the Education Board which he wished the government to establish should consist of two ministers of state together with three other members who, being 'irremovable' and able to outvote the ministers, would prevent the government from exercising complete control over the educational system. But this, of course, was shirking the problem rather than attempting to solve it, since a great deal would depend on the principle to be adopted when the non-government members of the Board were chosen: when pressed for information on this point later (15 July 1839) by the Bishop of

---

[1] Hansard, Third Series, Vol. XLIII, Col. 715.

[2] *Ibid.*, Col. 732. It will be remembered that Archbishop MacHale was complaining that Roman Catholics were not adequately represented on the Irish Board.

Chichester, Brougham replied that 'there was nothing in his bill which prevented a prelate from being one of the commissioners nominated by the Crown; but by putting a prelate on the board, they would be raising the question, whether a dissenting clergyman ought not to be there also'; and the Marquess of Lansdowne commented that 'that was the difficulty'.[1]

But by October 1838 the Liverpool Liberals appeared to have demonstrated that it was possible, without alienating public opinion, to leave the control of schools catering for the children of all denominations in the hands of laymen, and laymen chosen not with a view to achieving a balance between the various religious interests but simply selected from among those who could claim to be representatives of the citizens as a whole; it was particularly encouraging that the Roman Catholics in Liverpool had not insisted upon having one of their number appointed to the Education Committee. In short, the Liberals of Liverpool seemed to have proved, in the most important town in England outside London, that the difficulties which deterred the government from action were not so formidable as they seemed; and to have done so in spite of the special problem caused by the presence in the town of a far greater proportion of Roman Catholics than was to be found in most other parts of the country. The more active members of the Liverpool Education Committee had always hoped to turn the Corporation Schools into model schools for the training of teachers and to build additional schools in the town: now that the initial experiment had succeeded, they were prepared to bring their plans to fruition. They must certainly have felt justified in asking the government to note what they had done.

3

That Lord John Russell was not left in ignorance of the views of those who had been conducting the Liverpool experiment is quite certain. It can scarcely be doubted that Russell had heard of the Liverpool Corporation Schools before 1838, as indeed any attentive reader of the chief London newspapers, even if not furnished with other sources of information, must have done;[2] but now he was enabled to examine one of the schools for himself and to see the results of the policy pursued in them. According to reports published in the contemporary Dublin newspapers, Lord John Russell paid a short visit to

---

[1] *Ibid.*, Vol. XXXIX, Cols. 445–6; Vol. XLIX, Cols. 330–1.

[2] In addition to the references already mentioned, *The Times* had contained reports of speeches concerning the Corporation Schools on 20 October and 10 November 1836.

Ireland towards the end of September 1838,[1] and in view of what happened later it seems not unlikely that Russell, in making the visit, was actuated, at least in part, by a desire to obtain up-to-date information about the working of the 'Irish System' of education in Ireland.[2] He left Dublin on 1 October,[3] and arrived in Liverpool on 2 October; the next few days he spent in the town as the guest of William Rathbone, now Mayor. *The Albion* reported that Lord John and his party 'proceeded in his worship's carriage to Greenbank [Rathbone's house], where the noble lord had arranged to reside during his sojourn in this neighbourhood. . . . In the evening the noble lord dined with his worship and a very select party.' No time was lost in taking Russell to see one of the Corporation Schools; on 3 October, the day after his arrival,

. . . his lordship visited the South Corporation School. He was accompanied by the Mayor, Lord Ebrington,[4] Mr Stanley,[5] the Secretary for the Treasury, Sir Hesketh Fleetwood,[6] and several other gentlemen. He stayed for upwards of an hour and a half, during which time he made the most minute inquiries as to the system of instruction practised in the schools. He was present during the religious instruction given to the children, to which he paid the greatest attention, himself putting questions from time to time. He then remained to hear the children sing the hymn in which those of all sects unite every day before the school breaks up. His lordship and his party then left, after expressing their high satisfaction at everything which they had witnessed.[7]

It would certainly appear that Lord John Russell manifested more than a polite interest in the schools.

It was not the first time that William Rathbone had tried to persuade Lord John to adopt a given course of action; five years earlier Rathbone and a few of his friends had spent a weary period in London trying to convince Russell, Lord Althorp and others that steps ought to be taken to disfranchise the corrupt Liverpool freemen. On that occasion Rathbone had found Lord Althorp 'manly, frank and communicative', but he had described Lord John Russell's attitude as 'contemptible', and said of him:

[1] He arrived in Dublin on 22 September (*Dublin Evening Post*, 22 September 1838).
[2] According to Spencer Walpole, Russell went to Ireland 'with the object of seeing with his own eyes the condition of that country' (*The Life of Lord John Russell*, London, 1889, Vol. I, p. 310).
[3] *Dublin Evening Post*, 2 October 1838.
[4] Ebrington became Lord-Lieutenant of Ireland in the following year.
[5] Edward John Stanley (later second Baron Stanley of Alderley) was Patronage Secretary to the Treasury from 1835 to 1841. He represented North Cheshire in Parliament from 1832 to 1841.
[6] Member of Parliament for Preston.
[7] *The Albion*, 8 October 1838.

. . . he endeavoured to back out of his recommendation to pursue the general Petition, but he was not allowed to do so; said he should not be prepared to support a Bill even should we prove our case . . . endeavoured to back out of his admission . . . that the seat was purchased.[1]

Rathbone may therefore be forgiven, perhaps, if on this occasion he somewhat overstated his case, in the attempt to convince a man whom he considered over-hesitant and lacking in moral courage. But indeed William Rathbone appears to have been by this time sincerely persuaded that almost all of the political opponents of the Liberals were prepared to accept without criticism the policy which had been adopted in the Corporation Schools. As Mayor of the town he was most punctilious in avoiding political meetings at which he might be called upon to take sides with members of his own party,[2] so that when, on the evening following Lord John Russell's visit to the schools, Rathbone gave a dinner at the Town Hall in honour of his distinguished guest, men of 'all shades of politics' were invited. In order to emphasize the amicable, non-political nature of the function, journalists were not invited to report the speeches, and we owe our knowledge of what was said at the dinner to a single Liverpool newspaper, *The Albion*, which 'tried in every direction to get something like an accurate account of what fell from the several speakers in the course of the evening'; and, having 'pumped one, sifted another, and drawn as tightly as possible upon the memory of others', was able to publish short versions of the various speeches. It may be said that no one present at the dinner seems to have published any criticism of the versions given.

We learn from the *Albion* report that both Lord John Russell and William Rathbone at this time felt it possible at a friendly gathering of men of 'all shades of politics' to speak of the Liverpool Corporation Schools as if disagreement on the subject had virtually come to an end, so that all parties in Liverpool were at least prepared to acquiesce in what had been done. And it may well have been that Russell was not particularly surprised at this state of affairs: after all, the Conservative administration of Peel, as we have seen, had decided to support the 'Irish System' in Ireland, although many influential Conservatives had earlier bitterly criticized that system. The importance of all this to a harassed statesman who was eager to take action with regard to education but who had to keep in mind the realities of political warfare can

---

[1] Letter to his wife, dated 10 May 1833, printed in E. A. Rathbone (ed.), *Records of the Rathbone Family*, p. 193.

[2] Thus he refused to attend a meeting held to celebrate the electoral victory of his friend and supporter Thomas Blackburn in November 1837. Numerous other examples could be given.

easily be imagined. At any rate, Lord John began his speech by declaring that he would not 'wander into the field of politics', and concluded 'by expressing a hope that much would soon be done to raise the people, in a moral point of view, by an enlightened and religious education. He had visited the corporation schools in the course of that very day, and had witnessed the religious education of the children with the greatest pleasure'.

One of those who had accompanied Russell to Liverpool on this occasion was Mr E. J. Stanley, a member of Parliament for North Cheshire, a Secretary to the Treasury, and, it may be added, a nephew of the Bishop of Norwich, who, as has been shown, was taking an interest in the Corporation Schools at this time. Stanley,[1] like Russell, spoke at the Town Hall dinner as if he understood that the controversy concerning the schools had almost come to an end: he 'referred to the calumnies with which the corporation had been assailed, from interested motives, on the subject of the schools, and expressed his satisfaction with what he had that day seen, especially the religious instruction of the children. He hoped that the day of misrepresentation had gone by, and that the spirit of charity and kindly feeling, which, we were told, formed so important a feature in our holy religion, would once more prevail'. To complete the picture of harmony, the Rev. Mr Aspinall, one of the few Church of England clergymen who had co-operated with the Education Committee, said in reply to a toast proposed by the Mayor that 'he had thought it his duty to uphold the schools in question, and should have continued to do so had he remained alone and altogether unsupported. Still, he could not be otherwise than pleased with the great change of public opinion on this subject,[2] and with the testimony on their behalf which they had heard that evening'.

It seems safe to assume that Lord John Russell and his companions left Liverpool rather more hopeful about the prospects of eventually establishing some national system of education than Thomas Wyse and James Simpson could have felt when, after their brush with the Rev. Hugh M'Neile, they had set out from the same town to begin their 'educational tour' less than a year earlier. And since abridged versions

---

[1] E. J. Stanley had been among those who had spoken at the Theatre Royal meeting in Manchester a year earlier in favour of the establishment of a national system of education.

[2] A fortnight later Aspinall spoke of 'the success of that great Christian experiment, which has proved, without the sacrifice of one iota of principle on either side, that the children of those who constitute the different denominations of Christians, should be educated under the same roof, in Christian love, and harmony, and peace together' (*Liverpool Mercury*, 26 October 1838).

of the *Albion* report of 8 October 1838 appeared in the (London) *Times* and *Morning Chronicle* on the following day, the Liverpool Liberals must have felt that at last their efforts were winning recognition and might even soon lead to similar action being taken elsewhere.

Certainly they seem to have felt more confidence in Russell at the end of his visit than they had done when he first arrived. Several of the Liberal journals commented on the cold reception accorded to Lord John, even by Liberals, when he first appeared in public during his stay; and not even the fear of giving ammunition to their opponents prevented them from publishing editorials in which the lack of cordiality shown to the distinguished guest was accounted for and justified. The leading Liberal newspaper in the town went so far as to accuse Russell of 'truckling to the Tories' and, referring to the clear indications that Lord John had 'lost his popularity among the Reformers of Liverpool', wrote: 'The discipline is rough, but salutary, and if it works its proper effect, his Lordship's re-conversion, he may rely upon it that his reception on his next visit to Liverpool will be as different from this as day from night.'[1] But when the time came for Russell to leave Liverpool the Liberals appear to have been reassured about his general outlook, as they scarcely would have been had he been content during his stay in Liverpool to point to the difficulties in the way of taking some decisive action in the sphere of education. Thus the *Liverpool Chronicle* wrote:

We are pleased to hear in all quarters that Lord John Russell made a most favourable impression upon the minds of all who had any opportunity of conversing with him during his late visit. And of those who so informed us, many Reformers, discontented beyond measure at the late session of Parliament, approached him in no mood to be easily pleased, but, nevertheless, they left him with the conviction that he is yet unshaken in his firm attachment to the people and their cause.[2]

Immediately after his visit to Liverpool, Russell joined his wife in Brighton, and one of his biographers records that there, a few weeks later, 'during that melancholy week in which [he] was watching by his dying wife's bedside',[3] he at last made up his mind that the time had come for him to propose to the Cabinet measures to improve the provision of education for the people.

---

[1] *Liverpool Mercury*, 5 October 1838.
[2] 6 October 1838.
[3] S. Walpole, *The Life of Lord John Russell*, Vol. I, p. 329. Russell's wife died on 1 November 1838.

4

Because of the death of his wife, Russell was not present at the Cabinet meeting at which his first tentative plans were discussed soon afterwards. Lord Broughton later wrote:

At our Cabinet on November 26 [1838] we discussed Russell's Education scheme. Lord Melbourne confessed that he was against the thing altogether; on which Howick said, 'Thank God there are some things which even you cannot stop, and that is one of them'. Melbourne only smiled.[1]

Broughton remarked at this meeting that the opponents of the Liberals would not accept Russell's 'scheme', but 'would try to make a Church question out of it, and say we wanted to take education out of the hands of the clergy'.[2] On the following day Melbourne, as Prime Minister, wrote to Russell:

We talked much yesterday of measures and particularly of education. The general opinion was that the question could not be escaped nor deferred; that our relations with respect to it must be declared at the very commencement of the session. Upon the question itself I differ. I am against it. I think education at present stands in England upon a better ground than any new one upon which you will place it. I am convinced that if you attempt a combined system you will fail; but I have no objection to yield my opinion and try. But before you declare that you intend to propose a plan you must have a practical plan prepared. It appears to us all, therefore, that the sooner you mature your views upon this subject and reduce them to writing so that they may be submitted to some members of the Cabinet, the better.[3]

Russell at once replied (28 November 1838):

I will prepare the plan for education as soon as I can. But I do not think it should be brought forward early in the session.[4]

It is clear from all this that, although Russell did not make public his 'plan for Education' until some months later, he had begun to formulate such a plan by November 1838. It would seem also that at that time he was already putting forward two proposals which are of some interest to us: firstly, that the supervision of such provision for education as the government might make should not be entrusted to the clergy, and secondly (this to Melbourne's dismay), that the education provided

---

[1] Lord Broughton, *Recollections of a Long Life . . . With Additional Extracts from his Private Diaries*, edited by his daughter, Lady Dorchester, London, 1911, Vol. V, p. 168.

[2] *Ibid.*, Vol. V, p. 168.

[3] Lord Melbourne, *Papers . . .* , edited by Lloyd C. Sanders, London, 1889, pp. 384–5.

[4] Lord J. Russell, *Early Correspondence*, Vol. II, pp. 235–6.

by the state should be 'combined' education, i.e. it should be given in institutions each of which would be open to pupils of all denominations.

Whether, when Russell's tentative proposals were discussed at the Cabinet meeting of 26 November, there was any reference to Russell's recent visit to the Liverpool Corporation Schools, it is not possible to say; but there are at least two clear indications that the schools were not being ignored in Liberal circles in London during the period when Russell was 'maturing his views', in accordance with the Prime Minister's instructions, so as to be able to make definite recommendations to the Cabinet. On 11 January 1839 the *Morning Advertiser* (London) published the following report on its front page, entirely without comment, and evidently taking it for granted that no introductory remarks by way of explanation were necessary:

LIVERPOOL CORPORATION SCHOOLS

The Report of the Education Committee embodied the following statements of the number of Protestants, Catholics, &c., in the Corporation Schools:

North School.—Boys—Members of the Church of England 96, Methodists 25, Independents 14, Baptists 10, Presbyterians 5, Dissenters not classified 4—Total 154. Catholics 323. Total in the boys' school 477. Girls—Members of the Church of England 75, Methodists 4, Independents 7, Baptists 4, Presbyterians 5, not classified 4, Unitarians 1—Total 100. Catholics 221. Total in the girls' school 321. Infant—Members of the Church of England 54,[1] Methodists 12, Independents 12, Baptists 4, Presbyterians 3—Total 84. Catholics 65, denominations unknown 51. Total in the infant school 200. General state—Protestant boys 154, Protestant girls 100, Protestant infants 92—Total 333.[2] Catholic boys 323, Catholic girls 221, Catholic infants 65. Total 609. Unknown denominations 56. Total number in the North School on the 21st December 1838, 998.

South Schools.—Boys—Members of the Church of England 103, Church of Scotland 8, Independents 13, Baptists 16, Methodists 21, Presbyterians 6, Catholics 133—Total 300. Girls—Church of England 102, Baptists 4, Methodists 16, Catholics 118—Total 240. Infants—Church of England 89, Church of Scotland 4, Independents 2, Methodists 11, Catholics 74—Total 180. Totals—Number of children of the Church of England 294, Church of Scotland 12, Independents 15, Baptists 20, Methodists 48, Presbyterians 6, Catholics 325. Total number of the South Schools 720.

[1] The figure given in the minutes of the Education Committee is 53; this explains the error in the total (*Proceedings of Education Committee*, Vol. I, p. 90).

[2] This total, correctly copied from the official figures, is clearly wrong; moreover the number of 'Protestant infants' has just been given as 84.

Thus London readers were informed that at the beginning of 1839 more than one-third of the children attending the North Corporation School were Protestants; whilst of the children attending the South Corporation School *more than one half* were Protestants, the number of Church of England children (294) now being not much below that of the Roman Catholic children (325). This information had been derived from a report made to the Education Committee by the masters of the two schools and published in the Liverpool Press.

Soon after these figures appeared, the indefatigable James Simpson published in *The Courier* (London) a series of open letters on the need to establish in this country a national system of education. These were addressed to the Marquess of Lansdowne, Lord President of the Council, who had on several occasions been called upon to speak in the House of Lords in defence of the government's policy of supporting the national system of education which had been set up in Ireland. In one letter, which bore the heading 'Current Objections to Impartial Religious Education Examined', Simpson claimed that attempts to provide schools acceptable to members of all denominations were by no means doomed to fail, and said that: 'The experiment had been made, and the end attained, not only in Holland, but, nearer home, in Liverpool.'[1] In another letter he wrote:

I need not inform your lordship[2] that the arrangement is in most successful operation in the excellent, but grievously misrepresented Corporation Schools of Liverpool. I had the happiness to witness the gratifying spectacle of large classes of pupils, in different parts of the establishment, surrounding the pastors of their own persuasion. . . . The largest group was of the Establishment and the Rev. Mr Aspinall was the instructor. . . . After visiting all the groups, Church, Dissenting, and Catholic, I witnessed the conclusion: all the pupils, without distinction of sect, assembled in one hall, and, before being dismissed, sang a hymn of praise to their common Creator. I should not envy the feelings of the man who could be present on such an occasion and stand unmoved.[3]

5

A few days after the last of James Simpson's open letters to him had been published, the Marquess of Lansdowne received Lord John Russell's *Letter to the Lord President of the Council*, in which Russell announced

[1] 2 February 1839.

[2] It may be noted that Lansdowne had been Chairman of the Select Committee of the House of Lords on the New Plan of Education in Ireland (1837); he had been in the chair when the Liverpool Corporation Schools had been referred to (*Report*, Vol. II, p. 946).

[3] 29 January 1839.

the government's decision to set up 'a Board or Committee for the consideration of all matters affecting the Education of the People', and suggested that the state might usefully establish a Normal School for the training of teachers. His reference to the policy to be adopted with regard to the giving of religious instruction was a guarded one: 'Much . . . may be effected by a temperate attention to the fair claims of the Established Church, and the religious freedom sanctioned by law. On this subject I need only say that it is Her Majesty's wish that the youth of this kingdom should be religiously brought up, and that the right of conscience should be respected.' Lansdowne's reply, it is interesting to note, was rather more forthright; after remarking that the establishment of a Normal School was of great importance, he went on:

I at the same time beg leave to state . . . the strong conviction which I entertain that it should be a positive condition of such an establishment, that it should be so regulated and provided with sufficient means to enable the teachers who are trained there, to acquire and to give such religious instruction as may be required at all ordinary schools in the principles of the Church of England, without any exclusion of those who may be connected with such other religious persuasions as are known to prevail amongst a considerable portion of the population of the country, who may be desirous of and should be enabled to receive similar instruction from their own ministers. . . . That such a regulation should be distinctly promulgated and understood appears to me indispensable for its success.[1]

At this critical moment, whilst James Simpson and the Liverpool Liberals were pointing out to the government the good results which had followed the adoption of the 'Irish System' in the Liverpool Corporation Schools, others were becoming anxious lest the Liberal Cabinet should attempt to establish in England a national system of education based on the Irish model. Thus on 9 February 1839 a meeting was held[2] in London of 'Members and Friends of the Church of England'; in the course of it the government was repeatedly warned not to attempt to introduce any scheme similar to that in force in Ireland. It was resolved:

That the various schemes of national education which have lately been pressed upon the attention of the Government, proposing by the exclusion of the peculiar doctrines of Christianity, to introduce a system of instruction which should be thoroughly unobjectionable, are vain, delusive, and fraught with divers evils; inasmuch as such schemes would either wholly fail in

[1] Sessional Papers, House of Commons (Correspondence between the Home Secretary and the Lord President of the Council), 1839, Vol. XLI, pp. 255 ff.
[2] Reported in The Times of 12 February 1839.

accomplishing their professed object, or, if successful, would only be so, by effecting the establishment of a system fundamentally irreligious, and incapable of being made the basis of sound moral instruction. That the experience which has already been gained, of the working of similar schemes, has shown that, in effect, they operate to withdraw the education of the people from the hands of the clergy,—its natural and appointed guardians,—and to entrust the public funds devoted to this purpose, chiefly and almost exclusively, to those whose main object is to injure and destroy the religious establishment of these realms.

Lord Teignmouth, M.P., who proposed this motion, said that: 'It had been intimated that next week some such scheme [as the 'Irish System'] would be propounded to the nation.' Lord Ashley, with that system obviously in mind, asked all friends of the Established Church to declare that they 'would never consent to any suppression or mutilation of the Scriptures'.

Curiously enough, no reference was made to that modified form of the 'Irish System' which had been adopted in the Liverpool Corporation Schools—and this in spite of the fact that among the speakers were the Rev. Francis Close of Cheltenham, whose heated dispute with Samuel Wilderspin on the subject of those schools has been recorded; Viscount Sandon, one of the Members of Parliament for Liverpool, in whose last election campaign the agitation concerning the schools had figured so largely; and even—as principal speaker of the meeting—the redoubtable Rev. Hugh M'Neile himself! That none of these men, at a meeting called largely in order to warn the government not to 'introduce' the 'Irish System' of education into England, should have cared to mention the fact, very well known to them, that a version of that system had already been so introduced by the Liverpool Council, seems worthy of note. The truth seems to have been that, by leaving no doubt that the Authorized Version was read in its schools within school hours, and by demonstrating that many Church of England parents were willing to send their children to the Corporation Schools, the Liverpool Education Committee had deprived its critics of some of their most effective arguments.[1]

There is no doubt that at this time Lord John Russell did seriously consider the possibility of inaugurating in England a national system of education similar to that established in Ireland. When, on 12

---

[1] The Rev. F. Close had written a little earlier: '. . . to Romish Priests and Unitarian Counsellors [sic] the education of the poor of Liverpool is committed, as far as the influence of the corporate body extends'; but he had stated that, because of 'the noble stand' which had been made against them, 'the Liverpool Inquisitors' had been compelled 'to modify the severity of their system a little' (National Education and Lord Brougham's Bill Considered . . . , pp. 13–14).

February 1839, he somewhat vaguely indicated in the House of Commons what the government policy on education was to be, he went out of his way to express the opinion that the 'Irish System' had proved successful in Ireland in spite of the difficulties which it had been called upon to face:

> In Ireland there was a very great and broad distinction between the one portion of the people and the other. They did not consent to read the Scriptures according to the same version; and those who belonged to one religion required a comment on the Bible, while the other party contended that no such comment ought to be used.[1] Indeed there existed such a wide difference between these parties, that it was undoubtedly extremely difficult to form any united system of education. At the same time, he thought that great success had attended the experiment.

He went on to point out that such a system ought to prove more readily acceptable in England than in Ireland:

> In England, on the contrary, the Roman Catholics did not form any very great portion of the population, and the only other sect which did not agree in the general reading of the Bible in schools receiving children of all denominations, was the sect of Unitarians.[2] Therefore, as far as religious distinctions were concerned, there was not the same difficulty in this country as in Ireland in forming an united system of education.

He stated, however, that he had consulted 'several persons who might be taken as representatives' of the Church of England, and that as a result of these consultations 'he certainly had come to the conclusion that it would be quite hopeless to endeavour to induce those who held such opinions to concur in any one united plan of education by

[1] The difficulties with which Russell had to contend were even greater than he believed them to be. Thus it was usually claimed that the Church of England favoured the reading of the Bible in schools 'without note or comment', and M'Neile, as we have seen, had stated that one of the most serious defects of the Irish *Scripture Lessons* was that they were provided with notes, in accordance with 'Romish practice'. Yet no less a person than the Archbishop of Canterbury, when he came to criticize the system adopted in the schools of the British and Foreign School Society, remarked: '. . . some persons there were who said that the children must have the Bible put into their hands without note or comment. Now if that were done it must be perfectly clear, whilst the sacred book was unaccompanied with such note or comment, that the schoolmaster, be he who he might, necessarily became the commentator . . . to give them an education as to their religious and moral duties by merely placing the Bible in the hands of children, and saying, "There, read and judge for yourselves" did appear to him to be the most perfect mockery he had ever heard of' (Speech at a meeting of the National Society for the Promotion of the Education of the Poor in the Principles of the Established Church, reported in *The Times*, 2 May 1839).

[2] According to the report of the speech given in the *Mirror of Parliament*, Russell here added the words 'who do not form a considerable number' (Vol. I, 1839, p. 172).

which the views, intentions, and wishes of all might be consulted'.[1] It was therefore not possible for the government to recommend the general adoption of the 'Irish System' in England, since

they must not act upon what, taking an abstract view of the case, they would conclude would be the result. They must take the objections as they found them, and he feared, from what had been stated to him, that they were insuperable.[2]

Those who had attended the House prepared to oppose vehemently any attempt on the part of the government to introduce into England a system in any way resembling the 'Irish System' of education were manifestly relieved on hearing Russell's speech; thus Sir Robert Inglis, the member for Oxford University, at once congratulated the Home Secretary on having 'abandoned formally what was called the joint and comprehensive[3] system of education, as inapplicable to England'.[4] It seemed that the efforts of the Liverpool Liberals to influence the education policy of the government had, after all, been made in vain: Russell had tested the strength of the opposition and had found it too formidable to be defied.

Yet at this time Russell was not content merely to point to the obstacles in the way of action: he seemed much more confident than he had been in the previous June that the government might now take at least some small steps towards improving the provision for education in the country. It is true that when the Committee of Council on Education was appointed by Order in Council on 10 April 1839 the powers entrusted to it were much less sweeping than Russell had at first proposed: it was instructed merely to 'superintend the application of any sums voted by parliament for the purpose of promoting public Education'. Nevertheless, it is interesting that two important principles

[1] It may be noted that the Bishop of London wrote in his diary, 22 January 1839: 'Went with the Archbishop to Lord John Russell about education: asserted the claims of the Church to conduct the education of the people' (*A Memoir of Charles James Blomfield, D.D., Bishop of London, with Selections from his Correspondence,* edited by his son, Alfred Blomfield, 2 vols., London, 1863, Vol. I, p. 260).

[2] Hansard, Third Series, Vol. XLV, Cols. 276–7.

[3] Strictly speaking, in the educational jargon of the time a 'comprehensive' school was one connected with some religious body but attended by children of other denominations who were permitted to withdraw when religious instruction was given; a school in which secular instruction only was given by the schoolmaster and the religious instruction was given by the clergy of the different denominations was said to have adopted the 'combined' system. (See F. Adams, *History of the Elementary School Contest in England,* pp. 98–9.) But in practice both words were often loosely used to describe any arrangement by which children of different denominations were educated in the same school.

[4] Hansard, Third Series, Vol. XLV, Col. 287.

were laid down and firmly adhered to in spite of considerable opposition: that the Committee of Council should consist entirely of laymen, there being no attempt to appoint representatives of the various religious sects, as Thomas Wyse had proposed; and that the Committee should not include independent, non-government members, as Lord Brougham had recommended. The arrangement thus favoured by Lord John Russell was one which he had been urged to adopt by Dr Kay[1] (later Sir James Kay-Shuttleworth), soon to be appointed Secretary of the Committee of Council; but it seems not unlikely that Russell was the more inclined to consider the arrangement a practicable one because of his knowledge of what had been achieved by the purely lay Education Committee in Liverpool.

However, it was Russell's proposal to set up a state school for the training of teachers of all denominations which must have given most satisfaction to the Liverpool Liberals, and which eventually most angered Russell's opponents. At first the latter seem not to have appreciated the full implications of Lord John's plan, although some suspicions were at once aroused by his reference, in his letter to the Lord President of the Council, to 'her Majesty's wish . . . that the right of conscience should be respected'. Indeed, it was some time before the details of the plan were made known; and meanwhile, in view of Russell's reluctant acknowledgment that the general introduction of any system of education resembling the 'Irish System' would meet with the determined hostility of the leaders of the Established Church, it seemed most unlikely that he would be prepared to face the difficulties which would certainly arise if he persisted with his plan to educate pupils of all denominations in one state Normal School. He had himself spoken of the 'Religious Problem' often enough, as we have seen; the leaders of the Church of England had just reminded him that the difficulties which it presented were 'insuperable'; and even friends and collaborators among the Dissenters of the British and Foreign School Society had advised him not to allow a government Board of Education to 'interfere in religious instruction' or 'to undertake the training of teachers'.

We now know that almost all of the arrangements relating to the proposed state Normal School were drawn up for the Committee of Council by the able and trusted Dr Kay, but that the system of religious instruction was *not* recommended to the Committee by him. Kay's biographer has said: 'It seems evident that the proposal was not Dr Kay's, for it is unlike the rest of his policy, and he claimed afterwards to have foretold and warned Ministers of its failure.'[2] It would have been

---

[1] F. Smith, *The Life and Work of Sir James Kay-Shuttleworth*, London, 1923, pp. 148-9.
[2] *Ibid.*, p. 84.

quite open to Russell, Lansdowne and the other members[1] of the Committee, as Kay pointed out later,[2] to have proposed the establishment of four *separate* Normal Schools for members of the Church of England, Wesleyan Methodists, Orthodox Congregational Dissenters (with members of the Society of Friends) and Roman Catholics. Yet in spite of the opposition certain to be encountered and the advice and warnings it had received, the Committee decided in April 1839 to set up a single Normal School, to 'include a Model School in which children of all ages from three to fourteen would be taught'; and the Minutes of the Committee show that at its first meeting it drew up regulations concerning the giving of religious instruction in the Normal and Model Schools which were strikingly similar to the regulations in force in the Liverpool Corporation Schools. They were as follows:

Religious Instruction in Model School.—Religious instruction to be considered as general and special.

General.—Religion to be combined with the whole matter of instruction, and to regulate the entire system of discipline.

Special.—Periods to be set apart for such peculiar doctrinal instruction as may be required for the religious training of the children.

Chaplain.—To appoint a chaplain to conduct the religious instruction of children whose parents or guardians belong to the Established Church.

Dissenters.—The parent or natural guardian of any other child to be permitted to secure the attendance of the licensed minister of his own persuasion, at the period appointed for special religious instruction, in order to give such instruction apart.

Licensed Minister.—To appoint a licensed minister to give such special religious instruction wherever the number of children in attendance at the Model School belonging to any religious body dissenting from the Established Church is such as to appear to this Committee to require such special provision.

Scriptures read daily in School.—A portion of every day to be devoted to the reading of the Scriptures in the School, under the general direction of the Committee, and superintendence of the Rector. Roman Catholics.— Roman Catholics, if their parents or guardians require it, to read their own version of the Scriptures, either at the time fixed for reading the Scriptures, or at the hours of special instruction.

---

[1] They were Viscount Duncannon, Lord Privy Seal, and T. Spring Rice, Chancellor of the Exchequer.

[2] *Recent Measures for the Promotion of Education in England*, Fifth Edition, London, 1839, p. 59. Kay himself, it would appear, wished to see established a system of education based on the policy of 'retaining the intimate connection of every school with a particular Church or congregation' without 'excluding the children of other faiths', there being 'State inspection, popular control [and] popular management' (F. Smith, *op. cit.*, p. 150 n.).

NORMAL SCHOOL

Chaplain to instruct Teachers belonging to Established Church.—The religious instruction of all candidate teachers connected with the Established Church to be committed to the Chaplain, and the special religious instruction to be committed (in any case in which a wish to that effect is expressed) to the licensed Minister of the religious persuasion of the candidate teacher, who is to attend the school at stated periods, to assist and examine the candidate teachers in their reading on religious subjects, and to afford them spiritual advice.

It will be seen that, as in the Liverpool Corporation Schools, arrangements were to be made to educate together members of all denominations; to provide 'general' religious education acceptable to all and also to allow 'special' or denominational instruction to be given to the various sects by their respective ministers; to permit the reading of a version of the Bible acceptable to Roman Catholics, as well as of the Authorized Version; and all this to take place upon the school premises and in school hours. There was one difference between the modified form of the 'Irish System' in force in the Liverpool schools and the plan drawn up for the religious instruction of those who would attend the proposed Normal and Model Schools: in these latter there was to be a chaplain who would be a Church of England clergyman; he was not, of course, to interfere with the denominational religious instruction of Dissenters.

It is not difficult to see what policy the Committee of Council intended to pursue. Some years later Dr Kay observed in a letter to Lord John Russell that at this period (1839) the government had made up its mind to 'assert the claims of the civil power to the control of the education of the country', to 'vindicate the rights of conscience' and to 'lay the foundation of a system of combined education in which the young might be brought up in charity with each other, rather than in hostile camps for future strife'.[1] Russell's inquiries had shown him that a national system of education based on schools each of which was open to children of all denominations would be bitterly opposed by the leaders of the clergy of the Established Church; and obviously such a system could not be put into operation, however strongly the government might support it, if most of the Church of England clergy simply refused to give religious instruction in the schools. But Russell and his fellow-members of the Committee of Council might at least hope to establish *one* educational institution for pupils of all denominations, and then to ride out the storm which they well knew would inevitably

---

[1] F. Smith, *op. cit.*, p. 148.

follow, trusting that they would have the support of most of the Dissenters, and no doubt seeking to demonstrate eventually that the lay members of the Church of England were not so hostile to the policy favoured by the government as their leading clergymen had declared themselves to be.

In other words, the Committee of Council were preparing to undertake precisely the same task as that which had faced the Liverpool Education Committee three years before, when the representatives of the local Church of England clergy had made it clear that they would oppose the attempt to make the Corporation Schools available to children of all sects. We know that, of the members of the Committee of Council, Russell and Lansdowne, at least, were well aware of what had been happening in Liverpool, and had every reason to believe that the Liverpool Education Committee had succeeded in that task. It seems reasonable to suggest that the Committee of Council, when it decided to adopt a policy so similar to that pursued in the Corporation Schools, might well have been encouraged, if not inspired, to do so by the success which appeared to have attended the Liverpool experiment.

6

Meanwhile, during the six months following Lord John Russell's visit to the town, all had gone well with the Corporation Schools in Liverpool. Soon after the visit the annual municipal elections took place (November 1838), and even during that exciting period comparatively few references to the schools were made in public speeches and editorials. True, the *Liverpool Standard* denied that 'the school question' was 'set at rest for ever' and proclaimed that it 'never would be so until the Irish System' was 'banished from the Corporation Schools';[1] but other grievances were given much greater prominence; moreover, of the allusions made to the schools almost all took the form of abuse rather than of reasoned objections. Thus the schools were described as 'Popish seminaries',[2] and a member of the Gladstone family

. . . spoke strongly against the introduction of the Irish system of education, which was attempted to be introduced into general use in England through Liverpool, and which was calculated to sap and undermine the Protestant church establishment . . . he hoped that [his hearers] would by sending Conservative members into the council, prevent the Popish system of education from creeping through Liverpool into general and insidious use in the country.[3]

[1] *Liverpool Standard*, 26 October 1838.
[2] *Ibid.*, 30 October 1838.
[3] *Ibid.*, 9 November 1838.

But in general only the most half-hearted attempts were made to treat the 'Schools Question' as an election issue. The results of the elections showed that of the seventeen seats available the Conservatives had obtained six[1] and the Liberals eleven. Since only two of the retiring councillors had been Conservatives, the number of Conservative councillors was, as a consequence of the elections, increased by four; but this did not seriously perturb the Liberals, since the seats they were defending on this occasion were the last of those originally won in the landslide election of 1835 and some losses were to have been expected. The Liberal councillors now numbered thirty and the Conservative councillors eighteen; in addition, the Liberals had the support of sixteen aldermen. The *Liverpool Mercury*[2] considered that the result of the election 'taking all circumstances into consideration' was 'perfectly satisfactory' to the Liberals; and the Liberal *Albion*[3] remarked: 'The Municipal elections, running as they do, year after year, in the same current, are beginning to convince all waverers and trimmers that the hope of a Tory Town Council has set for ever.' The Conservatives had to be content to point out that their numbers in the Council were steadily, if slowly, rising; whilst Thomas Blackburn proclaimed to the Liberals that in the contest over the schools '. . . with the exception of a sixpenny snarl from Fielding Ould,[4] and an occasional growl from the lion of St Jude's, they had completely triumphed over all their opponents'.[5] He might have added that a new critic had begun to make himself heard: one Rev. D. James of Kirkdale had written to the local Press to proclaim that those councillors who supported the policy adopted in the Corporation Schools had 'forfeited their claim to Christian communion' and would be confronted 'at the great day of final retribution' by the children 'now ruined by the anti-Christian system' in force in the schools.[6] Such attacks now seemed of little importance and were not taken very seriously by those criticized.

In the two previous years, when the Town Council had assembled after the election results had been declared, the proposal had been made that the Corporation Schools should be sold; but at the corresponding meeting in November 1838 no such proposal was forthcoming; and indeed the Liberals now felt strong enough to contemplate

---

[1] For one of these James Lawrence, formerly a Liberal, was returned unopposed as a Conservative. (Since no fewer than five candidates were returned unopposed, it is not possible to make any useful comparisons with the percentages of votes cast for the two parties in previous elections.)

[2] 2 November 1838.

[3] 31 December 1838.

[4] An allusion to Ould's pamphlet concerning his correspondence with Cæsar Otway.

[5] *Liverpool Mercury*, 30 November 1838.

[6] *The Albion*, 24 December 1838.

building additional Corporation Schools in furtherance of the policy, originally advocated by William Rathbone in 1836, of establishing schools 'in every district' of the town. On 2 January 1839 the Liverpool Council passed the following resolution:

That this Council cannot reflect upon the depraved and degraded state of a large portion of the children of the working classes in this Town without feeling itself called upon to use its most strenuous exertions to ameliorate their condition: that in the opinion of this Council the most effectual means of accomplishing this end is to give their children the opportunity of obtaining a moral and religious education and that any surplus of the Corporate funds cannot be employed in a manner more noble or more conducive to the public welfare than in the furtherance of this object: that the Education Committee be therefore requested to take this subject into consideration and to report to the Council in what parts of the Town Schools are required, especially infant schools, to recommend situations for the same, and to obtain estimates of the cost of such buildings.[1]

The mover was Alderman Earle, who observed that 'it would be a proud thing for Liverpool if they introduced a general and effective system of education'. He pointed out that the government would gladly establish such a system but were 'fettered by the prejudices of the intolerant'; the members of the Liverpool Town Council, on the other hand, 'were free from those prejudices, and they could establish schools on the admirable system already adopted'. This was challenging the opposition with a vengeance, yet the response of the Conservatives was remarkably mild. David Hodgson (formerly a Liberal and a Quaker) moved that in the proposed new schools there should be 'a free, open and unrestricted system of Scriptural education', but refused to be drawn when asked whether that description did not apply to the system in force in the existing Corporation Schools. Isaac Holmes (also a convert to Conservatism and the Church of England) and Joseph Cooper were more forthright in expressing disapproval of that system; but there was little effective opposition, and it was finally resolved by thirty-seven votes to sixteen 'That the schools to be erected shall be conducted on the same system of open free and unrestricted Scriptural instruction adopted in those Schools already supported by this Council.'[2]

The Education Committee wasted no time: on 30 January 1839 the sub-committees concerned with the two Corporation Schools were asked to make inquiries in all of the sixteen wards of the town 'in order to ascertain what Schools now exist in those Wards and what number of Children are educated in them, and what additional Schools are

[1] *Proceedings of Council*, Vol. XVIII, p. 135.
[2] *Proceedings of Education Committee*, Vol. I, p. 91.

required and to fix upon situations for the same'.[1] Evidently the sub-committees recommended that a Corporation School should be established in each ward, since the minutes of the Education Committee record that on 5 March 1839 it was decided 'That the Reports concerning the building of a School in each of the Wards be referred to a Sub-Committee consisting of Mr Earle, Mr Harvey and Mr Sheil [a Roman Catholic], and that they be requested to prepare for this Committee a digest of the Reports, and to recommend situations where Schools are wanted.'[2] Meanwhile arrangements had been made to increase the accommodation at the North School by adding another storey to the infant school, thus making a school-room available for a further seventy or eighty children.[3]

Even the news that the Council was considering the establishment of at least fourteen additional Corporation Schools seems to have aroused little determined opposition in the town. On 25 February 1839 a meeting of the Liverpool Conservative Operative Association was addressed by the Rev. D. James and others on the subject of 'the evils of Popery'. At the conclusion of the meeting it was decided to address to the Town Council a petition relating to the proposal to establish new Corporation Schools.[4] On 4 March a further meeting, which 'persons friendly to Scriptural Education' were invited to attend, was held, with the purpose of forwarding 'the Object of the Education Petition' of what were now described as 'the Operative Protestants'. The Rev. Hugh M'Neile was in the chair: so far as can be ascertained he had said little about the Corporation Schools for a considerable time, and on this occasion his speech was, for him, remarkably restrained.[5] The 'memorial' subsequently presented to the Council (6 March 1839) stated that the petitioners had been compelled on conscientious grounds to withdraw their children from the existing Corporation Schools and had heard with dismay that the Council intended to build additional schools from which their children would be excluded: they suggested that it would be fair if the Council, having provided for those who wished their children to attend 'non-scriptural Schools', should now provide for those who preferred to send their children to 'Scriptural Schools'. It was suggested that the additional schools should be made available to the children of parents in the latter category.[6]

When the petition was discussed in Council, the Conservative support for the petitioners was not particularly strong, although one speaker, Isaac Holmes, suggested that 'schools paid for by a Protestant

[1] *Ibid.*, Vol. I, p. 93.   [2] *Ibid.*, Vol. I, p. 95.
[3] *Liverpool Mercury*, 8 February 1839.   [4] *Liverpool Standard*, 26 February 1839.
[5] *Ibid.*, 5 March 1839.   [6] *Proceedings of Council*, Vol. XVIII, p. 156.

Council' ought not to 'propagate Popish notions', and remarked that if the Council 'were determined to carry on the schools on the present system they ought to withdraw all sorts of catechisms'; or if they allowed the schools 'to be given to the Roman Catholics', they 'ought to build new ones for the Protestants'. The Liberal spokesmen, on the other hand, replied to the petitioners with considerable vigour, pointing out that the Corporation Schools were in every sense 'Scriptural Schools', that numbers of the 2,030 signatures were not above suspicion, and that far more operatives (including bachelors) claimed to have been obliged to withdraw children from the schools than could possibly have had children attending them. The Education Committee's formal reply was a minor masterpiece of confident irony.

At this juncture, just when it appeared that opposition to the Education Committee's policy might once more become important, and when the Committee must have been most anxious that nothing should occur to make Lord John Russell feel that the issue of the Liverpool experiment was in doubt, the opponents of the Committee suffered a damaging blow. In February 1839 one Dr Sleigh was made editor of the *Liverpool Standard*, a newspaper which, as will have been seen, was among the most vehement and abusive critics of the policy pursued in the Corporation Schools, and a fervent admirer of the Rev. Hugh M'Neile. Sleigh was an ultra-Conservative speaker and writer who seems to have made his first appearance in Liverpool in the previous October, when he delivered a series of lectures in which he undertook to prove 'that *republicanism* necessarily leads to *tyranny*, and is in direct opposition to the laws of nature and of nature's God; . . . that in proportion as the *elective franchise* is increased among the poor, their liberty and happiness are diminished; that *vote by ballot* . . . is demoralizing in its very nature, and a disgrace to any civilised nation'.[1] He was clearly well suited to become editor of the *Liverpool Standard*.

As soon as he was appointed he began to wield his pen with great energy. It was with something approaching horror that he heard that the Bible was excluded from the Corporation Schools, especially as he naturally failed to understand the somewhat esoteric sense in which M'Neile and some of his followers used the term 'excluded'. He was particularly moved when he read the petition of the Protestant Operatives ('drawn up at a public meeting of which a highly respectable Clergyman was chairman') complaining that the petitioners had been obliged to withdraw their children from the 'unscriptural' Corporation Schools. Full of fiery indignation, Sleigh wrote a number of eloquent editorials denouncing the Liverpool Liberals who supported

[1] Quoted in *Liverpool Mercury*, 26 October 1838.

such schools; but on one occasion (19 March 1839), after writing a very scathing article, he read in the Liberal *Albion* an extract from a letter in which William Rathbone 'unequivocally declared that the Bible was not only *not excluded from*, but actually *taught in*, the Corporation Schools'. Since he had already formed a very high opinion of Rathbone, Sleigh was puzzled, and at once added to his article a paragraph in which he announced that in view of Rathbone's statement he would visit the Corporation Schools, and if he found that he had been mistaken about the schools he would 'forthwith acknowledge the error . . . and cheerfully apologise for the same'.

To his astonishment, when his editorial appeared in print, he found that this final paragraph 'HAD BEEN STRICKEN OUT!' at the order of the proprietors of the newspaper,[1] and he at once ceased to be employed by the *Liverpool Standard*. On being reminded by the Liberals 'that the public expected, and were anxiously waiting for, a fulfilment of the promise made by him . . . that he would visit the Corporation Schools, judge for himself, and publish the result', Sleigh kept his word, and published a short pamphlet in which he gave an account of what he saw when he inspected the schools; writing, he said, 'as a man of honor and a Christian' he retracted 'most sincerely, all he ever said or wrote derogatory to the character of those Schools, *so far as the exclusion of the Bible be concerned*, and their general tendency'.[2] The reaction of the proprietors of the *Liverpool Standard* was not without its humorous side: in reply to Sleigh's statement that he did not become editor of the paper 'for the purpose of defending TORIES, and repudiating WHIGS and RADICALS, "*right* or *wrong*",'[3] they observed that it would be absurd to expect proprietors of newspapers, Liberal or Conservative, 'to intrust the editorial controul of their respective journals into the hands of parties *without any fixed principles* in politics'.[4]

Naturally the Liberal newspapers of the town made the most of Sleigh's published statements, and although the Conservative Press blustered somewhat vigorously, there was no doubt that Sleigh's one-month reign as editor did at least as much to help the Education Committee as the editors of the Liberal newspapers had been able to do in several years of political campaigning. Thus it was that in April 1839,

---

[1] *A Visit to the Corporation Schools in Liverpool (April 1839)*, Liverpool, 1839, p. 5. The proprietors of the *Liverpool Standard* subsequently explained that the paragraph referred to had been omitted because they did not wish Sleigh to 'make a fool of himself' by confessing '*his utter ignorance on the subject on which he had just been writing so confidently*' (*Liverpool Standard*, 30 April 1839).

[2] *A Visit to the Corporation Schools . . .*, p. 6.

[3] *Ibid.*, p. 4.

[4] *Liverpool Standard*, 30 April 1839.

when the Committee of Council began to formulate detailed proposals for its projected Normal and Model Schools, the triumph of the Liverpool Education Committee seemed to be almost complete; and there appeared to be every reason to suppose that it would not be long before the Liverpool Committee was in a position to begin establishing in the town what Alderman Earle had described as 'a general and effective system of education'.

7

It has been noted that one Church of England clergyman, the Rev. James Aspinall, had from the first supported the Liverpool Education Committee by giving religious instruction in one of the Corporation Schools, and by defending the Committee on several occasions against its numerous critics. Aspinall, it will be remembered, had been one of the speakers at the dinner given in honour of Lord John Russell in October 1838; his contribution towards the success of the schools had been referred to by James Simpson in one of his open letters to the Marquess of Lansdowne in January 1839. It is surely not without significance that Aspinall was, in May 1839, on the recommendation of Lord Melbourne,[1] appointed to the 'very handsome living'[2] of Althorpe in Lincolnshire: if there had been any doubt as to why the Prime Minister should select for preferment this hitherto little-known Liverpool clergyman, it would have been removed by the terms of the resolution passed by the Liverpool Town Council on 7 June 1839:

That this Council have learnt with much satisfaction that Her Most Gracious Majesty has been pleased to present the Rectory of Althorpe in Lincolnshire to the Reverend James Aspinall of this Town, a reward to which they consider him justly entitled for the exemplary manner in which he has discharged the sacred duties of his calling and the truly christianlike spirit he has evinced towards those who conscientiously differ from him on religious subjects.

[1] *The Albion*, 14 December 1840.
[2] *Liverpool Mercury*, 24 May 1839.

Chapter 9

RUSSELL'S PLAN AND
THE LIVERPOOL EXPERIMENT

1

I<small>T</small> was in April 1839 that the newly formed Committee of Council
on Education drew up the regulations designed to ensure that in the
proposed Normal and Model Schools appropriate religious instruction
should be given to pupils of all denominations: less than two months
later the Committee was obliged to inform the Queen that since it had
experienced 'so much difficulty in reconciling conflicting views respecting the provisions . . . that the children and teachers . . . should be
duly trained in the principles of the Christian religion, while the rights
of conscience should be respected', it would have to 'postpone taking
any steps' towards setting up the schools 'until greater concurrence of
opinion [was] found to prevail'.[1] On the day after this pronouncement
was made, Lord John Russell personally acknowledged defeat when he
informed the House of Commons (4 June 1839) 'that it was not the
intention of the Government to persist in the proposal to found the
normal school'.[2] The question at once arises: why did Lord John Russell and his colleagues fail so completely and so ignominiously quickly
in their attempt to achieve what the Liverpool Liberals appeared to have
accomplished as the result of an experiment which by this time had
been carried on for very nearly three years?

2

Some of the reasons are not very hard to find. There was, to begin
with, the fact that the Church of England was more strongly represented in the country as a whole than it was in Liverpool: as Lord
Brougham pointed out at this time, 'The dissenters . . . have much to
say in some of the large towns, especially those of recent growth; in the
counties their numbers and influence are extremely small.'[3] Again, the

[1] *Minutes of the Committee of Council on Education . . . 1839–1840*, London, 1840,
p. vii.
[2] Hansard, Third Series, Vol. XLVII, Col. 1381.
[3] *A Letter on National Education to the Duke of Bedford*, Edinburgh and London, 1839,
pp. 26–7.

Liberals of Liverpool had begun their experiment very soon after gaining control of the Town Council, at a time when they had an overwhelming majority and were in a position, therefore, to weather the first violent storms of opposition aroused by their decision to open the Corporation Schools to children of all sects; whereas when Lord John Russell and his colleagues published the details of their plan there was every indication that the Liberal administration might come to an end, almost unmourned, at any moment[1]—it was 'so weak and feeble as absolutely to be struggling for [its] political existence'[2]—and in fact the Cabinet resigned a few weeks later, resuming office only because of the Conservatives' dispute with the Queen over the 'Bedchamber Question'.

Moreover, the Liberals had come to power in Liverpool in 1835, when 'Reform' was still the watchword of the day, when even some of their bewildered and discouraged opponents were, like the Rev. Augustus Campbell, 'prepared to submit to change', since they realized, 'from the different constitution of the local government', that 'things could not go on under the old system';[3] but by 1839, on the other hand, the Liberal Cabinet had disappointed its supporters and encouraged the Conservatives by appearing to have lost the reforming zeal which it had once possessed. Indeed, as we have noted, Lord John Russell had on more than one occasion indicated that the government was unable to take any step towards establishing a national system of education, so formidable was the opposition to it likely to be; and the plan which he now put forward was, after all, a modified and small-scale version of a system which, only a few months earlier, he had regretfully declared himself unable to adopt—so that it was not surprising that the Bishop of London should now remind him that 'not long ago the noble Lord had declared that any such system as this was wholly impracticable'.[4]

We have observed that in Liverpool the opposition to the policy adopted in the Corporation Schools had, during the first years, been based almost entirely on the allegations that the system involved the exclusion and mutilation of the 'Protestant Bible' and encouraged the propagation of 'Popish' beliefs. After 1835 very little indeed had been

---

[1] Rathbone wrote to his son, William Rathbone (6th) on 3 April 1839: 'We are not going on well here in politics. Ministers are divided among themselves and the masses are very indifferent as to their continuance in office—probably before you get back the Tories will be in office' (*Rathbone Family Papers*).

[2] Lord Stanley (Hansard, Third Series, Vol. XLVIII, Col. 234).

[3] See p. 44.

[4] Hansard, Third Series, Vol. XLVII, Col. 762. Peel made the same point (*ibid.*, Vol. XLVIII, Col. 679).

heard of the claim that the Church of England ought to be granted a privileged position in the municipal schools, and it seems to have been fairly generally agreed, sometimes perhaps reluctantly, that the members of the Church could no longer expect to receive more favourable treatment from the Town Council than was accorded to Protestants as a whole. Indeed, there had been times, as has been pointed out, when even such an extremist as the Rev. H. M'Neile had been prepared to accept the possibility of municipal funds being made available even for Roman Catholic schools. In the country as a whole some members of the Established Church had genuinely welcomed the decision of the government in 1833 to distribute its grants in aid of the establishment of schools through both the National and the British and Foreign Societies, without favouring the one or the other; whilst others who had certainly not welcomed the decision had gradually come to accept it, so that they might have echoed the words of the Rev. H. Stowell when he said, in 1837:

Let us not be misunderstood in speaking approvingly of the Parliamentary grants, as though we regarded them with unmingled satisfaction; we do not hesitate to avow, that no plan of National Education would fully satisfy us, except it were to be conducted by the National Church; and this, spite of obloquy, would only be consistent in a nation upholding and acknowledging an ecclesiastical establishment as the queen and consort of the state. Still, in the existing position of affairs, the measure adopted by the government is perhaps the best, because the only practicable measure.[1]

But with surprising rapidity the atmosphere in Liverpool and elsewhere had begun to change, and the attitude of many members of the Church of England had hardened: from about 1838 the claim was heard much more frequently than in the immediately preceding years that the Established Church should occupy a privileged position within the general educational system of the country. It was quite often suggested, indeed, that the Church should in some sense superintend any national system of education which the government might introduce. It has often been said, with much justification, that this renewed insistence of the Church on what it believed to be its rights arose largely from the influence of the Oxford Movement, which 'created an influential group opposed to State control of education';[2] but it needs to be emphasized that very different forces were also at work, making many influential churchmen who regarded the Oxford Movement with deep suspicion yet feel that the Church should more vigorously assert its power in the state. We have seen how the meetings held in Manchester,

---

[1] *A Second Letter to the Inhabitants of Manchester* . . . , pp. 15–16.
[2] F. Smith, *The Life and Work of Sir James Kay-Shuttleworth*, p. 76.

Salford, Cheltenham and elsewhere to advocate the establishment of a national system of education had alarmed numbers of the Church of England clergy, and induced them to react in ways which had made them conscious of the strength of the support on which they could rely. Many churchmen who had made concessions to those of other faiths, more or less with good grace, began to feel that they would soon be called upon to concede far too much.

It must be added that the influence of the Protestant Association at this time has not been sufficiently recognized: whilst it is true that most of the Church of England clergy looked askance at the Association's activities, the many branches of the Association in different parts of the country provided platforms for eloquent, able and sincere men of the calibre of M'Neile, Stowell and Colquhoun, whose speeches were usually reported in great detail in local newspapers, and therefore made available to many who would have hesitated to attend the meetings. It must be remembered that it was from the accounts of such men as these that large numbers of people had learnt of the national system of education in Ireland[1] and of the state of affairs in the Corporation Schools in Liverpool;[2] it is therefore not surprising that by 1839 many churchmen all over the country were on their guard to prevent the development of similar systems in England, being convinced that the concessions which they had already made had merely led them to the edge of a dangerous slope from which the time had come to retrace their steps.

Moreover, one should not forget that most of the objections raised by responsible churchmen against earlier plans designed to make it possible for children of all denominations to be educated together had been taken carefully into account by the Liverpool Education Committee and the Committee of Council; the very success of these bodies in meeting the objections hitherto most discussed brought churchmen face to face with an issue which a fairly widespread movement in favour of toleration had made it seem desirable to avoid: within a state system of education was the Church of England prepared permanently to accept equality of status with all other Christian denominations—including, in the last resort, even Roman Catholicism? Many members of the Church of England in Liverpool had signified

---

[1] See, e.g., J. C. Colquhoun's The System of Education in Ireland: Its Principle and Practice, Cheltenham, 1838.

[2] Thus at a meeting in Sheffield a passing allusion to M'Neile's going 'into the schoolroom' with the Bible in his hand to cry 'No Popery' was at once understood and greeted with loud cheers (The Substance of Two Speeches Delivered at the General Meeting of the Sheffield Reformation and Protestant Association . . . , Nov. 13th 1839 by the Rev. Robert J. M'Ghee and the Rev. Hugh M'Neill [sic], Sheffield [n.d.], p. 33).

their readiness to accept such a situation, and elsewhere the Bishop of Norwich was not alone even among the clergy in wishing to see children of all sects educated together on equal terms. But it was not to be wondered at if large numbers even of fair-minded churchmen felt it difficult to grant to members of all denominations as a right what might have been accorded as an act of grace, or if many began to fear for the continued existence of the Church of England as the Established Church of the realm.

3

It has already been shown that when Lord John Russell and his colleagues on the Committee of Council drew up their plans for the establishment and regulation of the Normal and Model Schools, they knew well enough that they would meet with determined opposition from almost all of the clergy of the Established Church; if Russell had learnt nothing more from his visit to Liverpool he could not have avoided learning what the clergy were likely to think of such a scheme as that now proposed. For one particular argument the Committee was well prepared. No one reading accounts of the parliamentary debates on the Committee's proposals can fail to notice that, however conciliatory Russell and Lansdowne were when replying to other arguments, each spoke with the boldness of a man sure of the weakness of his adversary's case when it came to resisting the demand that the Church should control any national system of education which might be set up.[1] Both clearly felt that such a claim was politically absurd, and that in their resistance to it they could afford to be quite dogmatic, since they would be supported by large numbers of their countrymen. Unfortunately for them, however, their stand did not automatically win them the support of all the Protestant Dissenters, and that for two important reasons.

It seems fair to say that some historians of this period have tended to devote far too much attention to the more extreme demands of such men as Archdeacon Denison, F. D. Maurice[2] and W. E. Gladstone, whose proposals were comprehensive, attractively simple, but scarcely typical of those seriously put forward by responsible leaders of the Church or by such men as Peel among the political opponents of the Liberals. It is true, of course, that some intolerant churchmen

---

[1] See, e.g., Hansard, Third Series, Vol. XLV, Col. 278, and Vol. XLVIII, Cols. 656, 1256.

[2] See, e.g., F. Smith, *The Life of Sir James Kay-Shuttleworth*; F. Adams, *History of the Elementary School Contest in England*, London, 1882.

were to be found making the most extravagant claims. It would be possible to quote from contemporary speeches and pamphlets many declarations similar to that made by *The Times*: 'We would not merely say, though it be critically true, that the church of England has a right to the education of the people, exclusive of teachers of other sects, but that the people of England have a right to be educated by ministers of the Church of England, to the exclusion of teachers from alien sects.'[1] Lord Ashley, again, maintained that 'The State adopted the Church of England as the true Church, and if it did not enforce her tenets in education, it had no right to countenance others . . . if the State did not teach truth, it was far better that it should not teach anything at all'.[2] Sir R. Inglis informed the government that 'those holding office, and in possession of political power, were bound to exercise that power for the promotion of their belief, and not for the encouragement or advancement of anything which they disbelieved, or conceived to be erroneous'.[3] Mr Gladstone[4] claimed that the State 'had a conscience and could not be neutral in matters affecting religion'.[5] It was even suggested from time to time that all but a relatively few Dissenters would willingly send their children to Church schools if the government would assist the Church to provide such schools in sufficient numbers.[6]

But far more often the claims of the Church were put forward in terms which made it possible for the speakers to arouse the enthusiasm of churchmen without necessarily alienating all Dissenters by manifestly overstepping the bounds set by contemporary ideas on toleration.

[1] 21 June 1839.

[2] Hansard, Third Series, Vol. XLVIII, Col. 279.

[3] *Ibid.*, Col. 606.

[4] *Ibid.*, Col. 631.

[5] It would appear that the state's conscience was conceived as having a certain degree of elasticity. Among what he called '*Secret Political Memoranda*,' written by Gladstone at about this time, is the following note on the system of education which the state was supporting in Ireland: 'I said the value of a joint Education was so great that as long as there was any hope of giving effect to the original idea I would suspend condemnation although I saw much that was objectionable in the working of the system' (*Add. MSS.* 44819). Two years earlier, indeed, Gladstone had written a memorandum on Irish National Education with the purpose of suggesting modifications to the 'Irish System'; he had proposed, *inter alia*, to allow the reading of the Scriptures 'either in the authorized or Douay version, but without note or comment', and to make the reading of the much-criticized 'extracts' from the Bible compulsory for those who did not attend the 'Scriptural Readings'. A note made on the memorandum shows that it was read by 'Dr Elrington, Dean Murray, The Primate, The Bp of Exeter, Serjeant Jackson' (*Add. MSS.* 44727).

[6] See, e.g., the Rev. A. Campbell, *A Speech on the Subject of National Education . . .* , p. 15; the Rev. R. Burgess, *What May This System of National Education Be? An Inquiry Recommended to the Clergy of the Established Church*, London, 1838; *The Times* (leader), 3 June 1839.

Thus, when the Rev. Augustus Campbell spoke on the subject in Liverpool on 3 April 1839, he remarked that if 'a scheme of national education' could be carried on at all in England it 'should be in connexion at least with the established church'—otherwise he could not see how it would be 'national education'; but he added: 'To those who dissent from the establishment because they cannot conscientiously conform to it, we grudge no civil privileges, rights, or immunities . . . we value liberty of conscience quite as much as they do, and are as anxious to extend the benefits of it to the whole community as they are themselves.'[1] A little earlier the Rev. Francis Close had written: 'We will . . . call upon the clergy and laity of the Established Church to assert the great principle of that Church, as established in these realms, and to repudiate altogether the idea of *any national system of education* which is not connected with the Church and under her direction and control'; but he had claimed that this attitude did not involve oppression, and had said that no steps ought to be taken to 'withhold from the British and Foreign School Society, or from any *Scriptural School* assistance from public funds'.[2] Similarly the Bishop of London, at a meeting held in London, said: 'We say that the Church is the authorised and recognised organ and instrument of NATIONAL EDUCATION in its largest sense in this country'; he went on to say, however, that the Church of England clergy did not 'assert an empire over the conscience' of those not within their communion or 'presume to interfere' with Dissenters in the education of their own children.[3]

In the House of Lords on 5 July 1839 the same speaker remarked:

I do not claim for the Church the right of educating any other children than those of her own communion. I do maintain that she is, by the constitution of the country, the established and recognised organ of religious education; and she ought to have sufficient means for the discharge of her functions. If there be any . . . who refuse to accept the education we offer them, let them seek instruction according to their own views and methods. Let them even be assisted by the State, if the necessity should arise; but let it be done by way of charity to the dissidents from our Church, not as a matter of right: at all events let it not be done so as to make it appear to the people that the Government withholds its confidence from the Church.

In a series of carefully qualified statements he indicated that it was chiefly because the government plan was calculated to weaken the

[1] Rev. A. Campbell, *A Speech on the Subject of National Education Delivered at a Public Meeting in Liverpool on the 3rd April, 1839*, Liverpool [n.d.], pp. 5–6.

[2] Rev. F. Close, *National Education and Lord Brougham's Bill Considered . . .* , Cheltenham, 1838, pp. 55–8.

[3] *Speech of the Lord Bishop of London on National Education . . . on May 28, 1839*, London [n.d.], pp. 10–11.

Church that he disapproved of it, and he asked why the government might not continue 'at least for some time to come' to distribute grants through the National and British and Foreign Societies. This suggestion he further qualified with the remark: 'I do not mean to say, that the principle involved in that system is free from objection; or that it is altogether consistent with those which I have laid down. But almost all theories, when reduced to practice, must in some cases give way to unforeseen necessity, so long as no vital nor essential principle is compromised.'[1] A statement of the Bishop of Exeter further illustrates the somewhat confused and confusing claims made at this time: '. . . he was not of opinion that the Church had a right to claim the enforcement of any system of education on the people at large, least of all on that part of the people which did not belong to it. But the Church had a right to demand of the State . . . the means of offering education to them all, no matter whether they belonged to the Church or not.'[2]

The government decision to abandon the plan of establishing a Normal School, to throw 'one of our children to the wolf',[3] as Russell put it later, was taken partly as the result of the protests made at an important meeting held in London on 28 May 1839 of members and friends of the National Society; here a resolution was carried unanimously: 'That it is an object of the highest national importance to provide, that instruction in the truths and precepts of Christianity should form an essential part of every system of education of the people at large; and that such instruction should be under the superintendence of the clergy, and in conformity with the doctrines of the church of this realm, as the recognized teacher of religion.'[4] The meeting at which this sweeping claim was made was presided over by the Archbishop of Canterbury himself; but when he came to speak in the Lords he made a very mild demand indeed: 'As to their [the Established clergy's] arrogating to themselves the education of the people, all that they desired was, that the education of the children of the parents among their flocks who were attached to the Church might not be taken out of their hands.' He stated that the Church 'had never advanced any pretention' to controlling 'all the education of the country', and 'appealed in confirmation of his statement to the conduct of the clergy in general'. He was not, however, prepared to say 'that injudicious language might not have been occasionally used upon this subject'.[5]

This diversity of the claims made on behalf of the Church was

---

[1] Hansard, Third Series, Vol. XLVIII, Cols. 1306, 1307.
[2] Ibid., Col. 1275.
[3] Recollections and Suggestions, 1813–1873, London, 1875, p. 374.
[4] The Times, 29 May 1839.
[5] Hansard, Third Series, Vol. XLVIII, Cols. 1235, 1241.

a source of considerable strength to the Establishment, since it cor-
responded to, and arose naturally from, the wide diversity of opinion
within the Church itself, at this time of transition, as to its proper role
in the state. During the campaign against the policy adopted by the
Education Committee in Liverpool, many responsible members of
the Church of England had been repelled by the manifestly wild and
intolerant charges made against respected members of the Town
Council—that such councillors wished to propagate 'Popery', for
instance, and to exclude the Bible from the Corporation Schools. It had
not been difficult for a powerful Liberal majority to withstand these
accusations until the statements had been shown to be false and most
of the critics who made them had been reduced to silence. But the
Committee of Council now was faced with a form of opposition
capable of winning support from almost all shades of opinion in the
Church, and one extremely difficult to combat, since the general claim
that the rights of the Church should be respected embraced in fact so
many different demands, some of which no reasonable man could find
objectionable.

Moreover, those Dissenters, such as the Wesleyan Methodists, who
were normally fairly well-disposed towards the Church and inclined
to regard Roman Catholicism as a growing menace, were more easily
persuaded to support the Church in opposing the Committee's plan[1]
than they would have been if all of those who spoke on behalf of the
Church had adopted the uncompromising tones employed by some
of its members. Since the more responsible leaders of the Church of
England clergy and of the Conservative Party were agreed that the
Protestant Dissenters should continue to receive government grants
through the British and Foreign School Society, it was easy for some
of those Dissenters to feel that the Church of England was, after all,
a safer ally than the Church of Rome.

On the other hand, of course, many of the Dissenters resented what
they considered to be the arrogant claims of the Established Church,
and the Committee of Council probably hoped to win the same degree
of support from some of these as the Liverpool Education Committee
had obtained from many of the Liverpool Dissenters. Indeed, before

---

[1] At a meeting in London on 21 May 1839 representatives of the Wesleyans called
upon 'the Wesleyan societies and congregations throughout the kingdom' to send
petitions to Parliament condemning the government plan: it was claimed that the scheme
involved a 'direct violation of the first principles of the Protestant constitution', since it
contemplated 'the training and employing by the state of Romish (among other)
teachers', and recognized 'the corrupt Romish translations of the Holy Scriptures' as of
equal authority with the Authorized Version. It was also claimed that the plan was
impracticable and would give rise to 'a dangerous spirit of scepticism and unbelief'.

the full details of the government's plans were made known some such support appeared already to have been gained. At a meeting of Protestant Dissenters held in London in March 1839 Edward Baines, M.P.,[1] had declared that 'the only system of national education which could be generally approved of, would be that which, while it educated the nation, did not violate the rights or hurt the feelings of any particular denomination'; and the Rev. Dr Fletcher, after claiming that 'more than half the population of England and Wales did not belong to the established church', had gone on to say, amid applause, that 'all parties should receive a kind and beneficent notice from the government of the country in the application of funds for national education. It was true that in the case of Jews and Roman Catholics difficulties might present themselves, but there was no reason why these difficulties should not be obviated by providing distinct arrangements for the education of these parties'.[2] But many Dissenters who would have welcomed a government plan for education had it been proposed that all sects should be treated alike were angered by that one important feature of the government's scheme which distinguished it from the system in force in the Liverpool Corporation Schools, namely the regulation which provided that a clergyman of the Church of England should be appointed as chaplain to the proposed Normal and Model Schools.

This was scarcely a great concession to the Established Church and certainly, as events proved, not one considerable enough to disarm the Church's opposition; but many Dissenters felt aggrieved that definite provision was thus made for the denominational religious instruction of the children of churchmen, whereas similar instruction was to be given (by 'licensed Ministers') to the children of Nonconformists only wherever the number of such children in attendance appeared to the Committee of Council to justify 'such special provision'. Probably the practical effect of the different procedures for providing religious instructors would have been slight, but the apparent acquiescence in the Church's claim to receive favourable treatment was widely resented. Nor was the resentment altogether unjustified; in an important letter,[3] which seems hitherto to have escaped notice, Dr Kay, writing

[1] Baines must have been well acquainted with what was being achieved in the Liverpool Corporation Schools: his eldest son, Edward, who later became a leader of the 'voluntaryist' party in English educational circles, was married to a daughter of the Thomas Blackburn who had first advocated the adoption of the 'Irish System' in the Liverpool schools; a second son was editor of the *Liverpool Times*, which strongly supported the policy of the Liverpool Liberals.

[2] *Morning Chronicle*, 28 March 1839.

[3] Kay's letter, a very long one, was published in several of the London newspapers (see, e.g., *Morning Chronicle*, 27 May, and *Globe*, 28 May 1839). It was written in reply to

with the permission of the Committee of Council, attempted to appease the hostility of a Church of England clergyman who had criticized the Committee's plan, by saying: '. . . it forms one of the prominent features of the plan proposed to be adopted, that a chaplain should be appointed as a permanent officer of the Normal School, while the appointment of any other teacher is conditional.' Dissenters could hardly have been pleased to read such a surprisingly tactless declaration from such an authoritative source.

4

It is scarcely necessary to add that all of the insinuations and accusations which had been made against the Liverpool Education Committee were now made against the Committee of Council: cries of 'No Popery', warnings of a plot to destroy the Church, expressions of concern that latitudinarianism and scepticism were to be encouraged, all these were frequently to be heard. The London newspapers showed themselves in no way inferior to their Liverpool contemporaries in vehemence and fervour; *The Times* urged that public meetings should be 'called *instanter* in every town and city to protest against this anti-national and anti-Protestant measure',[1] and with a choice of epithet which revealed an interesting concurrence of ideas, *mutatis mutandis*, with those of the Archbishop of Tuam, spoke of the 'mischief' which would arise from allowing the children of Protestants to 'herd with the leprous young brood of Papists, Socinians, Freethinkers, and fanatics, about to be forced upon them by the Whigs'.[2]

Petitions rained upon Parliament, and on 5 July 1839 it was claimed by the Bishop of London that of these petitions only one hundred were in support of the Committee of Council's plan, whereas three thousand expressed disapproval.[3] Viscount Morpeth complained of what he called 'offensive, mendacious misrepresentations' conveyed in three-quarters of all the statements made by critics of the Committee's proposals;[4] Lord John Russell spoke of 'a perverse anxiety to exclude

one (printed first in the *Salopian Journal* and later in the *Morning Herald* of 25 May 1839) from the pen of the Rev. B. H. Kennedy, Headmaster of Shrewsbury School. Kay explained that in view of Kennedy's 'honourable and responsible position as head of one of the principal schools of this country', he (Kay) had been given permission by the Committee of Council to furnish some explanations of the Committee's plan.

[1] 18 May 1839.

[2] 3 June 1839.

[3] Hansard, Third Series, Vol. XLVIII, Col. 1293. On 20 June 1839 it was stated that 242 of the petitions presented to Parliament had been 'against any scheme of education which shall not be placed exclusively in the hands of the Established Church' (*ibid.*, Col. 640).

[4] *Ibid.*, Vol. XLVII, Cols. 1385, 1394.

the public from forming a correct notion of the plan', and referred to an allegation that it was the purpose of the Committee's scheme 'to expel religious instruction from the schools of this country'.[1] Lord Ashley claimed that the proposals were 'hostile to the Constitution, to the Church, and to revealed religion itself'.[2] The decision of the Wesleyan Methodists to side with the Established Church[3] made the opposition to the Committee of Council's scheme overwhelming; and what is surprising is not that the proposal to establish the Normal and Model Schools had to be abandoned, but that the Committee itself remained in being in spite of the vigorous attacks of its critics and the fairly widespread feeling that a committee concerned with education should not consist entirely of laymen.

5

At first scarcely any reference was made to the Liverpool Corporation Schools by either the supporters[4] or the opponents of the Committee of Council, and this was not surprising. So strong and vehement was the opposition to the proposal to erect the Normal and Model Schools that the Committee surrendered after striking only a single blow, in the form of the letter written by Dr Kay to the Rev. B. H. Kennedy. Thenceforward it was the task of the Committee to fight a courageous defensive battle in the hope of preserving its right to exist at all; to have quoted the example of the Liverpool Corporation Schools would have been merely to emphasize the fact that the Committee had deliberately adopted a policy similar to one which it well knew to have been opposed by almost all of the Established clergy in Liverpool. The attempt to appeal to public opinion over the heads of the clergy had failed, and it was with the indignant clergy that the Committee now had to deal. The Liberal Bishop of Norwich, who, as we know, was well informed about the Liverpool schools, prudently directed the attention of the Lords not to those establishments but to an attempt to educate together

[1] *Ibid.*, Col. 1380. (See also 'Ministerial Plan of Education—Church and Tory Misrepresentation' in *Edinburgh Review*, Vol. LXX, Edinburgh, 1840).

[2] Hansard, Third Series, Vol. XLVIII, Col. 270.

[3] For an account of the Methodist point of view at this time, see H. F. Mathews, *Methodism and the Education of the People*, London, 1949, pp. 132–4.

[4] See, however, P. Harwood, *National Education: Ought it to be Based upon Religion? A Sermon Preached at Bridport, February 24th, 1839*, London, 1839. Harwood described the Liverpool Corporation Schools as being among 'the best public schools in the country', and declared that no one could object to the system of religious instruction adopted in them except 'the bigot that sees damnation in every creed except his own, or the political churchman who fears that the unsectarianized millions of another generation may make a new appropriation of the ecclesiastical wealth of the country' (p. 24).

children of all sects which had been made in the diocese of Calcutta,[1] and the example was gratefully seized upon by Dr Kay.[2] Lord John Russell pointed out[3] that Protestant and Roman Catholic children living in workhouses received religious instruction from their respective pastors. The Marquess of Lansdowne maintained that the Committee of Council's plan had differed from the 'Irish System' of education in that the Committee had made provision for the giving within school hours of 'religious instruction as connected with the tenets of the Church of England';[4] he made no reference to the fact that in Liverpool the original version of the 'Irish System' had been modified in the same way.

The opposition also, possibly because they found the success which seemed to have attended the Liverpool experiment a little embarrassing, at first made no reference to the Corporation Schools. Instead, many critics preferred to make the much more damaging suggestion that the Committee's plan had been hatched by the very unpopular Central Society of Education.[5] It was chiefly in order to reply to this allegation that the Committee authorized Dr Kay to write to the Rev. B. H. Kennedy. Neither Kay nor Lord Brougham, when he replied to the Bishop of London in the Lords,[6] had any difficulty in disposing of the charge. The particular member of the Central Society most often referred to in this connection was James Simpson. It was true, of course, that the Committee of Council's plan was very similar to that adopted in the Liverpool Corporation Schools, and that this latter had been praised by Simpson. But what was claimed on this occasion was that the Committee had been influenced by Simpson's personal conviction that it was best to separate secular education completely from religious instruction, the latter being given by ministers of religion, and the secular teacher being prohibited from making 'in the course of his lessons' any reference 'to Christian doctrines or Christian history as such'.[7]

There was clearly no connection between these views and the arrangements made for giving religious instruction in the proposed Normal and Model Schools; and, indeed, Russell himself, it will be remembered, had earlier stated quite definitely that he considered the separation of religious from secular education to be highly undesirable.

---

[1] Hansard, Third Series, Vol. XLVIII, Col. 1290.
[2] *Recent Measures for the Promotion of Education in England*, pp. 69–74.
[3] Hansard, Third Series, Vol. XLVII, Col. 1379.
[4] *Ibid.*, Col. 760.
[5] See, e.g., speech of Bishop of London (*ibid.*, Vol. XLVIII, Col. 1295).
[6] *Ibid.*, Col. 1314.
[7] *Report from the Select Committee on Foundation Schools and Education in Ireland* (1835), Appendix No. 3, p. 185.

It had obviously been with the purpose of avoiding just such a separation that provision had been made in the Liverpool Corporation Schools for non-denominational religious instruction to be given by the secular teachers: and similarly the Committee of Council, in its turn, had gone out of its way to explain that in its proposed schools 'Religion [would] be combined with the whole matter of instruction and regulate the entire system of discipline'. Nevertheless, those who were determined to connect the Committee's plan with the detested Central Society, and especially with James Simpson, were quite inexorable in doing so.[1]

When it became obvious that the Committee of Council's opponents had not been appeased even by the withdrawal of the proposals concerning the Normal and Model Schools, and when it could be seen that no conciliatory measures short of complete and abject surrender could placate its critics, discretion on the part of the Committee's supporters appeared less important than before; and it was during what might be described as a spirited and well-fought rearguard action that the example set in the Liverpool Corporation Schools began to be quoted. On 18 June 1839 the *Manchester Guardian*, in the course of a leading article, declared:

It should be kept in mind that it is no new or untried plan which has been proposed. The system is essentially the same with that which has been for some time in most successful operation at the Liverpool Corporation Schools, and which, however abused by those who wilfully misrepresent it, has received—we may say has *extorted*—the applause of many who, until they had examined it for themselves, were grievously prejudiced against it.

Two days later, Mr Ewart, the former member for Liverpool[2] who had lost his seat in 1837 at the height of the campaign against the policy adopted in the Corporation Schools, informed the House of Commons of what had been achieved in those schools, and his speech was reported as follows:

The system of combined education without religious distinctions had been tried in Liverpool and had succeeded. He would not trouble the House with complicated statistics on this point, but he would refer to the statements of a converted opponent[3] to this scheme, who had watched its progress in Liverpool amongst a population of 200,000 persons. There were two great schools established in Liverpool under this system. The first was at the north end of the town, which was visited by the gentleman in question, and he put

[1] See J. C. Colquhoun's attack on Simpson, Hansard, Third Series, Vol. XLVIII, Col. 547, and Simpson's reply in *The Times*, 26 June 1839.
[2] Now member for Wigan.
[3] Evidently Dr Sleigh. See p. 172.

various questions to the master, who informed him that he was an Independent, and that he had two assistants, one of whom was a member of the Church of England, and the other a Roman Catholic. The number of children was nearly 500, and consisted of different religious denominations, including the children of members of the Church of England, Methodists, Baptists, Independents, Presbyterians, and Roman Catholics. The result of the observations of this gentleman was so satisfactory to his own mind, that from being an opponent he became a friend to the system; and although the orthodox party at first raised an outcry against it, subsequently the people were convinced that it was a most advantageous plan, and a general conviction prevailed that schools opened for all sects were public benefits. In the south end of the town the school was conducted by a master who was a member of the church of Scotland, with two assistants, one of whom was an Independent, and the other a member of the Church of England. The gentleman from whose statements he quoted found the schools going on well. The number of children under instruction in it, and the denominations, were as follows: Of the Church of England, 294; Roman Catholics, 325; Church of Scotland, twelve; Independents, fifteen; Baptists, twenty; and Methodists, forty-eight. Facts, then, proved the administration of education under a combined system to be quite practicable.[1]

On the same day no less a person than Daniel O'Connell also drew the attention of the House of Commons to the Liverpool Corporation Schools when he declared:

I do not hesitate to say, in the presence of the Honourable Member for Liverpool, that the experiment of a common education has succeeded there. Will you refuse to the poor population of other great towns the same advantage?[2]

This statement of O'Connell's[3] is particularly interesting in view of the fact that Archbishop MacHale of Tuam, who shared O'Connell's patriotic aspirations and collaborated closely with him, had recently appealed to O'Connell to 'do incalculable service' to their common religion 'by procuring a grant for the separate education of Catholic children'; MacHale had declared that those who favoured 'mixed education' were actuated by 'an erroneous feeling of liberality'.[4] Evidently 'The Liberator' was of a different opinion; and so, it appears, were almost all of the Roman Catholic members of Parliament, since

---

[1] Hansard, Third Series, Vol. XLVIII, Cols. 590–91.

[2] *Mirror of Parliament*, 1839, Vol. IV, p. 3163.

[3] O'Connell frequently passed through Liverpool on his way to and from Westminster, and he was on good terms with a number of the Liverpool Liberals; in January 1836 they had given a dinner in his honour, and William Rathbone had conducted him on a tour of some parts of the town. See *The Times* (London), 25, 30 January 1836.

[4] Letter printed in Rt Rev. B. O'Reilly, *John MacHale, Archbishop of Tuam, His Life, Times and Correspondence* (Vol. I, p. 418).

when the member for Mayo, Mr Dillon Browne, praised MacHale's stand against the 'Irish System' of education as established in Ireland, and moved that important modifications should be made in it, he failed to find a seconder for his motion.[1]

It was now clearly necessary for the opposition to attempt to rebut the claims made in favour of the Liverpool schools, and this task was undertaken by one of the members of Parliament for Liverpool, Cresswell Cresswell, in the course of a speech made in the Commons on 24 June 1839. The relevant parts of his address were reported as follows:

It had been said, that the experiment of teaching children of different religious persuasions in common, had been already tried, and found successful. Now, he would put the House in possession of the facts of the case; and they would then be enabled to judge how far the experiments which had been tried had proved successful. It was said there was a neutral ground in religion, upon which children of all creeds might meet, and this they would ascertain from the result of this experiment. About three years ago, the corporation of Liverpool devoted part of their funds to the purposes of that experiment, and they accordingly established[2] two schools, in which children of all sects were received, and in which ministers of each creed were allowed to attend to instruct the children in their several doctines, at particular times. The hon. gentleman at the other side had alluded to the success of the scheme, but he had very much exaggerated the results of the experiment. At that period there was a strong Protestant feeling in Liverpool, and the consequence was, that the greater part of the Protestants, whose children had previously been receiving instruction at the schools, withdrew them when the new arrangement was brought into operation. Those who were opposed to the system of mixed religious instruction, had been accused of a disinclination to afford instruction: but how was that proved? By their subscribing a sum of 10,000 l. for the purpose of affording education to those who were not inclined to avail themselves of the schools which had been established by the corporation of Liverpool. In the corporation schools, in the first instance, extracts from the Bible were given to the children, and not the whole Bible; of course he meant during the hours in which they were under the master of the school. The cry, however, against this part of the plan became so strong, that they were obliged to abandon it, and the whole Bible was placed in the hands of the children, with the exception of Roman Catholics, who still had the extracts. But how had the special religious education gone on? In the year 1837 there were 320 Roman Catholic children in these schools, and no Roman Catholic [?priest] had ever attended, nor had any Dissenting minister. The only person who ever attended was a minister of the Church of England. Here, then, was an end to the system of combined religious

[1] Hansard, Third Series, Vol. XLIX, Col. 1270.
[2] The Corporation schools had, of course, been established not three years earlier, but twelve.

education. It was possible to have a combined secular education but not an united religious system.

After quoting figures showing the numbers of children in the schools established by the different sects in the town, the speaker continued:

Now how any body [*sic*] could say that the combined system of education had been introduced in Liverpool with the most perfect success, he could not imagine. There was no neutral ground in religion. A clergyman, who felt much interest in the success of the system tried by the corporation at Liverpool, offered his services upon the condition that the children should begin the day with some form of divine worship in which all might join. But this plan failed. Objection was started after objection, and at last it was proposed that they should repeat the Lord's Prayer. But that also was refused. The Roman Catholic priest refused to allow the Roman Catholic children to join in repeating that prayer, although it was given to them by an authority whom all reverenced. Where, then, would they find neutral ground on which might be built an altar at which all could worship? Combined religious education was, in his opinion, perfectly hopeless.[1]

It is necessary to point out that some of Cresswell's remarks were seriously inaccurate, partly, no doubt, because he was not resident in Liverpool and had not been well briefed concerning the schools. The reports of his speech given by Hansard and in the *Mirror of Parliament* must have conveyed the impression that the Roman Catholic children were kept without a complete version of the Bible, and that only they 'still had the extracts'. There is in fact ample evidence, some of which has already been quoted, that both statements were untrue. More seriously misleading was the statement in the reports that, 'In the year 1837 there were 320 Roman Catholic children in these schools, and no Roman Catholic [?priest] had ever attended.' This remark must have convinced many readers that the Liverpool Education Committee had utterly failed to win the support of the Roman Catholic clergy of the town.

The truth was that in the year mentioned there were far more than 320 Roman Catholic children in the schools and that both schools *had* been attended by Roman Catholic priests, although for the past two years, as we shall see, the task of giving denominational religious instruction to the Roman Catholic children in the South School had been delegated by the priests to Roman Catholic monitors selected and trained for the purpose. It might be said that even if Cresswell (or his informant) believed that the non-attendance of a priest at this school was evidence of some unwillingness to support the system in force in the Corporation Schools, it was rather disingenuous to omit all

[1] *Ibid.*, Vol. XLVIII, Cols. 766–8.

reference to the continued attendance of a priest at the North School. This apart, however, the misleading statements concerning the schools which were spread abroad in the reports of Cresswell's speech probably arose merely from errors made by some of the parliamentary reporters; and the version of the speech published in the *Liverpool Standard* (28 June 1839) probably gives the best indication of what Cresswell actually said in this part of his address: '. . . from the summer of 1837, a school having 327 Roman Catholics in it, had never been visited by a Roman Catholic priest.' This, of course, was a very different, and strictly true, observation.

Evidently careful plans had been laid by both sides for a parliamentary battle concerning the Liverpool Corporation Schools, since Cresswell was at once answered by Richard Sheil, member for Tipperary, in a well-documented speech, during the course of which he said:

That learned Gentleman [i.e. Cresswell] has made certain statements regarding the corporation schools utterly at variance with the information which I have received upon the subject. I wrote to Mr Rathbone, a gentleman of the highest respectability, in order that he might ascertain the exact state of facts. Previous to the passing of the Corporation Reform Bill no more than two or three Catholics had attended the corporation schools. When the Corporation Reform Bill had passed, the council had to determine what course they would take in regard to the schools.

Sheil then quoted at length from Thomas Blackburn's *A Defence of the System Adopted in the Corporation Schools of Liverpool* to show that the Liverpool Council had felt obliged to make the schools available to children of all sects, and had therefore adopted the 'Irish System' as being peculiarly fitted for their purpose and 'founded on enlightened and truly scriptural principles'. Sheil then read to the House the following letter from William Rathbone, written, it may be observed, a week before the government had announced its decision not to proceed with its plan to establish the Normal and Model Schools:

Liverpool, May 25, 1839.

Sir—I . . . beg leave to assure you, that I shall have the highest gratification in giving you any information in my power respecting our corporation schools. I have been on our education committee from the time the schools came under the management of the reformed town council; I speak, therefore, from my own knowledge, and pledge myself to the accuracy of my statements.

We have the gratification of believing, that the system works admirably, and that, too, though opposed with reckless misrepresentation, and with unscrupulous hostility. The Catholic clergy have acted with great liberality, and with a most gratifying confidence in us, allowing and encouraging the children to come to schools under the direction of a committee at one time wholly Protestant, and the teachers also, and ready to concede and conciliate wherever it could be done without the violation of a principle. We are bold enough to think, that we have demonstrated the fact, that a system of national education is practicable; to give to all the best possible secular education, a morality which may guard against the dram shop, and keep out of gaol, without interfering with each being well instructed in their own peculiar religious dogmas, and all proving, that they are christians by their love to one another. The examinations have proved how well the religious instruction has in the mean time been completed. I believe there is not a school in Liverpool where there is the same quantity of sound religious instruction and knowledge. Although you do not mention it in your letter, I may as well even at the risk of being tedious, refer to the cry especially raised against us, viz., that the Bible was excluded the schools [sic]. It is true, that the Catholics are not compelled to read or hear read the authorised version of the scriptures, but are furnished with the Douay version; but to the Protestants, the authorised version is read; they are taught to read it, and have been from the first day the schools came into our hands. I may repeat, that they are not merely taught to read, but to understand what they read, and to apply its glorious precepts and principles to the daily duties of life. If at any time you should be going through Liverpool . . . I should have great pleasure in waiting upon and showing you our schools; every one is admitted to see them even without introduction, on writing their names in a visitors' book, and at all hours. We have nothing to conceal, and have, therefore, no mysteries. . . .

Sheil added:

Such are the results, according to a very high authority, of the system of instruction adopted at Liverpool. If a different system had been followed, how large a portion of the population would have been deprived of the elements of literary, moral, and religious education?[1]

By 24 June 1839, when this speech was made, it could no longer be hoped that the government would set up schools throughout the country similar to those which Sheil felt had been so successful in Liverpool; nevertheless, he maintained that the success of the Liverpool Corporation Schools ought to convince the government and others that Roman Catholics in particular areas might yet be brought within a national system of education if the 'Irish system' were adopted in those areas. Sheil said:

I am very far from saying, that the Irish system of education should be adopted generally through this country. But in particular localities, circumstanced exactly as districts in Ireland are confessed to be, such a plan ought to

[1] Ibid., Vol. XLVIII, Cols. 777–80.

be adopted as shall admit those children to the benefit of a Parliamentary grant, who might otherwise be excluded from its advantages.[1]

But Sheil's praise of the Corporation Schools was balanced by Cresswell's condemnation of them; each of the London newspapers adopted whichever of the two views suited its own political beliefs; and the result was that those who had no means of verifying the various statements made about the schools were left in doubt as to whether the outcome of the Liverpool experiment had been triumphant success or miserable failure. And it need hardly be said that such doubt concerning the results of the policy followed in the Corporation Schools worked in favour of those who were anxious that that policy should not be adopted elsewhere.

6

Meanwhile, as was to have been expected, the Committee of Council's proposal to set up educational establishments open to pupils of all denominations had aroused considerable interest in Liverpool, and supporters of the Liverpool Liberals were quick to point out that, in the words of the *Liverpool Mercury*, the plan drawn up by the Committee was 'precisely similar in principle to that adopted with signal success in the Liverpool Corporation Schools'.[2] Those who had long criticized the policy pursued by the local Education Committee naturally prepared at once to give battle, and some of the opposition offered in Liverpool to the government scheme was at least as vigorous as that to be found elsewhere.

True, the local clergy of the Established Church seem often to have gone out of their way to voice their criticisms in a way which would give as little offence as possible to Protestant Dissenters. It has already been noticed that at the meeting held in Liverpool on 3 April 1839 the Rev. A. Campbell had carefully qualified the claims which he then advanced on behalf of the Church of England; on the same occasion he had proposed a motion 'That it is highly expedient to extend and improve the education of the labouring and middle classes; but that such extension and improvement should take place in connexion with the Established Church'; he had, however, added the words 'so far as it can be done without restricting the religious liberty of the people'[3]. The Rev. H. M'Neile claimed at a London meeting that 'to the clergy of right belonged the education of the people, and he must protest against its being taken away from their superintendence';[4] but for

---

[1] *Ibid.*, Vol. XLVIII, Cols. 782–3. [2] 31 May 1839.
[3] *Liverpool Courier*, 10 April 1839. [4] *The Times*, 12 February 1839.

M'Neile the real enemy was 'Popery', and at this time he was usually to be found demanding that the state should make grants only to schools which were 'Scriptural' (that is, which made use of the Authorized Version); he did not stipulate that the schools should be only those attached to the Established Church.

However, the claims made were not always so moderate, and even Campbell alleged on one occasion, in a letter to the Press, that the government scheme degraded the ministers of the national religion, undermined the Word of God, surrendered the principle of a Church establishment, weakened Christianity itself 'by disowning any fixed standard of religious truth' and endowed religious error by law. He remarked: 'If the queen's government cannot teach religious truth without teaching irreligious error, they had better let religion alone'.[1] These were strong words from a man who had once admired the 'Irish System', and who, only three years earlier, according to his own admission, had come very close to co-operating with the Liverpool Education Committee. But in Liverpool, as in London, the most fervent and uncompromising devotion to the interests of the Established Church was expressed by the journalists. The *Liverpool Courier* observed: 'If we are to have an established church, however painful the alternative, however rigorous and unequal, under present circumstances, the restriction may appear, it can only be *by confining the legal provision for religious instruction to the teachers of a particular sect of Christianity.*'[2] This newspaper even went so far as to say: 'We have never been able either to subscribe to or understand the laudatory terms in which the principle and mode of bestowing government aid upon two societies, one propagating orthodoxy and the other dissent, have been spoken of.'[3] The *Liverpool Standard* maintained that no measure which accorded equal treatment to all sects could 'be recommended to Her Majesty without committing *high treason*',[4] and went on to accuse the government of 'infamy', of 'offering a gross and flagrant insult to the Protestant population', of 'abject truckling to the Popish and infidel factions', of being 'profligate politicians' who had evolved a 'most pernicious' scheme.[5]

Apparently one of the first groups of citizens to draw up a petition against the government plan was the congregation of the Rev. H. M'Neile, and the *Liverpool Standard* seems to have been anxious that the example thus set should be widely followed. A leader-writer in that journal remarked:

[1] *Liverpool Courier*, 5 June 1839.   [2] *Ibid.*, 19 June 1839.
[3] *Ibid.*   [4] 22 February 1839.
[5] *Liverpool Standard*, 24 May and 25 June 1839.

Petitions must be forthwith got up in every town and hamlet against this novel scheme. . . . There is no time to be lost. We have elsewhere given the form of petition which will serve for the purpose. Let Liverpool be one of the first places to stir in this matter. The people of Liverpool have had the first experience of the Irish system—they have protested most nobly against it—let them once more show that they hold it in utter detestation. The clergy of the town are bound by every motive of consistency—of duty to their flocks—of regard to the welfare of this nation—and of allegiance for their Great Master, to enter their solemn protest against this infidel scheme.[1]

The *Liverpool Courier* made a similar appeal in words which probably caused numbers of its readers to lose sight of the fact that the government was proposing merely to provide a single institution for the training of teachers of all sects, and to entrust the distribution of the annual education grant to a Committee of Council:

Those who desire the preservation of the church establishment, and who do not wish to see all distinctions between right and wrong obliterated, and anarchy and unbelief enthroned upon the ruins of religion, order, happiness, and good faith, should hasten to protest, while yet there is time, against this unhallowed and insidious scheme.[2]

Petitions from Liverpool against the government's proposals were presented to Parliament on 12 April[3] and on 15 May,[4] the latter expressing opposition to the establishment of 'any system of education not founded on the principles of the established church'. On 12 June[5] a further three petitions were submitted, and two days later 'Lord Viscount Sandon presented petitions from 6,500 inhabitants of Liverpool; from the Mariners' Church at Liverpool; from the congregation of All Saints' Church; and Christ Church; and several other congregations at Liverpool, against the government plan'.[6] A report published later in *The Times*[7] (London) stated that seven of these petitions had been organized by the Liverpool branch of the Protestant Association. The local Wesleyan Methodists obeyed the call sent to them from London 'to forward . . . petitions without delay';[8] and the *Liverpool Mercury* complained bitterly that 'petitions cut and dried' were 'sent about the country like brokers' circulars'.[9] In Liverpool the results of all this activity turned out to be surprisingly small, and seem to indicate that the opposition in the town to the government scheme was not very great; for the *Liverpool Standard* could claim only that the signatures to

---

[1] *Ibid.*, 24 May 1839.
[2] 29 May 1839.
[3] *Mirror of Parliament*, 1839, Vol. II, p. 1675.
[4] *Ibid.*, Vol. III, p. 2446.
[5] *Ibid.*, Vol. IV, p. 2856.
[6] *Ibid.*, p. 2929.
[7] 7 October 1839.
[8] See p. 182.
[9] 14 June 1839.

all the petitions from Liverpool and its suburbs against the government plan probably numbered not less than 11,000;[1] and this was scarcely an impressive figure in view of the fact that in Manchester a petition in favour of the admittedly unpopular proposals was signed 'in the short space of a week, *by upwards of twenty-one thousand persons*'.[2]

The Liverpool Liberals, however, seem to have been as much taken aback as was the government by the bitterness of much of the criticism offered, the widespread misunderstanding and misrepresentation of the government's intentions, and the varied claims made on behalf of the Established Church. Moreover, some of the local Protestant Dissenters who had supported the policy adopted in the Corporation Schools probably felt misgivings similar to those of some Dissenters elsewhere, about a plan which the Committee of Council's own secretary had shown to favour members of the Established Church. But the Roman Catholics in the town remained firm in their support of the Liverpool Education Committee's policy and of the government plan;[3] indeed, at the time when the agitation against that plan was at its height the pro-Catholic *Liverpool Journal* made a declaration which reads a little oddly today, especially since it clearly approved of the use of what we should now call an 'Agreed Syllabus':

. . . it is but too evident that, with the exception of the Catholics, there is no considerable body of religionists in the kingdom willing to regard secular education in conjunction with such religious and moral doctrines as all hold in common, and leaving religious education from the point at which they diverge to the care of separate ministers, as a public duty. . . . In Holland, a

[1] 14 June 1839.

[2] *Manchester Guardian*, 12 June 1839.

[3] It may here be noted that on 26 July 1839 a petition concerning the plan was submitted to the House of Commons on behalf of nearly four thousand Roman Catholics of London, among them 'Nicholas Wiseman, D.D.' According to the *Mirror of Parliament* (1839, Vol. V, p. 4371), Mr Langdale, when presenting the petition, said: ' . . . the petitioners claim for the pastors of their church the exclusive control over the education and religious instruction of their flocks.' (This speech was not reported by Hansard.) Reference to a copy of the petition itself, however, shows that 'control over the education' of Roman Catholic children was *not* asked for. The petition was evidently intended as a reply to the many petitions which had been addressed to Parliament suggesting that the Church of England should superintend the religious instruction given in any educational institutions established by the government. The Roman Catholic petitioners declared that they 'would consider any scheme of distribution of the Educational Grant, which would give a preference to the Established Church, or any powers to the clergy or members of that Church to regulate or control the religious instruction of Catholics or of Protestant Dissenters, to be manifestly unjust'; they 'respectfully demanded' that 'the religious instruction of Catholic children should be placed under the exclusive inspection and management of the prelates and pastors of the Catholic Church'. The petitioners were opposed to state control of religious instruction, but raised no objection to the state control of *secular* education (*Appendix to the Reports of the Select Committee of the House of Commons on Public Petitions, 1839*, p. 531).

protestant and highly civilised country, where a strong religious feeling prevails, the government has adopted a system of education precisely similar to that practised in the corporation schools of Liverpool, and, as appears from statistical returns, and the concurrent report of all travellers, with the happiest effects.[1]

A week later the same newspaper made clear its attitude to the policy of Dr MacHale when it said of a petition criticizing the 'Irish System' which had recently been presented to the House of Commons on behalf of the Archbishop and clergy of the diocese of Tuam:

> It [the petition] must be set *pro tanto* to the debit side of catholic liberality, on which we hope, however, it will not be considered seriously to reflect, so long as Dr MacHale is alone, in the hierarchy to which he belongs,[2] in holding it to be irreligious in Christians, of different denominations, to receive instruction in their common duties under one roof. For one intolerant prelate of the catholic church, the church of England can show sixteen . . . the only difference that we can discover between the principles of the Archbishop of Canterbury and the Archbishop of Tuam being, that the one would exclude catholics, and the other protestants.[3]

It would possibly be wrong to assume that such opinions were shared by all of the Roman Catholic laity in Liverpool, by all of the Roman Catholic clergy in the town or by all of those whose duty it was to guide the local clergy on matters of policy. Nevertheless, it is worthy of note that it was at this time possible to ascribe such views publicly to Roman Catholics in general without being called upon by the clergy or others to contradict or qualify the statements.[4] There is every indication that in Roman Catholic circles in Liverpool there was wholehearted support for the ideas of the Roman Catholic Archbishop of Dublin and little or none for the sentiments of 'John of Tuam'.

No doubt many of those in the town who had for some time supported the policy followed by the Liverpool Education Committee would readily have signed petitions in favour of the Committee of Council's proposals, but, curiously enough, no arrangements seem to have been made for the drawing up of petitions to be signed by members of the general public; perhaps this was because it was felt that

---

[1] 8 June 1839.
[2] By this time this statement was probably no longer strictly true, since early in the following year ten of the twenty-eight Irish Roman Catholic prelates expressed dissatisfaction with the 'Irish System'. See p. 137.
[3] 15 June 1839.
[4] It will be remembered that the *Rescript* referred to earlier, in which the highest authorities of the Roman Catholic Church described as 'very dangerous' the practice of teaching children 'in common' the 'articles in which all Christians agree', was not published until 1841.

representations on behalf of those who favoured the proposals could best be made by the Town Council. Two days before the announcement of the government's decision to 'postpone' the establishment of the Normal and Model Schools, the *Liverpool Chronicle* declared:

. . . we do especially complain that no movement in support of the Ministerial Plan of Education has yet taken place in Liverpool. Liverpool ought to be the first in the field in so holy and good a cause. Here the battle has already been fought and won on this very subject. Here our Town Council have fully tried the experiment which the Ministers are about to attempt on a larger scale—and they have not only nobly tried it but they have gloriously succeeded in it . . . they have persevered until they have brought what at first was only an experiment for the event of which even some of their best friends trembled and were alarmed, to a successful and triumphant issue. . . . The inhabitants of Liverpool . . . have beheld the cause of general Education stoutly fought against by all the array which bigotry could set against it, and yet victorious over all its assailants. They, therefore, are bound above all others to step forward at this juncture, and to pray the government of the country to extend to the people generally the same advantages of education, education open and free to all sects, which have been bestowed upon the children of the operative classes in this community. A petition from Liverpool upon this subject would not simply be a petition. It would . . . be an evidence and a testimony of the success which has attended the educational experiment of our 'Town Council'.[1]

On 7 June 1839, at a special meeting of the Council, Thomas Blackburn informed his fellow-councillors that it was 'their duty to come boldly forward and tell the Minister the results of the working of that great and glorious experiment' which had been carried on in the town. Naturally, some opposition was expressed, and D. Hodgson told the Liberal members of the Council that 'he would as soon think of going into the gambling houses in London to look for honesty, as to find true religion emanating from the system of instruction pursued in their schools'. The Conservatives moved as an amendment that a petition should be presented to the House of Commons praying that 'in any system of national education which may be introduced, the Scriptures in the authorized version only be used in the Schools and that nothing shall be taught under the name of religion, and with the authority of Government, inconsistent with the principles of the Protestant Reformation'.[2] But the Conservative amendment was defeated,

---

[1] 1 June 1839.

[2] *Liverpool Mercury*, 14 June 1839. Among those who voted for the amendment and against Blackburn's proposal was Robertson Gladstone (brother of William Ewart Gladstone), who had become a member of the Council in the previous year.

and Blackburn's motion carried by thirty-one votes to nine. It will perhaps be best to allow the formal Council record to speak for itself:

Extract from the Minutes of the Meeting of the Liverpool Town Council Held on 7 June 1839 (Proceedings of Council, Vol. XVIII, pp. 201–4).
Resolved
That the following Petition be presented to the House of Commons.

To the Honourable the Commons of the United Kingdom of Great Britain and Ireland in Parliament assembled.
The Petition of the Mayor, Aldermen and Burgesses of the Borough of Liverpool,

Humbly Sheweth
That your Petitioners are deeply sensible of the importance of education as the only effectual means of improving the Physical and Social as well as the moral and religious condition of the People and regard it to be one of the most important duties of Government to devise and carry into speedy operation some plan for placing its advantages within the reach of all classes of Her Majesty's subjects.

That your petitioners considered it their duty to appropriate a portion of the revenue placed at their disposal to the promotion of this important object and were anxiously concerned as trustees of public property to introduce such arrangements into their schools as should render them accessible to every part of the community.

That with this view your Petitioners adopted and have now for three years successfully acted upon a plan of combined secular and separate religious instruction similar in its main features to the national system of education for Ireland, as well as that recently proposed in the minutes of Council issued by the Commissioners of the Board of Education for England.

Under the present circumstances of Excitement on this subject and while efforts the most determined are made by one party to secure the support of Government to themselves and exclude all others from a participation in it, your Petitioners are impelled by a sense of public duty to lay before your Honourable House the results of their own observation and experience on the working of a system which knows no distinction of sect or party but throws open the Schools for the free entrance of all.

There are now in one of the Schools supported by this Corporation an equal number of protestants and Roman Catholics and in the other, two-thirds are Roman Catholics and one-third protestants; the protestants are chiefly the children of members of the Established Church, though there are dissenters of almost every denomination and your petitioners can testify with unhesitating confidence that religious feuds and dissentions have been entirely unknown among the children, that in their classes for secular learning and in their hours of play, distinctions of sect are never thought of and that the spirit of harmony, peace and good will towards each other pervades these schools as perfectly as if the children were all of one denomination.

Your Petitioners humbly submit that in a state of society such as now exists in this empire where religious differences are the main source of internal dissention no school system is worthy of legislative support, or deserves the name of National which has not a tendency to abate this giant evil so inconsistent with the due influence of true religion and so fatal to the happiness and welfare of society, for where envying and strife is, there is confusion and every evil work.

Your Petitioners yield to no body of men in the strength of their conviction that the true and permanent improvement of a nation can never be effected but by the diffusion of religious knowledge; and that the Bible is the source of that knowledge which is the stability of the times. They have a conviction equally strong, that force and compulsion in matters of conscience are utterly at variance with the spirit of Christianity, that the conscience of every man is entitled to be treated with respect, and that all attempts to confer religious benefit must necessarily fail when they commence by trampling upon its rights. Influenced by these vital principles which lie at the root of all sound legislation in reference to religion, your petitioners recognise the inalienable right of the parent to direct the instruction of his children, and while they place the Bible within the reach of all, they do not force it upon any, nor make the reading of it a condition of admission to their schools.

The result of the system of Freedom thus pursued has been that all the children unite in reading those admirable selections of the Bible—The Irish scripture lessons—that all the protestant children unite in reading the authorized version and that, during the hour of each day set apart for religious instruction, when the Ministers of religion are invited to attend, the children belonging to the establishment, in addition to scripture reading, learn the Church Catechism and other formularies, and the children of Roman Catholics read the Douay version of the scriptures and learn their own Catechism. Several public examinations of the schools have taken place in order to afford an opportunity of ascertaining the progress of the children, particularly in religious knowledge, and your petitioners are not afraid of contradiction when they affirm that these examinations have afforded proof that the children of protestants obtain in these Schools a sound scriptural education equal at least to that which is given in any other educational institutions in the Country.

In earnestly intreating the attention of your Honorable House to this statement of facts your petitioners venture with great deference, but at the same time with confidence, to maintain that the experiment which they have had the honor to conduct justifies the following conclusions.

1st. That the assembling of children of different religious sects in the same School, so far from tending to excite discord and alienation, is calculated to produce a contrary effect and to promote peace harmony and good feeling.

2. That in an institution thus constituted and conducted though the reading

of the same scriptures is optional considerable portions will be read by all sects and parties, and that the use of the authorized version by the protestant children will be as certainly secured and as fully attended to as it can be in those schools where it is peremptorily enforced.

3. That the appropriation of a separate hour for the sole purpose of religious instruction affords a better method of communicating a knowledge of the truths of Christianity to the children of the poor than any that has yet been devised—a method which, if its advantages be not lost by a neglect which would be criminal on the part of the teachers of religion, cannot fail to insure incalculable benefits to the great mass of the people.

Your Petitioners therefore pray that your Honorable House will refuse its support to every system which has the effect of excluding from its benefits any section of the inhabitants of the empire and will speedily confer on the nation at large—what your Petitioners have already awarded to the inhabitants of Liverpool, a liberal, and comprehensive scheme of Education in which the children of every sect in religion and every party in politics may freely and equally participate.

And your Petitioners will ever pray &c.

Resolved
    That the Right Honorable Lord John Russell be requested to present the said Petition to the House of Commons.

Chapter 10

'IF NECESSARY, ALONE'

I

IF, as seems certain, it was the apparently successful outcome of the Liverpool experiment which had persuaded Lord John Russell and the other members of the Committee of Council to formulate some of the proposals which they had made in April 1839, then it must be admitted that the ultimate consequences of the policy adopted in the Liverpool Corporation Schools were far different from those which Rathbone and his friends had hoped for. It is true that the Committee managed to survive, and that the government was able so to modify the regulations concerning the distribution of grants in aid of school building that the Committee was empowered to make grants 'in particular cases' otherwise than through the National and the British and Foreign School Societies. But the immediate result of the Committee's proposal to educate together pupils of all sects was to arouse those passions of which Russell himself had spoken in November 1837, when, it will be recalled, he had warned his hearers that 'if they unhappily introduced a plan which excited either resentment or repugnance on account of religious feelings, or which gave additional motives for dissension between the Established Church and the great body of Dissenters, they would not be furthering, they would only be obstructing, the great cause which they had at heart.'[1] Whether *any* decisive step towards introducing a national system of education could possibly have been taken at this time without exciting 'resentment or repugnance' is open to question; but certainly the reception accorded to the Committee of Council's plan was extremely discouraging to those anxious to see such a system established. Brougham wrote in September 1839:

So far we must make up our minds, looking our position steadily in the face, to admit that we are completely defeated, and defeated without any hope of a favourable reverse of fortune another time. A controversy of thirty years, with all the reason and almost all the skill, and, until very lately, all the zeal on our side, has ended in an overthrow somewhat more complete than we should in all probability have sustained at the commencement of our long and well-fought campaign.

[1] See p. 132.

The opposition aroused by the Committee's proposals, and by the second reading of his own Education Bill in July 1839, had by this time convinced Brougham that 'the alternative of refusing all National Education' was 'to allow some preference, some interference to the Church'; and he was prepared to accept 'such preference, such interference' provided that 'the sacred rights of conscience' should be respected.[1] It is not at all easy to see how Dissenters were to be won over to Brougham's views, but it is at least clear that Brougham was deeply disturbed at the turn which events had taken, and was prepared to surrender much for which he had quite recently fought.

A letter written by Richard Cobden to Thomas Wyse and found among the latter's papers in Dublin illustrates the confusion of mind produced by the Committee of Council's plan and the opposition to which it had given rise. The letter was written only one day before the Committee announced that the plan to establish the Normal and Model Schools had been 'postponed'; since, so far as this writer is aware, it has not previously been published, it is here given in full:

Man[r] 2 June 1839

My dear Sir

I return you thanks for your attention to my request about Dorsey.

Your letter is gratifying because I can see you are still *hoping*—I fear the ministry have blundered in their measure, and that we shall be temporarily at least thrown back—The methodist howl, and the high church crusade, will succeed, because the ministers have not secured the dissenters or the liberal party by their plan—First, they have done wrong in making provision for the visits of chaplains and ministers to their schools. The next mistake is in alluding to the Douay bible, which is not necessary in this country, where Protestantism is the rule and Catholicism the exception—Had they adopted the British and Foreign rule, as regards religion, it would have demolished the cry of infidelity on one hand; and rallied around them the dissenters, quakers, and the liberal party—whilst the methodists would have been neutralised—whilst on the other, they would have put the church party in the position of fighting for exclusive control against a system which is now working well throughout the country. Again they have put sad nonsense into their minutes, when they talk of making religion provide the whole course of instruction. How will they teach the rule-of-three or modern geography *religiously*! In this they have fallen into a senseless prejudice.

We think of trying to get up a petition here to break the fall of the ministerial scheme. But the dissenters, generally, though favourably disposed towards the government, cannot approve altogether of the plan; and therefore we shall be obliged to word the petition very vaguely. In fact it will not support *the* plan of the Ministry, but pray for a liberal and comprehensive one. We shall endeavour rather to oppose the rabid and factious opponents

[1] *A Letter on National Education to the Duke of Bedford*, pp. 17–18, 36–7.

than to support the present plan. It is difficult under such circumstances to do anything very satisfactorily. I repeat the ministry have blundered!

The more I think of the subject, the more I am convinced, that the British system is the best, for evading the factious opposition, which will take the cloak of religion against any scheme if possible. As regards the districts where Catholics abound, as here & Liverpool, some *practical* modification might be afterwards introduced. But in *thousands* of parishes where no Roman Catholics are to be found, the British system might work without difficulty on that score.[1]

Thus whilst Brougham was preparing to 'allow some preference, some interference' to the Church of England, Cobden was proposing—surely not very hopefully—that a national system of education should be set up in defiance of the Church and based on principles favoured by the Protestant Dissenters. Moreover, the last few sentences of Cobden's letter seem to indicate that, considering impracticable a policy which he had praised when he had seen it at work in the Liverpool Corporation Schools, he was now willing to leave the Roman Catholics out of a national system of education, hoping that 'some *practical* modification might be afterwards introduced'; nothing shows more clearly than this the despair which Cobden must have been feeling in face of the opposition aroused by the Committee of Council's plan, for he was usually most insistent that, as he put it later: 'Any system which does not embrace that part of the population [the Roman Catholics] cannot be entertained for one moment as a system.'[2]

As it turned out, Cobden had taken too gloomy a view of the attitude likely to be adopted towards the Committee of Council's plan by those in and around Manchester who hoped for the establishment of a national system of education. A petition drawn up by 'the Manchester Society for Promoting National Education' and 'signed in the short space of a week *by upwards of twenty-one thousand persons*'[3] was by no means half-hearted in its support for the plan. The petitioners 'hailed with great satisfaction and gratitude the establishment of a Board of Education in Her Majesty's Privy Council, as the first step in the performance of a duty which is imperative on every enlightened government'; and the petition continued:

. . . your Petitioners also hold it to be an indispensable principle of justice, that all schools supported by the public funds should be, without an infringement of the rights of conscience, open to all denominations of Her Majesty's subjects. Your Petitioners therefore pray that your Honourable House will support Her Majesty's Government in the establishment of Model and

---

[1] *Wyse MSS.* (National Library of Ireland). Uncatalogued.
[2] *Speeches on Questions of Public Policy*, Vol. II, p. 572.
[3] *Manchester Guardian*, 12 June 1839.

Normal Schools, based upon principles of perfect religious freedom, and that your Honourable House will make a liberal grant in aid of this object.[1]

2

The Liverpool Liberals, for their part, appear to have remained unshaken in their support of the Committee of Council's proposals, and the abandonment of the plan to set up the Normal and Model Schools seems merely to have made them determined to show that the policy which they had adopted in the Corporation Schools, even if not as yet acceptable to the country as a whole, could in practice solve the problem set up by the presence of large numbers of poor Roman Catholic children in particular areas, and thus remove what was probably the most serious obstacle to the establishment of a national system of education. The Liverpool Education Committee therefore pressed vigorously on with its plans to establish additional schools to be conducted on similar lines. At the beginning of July 1839, the Committee agreed that in view of the inadequate provision for the education of the poor of the town it was 'highly desirable to establish as extensively as possible such schools as those already supported by the Corporation'; they announced, however, that they could not, as they would have wished, recommend the establishment of a Corporation School in every ward of the town, since the municipal funds were not 'sufficiently large'. But they proposed to the Council that 'Schools for Children as well as for Infants' similar to the existing Corporation Schools should be set up 'at Windsor in West Derby Ward, in Castle Street Ward, and in St Paul's Ward'.[2] Shortly afterwards the Committee recommended that 'a School be erected immediately in Myrtle Street South, on land belonging to the Corporation', and also pointed out that when the Islington Market was discontinued its site would provide 'an excellent situation for a school'.[3] The Finance Committee, to whom the Education Committee's recommendation had been passed by the Council, ordered the Surveyor to prepare plans and estimates of the cost of erecting a school in Myrtle Street South.[4]

Anxious that the proposed schools should be thoroughly up to date, the Education Committee decided in October 1839 to ask Dr Kay, as Secretary to the Committee of Council on Education, 'to favor this Committee with any suggestions concerning the plan

[1] *Appendix to the Reports of the Select Committee of the House of Commons on Public Petitions*, Session 1839. The number of signatures is here given as 22,000.

[2] *Proceedings of Education Committee*, Vol. I, pp. 109–10.

[3] *Ibid.*, Vol. I, p. 116. Permission to 'appropriate' this site was at first granted by the Council but later withdrawn (*ibid.*, p. 121).

[4] *Proceedings of Finance Committee*, Vol. X, p. 250.

of Schools, with a view to their guidance in the erection of those directed by the Town Council'.[1] Kay sent copies of a plan for a school, and also 'copies of the Reports on the training of Pauper Children published by the Poor Law Commissioners';[2] as a result, the Committee were evidently tempted to set up something in the nature of municipal industrial schools, since they resolved that 'the Surveyor be directed to submit an Estimate of the Expence of the erection of a School according to the plan with and without Workshops'.[3] Curiously enough, at about this time information on the subject of school 'workshops' was probably also available to the Committee from an even more authoritative source, for Lady Noel Byron,[4] a friend and correspondent of Mrs Rathbone's, was staying in the town;[5] and since Rathbone's wife was an enthusiastic member of the committee of ladies who helped to run the girls' department at the South School, and frequently wrote to Lady Noel Byron about the Corporation Schools, it would be surprising if such a distinguished educationist were not asked for advice. On 26 October 1839 the Town Clerk stated that sanction had been given for the building of three new schools at a total cost of £10,000, the probable expenditure during the current year being £3,300, presumably for the erection of a single school. It must be remembered that the Council's plans could not have been more ambitious since it had no power to levy a rate for the erection of schools, and the money required could come only from the surplus revenues of the town.

The Education Committee's determination to make the Corporation Schools as efficient as possible, and perhaps also its lingering desire to establish eventually something in the nature of a Normal School, were well shown by the arrangements that it now began to make for the training of teachers, arrangements which indicated clearly enough that the members of the Committee must have been among the earliest disciples of Dr Kay, and admirers of his 'apprentice-teacher' system.[6] Just as Kay, in his search for well-trained teachers, had been obliged to seek them in Scotland,[7] so the Liverpool Education Committee had appointed Scotsmen as masters of its two schools; but the number of

---

[1] *Ibid.*, Vol. I, pp. 120–1.   [2] *Ibid.*, Vol. I, p. 124.   [3] *Ibid.*

[4] For an account of the 'Industrial School' set up in Ealing Grove by Lady Noel Byron (widow of the poet) in 1834, see B. F. Duppa, 'Industrial Schools for the Peasantry' in the first volume of publications of the Central Society, 1837; 'Report on Schools of Industry' in *Minutes of Committee of Council on Education, 1842–43*. As a result of Lady Noel Byron's example, James Cropper, a close friend and former business partner of the Rathbone family, had set up an agricultural school near Warrington in 1835.

[5] 'Lady Noel Byron has been staying at the Adelphi during the last month' (*Liverpool Standard*, 24 September 1839).

[6] For an account of the origin of this system in England a little earlier, see F. Smith, *The Life and Work of Sir James Kay-Shuttleworth*, pp. 50–1.

[7] F. Smith, *op. cit.*, pp. 49, 58.

such teachers available was small, and it is not surprising that the Liverpool Committee was glad to adopt a system which Kay had found to work well.

It should be pointed out that the Education Committee was faced with a particularly difficult problem: although anxious not to stress religious differences in the schools, it naturally wished to appoint teachers of various denominations, so long as this could be done without lowering standards. There was, however, some difficulty in recruiting able Church of England teachers, partly because few such were to be found, and also because almost all of the local Church of England clergy were opposed to the system in force in the schools. It was even more difficult to obtain good Roman Catholic teachers, owing to the lack of facilities for their training; it is a remarkable fact that some of the Roman Catholic teachers in the town had actually been obliged to go for training to the Liverpool Bluecoat Hospital,[1] one of the most important training centres of the National Society for Promoting the Education of the Poor in the Principles of the Established Church. At the beginning of 1840 the staffing position in the Corporation Schools was described as follows:

Five of the teachers belong to the Church of England, three are Roman Catholics, four are Scotch Presbyterians, two Baptists, two Independents, and two Wesleyan Methodists. There is not a single Roman Catholic master or mistress in the South School establishment, although there are 329 Roman Catholic children belonging to it. There is no Church of England master in the South Boys' School. The head teachers of both the boys' schools are Scotchmen, one of them a Presbyterian of the Established Church and the other an Independent; and the head teachers of both the girls' schools belong to the Church of England. There is not a single Unitarian teacher on either establishment.[2]

In April 1839 the Education Committee, claiming it to be 'universally admitted that [there was] the greatest possible difficulty in procuring good Masters for the Education of the lower Orders', recommended that the Council should pay fees to enable a few of the most suitable boys leaving the Corporation Schools to attend the Evening School attached to the Liverpool Mechanics' Institution. It is interesting that 'no pledge was to be exacted' that the boys would in fact become teachers.[3] Shortly afterwards it was agreed that a number of boys and

---

[1] Forster, the Master, wrote to Dr Bell in 1831: 'There are besides eleven masters and mistresses at present with us, two of whom are for the Catholic schools in the town; and we have before had either five or seven of their teachers' (C. C. Southey, *The Life of the Rev. Andrew Bell*, Vol. III, p. 448).

[2] C. E. Trevelyan, *The Liverpool Corporation Schools*, Liverpool, 1840, p. 15.

[3] *Liverpool Mercury*, 3 May 1839.

girls should be engaged as 'Assistant Teachers', receiving two shillings and sixpence a week; and in January 1840 a formal 'Apprenticeship System' was introduced, with the purpose of engaging 'by Indenture for a Term of Years as many of the Pupils in the schools as can be usefully employed in the capacity of Assistant Teachers, the apprentices to be paid 'at a rate not exceeding two shillings and six pence per Week in the last Year of the period for which they may be bound'.[1]

Few details are available of the provision for instructing these apprentices, but on one occasion a headmaster reported on the progress which six of his apprentices were making in mathematics under his instruction: one of them, who had been studying 'the higher parts of Algebra and Trigonometry', had completed that course and had 'commenced the Differential Calculus', in which he was making 'rapid and effective progress', so that he appeared 'likely to become a Mathematician of the highest order'. The master was 'endeavouring to give these boys a little Latin', which he thought might be 'useful in extending their acquaintance with language generally'.[2] Perhaps the most interesting fact in connection with these arrangements for providing teachers is that one boy, John Buckley, after having been a pupil and later a paid monitor in one of the Corporation Schools, was helped financially by the Education Committee to fit himself for the teaching profession by becoming a student at Queens' College, Cambridge.

Notes found among the minutes of the Education Committee and evidently written not long after June 1841 show that at that time there were in the two schools seventeen regular teachers (including a music teacher) of whom eight belonged to the Church of England, five were Protestant Dissenters and three were Roman Catholics. (The religion of the remaining teacher is not given.) There were also eighteen apprentices, of whom four belonged to the Church of England, five were Protestant Dissenters, one was a Unitarian, and no fewer than eight were Roman Catholics. As in Dr Kay's establishment at Norwood, apprentices were bound for five years.

3

In view of the Committee of Council's decision to bow before the storm aroused by its proposal to establish the Normal and Model Schools, it is not surprising that the experiment being carried on in Liverpool now appeared to most people living outside the town to have less significance than before; although in fact there seemed to be good

---

[1] *Proceedings of Education Committee*, Vol. I, pp. 128–9.
[2] *Ibid.*, Vol. I, pp. 175–6.

prospects that the policy of the Liverpool Education Committee would be generally either supported or more or less reluctantly accepted in the town itself; and if it had been possible, as the Liberals still hoped it would be, to increase gradually the number of Corporation Schools, other parts of England might well have come in time to see the importance of what had been achieved in Liverpool. Even as matters stood, some observers not resident in the town continued to hope that the example set in Liverpool would be copied elsewhere. Thus the Rev. Baden Powell referred with approval to the system in force in the Corporation Schools when he wrote his *State Education Considered with Reference to Prevalent Misconceptions on Religious Grounds*, London and Oxford, 1840; whilst the Bishop of Norwich visited the schools on 23 October 1839[1] and again on 11 March 1840,[2] the first of his visits being reported and commented upon in these terms:

... the Bishop ... spent nearly two hours in the examination of the children, particularly with reference to their scriptural knowledge and religious subject [*sic*]. . . . we understand that he both felt and expressed the highest gratification at the results. . . . A meeting of the intolerants is about to be held at Norwich, and we doubt not in the least that the good Bishop will be enabled to avail himself on the occasion of the personal knowledge he has obtained, both there and in his place in Parliament, whenever a proper occasion shall offer, in a manner highly conducive to the success of the great cause of national education.

But the most interesting and interested visitor to the schools at this period was Charles Edward Trevelyan[3] (1807–1886), brother-in-law and close friend of Macaulay, and later Governor of Madras. After serving for a time in India, Trevelyan returned to England with Macaulay in 1838, and was at once struck by the increase in religious bigotry and strife which had taken place since he had left England. His interest in education[4] led him to visit the Liverpool Corporation Schools towards the end of 1839 (shortly before he became an assistant secretary to the Treasury); but before writing an account of the schools he felt it necessary to call attention to the evils of the agitation against Roman Catholicism then being carried on in Liverpool as elsewhere, more especially by the Rev. H. M'Neile. Using the pseudonym 'Philalethes', Trevelyan published a pamphlet entitled *The No-Popery Agitation* (Liverpool, 1840) in which he remarked that it was not until he came to Liverpool that he saw 'political and religious bigotry carried to the greatest possible height'. He heard M'Neile, in the course of a sermon,

---

[1] *Liverpool Mercury*, 25 October 1839.   [2] *Ibid.*, 13 March 1840.
[3] He was the grandfather of the modern historian, G. M. Trevelyan.
[4] He published a book on the education of the people of India in 1838.

. . . ranting in the most furious manner against the Roman Catholics. . . . The struggle, which he announced had already begun, was to end only in the entire subjection of either Catholics or Protestants. . . . His whole sermon was a savage declaration of war. It was absolutely incendiary, and if the public mind had been in an equally inflammable state, there is no degree of excess to which it might not have led.

After expressing something almost approaching horror at hearing M'Neile's remarks, and deploring the effect on those who came to share such opinions, Trevelyan wrote:

In the Corporation schools at Liverpool the Roman Catholic children receive, with the full knowledge and consent of their Priests, as sound evangelical instruction as the children in any school belonging to the Church of England or Protestant Dissenters. . . . By means of the system of education which has been established in Ireland and at Liverpool . . . we have it in our power to give the rising generation of Roman Catholics the solid Christian instruction of which I have been speaking. Can it be doubted what we ought to do in such a case?

In the hope that the same system might 'soon be extended to the remaining masses of the Roman Catholic population in England and Scotland', Trevelyan next produced a longer pamphlet entitled *The Liverpool Corporation Schools*, Liverpool, 1840;[1] this is important not merely as giving Trevelyan's views but because it provides a good deal of information about the schools as they were after the Education Committee's policy had been in operation for a few years. Thus we learn that at the end of 1839 the schools were constituted as follows:

	Boys	Girls	Infants	Total
Church of England	185	172	179	536
Roman Catholics	419	339	178	936
Church of Scotland	11	14	12	37
Methodists	38	29	9	76
Independents	20	22	20	62
Baptists	12	18	—	30
Irvingites	—	2	—	2
Unitarians	2	1	3	6
Socialist	1	—	—	1
	688	597	401	1686

Trevelyan commented: 'The small proportion of children of Protestant Dissenters attending the schools is remarkable, considering that the Dissenters defend the principle on which they are conducted': he explained that this was because most of the Protestant Dissenters in

[1] At least four editions of this pamphlet were published; after a short time both pamphlets were published under one cover.

Liverpool 'did not stand in need of charitable aid for their children', and to meet such need as there was 'large and efficient schools' supported by Dissenters were available. Therefore, in Trevelyan's words, although 'the ministers of the Liverpool Protestant Dissenters have attended now and then to examine the schools . . . they seem to think that the number of children of their own persuasions receiving instruction at them is too small to require separate attention'. The writer emphasized that 'in proportion to the progress which the schools have made in public opinion, the number of Protestant children attending them has increased, and has gradually risen from 52 to 750, of whom 536 belong to the Church of England'. That such 'progress . . . in public opinion' had been made he attributed partly to the fact that a deputation consisting of (Liberal) representatives from all the wards in the town had 'examined the children in the Bible, and the favourable report given in by them of the manner in which their religious instruction had been attended to, secured the confidence both of the respectable class which adopted these means of ascertaining the truth, and of a great proportion of the people at large'.

In general, of course, Trevelyan confirms what has already been learned from other sources about the system of religious instruction adopted in the schools, but he gives one or two interesting details and, as we shall see, at least one surprising piece of new information. We are informed that, although there were now six Unitarians and one Socialist attending the schools, no alteration had been made 'in the nature of the common religious instruction' on their account, 'since the plan of cutting down religious instruction to the standard of those who believe least has never been acted upon in these schools'. He explains that the Protestant children were 'all taught the Bible together, through the medium of the authorized version' on all but one day of the week, when the Protestant Dissenters were 'taught Watts's catechism', whilst the children belonging to the Established Church were 'taught the Church catechism by masters or monitors belonging to the Church of England, or by a clergyman if there be any present'.

The Roman Catholic clergymen were said to be 'very exemplary in their attendance on the North School, but at the South School they seem disposed to leave the secular teachers to take their own course about the religious instruction,[1] which is the more remarkable as all these teachers are Protestants'; this is explained elsewhere when Tre-

---

[1] It will be remembered that Sleigh had reported that no priest had visited the South School since 1837 (op. cit., p. 11). Apparently attendance at the South School by a Roman Catholic priest was resumed before January 1842 when the Rev. William Parker stated that he had been 'in the habit of visiting the school' (Liverpool Mercury, 21 January 1842).

velyan informs us that 'The Roman Catholic monitors, acting under the direction of their priests, instruct [the Roman Catholic children] in their catechism. The Roman Catholic teachers, where there are any, hear them read their Bible; and in the South School, where there are no teachers of that persuasion, the Roman Catholic children are taught the Bible by one of the Protestant teachers, who explains it to them in strict accordance with those essential doctrines of Christianity which are held in common by Protestants and Roman Catholics'.[1] Of course only the Rheims and Douay versions of the Bible were employed for the instruction of Roman Catholic children. It had been found advisable not to allow monitors to give 'instruction in the Bible', since they taught 'in too formal and mechanical a manner to produce the proper effect upon the minds and characters of children'.

But certainly the most striking piece of information provided by Trevelyan concerns the arrangements made for the religious instruction of those children attending the Infants' Schools, whose ages ranged from two to six. He writes:

The business of each day commences with the prayer, of which a copy is annexed, in which all unite. No distinctions of any kind are allowed in the infant schools. Girls and boys, Protestants and Roman Catholics, are all taught together to fear their God, to love and adore their Saviour, and to grow up in habits of good fellowship with one another. The religious instruction given cannot be termed peculiarly Church of England, Church of Scotland, or Church of Rome. It is only peculiarly Christian. . . . Infant schools, conducted on the principle of these schools, ought to form the basis of any system of national instruction that may be adopted. We shall then at any rate set out right. The first formation of the national character will be on the foundation of Christian union.

The interesting fact here revealed is that, although the Roman Catholic priests had refused to allow the older Roman Catholic children to join in prayer with their non-Catholic fellows, and had incurred a great deal of criticism and jeopardized the success of the Education Committee's policy by doing so, they had nevertheless agreed to permit the very young children of their faith to unite in a common form of prayer with Protestant children. When the consent of the priests had been given is not stated, but if an otherwise somewhat obscure observation of Samuel Wilderspin's[2] is read in conjunction with

---

[1] Such Biblical instruction was sometimes given in the girls' schools by members of the committee of ladies who helped to run the schools. Mrs Rathbone was one who read the Bible with Roman Catholic children (*Liverpool Mercury*, 7 January 1842).

[2] 'The mistress of the Infant School has assured me that prayer was *always* adopted in the Infant Schools, and the [head] master also assures me that he has continued it' (Letter published in *Liverpool Chronicle*, 8 April 1837).

Trevelyan's remarks it becomes possible to infer that the infants of all denominations prayed together from the first day that the new system was introduced into the schools.

Trevelyan gives some interesting information about the day-to-day working of the schools: he refers to the attempt made to 'engraft' upon the monitorial system the 'methods recommended by Pestalozzi, Wood, &c.', and he speaks of the importance attached to 'gymnastic exercises', and to the 'jury system', by which children passed judgment on their fellows; he mentions also that once each day boys and girls were 'assembled together in the gallery and ... lectured and closely examined by the [head] masters in arithmetic, natural history, geography, or astronomy', the lectures being 'illustrated by maps, globes, and any simple experiments which may be available for the purpose'. Trevelyan adds the comment: 'This mode of accustoming the boys and girls to each others' society is ... found to have a good effect upon both.' But what most impressed him was the absence of ill-feeling between the children of the different denominations; he gives a convincing account of his attempts to discover signs of discord, which elicited from the children only the smiling admission that the Protestants sometimes played tug-of-war with the Roman Catholics, the teacher helping whichever side seemed the weaker!

Summing up, Trevelyan stated that, after a careful consideration of the principle on which the schools were conducted and a searching examination into its practical working, he was convinced that the arrangements made were 'extremely well adapted both for giving a sound religious education, and for teaching the tenets peculiar to each religious persuasion, without interfering with the harmony which it is so desirable to cultivate among them all'. He described the schools as 'very decidedly the most religious schools' he had ever seen; and he went on:

The success which has attended this experiment has a very important bearing upon the great education question which is now dividing the nation. If it be practicable to give a sound religious education to Protestants and Roman Catholics in common, it must be still easier to obtain the same result where none but Protestants have to be taught, which is the case in ninety-nine places out of a hundred in this island.

But if Trevelyan had found cheerful toleration within the Liverpool Corporation Schools, he had also, as we have seen, learned something of the efforts which were being made outside the schools to create a very different atmosphere in the town and, indeed, in the country as a whole. He himself remarked: 'The perfect harmony which prevails

inside the Corporation Schools, and the deadly hatred and open violence which prevail outside, are an awful reproof to those ministers of
discord who openly glory from the pulpit in having set one half of the
country against the other half.'

4

It might have been expected that the decision of the Liberal councillors to establish additional Corporation Schools would not be accepted without protest, especially in view of the fact that the Committee
of Council had just been compelled to abandon its plan to set up the
Normal and Model Schools. Yet there seems to have been little spon-
taneous opposition to the new proposals. In June 1839 a somewhat
vaguely worded petition 'from certain Municipal Voters and others
resident in Abercromby Ward' begged that the Council would, in any
Corporation Schools which might be established in that ward, establish
a system of education which would be in 'conformity to the Established
religion of this Kingdom', would permit the 'free and unrestricted use
of the bible' and would allow 'a complete toleration of all dissenters
from the Established Church without any limitation or exception other
than what arises from the conjunction of dangerous political dispositions
with certain religious tenets'.[1] This petition aroused little interest, it
would appear, either in the Council Chamber or elsewhere.

The news that the Council intended to erect a school in West
Derby Ward brought a protest from some of those resident in that
ward, who, in the words of their representative, John Smith, asked the
Council to leave them to themselves 'and not to interfere with the
education of their poor'; they pointed out that they had established
schools by voluntary effort, and would provide additional schools
when such were required. The discussion which followed the presen-
tation of this protest[2] was of some interest as showing the differences
of opinion among the Conservative members of the Council. One,
Joseph Cooper, claimed that the majority of the inhabitants of Liverpool were opposed to the policy adopted in the Corporation Schools,
and that 'no real Protestant' could send his child to them. Mr Sands
proposed that no denominational religious instruction whatever
should be given in the Corporation Schools, but felt that all the
children should read the Authorized Version of the Bible.

Isaac Holmes, a determined critic of the Liberal policy, made the
same proposal, but was also willing to allow the Council to establish

[1] *Proceedings of Council*, Vol. XVIII, p. 199.
[2] *Liverpool Courier*, 10 July 1839.

separate schools for Protestants and Roman Catholics. Thomas Case was another Conservative who favoured the building of separate schools for Roman Catholic children, arguing that all who contributed to the town's revenues should 'share in the benefits of public education'. The readiness of a number of the Conservatives to compromise, or even to accept without further opposition what had been done, is well shown by the remarks of G. H. Lawrence, who is reported to have said that he 'had really felt until very lately, that there might be some modification of the system to meet the wishes of all parties, but it seemed to be impracticable now, and he thought it quite in vain to discuss the matter over and over again in this manner. Sir Robert Peel was satisfied after two divisions in the House of Commons[1] to abandon his opposition . . . and he [Mr Lawrence] thought that, having tested the opinion of the Council on the matter more than once, they might now allow it to remain as it stood'.

Two Liberals, Sir Joshua Walmsley and Richard Sheil, suggested that a compromise might be effected if secular instruction only were to be given in the Corporation Schools; Sheil alluded to the well-known fact that many members of the middle class in Liverpool sent their children to schools in which no religious instruction was given; he remarked that, although a Roman Catholic, he had unhesitatingly sent his children to such a school, even though it was under the control of a clergyman of the Established Church.[2] After some discussion the decision to build a school in West Derby Ward was confirmed by thirty-three votes to eight, two of the Conservatives, Thomas Case and Charles Lawrence, voting with the Liberals.

A more impressive protest against the Liberals' proposal to establish new Corporation Schools was made a few months later (December 1839) when 'certain Operative Inhabitants of the Borough' renewed the appeal which they had made in the previous March that the new schools should cater for those who could not conscientiously send their children to the existing 'unscriptural' schools. As on the former occasion, this petition had been drawn up at a meeting of the Liverpool

[1] The allusion was to the recent debates during which the constitution and powers of the Committee of Council had been discussed.

[2] Probably Sheil was referring to the Royal Institution School in Liverpool, the Principal of which had been the Rev. J. B. Monk. It is an interesting fact that Monk and the Rev. Augustus Campbell (who had sent his children to this school) both firmly believed that it was better not to educate the poor at all than to give them education without religious instruction, and both men were moved to indignant protests when they thought that the Bible was being excluded from the Corporation Schools; yet neither of them was at all concerned about the absence of religious instruction or Bible-reading from the curriculum of the Royal Institution School, which catered for children of the middle class. This attitude was, of course, by no means uncommon.

Protestant Operative Association, a meeting at which the Rev. H. M'Neile had agreed that Bible reading was 'bona fide a part of the system' in force in the Corporation Schools, but yet contended that the schools were not 'Scriptural', since the teaching of 'Popery' was also part of the system; he had told his hearers:

> There is no use in being moderately and quietly right in these days; you should be determinedly right. The great agitator can now only obtain any thing. They will mistake moderation for weakness.[1]

Once again the Council was asked to consider the proposal that the existing schools might remain as they were, but that 'in all schools which might hereafter be erected at the expense of the Corporation . . . the authorized version of the scriptures' might be taught to all the pupils; and once again the motion was lost, on this occasion by thirty-three votes to seven. Even the moderate proposal of the Conservative Thomas Case that *one* of the new schools should be such as would satisfy the wishes of the petitioners was ignored; whilst the Liberal Alderman Earle suggested that the operatives' petition scarcely merited a courteous reply, as it might have done if it 'had come from a body of their fellow-townsmen speaking their own sentiments, without being under the control of any priestly influence'.[2]

In the end, however, although the Liberals continued to hope that they might be able to build additional Corporation Schools, they found it impossible to do so. As late as October 1840 Thomas Blackburn said:

> In referring to the Corporation Schools . . . it was not the fault of the Education Committee but for the want of funds, that other schools, to be conducted on the same plan, had not been erected; a site, however, had been fixed on for an additional school, and he hoped by the next Municipal election that it would be completed.[3]

But the claims on the not very considerable surplus funds of the Corporation were many, and the existing schools were proving expensive to run: early in 1840 an indignant critic objected that the schools then cost twice as much to run as they had done under the old Council, and William Rathbone was obliged to explain that it had been necessary to engage better masters, and that, finding 'the monitorial system not a good one . . ., they had now teachers, which, of course, incurred additional expense'.[4] At one time the Education Committee was

---

[1] *Liverpool Mercury*, 25 October 1839.
[2] *Ibid.*, 13 December 1839.
[3] *Ibid.*, 23 October 1840.
[4] *Liverpool Mercury*, 14 February 1840. In 1828 the salaries bill had amounted to £370; it now amounted to over £1,350 (*Accounts of the Corporation of Liverpool*).

anxious to take over the Hibernian (St Patrick's) School in Pleasant Street—the school which Thomas Wyse had praised in Parliament when the 'Irish System' of education was first being planned; but the negotiations with the trustees of the school came to nothing.[1] The Education Committee had to be content with adding 'four Class Rooms . . . at the North School, two for the Boys and two for the Girls',[2] at a cost of about £700.

5

Those local historians[3] who have made any reference in their works to the Liverpool Corporation Schools have tended to accept without question the claim made by the Liberals[4] that when they lost control of the Town Council in 1841 it was almost entirely because of the opposition aroused by their policy of making the Corporation Schools available to children of all denominations—such opposition having been stimulated and organized almost solely by the Rev. H. M'Neile. The claim is rather too sweeping; it is not unusual for political parties to give over-simplified explanations of their victories and defeats, or to over-emphasize such factors as they consider to redound to their credit. But in any case the explanation given by the Liberals itself raises a problem. There is not the least doubt that at the time of Lord John Russell's visit in October 1838 the policy adopted in the Corporation Schools had almost ceased to be a live political issue, in spite of the fact that for more than two years it had encountered the most determined opposition not only of M'Neile and his followers but of almost all of the most highly respected Church of England clergymen in the town. M'Neile himself, it will be remembered, had acknowledged his despair and his defeat. How, then, did he and the forces he stood for become powerful enough within a few years to sweep the Liberals from power in the town?

Part of the answer seems to be that at this time there would in any case have appeared in traditionally Conservative Liverpool signs of that widespread Conservative reaction which eventually brought Peel to power in 1841; the case scarcely needs to be argued, but it may perhaps be noted that *The Times*, after the municipal elections of 1840, could with much justification claim that:

In Manchester and Birmingham the conservatives contest the validity of the charters, and consequently refuse to interfere in the elections. But with

---

[1] April–May 1839 (*Proceedings of Education Committee*, Vol. I, p. 106).
[2] *Proceedings of Council*, Vol. XVIII, p. 443 (5 August 1840).
[3] See, e.g., R. Muir, *A History of Liverpool*, London, 1907, p. 312.
[4] See, e.g., E. A. Rathbone (ed.), *Records of the Rathbone Family*, p. 211.

these two exceptions, and perhaps one or two others in which the conservatives have made no exertions, every town of England of the first class, and almost every one of the second and third classes, has given a verdict of reprobation of the ministerial adherents.[1]

It is true, of course, that the Protestant Association as a whole, and M'Neile in particular, had to some extent helped to bring about the general reaction referred to, by proclaiming repeatedly that the Church was being endangered as the result of policies pursued by the Liberals; but most people would agree that the *Liverpool Standard* was being very much carried away by partiality when it claimed, after the Conservatives had been successful in the General Election of 1841, that 'no one individual in the kingdom' had 'contributed more than Mr M'Neile to our late anti-revolutionary reaction'.[2] It is important to note that, just as the Liberals in the country as a whole were divided among themselves, so also in Liverpool they played into the hands of their opponents during the years 1839-41 by allowing disunity and dissension to diminish their strength, and they were far from being in a position to resist as a united and well-led party the general movement towards Conservatism: matters even reached such a pass that during the Parliamentary election campaign of 1841 their chosen candidate, Sir Joshua Walmsley, publicly acknowledged that he was without the support of many of his party![3] In short, whereas a writer in the *Dictionary of National Biography* claims that M'Neile 'defeated the town council of Liverpool in a dispute about the management of the corporation school' [sic], it would probably be more accurate to say that the Liverpool Liberals would have been 'defeated' when they were even if M'Neile had never been heard of; but that it was very largely because of his efforts that the victory of the Conservatives was so decisive and led to such a great change of policy in the Corporation Schools.

For it seems very likely that if it had not been for the work of the Rev. H. M'Neile and, to a much lesser extent, of his fellow-members of the Protestant Association, the Rev. Fielding Ould and the Rev. D. James, either the system adopted in the Corporation Schools would have continued to establish itself, and to win at least grudging acceptance among most of those interested in the schools, or at any rate some compromise reasonably acceptable to members of all denominations would have been found. Indeed, for periods of months at a time no reference to the schools was to be seen in the Conservative or Liberal Press; and sometimes even at meetings of the Protestant Association only brief allusions to the schools were made. In 1837, according to

---

[1] 6 November 1840.   [2] *Liverpool Standard*, 19 October 1841.
[3] *Liverpool Mercury*, 18 June 1841.

M'Neile, the Protestant Association had provided 'for the people of England' what he called 'three watchwords': 'Scriptural Education', 'Church Extension', and 'The Repeal of the [Roman Catholic] Emancipation Bill';[1] but from 1839 onwards it was the last of these aims which most engaged M'Neile's attention, so that, except at election times, the meetings of the Protestant Association tended to be concerned more with discussions of the perfidy and general undesirability of 'Popery' than with the particular shortcomings of the Corporation Schools.

At the annual meeting of the Protestant Association held in October 1839 about twenty-six of the Protestant clergy of Liverpool were present; this represented about one-third of all the Protestant clergy in the town. Usually, however, the number of such clergy present was very much smaller, and it was noticeable that most of the better-known clergymen, including the two Rectors, did not attend the meetings of the Association. It was not, indeed, surprising that the more responsible English clergymen in the town should have wished to keep away from gatherings at which the staple fare consisted of vehement denunciations of 'Popery' made by crudely intolerant Irish clerics whose every word was an implied criticism of the lukewarmness of the Englishmen's attachment to their Protestant beliefs. And there is evidence that M'Neile's influence on middle-class opinion in general was at this period not particularly strong.

At one Protestant Association meeting the Rev. F. Parry remarked:

How can I but feel pain . . . when we learn that the support given to the Protestant Association of Liverpool by the Protestant public of Liverpool is so inadequate to its wants, and so far from commensurate to its objects? Surely that object has not been fully appreciated?

On the same occasion the Rev. H. M'Neile, after remarking that the victory of the Conservatives in the recent parliamentary elections would make political activity less necessary, told members of the local association that they were 'supported to-day in some degree as they ought always to have been supported'; but he went on:

Upon one or two occasions lately the support has seemed to have fallen away. There were in this town some who began to murmur, to look coldly upon these proceedings . . . I have good hope, sir, that we shall find such support from many seriously-minded men who were alarmed at what they called a political movement, but who now seeing it divested of party politics, will join it as a Protestant movement.[2]

[1] *Jezebel, a Type of Popery* . . . , Liverpool, MDCCCXL, p. 39.
[2] *Liverpool Courier*, 6 October 1841.

The Rev. Hugh Stowell somewhat pointedly stated that the Manchester branch of the Protestant Association did not owe sixpence and had a credit of ten or twelve pounds, whereas the Liverpool branch was more than a hundred pounds in debt.[1] All these statements were made, it must be noted, within a month of the date when the Liberals lost control of the Council. Somewhat earlier Rathbone had declared in a letter to his son:

. . . I think the poor Parson has missed his mark sadly, even the Tories say it is too bad, and he has proved to my mind that he is capable of being a zealous and a bitter partisan, but incapable of appreciating or acting upon those high principles which give consistency or claim respect, he may yet be made use of as a tool by some, but none whose opinion is worth having or any side will respect, and no one will trust.[2]

It must be said, in support of Rathbone's opinion, that, up to the time when he was writing, very few of the Conservative members of the Council seem to have echoed the extreme and uncompromising opinions of M'Neile.

Whence, then, did M'Neile derive his influence and support? There seems to be good reason to believe that a writer in *The Albion* of 21 October 1839, although of course a biased witness, was not altogether wide of the mark when he stated that M'Neile, having failed to influence for long the 'respectable' and 'educated' classes in the town, was being compelled to turn for support to 'the ignorant and unlettered'. What had given rise to this observation was the speech which M'Neile had recently delivered at a meeting of the Liverpool Operative Protestant Association, when he had counselled against moderation and advised his hearers that 'the great agitator can now only obtain any thing'. M'Neile had by this time grasped several important facts: that although many members of the English middle class had no love for Roman Catholicism, most of them had a considerable respect for the principle of toleration; that some part of the 'working classes', on the other hand, could be much more easily swayed; that an exciting public meeting was far more effective than a carefully reasoned article in an expensive newspaper; and, above all, that in the new, still small, constituencies a well-organized 'pressure group' could not only help to defeat opponents but, perhaps even more important, could hope to dictate the policy of allies.

So pleased was M'Neile with the enthusiasm of the 'operative Protestants' that he helped to organize branch groups in various Liverpool

---

[1] *Liverpool Standard*, 5 October 1841.
[2] Letter dated 16/17 March 1840 (*Rathbone Family Papers*).

parishes;[1] soon he was able to boast that when he had first discussed the foundation of 'Operative Protestant Associations' with his 'reverend and beloved namesake' (Rev. Hugh Stowell), the latter had 'had some doubts . . . about the practicability of doing it right'; however, Stowell had called a meeting of operatives and now had become 'the most powerful man in Manchester'. But this, M'Neile remarked, was not all. He went on:

I suppose if the Protestant feeling had been confined to Exeter Hall, and Liverpool and Manchester, our rulers would have gone on dozing quietly as usual; that they would have said, 'these manufacturers are gone mad—do not mind them.' But, lo! another and another fire broke out—one in Bristol, another in Bath, another in Hereford. No wonder Dr. Murray calls us smoking firebrands. We have been agitators for Protestantism throughout England. We have animated the country, we have had meetings in Glasgow, Edinburgh, York, Newcastle, Hull, and next week if all be well, I shall be at Norwich.[2]

The *Liverpool Standard* proudly claimed that: 'From this town . . . the fervid eloquence of M'Neile has reverberated from the shores of the Mersey to the Clyde and the Thames, palsying at its sound the steps of the unclean spirit of Belial, whose polluting foot was already upon the altar, and whose defiling hand was grasping at the sacred things of the sanctuary.'[3] Shortly afterwards the *Liverpool Courier* quoted the annual report of the Liverpool Protestant Operative Association as saying that 'the influence of this Association was not confined to Liverpool but that similar combinations, in consequence of its formation, had sprung up in several districts of the metropolis, as well as in Manchester, Sheffield, Norwich, Bristol, Wigan and other places.'[4]

The 'operative associations' seem to have existed chiefly in order to hear speeches on the evils of 'Popery', but at election times the members were given clear-cut instructions as to how they should vote; and the speeches on free trade[5] which M'Neile delivered to some of these supposedly religious organizations[6] during the parliamentary

---

[1] See accounts of the inauguration of such branches at Toxteth Park and in St Simon's Parish (*Liverpool Mercury*, 2 October and 16 October 1840).

[2] *Liverpool Courier*, 14 October 1840.

[3] 26 June 1840.

[4] *Liverpool Courier*, 11 November 1840.

[5] Richard Cobden replied to M'Neile's arguments in a letter to Lawrence Heyworth, Chairman of the Liverpool Anti-Corn Law Association; extracts were printed in the *Liverpool Mercury*, 25 June 1841.

[6] M'Neile spoke on the Corn Laws to the London Protestant Operative Association, 16 June 1841 (*Times*, 17 June 1841), and also to its counterpart in Liverpool on 11 June 1841. A sample of his oratory when addressing 'operatives' may be of interest:
The Operative Protestants were all exhorted to favour 'English manufacturers,

election campaign of 1841 must have helped the Conservatives more than did many more dignified and learned disquisitions in favour of the Corn Laws. One curious, if not altogether surprising, result of M'Neile's varied activities was that on at least one occasion bands of workmen who held opposing views concerning the Corn Laws first broke up each other's meetings and then proceeded to smash windows in Roman Catholic and Church of England churches and schools.[1]

With each month that passed, the vehemence of M'Neile and his supporters increased. Only occasionally did they refer specifically to the Corporation Schools, as when the Rev. D. James, after a visit to the schools, reported that in them provision was made 'for teaching the *bad*, the *immoral*, the *barbarous*, and the *heretical*, as well as the "pure and undefiled".'[2] It became a commonplace for M'Neile to 'advise his hearers by all they valued, to join in the cry of "No Popery",'[3] whilst Stowell was to be heard asking Liverpool audiences never to rest 'till the reformed faith of our fathers fills all England and Ireland and the Pope of Rome has not one vassal left within the dominions of the Queen'.[4] Some of the newspapers showed their appreciation of M'Neile's support of the Conservative cause by echoing his sentiments; so that the *Liverpool Standard* was to be found remarking that if the 'Papists' were ever again allowed to parade through the town on St Patrick's Day 'all we can say is that the public authorities of the town are willing to be considered as conniving at treason, and that the Protestant inhabitants of the town have consented to place their necks under the yoke of Popish tyranny'. There was something dangerously near to incitement to riot in the *Standard's* final exhortation on this occasion: 'Protestants of Liverpool! shame upon your cowardly dere-

English machinery, English commerce, English sailors, ready and prepared for every occasion, and every enterprise alike of bravery and humanity, English navy, English army, English church—(tremendous applause)—English constitution, securing the splendour and prerogatives of the crown, the dignity and hereditary possessions of the nobles, and the liberties and security of the people. (Enthusiastic burst of applause). English oxen, and sheep, and hogs, and poultry,—yes, and the best, safest, and most nutritious food for all these, English Corn! O! gentlemen be not deceived by the new-fashioned cant of cosmopolitan liberalism as if patriotism had become a crime. (Hear, hear, hear.) No; cultivate patriotism in wheat. (Cheers). Patriotism in wheat! (Renewed cheers). Instead of looking upon patriotism as a prejudice, cultivate all that is dear to England—yes, and make the welkin ring with the cheers of honest hearts and hands and tongues for old England—for OLD HOME-FED ENGLAND! (Most enthusiastic burst of applause.)' (*The Corn Laws. Extracts from the Speech of the Rev. Hugh M'Neile at the Meeting of the Liverpool Operative Protestant Association . . . , 11th June 1841*, Liverpool [n.d.]).

[1] *Liverpool Mercury*, 11 June and 18 June 1841.
[2] *Liverpool Courier*, 18 November 1840.
[3] *Liverpool Mercury*, 9 October 1840.
[4] *Liverpool Courier*, 6 October 1841.

liction of principle! How long will you permit a horde of beggarly aliens to trample upon you and insult you? Shake off your lethargy and be men.'[1]

It was perhaps not surprising that on the day of the General Election in July 1841 serious disorders broke out and a hundred arrests were made; indeed, that more serious riots did not take place could have been due only to the fact that, as Trevelyan had put it, the public mind was not generally in the same 'inflammable state' as were the minds of some of its counsellors. Perhaps the most revealing comment on the situation in Liverpool at this time is that of one citizen who, after spending a short time in London, expressed his astonishment and delight that he had been able to traverse the metropolis without seeing a single 'No Popery' placard![2]

6

In the midst of all this clamour it was not surprising that the voice of the great majority of the Protestant clergymen of the town was not to be heard; unable to support either M'Neile or those whose opinions he so fiercely denounced, they were significantly and, in a sense, impressively silent. On one occasion, however, there was an interesting exchange of views among the Church of England clergy as a whole; this occurred when in 1839 plans were being made to establish in Liverpool under the control of members of the Established Church a Collegiate Institution which would 'provide the commercial, trading, and working classes with an education in which secular instruction should be combined with religious instruction in the doctrines of the Established Church.'[3] The question at once arose whether Protestant Dissenters might be admitted to this institution for higher education. The problem was left for the clergy to solve, and after two meetings it was decided to recommend that in the new school, although all children would read the Authorized Version of the Bible, only members of the Church of England would be obliged to study the Church Catechism.[4] This decision found favour with almost all of the Church of England clergy, including M'Neile; a small High Church group led by the Rev. Cecil Wray protested in vain that the Church alone had the power to control the education of the people, and should insist on teaching its doctrines to all who attended its schools.[5]

The decision to establish the Collegiate Institution gave rise to an interesting situation in the following year. Lord Stanley, as a local

[1] 20 March 1840. [2] *Liverpool Mercury*, 10 September 1841.
[3] *Liverpool Courier*, 27 November 1839. [4] *Ibid.*
[5] *Ibid.*, 27 November and 4 December 1839.

representative of the aristocracy, a leading Conservative and a champion of the Church of England, was the obvious choice for the honour of laying the foundation-stone of the new building; had he not during the stormy debates concerning the constitution of the Committee of Council on Education even gone back to the reign of Henry IV to find support for the contention that in England education should be directed by the clergy?[1] On the other hand, neither Stanley nor his hearers were likely to have forgotten that it was he who had first sanctioned the introduction of the 'Irish System of Education' into Ireland; so that all those who had taken part in the struggle concerning the Corporation Schools were likely to provide an audience markedly attentive to what he had to say about education. It is not surprising, therefore, that when he came to discuss the duties of the state in relation to education his remarks were somewhat lacking in forthrightness; yet the speech represented an unmistakable, if somewhat muted, defiance of such men as M'Neile, and, therefore, must have pleased those who hoped that the Conservatives in the Government and in the local Council would resist the pressure being put upon them by the more intolerant of their supporters. Stanley stated that he did not believe that it was the duty of the Government to 'provide for the education of all the people', since this would involve a 'government controul over the education of the people, which was at variance with that freedom of conscience which, if they claimed it for themselves, they freely gave and conceded to all others'. The report continued:

But he admitted,—nay, more, he contended, that it was the duty of the Government to promote the education of the people, and to aid individual exertions. Various questions might arise, nice and difficult and complicated questions, which were not to be hastily decided upon, but upon which much might be said on both sides, as to the degree in which a State was bound to enforce on a people its own views, with regard to education; and when he used the word education he comprised and included the diffusion of religious knowledge also. There might be no circumstances, or there might be few and doubtful circumstances, in which it might be the duty of the State as a State to promote by its assistance even the diffusion of a religion erroneous, professed by a large portion of the community. On this subject there must be many opinions, and he hesitated not to state his own opinions frankly and fairly. They would not respect him if he did not do so, and he hesitated not to say that there were many circumstances in which it must be the duty of the State to be satisfied with the promotion of important truths, not with an admixture of error, but with an imperfection of truths.[2]

[1] Hansard, Third Series, Vol. XLVIII, Col. 238.
[2] *Liverpool Mercury*, 23 October 1840; *Liverpool Courier*, 28 October 1840.

The comments of the Rev. Hugh M'Neile on this declaration seem not to have been recorded, but his chief lieutenant in Liverpool, the Rev. Fielding Ould, at the next meeting of the Protestant Operative Association of the town, promptly 'combated the opinion laid down by Lord Stanley that it was the duty of the state to promote religious error when that error was shared in by a large portion of the community'.[1]

7

Meanwhile the general reaction in favour of Conservatism, the divisions of opinion among the Liberals in the town, a certain degree of dissatisfaction with some of the Liberals' measures, the discontent brought on by a period of economic depression and, of course, the prolonged campaign led by M'Neile, had begun seriously to weaken the position of the Liverpool Liberals. In the municipal elections of 1839 nine Liberal councillors and eight Conservative councillors had to seek re-election; eight Liberals and nine Conservatives were elected, and of the eight contests in which Liberals were successful four were won by a total majority of only ten votes. Between 1837 and 1839 the percentage of the votes cast which had gone to Liberal candidates had dropped from about 52 to nearly 48.6.[2]

It can be said that on this occasion the 'Schools Question' was certainly not the only important issue at stake; true, M'Neile urged the householders among the members of the Protestant Operative Association to 'shout in every street and in every polling place—"Scriptural schools or no schools, put the Bible into the hands of our children or we will not put you into the Town Hall" ';[3] whilst at the pre-election meeting of the Tradesmen's Reform Association much was said in praise of the system adopted in the Corporation Schools, and two Roman Catholic speakers called on their co-religionists to support the Liberals.[4] But both the victorious and the defeated parties appear to have believed that the election results were also influenced by opposition to the Liberals' decision to build warehouses on the dock quays, by resentment at the creation of new by-laws, by the indignation of influential publicans at the granting of many new licences, and by apathy among the Reformers. Commenting on this last factor in the

[1] *Liverpool Courier*, 11 November 1840.

[2] One Conservative was returned unopposed.

[3] *Liverpool Mercury*, 25 October 1839. This was said at the meeting at which M'Neile agreed that the Bible was '*bona fide* a part of the system' in force in the Corporation Schools, but nevertheless claimed that these schools were 'unscriptural'. See p. 216.

[4] *Ibid.*, 1 November 1839.

defeat of the Liberals, the *Liverpool Journal*[1] observed that in the recent municipal elections the Conservatives had 'considerably strengthened their influence in the municipal councils of the nation generally'; and the *Liverpool Mercury*[2] wrote that Liberals, in Liverpool as elsewhere, had become 'to some extent, indifferent and lukewarm, in consequence of the slow, or rather, backward progress made in the attainment of just and salutary reforms'.

It was possible for some of the Liberal journals to speak of the Liberals' lack of success in the municipal elections of 1839 as a 'slight discomfiture'[3] and as 'a little reverse of fortune',[4] but in fact it marked the beginning of a series of defeats which were to lose them control of the Council. The municipal elections of 1840 were disastrous for the Liberals: although their share of the total votes cast declined only very slightly (from about 48·6 to about 48·5 per cent),[5] so many of their seats were at stake on this occasion that the defeat of the Liberals was much more serious than that suffered in the previous year. Conservatives were returned in eleven wards and Liberals in only five; as a result of these elections the Conservatives gained seven seats, so that now there were twenty-seven Conservatives in the Council to twenty-one Liberals, the latter retaining control of the Council only because of the presence in it of sixteen Liberal aldermen, eight of whom would have to seek re-election in the following year. William Rathbone was defeated by one vote and Thomas Blackburn by four. (Shortly after the elections W. W. Currie, the Liberal member for North Toxteth Ward, died, and in the by-election which followed Rathbone was again defeated, on this occasion by three votes in a total poll of 515.)[6] Again the 'Schools Question' was an important, but by no means the only, and perhaps not even the dominant, issue, for a very great deal of attention was again paid to the 'Warehouse Question',[7] especially since allegations were made that the Liberal policy in the matter would cause much unemployment in the town.

For months at a time, until the election period drew near, there had been no references to the Corporation Schools in the local Press; and even during the election campaign there were only brief references to

[1] 2 November 1839.
[2] 8 November 1839.
[3] *The Albion*, 4 November 1839.
[4] *Liverpool Journal*, 2 November 1839.
[5] The figures given relate to all the municipal elections for the year specified, including by-elections.
[6] *The Times* printed the news under the heading 'Glorious Radical Defeat' (21 November 1840).
[7] William Rathbone's electoral address in October 1840 was almost entirely devoted to a discussion of the subject (*Rathbone Family Papers*).

the schools at most of the ward meetings, although at some such meetings Conservatives and Liberals attacked or defended with vigour the system in force in the schools. Certainly, when the elections were over most of the victorious Conservative candidates had no need to feel that they had committed themselves to any agreed course of action with regard to the Corporation Schools. The Liberals had claimed before the elections that they had established in the Corporation Schools 'a system of education so excellent, that it has lived down all open attack, though still exposed to secret calumny', thereby winning for themselves 'immortal honour'. They had said: 'If the Reformers remain in power, they will ultimately establish a school or schools on the same principle in every ward of the town, so that a good, sound, and scriptural education will be within the reach of the poor of all classes.' They had pointed out that if the Conservatives obtained power they would be obliged 'in consistency, either to shut up the Corporation Schools altogether, or restore the former exclusive system'.[1] But by this time the opinions of the Liberals were losing their importance, and it remained to be seen what action the Conservatives would in fact take when, as now seemed inevitable, they gained control of the Council during the following year.

[1] *Liverpool Mercury*, 30 October 1840.

Chapter 11

THE END OF THE EXPERIMENT

I

AFTER their defeat in the municipal elections of 1840, most of the Liverpool Liberals appear to have taken it for granted that they could not retain control of the Council for very much longer;[1] but many of them still hoped that the policy which they had followed in the Corporation Schools would be continued, perhaps with some slight modifications, by their successors. Nor was this hope altogether unreasonable. Most of those who had hitherto represented the Conservatives in the Council had been willing to discuss the 'Schools Question' with a surprising degree of detachment and independence, refusing to join in the heated controversy which had sometimes raged outside the Council Chamber, and, as we have seen, not always following the lead of even the more restrained of the Church of England clergy. It was not unlikely that those whom one might describe as councillors of the old-fashioned kind, men whose families had long considered membership of the Council an honourable and dignified service to the community, would find it difficult to co-operate whole-heartedly with the self-proclaimed religious agitator M'Neile.

When Peel and his followers had come to power for a brief period in 1835 they had found it wise or expedient, as we have seen, not to withdraw their support from the Irish Board of Education, in spite of the outspoken criticisms of the 'Irish System' which had so often been voiced earlier by important members of the Conservative Party; it had been made clear that there was, after all, not a great deal in common between men like Peel and Stanley, or even the Duke of Wellington, and such extremists as Bishop Phillpotts. In Liverpool, therefore, it would not have been very surprising if many Conservative councillors, although ready enough to accept whatever votes M'Neile's efforts might obtain for them, had yet hesitated, when the decision lay in their power, to adopt policies which would have the effect of depriving of school education more than nine hundred of the poorest Roman

---

[1] 'The result of last Monday's struggle, not only in Liverpool, but throughout the country, . . . leaves a melancholy impression . . . that the future is partially without hope' (*The Albion*, 9 November 1840).

Catholic children of the town. Clearly, the attitude of moderate Conservatives would be of the highest importance, since, if their efforts led to the continuance in the Corporation Schools of the policy pursued hitherto, this would be to establish a precedent all the more important from the fact that it had the support of both parties. On the other hand, if measures unacceptable to Roman Catholic parents and their advisers were adopted it would be made known throughout the kingdom that an important attempt to devise a system of education acceptable to all denominations had ended in failure—and this at a time when a new Conservative government was, in its turn, beginning to devote its attention to the 'Education Question'.

It is interesting to note that, in one important respect, a lead was given to the Liverpool Conservatives by some of those influential in the highest Conservative circles. *The Times* had for some years praised the activities of the Protestant Association and its various branches throughout the country;[1] it had published long reports of proceedings at Association meetings; and the Conservative Party had undoubtedly benefited from the attacks so frequently and forcefully launched by the Association against the Liberal Party's policies and proposals, especially those relating to education and to the administration of Ireland. But an ally useful when the Conservatives were out of office might well have been a considerable encumbrance when they were called upon to formulate practicable policies and act upon them; clearly it was no longer possible in 1841 to contemplate seriously such measures as the repeal of the 'Roman Catholic Emancipation Act'. It was not surprising, therefore, that, only a month after the Conservatives came to power as the result of the General Election of 1841, *The Times*, in effect, formally announced to such men as the Rev. H. M'Neile and the Rev. H. Stowell that their help was no longer required. On 9 August 1841 *The Times* said of the Protestant Association:

. . . we very decidedly disapprove of the proceedings of that body and more especially of its interference with politics. The violent fanaticism and vituperative fury by which its orators are distinguished, are in no degree calculated to advance the objects which they profess to have at heart.

The writer admitted that *The Times* had sometimes denounced Roman Catholic priests as 'ruffians' for 'prostituting their influence for electioneering purposes' and 'instigating the ferocious passions of a misguided populace to criminal actions'; but he went on:

[1] It had, for example, spoken of the Liverpool Protestant Operative Association as 'this valuable association'(12 September 1839).

. . . When we find a professedly religious society speaking of the collective clergy of that communion [i.e. Roman Catholic] in the sister island as 'not more honest than those of Mahomet, not more pure than those of Paganism, not less inhuman than those of Juggernaut'; we really cannot sympathise with so wholesale and monstrous an accusation. It is too like an assertion made last year, at a meeting of this same society, that 'Popery is the religion of the Devil'. Words such as these are foolish, intemperate and profane; they excite nothing but disgust in the minds of practical and moderate men; their inevitable effect is to recoil upon those who use them.

Most definite of all, as giving notice of a dissolution of partnership, were the accusations that 'the agitators of the Protestant Association' were 'likely to make, if they had not already made, many more Papists than Protestants', and that those agitators were 'chargeable with fanning the flame of that truculent political Popery which [was] so grievous a curse to Ireland'.

Such a display of ingratitude must have been a severe shock to the Rev. H. M'Neile, particularly since it came at a time when some of his Liverpool supporters were discussing the possibility of his being made a bishop[1] by a grateful Conservative government; however, he gave no comfort to his opponents by showing signs of resentment, but mildly observed that although he could not approve of the Conservative government's decision to continue making a grant to Maynooth College, nevertheless the members of the Liverpool Protestant Association might thank God that they had 'the very best men on the face of the earth for a government'. He added the remark already quoted, to the effect that, since a Conservative government was now in power, the Protestant Association need no longer concern itself with politics. The Rev. H. Stowell, however, lacked M'Neile's resilience, and at the annual meeting of the Liverpool Protestant Association in October 1841 he complained of the criticism of *The Times*:

When they (the conductors of the paper) thought that the efforts of the Protestant Associations might be made useful in securing the triumph of the Conservative party, they were silent; but when the efforts seemed likely to embarrass a Conservative government, the Protestant Association was denounced as a political institution and some of its leading members denounced as excessively wild and hot declaimers, who said strong things at random.[2]

[1] *Liverpool Standard*, 19 October 1841. M'Neile is reported to have claimed in later life that he would have become a bishop had he been less hostile to Roman Catholicism. (Liverpool) *Daily Courier*, 1 February 1879.

[2] *Liverpool Courier*, 8 October 1841. Two of the 'leading members' singled out for mention by *The Times* had been the Rev. R. J. M'Ghee and the Rev. H. Stowell himself.

It may perhaps have appeared a little ominous to him that the Conservative *Liverpool Courier* omitted these remarks from its report of his speech.

The apprehensions concerning the future of the Corporation Schools expressed in the Liberal newspapers after the municipal elections of 1840 led to renewed discussions on the subject, but after a short time references to the schools in the Press became few and far between. The General Election of 1841 was fought almost entirely on the issue of free trade, and the Liberals were defeated before the contest began, largely, as we have seen, because of their lack of unity; they were not helped by their choice as second candidate of Lord Palmerston, who did not even visit the town at the time of the election. Little was said on this occasion of the Corporation Schools. Indeed, the Rev. H. Stowell complained in Liverpool that he had 'looked at' the addresses of the Conservative candidates, and was 'sorry to see, that though the corn laws, and free trade, and other topics were touched upon, there was not a single syllable about our Protestant interests and institutions';[1] this observation was not strictly accurate, as the Rev. H. M'Neile hastened to point out, but Stowell's remark indicates how very different was the atmosphere on this occasion from that which had prevailed during the previous parliamentary election—the 'wooden-Bible election'—in 1837.

There were other signs that the system adopted in the Corporation Schools might eventually become less of a source of strife between the two political parties. Foreseeing clearly enough that the Conservatives would almost certainly become responsible for the administration of the schools in a year's time, one of the Liberal councillors, H. Hornby, at the first meeting of the Council after the 1840 elections, proposed that a number of Conservatives should become members of the Education Committee. He explained that: 'All that he wished was, that the system now followed in the Corporation schools might be understood practically as well as theoretically, so that the gentlemen might have an opportunity of giving testimony by which the party then in power, if they [i.e. the Conservatives] should be in power, would be enabled to come to a safe conclusion.' Alderman Evans appealed to those who criticized the Liberal policy in the schools to 'endeavour to get upon the committee in order that they might be enabled to change what was wrong when they got to close quarters with it'. D. Hodgson, uncompromising as ever, denounced that policy as 'ungodly and anti-Christian', and expressed the hope 'that the first act of the Conserva-

---

[1] *Liverpool Standard*, 5 October 1841. Viscount Sandon's election address referred to his wish to further the promotion of order and security 'by encouraging the spread of religion and education on definite but tolerant principles'.

tives will be to put an end to it'; whilst another councillor, one W. Birkett, described the system in force in the schools as 'very little better than heathenism'. Nevertheless, four Conservative councillors, Messrs. G. H. Lawrence, Sandbach, Sands and Case, ultimately agreed to become members of the Education Committee, indicating that their doing so was not to be understood as implying approval of the existing system.[1]

One of these Conservative members, Mr Sands, soon afterwards wrote to Hornby, who was chairman of the sub-committee which supervised the working of the South Corporation School, courteously and with evident sincerity urging that the children attending that school should begin the school day with prayer; Hornby as courteously replied, and expressed agreement, but pointed out that care would have to be taken not to introduce any practice which would prevent Roman Catholic children from attending.[2] Apparently as a result of Sands's remarks, arrangements were made at the South School for all children to begin the day with prayer; but Roman Catholics and Protestants were separated for the purpose.[3] A more striking indication of readiness to compromise was given when one of the Conservative members of the Education Committee, G. H. Lawrence, agreed to allow William Rathbone, the arch-enemy of some of the Conservatives in this matter of the schools and now no longer a member of the Council, to attend meetings of the South School Sub-committee in order to give help and advice.[4]

On the other hand, if criticism of the system in force in the Corporation Schools was now less frequently heard than in some earlier years, this was very largely because the most vehement and determined of the critics were at this time engaged, as we have said, in a more general campaign against 'Popery'. During the year 1841, as the Liberals became more and more disheartened and the leading Conservatives in the town hesitated to follow the example of *The Times* by dissociating themselves publicly from the less tolerant of their supporters, the latter were encouraged to hope that they would soon enjoy the fruits of political power. Their increasingly vehement and unrestrained speeches were arousing in many Protestants and Roman Catholics such bitter

[1] *Liverpool Mercury*, 13 November 1840.
[2] *The Albion*, 18 January 1841.
[3] There is some conflict of evidence about the precise arrangements: one witness, C. Bushell, speaking of the two groups, after being separated by a large curtain, 'saying parts of the same prayer'; another saying that 'a screen was let down when the prayer was read to the Protestant children, and afterwards to the Catholic children' (*Liverpool Mercury*, 7 January 1842).
[4] *Liverpool Courier*, 10 February 1841.

animosity and suspicion that it was becoming increasingly difficult for all but the strongest characters to remain capable of judging calmly and rationally in any matters connected with religious beliefs; indeed, religion and party politics seemed to many to have become inextricably entangled, with the growing strength of the Conservative Party becoming more and more committed to the support of the group of religious extremists who followed the Rev. H. M'Neile.

Moreover, it must be said that many of the newer councillors were men of very different calibre from their predecessors, men who had been drawn into politics by their desire to take part in a controversy which had inspired in more sensitive and intelligent men only repugnance and dismay;[1] at first more than one of the Liberal councillors poked fun at the lack of education of some of these newcomers, as revealed in their faulty grammar; but it was not long before the Liberals discovered that a lack of education can often manifest itself in other, less amusing, ways. Conservatives and Liberals alike were to learn how much power could be wielded by crude men whose natural and unrestrained leaning towards intolerance derived sanction and strength from their honest belief that they were working for a cause higher than themselves. Mild-mannered men could scarcely make themselves heard amid the clamour raised by such adversaries, and often they themselves became infected with the virus of intolerance, or at least anxious to avoid the vehement attacks of less tolerant men. It is the behaviour of these 'moderate' men, and of those who discovered too late that religious intolerance is a dangerously uncontrollable weapon, which principally concerns us here.

2

As the decisive municipal elections of November 1841 drew near some of the Conservatives began to have doubts concerning the policy which they ought to pursue in the Corporation Schools when their control of the Council was assured; and for a time it appeared possible that a solution to the 'Schools Question' acceptable to all parties would be sought and found. It is true that a number of Conservative candidates spoke of 'returning to the old system' in the schools,[2] but at some of the Conservative ward meetings which preceded the elections no references

[1] One Conservative remarked at a meeting of the Town Council in December 1842 that: 'The town was suffering from the continual agitation of this question. Some of their leading men had been shut out by it from coming there, men honourable in social life, and men who would do honour to the Council, but they said, "We cannot do with that question. We cannot deal with it"' (*Liverpool Mercury*, 16 December 1842).

[2] *Ibid.*, 29 October 1841.

whatever were made to the Corporation Schools, and at one such meeting, in Great George Ward, where William Rathbone was being opposed, G. H. Lawrence, now one of the Conservative members of the Education Committee, assured his hearers that the Conservative candidate, James Lawrence, was 'not anxious to employ the Corporation funds for the maintenance of the Church of England children alone'.[1] The *Liverpool Mail* was as wildly uncompromising as ever, but the *Liverpool Courier* scarcely mentioned the schools before the elections, and gave little indication of what policy it would in future advocate with respect to them.

The third Conservative newspaper in the town, however, the *Liverpool Standard*, clearly indicated that it was meditating a change of policy scarcely less remarkable than that made a few months earlier by *The Times*: evidently some of the leading Conservatives were at this time considering the possibility of detaching themselves from M'Neile and his followers so as to regain complete freedom of action and then seek some means of keeping the Corporation Schools available to children of all sects, including Roman Catholics. Barely a week before the elections the *Liverpool Standard* surprised its opponents, and, no doubt, almost all of its supporters, by making the following comments concerning the 'Schools Question':

What we would expect of a *Conservative* council would be the establishment in the schools of the religious ascendancy of the national church, but *not* in such a way as to be intolerant of religious liberty in such as may conscientiously, though erroneously, dissent from it. This is the principle which has been adopted by the Presbyterians of Ireland, and upon which they now receive aid from the National Board of Education in that country.[2] The *rule* of their schools is Scriptural Education, and the Catechism of the General Assembly . . . this is their *rule*, but it is not a rule to which they make no exception; it is the rule but they relax it in behalf of Roman Catholic children whose parents come forward and record their disapprobation. By this means Roman Catholic and other children are not debarred the general education conveyed in their schools. . . . We are no friends to any intolerant, persecuting, or exclusive system; we wish men first to act conscientiously, and then with a proper feeling towards the weakness and errors of others, and a due allowance of a conscientious liberty.[3]

---

[1] *Ibid.*, 22 October 1841.

[2] After negotiations begun in 1833 (see p. 24), resumed in 1839 and concluded in 1840, the government had agreed to allow the Irish Board of Education to make grants to Irish Presbyterian Schools in which denominational religious instruction was given during school hours, provided that children whose parents objected to their receiving such instruction should be allowed to attend for secular instruction only.

[3] 22 October 1841.

Such an abandonment of the arguments that purely secular education was worse than none, and that the Authorized Version was 'excluded' from schools in which *all* the children did not read it, was indeed astonishing, especially coming from a journal which had always devotedly supported the Rev. H. M'Neile. In its next issue the *Standard* seemed positively hurt that its remarks had been received with suspicion by the pro-Roman Catholic *Liverpool Journal*: 'The *Liverpool Journal* is quite astonished at our having referred to the practice of the Presbyterians of Ireland. . . . "It really requires", says our cautious contemporary, "something more than the *ipse dixit* of an anonymous writer, however respectable his position, to believe that *the Tory party in a body* meditate such an *entire desertion of principle as this implies*".'[1] How far the 'contemporary' was justified in being 'cautious' we shall see. With extraordinary aplomb the *Standard* next rebuked the *Liverpool Mercury*:

We do not deny that education is a subject of very great importance, and that the trust committed to the members of the Municipal Council, with regard to the management of the Corporation Schools is one of great responsibility; but we do . . . protest against the agitation of the subject *now*, as a mere electioneering *ruse*.

Annoyed by the unusual vagueness of the *Standard's* remarks about the future policy of the Conservatives, the *Liverpool Mercury* observed:

. . . the school system may, or may not be subverted, when the Tories have a majority in the Town Council; but the mystery advocated by our contemporary, however prudent, is by no means honest. . . . If our contemporary and his friends were honest, they should say at once what they intend to do, and then the electors would have full opportunity for consideration whether it would be wise and prudent to give them the means of doing it. . . . We again urge the Tories to speak out on the school question; they were not wont to be so mealy-mouthed upon it.[2]

The *Liverpool Standard* maintained that the Conservatives could 'fairly rely on their general principles, and on their character, for obtaining the suffrages of the electors, without pledging themselves to any particular plan or system in the matter of the schools'. In reply to '*liberal* insinuations that Conservatives would do all manner of illiberal things immediately on gaining the desired ascendancy', the *Standard* declared 'that the Conservatives were unpledged as to any particular scholastic system'. Nevertheless the journal, after emphasizing that the Church of England was never exclusive or intolerant, once again

[1] 26 October 1841.
[2] 22 October 1841.

praised 'The Presbyterian system in Ireland', suggested that it might be adopted in the Corporation Schools, and added: '. . . so much we certainly do expect, and shall look for, from a Conservative Council, when established, in Liverpool.'[1]

In the ensuing elections the Conservatives were successful in thirteen of the sixteen wards;[2] the control of the Council passed to them; and both their supporters and their opponents waited anxiously to see what policy would be recommended for adoption in the Corporation Schools. No other subject was thought to approach this in interest and importance; and discussion turned almost entirely on the question whether Roman Catholic children might, as the *Liverpool Standard* had suggested, be permitted to attend the Corporation Schools to receive secular instruction only. At the first meeting of the new Council, on 9 November 1841, Mr T. Sands put forward the names of fifteen councillors who, he proposed, might constitute the new Education Committee. The list included the names of three Liberals, but also those of the four Conservatives whose views on the 'Schools Question' were known to all to be the most extreme and uncompromising—David Hodgson, James Parker, Richard Harbord and William Birkett. In view of the proposal to choose these men, some difficulty was experienced in persuading Liberals to join the Committee, and their protests were echoed by H. R. Sandbach, a Conservative who had served on the Education Committee during the previous year, and who now remarked that 'he did not see, from the constitution of the [proposed] Committee, the possibility of the good working of any system at all. He felt that he could not go into the committee with any chance of working the schools with any good result to the town'. Instead of ignoring these objections, the Council agreed to postpone the choice of a Committee until its next meeting.

Coming after the articles in the *Liverpool Standard*, this appeared to constitute a second challenge to the extremists. The Liberals began to breathe more freely, and *The Albion* reflected that the Conservatives, now that they were 'firmly fixed in their seats', felt that it would be 'impolitic to abolish a system which, with some few, to them, objectionable parts, works better in practice than, as they pretend, they had thought when in opposition!' The *Liverpool Journal* spoke of 'the tory party' being 'very much divided', and suggested that 'the only solution of the difficulty' concerning the schools was 'a compromise in the shape of an equitable distribution of the funds in the ratio . . . of

---

[1] 26 October 1841.

[2] They obtained about 53·3 per cent of the votes cast. William Rathbone was again defeated—on this occasion by 22 votes—whilst Thomas Blackburn did not stand.

numbers and necessity'.[1] The Conservative *Liverpool Courier* had already expressed the hope that the Conservatives would 'use their victory with moderation' and had spoken of paying 'judicious homage to the spirit of the times'.[2]

Meanwhile the *Liverpool Standard* was defending the conciliatory policy it had recommended against the criticism which its remarks had aroused. It denied that to allow a Catholic parent to withdraw his child from 'scriptural education' was to 'sanction' such conduct, and, with a display of liberality which must have amazed some of its readers, continued:

> But if the authorities of a school refuse to allow such withdrawal and the R.C. parent does not therefore allow his child to attend, will not the representative of the school, in that case, be . . . in some degree a party to the child's abandonment to the education of the streets—a sanctioner of his being brought up in total ignorance of all useful instruction?

As for the argument that secular instruction without religious knowledge would prove a curse, the writer maintained that 'such secular instruction as would be attainable in scriptural schools such as we speak of would not be hurtful, but the contrary . . . of its secular uses and importance, and, we may add, of its advantage to society generally, there cannot, we think, be a question'. In short, the policy of converting the Corporation Schools into Church of England schools whilst allowing all who wished to do so to send their children merely for secular education appeared to the *Liverpool Standard* a fair and sensible one, which did not involve 'the smallest compromise nor guilty sanction of any sort'.[3]

It was not without some justification that at the next Council meeting (on 15 November 1841) Alderman Earle remarked that the Corporation Schools, like the Poor Law and the Protestant Association, had been used 'as machines for the purpose of raising certain parties to power . . . [but] it now appeared that the discriminating and observant Tories did not choose to wield these weapons any longer. In justification of this assertion he had only to appeal to *The Times*.'[4] It now appeared that at last the Liverpool Town Council would be able to exhibit to the rest of England a practical solution of the 'Religious Problem' which would for some time to come prove reasonably acceptable to almost everyone concerned.

[1] 6 November 1841.
[2] 3 November 1841.
[3] 9 November 1841.
[4] This, of course, was a reference to the attack which *The Times* had made on the Protestant Association shortly before.

3

But Earle, when he made the remark quoted, was already a little behind the times. Three days earlier the *Liverpool Standard* had published two letters protesting against the kind of compromise which it had been advocating; one letter, which was signed 'Fidus Achates', was believed by some to have come from the Rev. H. M'Neile himself;[1] the other was from one of his chief lieutenants, the Rev. D. James. Both were addressed to 'The Conservative Members of the Town Council of Liverpool', and both insisted that there could be no compromise over the 'Religious Problem'. The first of the letters recalled much of what had been said at the great protest meeting in the Amphitheatre in 1836, and pointed out how inconsistent it would be now to exempt any children attending the Corporation Schools from reading the Authorized Version of the Bible. The second letter, that from the Rev. D. James, declared that it was the duty of the Conservative councillors to follow the dictates of their own consciences, not the wishes of parents; councillors ought to give to all the children in the Corporation Schools the same 'scriptural instruction' as they gave to their own offspring: this would 'leave the objectors no fair ground of opposition'. As for the objection that all children were entitled to attend the schools, 'what could be fairer' than to let them all share 'in what is the best education available'? The argument that because all contributed to the schools all had a right to be educated in their own way was quite fallacious: once ratepayers had paid their rates 'they had fulfilled their duty, and their conscience was not further affected'. The responsibility thereafter lay entirely with the councillors, who should 'love their neighbours as themselves' and 'not have one description of education at home and another of diametrically opposite character in the Corporation Schools'.[2]

When the Town Council met on 15 November 1841 to resume its discussions on the composition of the Education Committee, there were indications that the Conservatives were becoming anxious to prevent a split in their ranks. To the astonishment of some of the Liberals, Conservatives who had earlier deprecated the appointment to the Education Committee of men holding extreme opinions now voted for the inclusion of such men; thus only one Conservative, John Smith, voted against the appointment of David Hodgson, and the equally uncompromising Richard Harbord was chosen in preference to a more moderate Conservative. Sandbach, the Conservative whose unwilling-

---

[1] *The Albion*, 15 November 1841.
[2] 12 November 1841.

ness to have men of extreme opinions appointed to the Committee had earlier heartened the Liberals, now explained that at the last Council meeting he had feared that 'some measure was to be proposed of so exclusive and extreme a nature that he could not be a party to it. He was now, however, better informed, and he was happy to say that there was no intention of proposing any such measure, or any measure in which he did not frankly and cordially concur.... He trusted that when the Council heard what was intended to be done, they would all see that they had been entirely mistaken in supposing that any such extreme measures were in contemplation'. He added that 'it was with him, and he knew it was with many others also, he thought he might say, with the town at large, an object of intense anxiety that the Roman Catholic part of the population, in common with the rest, should send their children [to the schools] ... he hoped every person would avoid every expression that might give needless offence to the Roman Catholics, or tend to prevent them sending their children to the schools, which he most earnestly desired they should do.'[1]

There is no doubt that numbers of Conservatives would have echoed these words, and probably more than one hoped that the few extremists of Hodgson's stamp could be fairly easily controlled in committee. One Liberal member of the Council, Alderman Earle, revealed later that at this time he had warned individual Conservatives of the probable consequences of appointing certain men to the Committee, but those to whom he had spoken 'had treated his warning very lightly, and they had spurned the idea of being influenced by men so inferior to themselves in intellect.... They had voted for certain men to be upon the Committee, and then when their backs were turned they treated the prejudices of those men with scorn.'[2] He was not contradicted when he claimed in open Council that one such Conservative, whom he named, had said of Hodgson: 'We can easily manage him.'[3] Apparently few of the more moderate Conservatives yet realized that such support as the extremists might need they could by this time easily obtain from outside the committee-room and Council Chamber.

Still, the issue was not yet decided. By the beginning of December 1841 it seemed likely that the new Education Committee would eventually propose that in the Corporation Schools the Church Catechism would be taught only to those children whose parents did not object, but that all children, without exception, should be obliged to read the Authorized Version of the Bible and to join in the common form of

[1] *Liverpool Mercury*, 19 November 1841.   [2] *Ibid.*, 7 January 1842.
[3] *Ibid.*, 11 February 1842.

prayer. Four of the Roman Catholic priests of the town, writing 'on their own behalf, and on behalf of the rest of the clergy', therefore warned the Council that they could not 'concur in such an arrangement, whereby the religious principles of the Catholic children attending the schools would be compromised'; they prayed that 'the contemplated scheme might not be adopted'.[1] This protest encouraged a few Conservatives to express in Council the fears which not a few members of their party were feeling: that, in fact, the Roman Catholic children would soon be prevented from attending the Corporation Schools.

One of them, John Smith, said that

... nothing would give him greater pleasure than to see this momentous and heart-burning question brought to a satisfactory decision. . . . Never could the cause of true Conservatism in the town be placed on a firm and lasting footing until this religious fire-brand was altogether extinguished. Ardently and sincerely attached to the church to which he belonged [sic], yet he was not so uncharitable as to wish to withhold the benefits of education from the children of Roman Catholics. To act on any such principles of exclusiveness would indeed be to display very little of the genuine spirit of true Christianity . . . it would be sacrificing countless numbers of the most destitute of their fellow-creatures at the shrine of bigotry and intolerance.

After observing that, by refusing to allow the Roman Catholic children that education which their parents could conscientiously allow them to receive, the Council would be compelling those children to 'tread the path of infamy, wretchedness, and crime', Smith went on to propose his solution to the difficulty:

Let these schools be placed on their original [Church of England] footing, and erect two schools, the one at the north end and the other at the south, for the Roman Catholics . . . peace and harmony would again prevail, and they would have the proud satisfaction of knowing that they had once and for ever consigned to the tomb of oblivion this demon of religious discord.[2]

This was a solution similar to those which the Conservatives in the Council had once heartily supported,[3] which the *Liverpool Courier* had several times put forward,[4] and which the Rev. H. M'Neile himself had earlier declared to be tolerable;[5] whilst the Protestant Operatives, at M'Neile's suggestion, had actually prayed the Council only two years earlier to introduce some such arrangement.[6] But now Smith was informed by J. Parker, a devoted follower of M'Neile's, that Christian

---

[1] *Ibid.*, 3 December 1841.   *Ibid.*
[3] See p. 88.   [4] See p. 80.
[5] See pp. 79, 80.   [6] See p. 170.

charity could never consist of being 'instrumental in teaching others error', and that to teach error in separate schools was quite as objectionable as to teach it 'under one roof'.

Another Conservative, G. H. Lawrence, who had already been a member of the Education Committee for one year, and, who, therefore, knew something of the working of the schools under the Liberal Committee, was almost pathetically anxious not to have the Roman Catholic children removed from the schools. He declared that he wished to see no form of religious instruction given in the schools other than that which was in accord with Church of England doctrine, but he appealed to the Council, to the clergy of the Established Church, and to the Roman Catholic clergy, to allow the Roman Catholic children to attend the schools to receive secular instruction only; he added that he

was perhaps in some degree departing from the stern path of principle to that of expediency. . . . He dared say he was in error, but he hoped he would be judged charitably. He could not help but feel an interest in children, Protestant and Catholic. He could not help thinking how many there were who would be turned loose on the world; he did think that if they could, without any material sacrifice of principle, continue them, it would be well. The schools belonged to the people after all, and the funds by which they were provided were the people's, and it was their [the Council's] duty to administer the funds impartially.

Yet another Conservative, T. Robinson, agreed that the Douay version of the Bible should be withdrawn from the Corporation Schools, but stated that 'with respect to the Irish Extracts, so far as he could form an opinion, . . . they were like the authorized version. He wished other gentlemen would look to them with a little consideration, and let them continue in the school for the use of the Roman Catholic children. They were representatives of the whole community there, and anything that was done to exclude the Roman Catholics would be a great injury to them'. Alderman Turner, also a Conservative, informed the Council that 'he hoped and believed he was a staunch supporter of the Protestant Church, but as great an enemy to intolerance of any kind, and the bringing forward of any resolution that would deprive the Roman Catholic people of the instruction they now received, would be an act of injustice. There was no sect exempted from town dues because of their religion, and therefore they had all as much right to participate in any advantages the Corporation had the satisfaction of affording as they [the Protestants] had'. It is true that D. Hodgson announced that he 'could not consent on any terms to become the patron and inculcator of what he believed to be a lie', and that the

building of separate schools would be 'only another attempt to shuffle off an iniquity'; but in spite of this and similar declarations from Hodgson and a few others it still seemed possible that some compromise would be found, and one of the Liberals was able to state that 'he did not yet despair that some plan would be adopted for continuing the schools on such principles as would allow every class to attend them'.[1]

The new Education Committee had come to the Council meeting here referred to with the proposal that all of the regulations of the previous Committee concerning the management of the schools should be at once rescinded; it was not difficult for their Liberal opponents to elicit the admission that the Committee had been so anxious to inaugurate the new régime that it had put forward the proposal without reading the regulations concerned. It seemed reasonable to suggest that regulations of *some* kind would have to remain in force until the Committee had prepared others. The Town Clerk admitted that he had advised the Committee to put forward their proposal, but he now felt that it would be better to allow the old regulations to continue in being until new ones had been drawn up; so unyielding was the Committee, however, that a vote had to be taken and the decision went against it by thirty votes to twenty-three.

Outside the Council this appeared as an act of defiance to the new Education Committee, resulting, as it seemed, from the appeals for compromise made by some of the Conservative speakers. At once the Rev. H. M'Neile sprang to the attack, and, in the course of a sermon preached in his church, St. Jude's, on the following Sunday, he very forcefully criticized those who had voted against the Education Committee, even, it would appear, requesting or commanding one of the councillors, Christopher Bushell, who was a parishioner, to leave the church.[2] Evidently explanations and excuses were at once made to him, and he was able to assure his hearers at a meeting of the Protestant Operative Association shortly afterwards that all was well: the action of those who had voted against the Education Committee had been misconstrued because the Town Clerk's speech had not been accurately reported; Mr Bushell had explained and was his friend once again. Nevertheless, M'Neile felt that the 'strong expression of feeling' to which the mistake had given rise 'had been attended with beneficial results'. He 'believed that he might say to them now that there was very little doubt, speaking after the manner of men, he should say no doubt, that a true Protestant system, with the authorised version of the Bible, and that version alone, would be introduced into the Corporation Schools of this town . . . the Douay [*sic*] was to go out, and the

<hr />

[1] *Liverpool Mercury*, 3 December 1841.   [2] *Ibid.*, 24 December 1841.

Irish extracts also. He believed that he might tell them that all the Conservative members of the education committee were unanimous on the point, and that the recommendation would be submitted to the Council in due time'. It was thus that Liverpool was told what was to be the future policy of its Education Committee. Having received the assurance, the meeting passed to its more normal business of considering the possibility that recent fires, such as those at the House of Commons, had been caused by Jesuits.[1]

4

The division of opinion over the proposal that all the regulations in force in the Corporation Schools should be at once rescinded, and the consequent sharp rebuke administered by the Rev. H. M'Neile, evidently forced the Conservatives to recognize clearly that a dangerous lack of unity was beginning to manifest itself and that they would have to close their ranks. One of their journals even spoke of 'the recent proceedings . . . relative to the education question' having caused 'intense grief and consternation among them'.[2] The *Liverpool Mail* had never ceased to thunder against those Conservatives whose views on the 'Schools Question' were less extreme than its own; and by now it had been joined by the *Liverpool Standard*, which, on 23 November 1841, had, without a word of explanation, begun to denounce in the severest terms the kind of compromise solution which it had strongly advocated only two weeks earlier. It now had become necessary, in the opinion of that paper, for every Protestant to 'stand by his profession, and require the unreserved use of the Bible [in the schools] as a necessary evidence that he does not in any degree, or in any particular, recede from it'.[3] The *Liverpool Standard* now felt that '*merely temporal* education' would not be 'of much use to Romanists; . . . and if they will not have our moral and religious instruction, they have no right to take up the room of those who will gladly abide by all our rules'.[4] The *Liverpool Courier* had even more rapidly ceased to speak of 'paying judicious homage to the spirit of the times', and now addressed argument after argument to those 'benevolent' and 'conscientious' Conservatives who found it difficult to bring themselves to take steps which would result in the children of Roman Catholics being withdrawn from the schools.

All three of the Conservative journals informed the 'moderate' Conservatives that any compromise with 'Popery' would be a breach of the trust reposed in them by the electors; that to 'withhold' the

---

[1] *Liverpool Courier*, 22 December 1841.
[2] *Ibid.*, 8 December 1841.
[3] 23 November 1841.
[4] 3 December 1841.

Authorized Version of the Bible from any child was to allow it to take the path to 'eternal ruin';[1] that Roman Catholics contributed little to the town's revenues; that it would be the responsibility of the priests if Roman Catholic children were withdrawn from the schools; that to teach 'Popery' would be wicked; and that purely secular knowledge was worse than none. But undoubtedly the most influential and plausible of all the arguments adduced in the Conservative Press and in the course of the discussions in the Council Chamber was to the effect that even if all the children attending the Corporation Schools were required to join in prayer and in the reading of the Authorized Version of the Bible, the Roman Catholic children would not, in fact, permanently leave the schools; although they might be withdrawn for a time, under the influence of the priests, such children would soon return,[2] as many Church of England children had done after at first quitting the Corporation Schools in 1836. There is no doubt that this reasoning had its effect on numbers of humane and charitable men,[3] and no doubt it provided a means of easing the consciences of some who were under strong pressure because of the fear of appearing inconsistent, the desire to preserve the unity of the party in its moment of victory, the natural unwillingness to become the target for the attacks of M'Neile and his followers, and, of course, the need to please and placate an organized group of electors.

On 1 January 1842 the Education Committee submitted for the Council's approval the regulations which it had drawn up for the Corporation Schools; as had been expected, the rules provided for the instruction of the children in the doctrines of the Church of England, but permitted absence from such instruction on conscientious grounds; *all* the children, however, were to be required to read the Authorized Version of the Bible and to join in prayer at the beginning and end of each school day. Once again the Council discussed the matter at great length, and once again some of the Liberals and also the Conservatives John Smith, Alderman Turner, G. H. Lawrence and T. Robinson,

---

[1] *Liverpool Courier*, 8 December 1841.

[2] 'With regard to the threat held out by some that the children of Roman Catholics would be turned upon the streets in the event of the new system being carried, there is nothing in it. However willing the priests might be that such a result should take place, they could not effect it; parental affection would prove stronger than priestly authority; there is no cause for apprehension on this score' (*Liverpool Standard*, 11 January 1842). This suggestion was put forward on almost all occasions on which the change of policy was discussed.

[3] 'The Tory majority in the Committee seem to be of opinion, that, though the children of Roman Catholic parents may, when the new system shall come into effect, withdraw from the schools, they will afterwards return. This is the hope of the moderate men among the Tories' (*The Albion*, 13 December 1841).

urged that arrangements should be made for the education of Roman Catholic children, at least by permitting them to attend for secular instruction only. In the end, however, an amendment in that sense was lost by thirty-two votes to twenty-four, and the Education Committee was authorized to enforce its new regulations in the Corporation Schools.

Within a week the Roman Catholic clergy had conferred together and drawn up a statement to be read in their chapels and displayed on placards in the town; in this they said:

By the new arrangement the catholic translation of the Scripture has been excluded from the schools, so that all the children will be required to use the protestant Bible, which, for different reasons, the catholic clergy cannot sanction. Another objection is that should any Catholic children attend, they will be required to join with the rest in a form of worship, from which, both in practice and belief, they must conscientiously differ . . . the catholic clergy feel it their duty, under present circumstances, to denounce these schools, and to tell catholic parents they cannot conscientiously send their children to them.[1]

On the day when the new régime began in the schools a Roman Catholic priest addressed the Roman Catholic children present, and asked to be provided with the names and addresses of those children of his faith who continued to attend the schools.[2]

Evidently as a reply and challenge to the priests, the Education Committee also published a declaration, which appeared in the advertisement columns of the newspapers and on placards; in this it was stated that the Committee deemed it right 'on account of the misrepresentations that have been repeatedly set forth, to take this method of informing the Community, and especially the poor inhabitants of the Borough, who desire to obtain a good education for their children, what the principle is on which the schools are conducted, namely, the equal maintenance of Religious Truth and of Liberty of Conscience'. The Committee explained that, whilst the Council was responsible for the education which it provided, and therefore felt 'bound to provide what it considered a sound education', it also recognized the obligation 'to secure this advantage as far as possible, alike to all, whatever may be their difference of creed'. It was pointed out that there would be nothing in the prayers said in the schools which would 'wound the conscience of any Christian of any denomination'; that no children would

---

[1] *Liverpool Journal*, 15 January 1842.

[2] Allegations that the priest had 'threatened and frightened the children' were made at a Council meeting on 12 January 1842, and denied in a letter from the priest concerned (*Liverpool Mercury*, 21 January 1842).

be 'required to learn any Catechism, or to go to church, if their parents object'. The declaration concluded:

The Committee, therefore, invite all their poor fellow-townsmen to send their children to the School, and not to be prevented by the representations of others, but to judge for themselves. They will not believe that there are many individuals among their fellow-townsmen who will object to their Children reading the Bible, and praying together with the Children of their neighbours.[1]

There was here, clearly enough, a strong and sincere desire that Roman Catholic children should continue to attend the schools. But as soon as the regulations of the new Committee came into force, in January 1842, almost all of the 936 Roman Catholic children in attendance were withdrawn, and the hope which had been expressed that, after a time, many of them would return to the schools was not fulfilled. The Liverpool experiment had come to an end.

5

It now becomes possible to see how it came about that Liverpool, after 'certainly taking the lead upon the great and important subject of national education',[2] ceased for a very long time after 1842 to be remarkable for its interest in educational progress. Manchester, it is true, had to bear with its Rev. Hugh Stowell, and no one who studies the history of the period is likely to underrate the importance of that clergyman's opposition to the various plans for establishing a national system of education which were drawn up and supported in the town. It is certainly true, as the writer of one of M'Neile's obituary notices observed, that 'the career of the two clergymen in those immense neighbouring towns is a remarkable chapter of provincial history'.[3] But the influence of the Rev. H. M'Neile in Liverpool was for a time far greater than Stowell's ever became in Manchester, as the writer hopes to show.

It was not to be expected that an Education Committee dominated by M'Neile's more ardent followers would feel much admiration for the efforts which had hitherto been made to make the Corporation Schools among the most up to date in England. M'Neile himself had, a few years earlier, deplored 'the loud outcry' which had been made 'against teaching children, as so many parrots, to say words which they do not understand'. He had criticized the notions that education should

[1] Ibid., 14 January 1842.   [2] See p. 131.
[3] Liverpool Mercury, 29 January 1879.

'draw out the reasoning faculties' and that 'the right way is to communicate only so much at a time as the youthful mind can understand'. The chief reason given in support of his opinion was attractively simple:

> What are the reasons against this mode of education? The first and crowning reason is, that it is not God's plan in the Bible. . . . God spake words that man did not and could not understand. . . . The prophets did not understand what they were saying. This is God's mode of teaching. The modern fashionable system reverses this mode: it simplifies the language so that the human mind is able to comprehend every step as it goes along. . . . Let them, therefore, call our old system the parrot system: it is the education of the mind to receive a mystery, and so a preparation for receiving the Bible.[1]

Such a doctrine, one might suppose, made it scarcely necessary to have highly skilled teachers in the Corporation Schools, or, for that matter, a very enlightened Education Committee to supervise them; and it soon became obvious that in both of these respects a new era had begun for the Corporation Schools. When the new regulations began to be enforced in the schools, the two headmasters intimated that they could not conscientiously oblige Roman Catholic children to read the Authorized Version of the Bible; thereupon they were informed that their refusal would be taken to mean that they had resigned from their posts. Three Roman Catholics ceased to teach in the schools for the same reason. A superintendent for both schools was then appointed— a Mr Stone, who seems to have been not very well qualified by training or experience for the work he was called upon to do, and whose powers of expression in his letters left a good deal to be desired (as the Liberals were not slow to point out), but who had been a teacher in the Sunday-school attached to the church of the Rev. H. M'Neile.

When it was claimed, at a meeting of the Council, that Stone had been chosen in preference to much more experienced and better-qualified candidates, and that he could not give the apprentices such advanced instruction as his predecessors had done, a spokesman of the Education Committee replied that 'he did not think it important that the working classes should be taught the higher branches of education as they called them. All that was wanted was a plain education. There was no education for the higher branches of mathematics, the derivation of words, or the classics as taught under the old system. A man giving a plain education was all they wanted'. D. Hodgson later complained that the Liberals had been 'wasting the public property, injur-

[1] *Liverpool Courier*, 4 January 1837.

ing the morals of the poor' by instructing 'poor barefooted children in geography, in the derivation of words from Greek and Latin'.[1]

The Roman Catholic apprentices were dismissed when they refused to give instruction in the Church Catechism; it was held that Roman Catholic children might absent themselves from such instruction, but that Roman Catholic apprentices, as teachers, could not be exempted from giving it.[2] Some of the Protestant apprentices felt aggrieved that, by the terms of their indentures, they were now bound to Stone, who was not able to give them the advanced instruction which they had hoped to receive; when they objected, they also were dismissed. The Committee had already agreed that no further apprentices should be engaged for the schools, and the monitorial system was reintroduced. When John Buckley, the former pupil of the North Corporation School who was now studying at Cambridge, wrote 'requesting the continued patronage of the Committee in furnishing him with the means of support at Queens' College' the Committee refused to help him.[3] On another occasion the committee of the Pleasant Street School, which, as we have seen, admitted children of all denominations, asked to be given the now unused copies of the Douay version of the Bible and of 'the Irish Scripture Lessons' formerly read in the Corporation Schools. Some of the members of the Education Committee were horrified at receiving such a request; one, Mr Birkett, 'rose to express his strongest disapprobation of the existence of such a school in the town of which he had the honour to be a native'; whilst another extremist, Mr Parker, a leading brewer who was now becoming acknowledged as a leader of the Conservatives in the Council, and who was a firm supporter of the Rev. H. M'Neile, remarked that he 'would have the books put into chests, cased with iron, and put into the lowest sinks of the filth of the Corporation, and there he would have them kept *ad infinitum*'.[4] The Town Clerk, without discussing this suggestion, ruled that the Council had no power to give away its property.

But the ever-mounting intolerance of M'Neile and his followers, and their growing power in the town, were soon displayed in more important ways. It has been shown that among those Conservatives who had wished to have concessions made so that Roman Catholic children might be instructed in the existing, or additional, Corporation

[1] *Ibid.*, 9 December 1842.
[2] *Ibid.*, 6 May 1842. Mrs Rathbone endeavoured to find teaching posts for the displaced apprentices, but on 15 April 1842 she wrote to Lady Noel Byron: 'I can find no schools where it would be satisfactory to place such of our apprentices as are but half educated' (*Rathbone Family Papers*).
[3] *Proceedings of Education Committee*, Vol. I, p. 242.
[4] *Liverpool Mercury*, 22 July 1842.

Schools were Alderman Turner, G. H. Lawrence, John Smith and Thomas Robinson. It was to such men as these that M'Neile referred when he addressed the Toxteth Park Branch of the Protestant Operative Association in July 1842. Four months earlier Lord Eliot, the Conservative Chief Secretary for Ireland, had informed the House of Commons that the government intended 'to include in the estimates for the ensuing year a grant for national education in Ireland, without proposing any alteration in the principles which had regulated its distribution'.[1] Now in July 1842 Lord Eliot was to be found informing the House that the 'Irish Scripture Lessons' had never been intended 'to supersede the use of the Scriptures'; he went on to state that 'the accusations made against the Irish Board, of garbling the Holy Scriptures were entirely unfounded'.[2]

Worse still, from M'Neile's point of view, was the fact that Eliot had been supported, not only by Lord Stanley but by Viscount Sandon, who admitted having criticized the 'Irish System' earlier, but who now felt that, since the opposition had failed and the system had now been established for a considerable time, 'He, for one, should be most unwilling to disturb a great question like that, without being able to substitute another system more likely to succeed; and he confessed that he was not aware of any such system'.[3] This last declaration, from one of the successful Conservative candidates in the famous 'wooden-Bible election', must have been a particularly severe blow for M'Neile, and he was most determined that such ideas should not be allowed to spread in Conservative circles in Liverpool. After quoting and discussing Lord Eliot's remarks about the 'Irish Scripture Lessons', M'Neile went on to say to the Protestant Operatives:

Now because of that speech of the noble lord, we have councillors saying in this town, 'The government is with us, after all, upon education'. I hope we shall have no councillors trimming and changing, after getting in as friends of scriptural education. (Loud cheers.) I hope we shall have no narrow majorities upon that subject when the Council divides again. (Renewed cheers.) Watch them! (Loud cries of 'We will watch them!') The time for watching is now, without much talk; the time for action is coming. November is very near![4]

As the November elections drew close it was made very clear to John Smith and Thomas Robinson that they were no longer wanted in the Conservative Party by the extremists. Thus the Liverpool Standard

[1] Hansard, Third Series, Vol. LXI, Cols. 936-7.
[2] Ibid., Vol. LXV, Col. 209.
[3] Ibid., Vol. LXV, Col. 218.
[4] Liverpool Courier, 27 July 1842.

on 4 September 1842 publicly informed Smith and Robinson that they were not the kind of Conservatives 'required in these days'; and it continued: 'The Conservative electors . . . are bound to put in nomination and to return . . . two very different men—two *sound* Conservatives.'[1] At first Robinson refused to stand down, feeling that 'retirement at this time would imply a desertion of duty, and involve a principle of right, which it is the interest of all parties to vindicate and uphold'.[2] In the end, however, he yielded to the clamour against him and withdrew.[3] But John Smith decided to fight for his right to express his opinions freely in the Council Chamber. On 18 October 1842 his Conservative critics held a ward meeting in West Derby Ward at which the chief speaker and, as it were, counsel for the prosecution, was no other than Edward Ratcliffe, clerk to the Rev. H. M'Neile. It was pointed out that Smith had spoken of a 'religious firebrand', had stated that he did not wish to 'withhold the benefits and blessings of education from the children of the Roman Catholics', and had suggested that separate schools might be provided for them. By expressing such views Smith had 'betrayed the confidence reposed in him' when he had been elected as a Conservative. Ratcliffe observed: 'It was their duty to instruct the Roman Catholics. In Popery? No, in Protestantism.' He warned his hearers to beware of 'trimmers, miners and sappers'; and the meeting accordingly adopted as the official Conservative candidate one who was said to have 'an undying hostility to the late system of education adopted in the schools' and 'to any system not based on the unrestricted and unmutilated Word of God'.[4] John Smith contested the seat in the subsequent election, but was defeated by 182 votes to 112.[5]

It would scarcely have been surprising had the greater part of the Conservative Party and Press united in an immediate protest against such a naked display of clerical power, but, curiously enough, the only Conservative protest seems to have come from the *Liverpool Mail*, a journal hitherto so vehemently opposed to Roman Catholicism and so whole-heartedly devoted to M'Neile that its remarks on those subjects had often verged on the absurd. Its statements on this occasion clearly had their source in long-repressed irritation, and must surely have given some satisfaction to a number of moderate Conservatives, who could hardly have failed to see the significance of M'Neile's successful

[1] *Liverpool Standard*, 4 September 1842.
[2] *Liverpool Mercury*, 28 October 1842.
[3] As an alderman with five years more to serve, Turner was beyond the reach of his critics; G. H. Lawrence was merely subjected to contemptuous abuse and warnings that he would lose his seat.
[4] *Liverpool Mercury*, 21 October 1842.
[5] There was no Liberal candidate.

attempt to dictate Conservative policy. The writer in the *Liverpool Mail* declared:

We must tell certain parties in the Town Council that however earnest and honest may be their zeal, their ultra-pious and dictatorial conduct will not be endured in the town of Liverpool. Who is to be a Councillor and who is not to be a Councillor must not be declared from any pulpit, without meeting the unsparing opposition of every well-educated and intelligent man. Trinity College, Dublin, must not be presumed [*sic*] to dictate to Oxford and Cambridge, even in this neglected locality. We have had too much of this and we can stand it no longer. We will not permit the remaining fragments of a Quaker[1] moulded into a disciple of M'Neile or Fielding Ould to usurp the part of a religious Cincinnatus. . . . Perfect unanimity in a mixed body of men is impossible with any regard to honesty . . . we must condemn the unworthiness of taking exceptions [*sic*] or of offering opposition to one or two members who, from sincere conviction, differ on one question only from the rest. . . . If the majority persist in this unhappy course what will the Town-hall become? Nothing more than an adjunct vestry for St. Jude's, a place of indulgence for lay preachers, a sheepfold for prayer meetings. What honourable man will aspire to a seat in the Town Council if he is to be perpetually worried with religious questions, and forbidden to think except through the mind of the little lion of the day?[2]

When M'Neile next spoke in public he described the *Liverpool Mail* as 'the apostate portion of the public press of this town', and spoke of not stooping to pick up a stone to cast at a cur;[3] but it must have seemed to M'Neile, as to many others, that the most effective reply to those Conservatives who wished to contest the Irish cleric's position in the town, was the electoral defeat of the rebellious John Smith by the man so significantly supported against him by M'Neile's clerk. The *Liverpool Courier*, far from echoing the complaints of its contemporary, pointed out that Smith's defeat would have 'a useful effect upon other members of the Council who may be inclined to waver from their principles';[4] and such warnings now became the order of the day.

A letter written a year earlier than the events we have been considering shows what one intelligent, if not altogether unbiased, observer thought about the state of affairs in Liverpool at this time. William Ballantyne Hodgson, later a distinguished educational reformer,[5] had come to Liverpool in 1839 to become Secretary to the Liverpool

[1] This was a reference to D. Hodgson who, as has been said, had been a Quaker before joining the Church of England.
[2] *Liverpool Mail*, 19 October 1842.
[3] *Liverpool Mercury*, 28 October 1842.
[4] 2 November 1842.
[5] See *D.N.B.*

Mechanics' Institution. On 28 September 1841 he thus described the situation in Liverpool:

Toryism and Churchism are in the ascendant, and reign with undisputed sway. The Liberal party are disheartened, and have virtually (not virtuously) abandoned the contest. Bigotry, encouraged by the want of opposition, speaks out more and more boldly. 'Every Jew, dying as a Jew, is irretrievably lost,' said the Rev. Hugh McNeile the other day; 'it is godlike love to tell them of their miserable condition; godless liberalism to conceal it from them.' The tyranny of the priesthood is said to be great in Scotland, but really I think it is much worse here. More complete spiritual subjection I never saw.[1]

6

Such was the unpromising state of affairs when some of the Conservatives, supported by the Liberals, made a last desperate attempt to bring about a change in the policy pursued in the Corporation Schools so as to make it possible for Roman Catholic children to attend them. A number of Conservatives, as we have seen, had been persuaded to accept the new policy by the constantly repeated argument that the Roman Catholic children, even if they were withdrawn from the schools when the new regulations began to be enforced, would soon return. In December 1842, when the new system had been in operation almost a year, these Conservatives had to face the fact that, although the Committee had claimed that the number of Roman Catholic children in the schools was constantly rising, there were on the books of the schools 1,149 members of the Church of England, 312 Protestant Dissenters and only 120 Roman Catholics: one member of the Committee remarked that 'with the exception of children sent to the infant schools to be out of harm's way, the Roman Catholics would not send their children to these schools'.[2] Immediately before the new regulations had been introduced there had been 936 children in the schools: some of these children had been accommodated in the newly opened St Anthony's Roman Catholic school,[3] but many had been left without schooling.

Typical of those among the Conservatives who felt concern about this situation was William Ewart Gladstone's brother, Robertson, a

[1] J. M. D. Meiklejohn (ed.), *Life and Letters of William Ballantyne Hodgson*, Edinburgh, 1883, pp. 35–6.

[2] *Liverpool Mercury*, 9 December 1842. The children actually attending the schools at this time numbered 1,168, about three-quarters of those 'on the books'.

[3] At the opening ceremony a priest had pointedly announced that the school was for Catholic children, but that if room could be found for children of other persuasions he would be pleased 'to bestow on them a good secular education—without tampering with their religion' (*Liverpool Journal*, 22 January 1842).

member of the Education Committee. Few had more forcefully denounced the policy pursued in the schools by the Liberals than he had done, but it was not long before the consequences of victory began to inspire anxiety in the victor. Two months after the new policy had been introduced by the Conservatives he had promised that if the schools were not in fact attended by Roman Catholics he would consider the new system to have failed;[1] three months later still, in June 1842, he informed the Council that 'unless the schools were filled by all classes and denominations—he did not mean to contend for the proportion, but generally available for all . . . he would propose some change that would make it so. . . . It was the intention of Parliament, so far as he could understand the subject, that the funds of the Corporation should be made available, without distinction, to all classes, and, therefore, to that extent, he should be prepared to propose such a change.' In the meantime he asked that bickering should cease, whilst the existing system was given a fair trial.[2] Such a declaration from a representative of the leading Conservative family in the town could not easily be ignored; but a Gladstone was not lightly to be attacked in Liverpool, and the Rev. H. M'Neile and his supporters appear to have remained silent.

The Liberals, naturally enough, did not allow Gladstone to forget his promise, and Thomas Bolton reminded him of it in October 1842.[3] In the elections of November 1842 the Conservatives were again successful in thirteen of the sixteen wards, but one of the Liberals returned was Thomas Blackburn, who was thus able to resume his role as a champion in the Council Chamber of the policy of making the Corporation Schools available to children of all sects. When he gave notice that he would propose a change in the policy pursued in the schools, it was obvious to all that he wished to force the hand of Gladstone and such of the other Conservatives as might be similarly inclined to deplore the results which had followed the change of system in the schools. Before Blackburn's motion came up for consideration, however, the Conservative G. H. Lawrence initiated a debate on the same subject, and it was therefore through him that the challenge to the extremists on the Education Committee was delivered. That challenge was at once taken up, both sides agreeing that the point at issue was whether or not Roman Catholics might be allowed to attend the Corporation Schools to receive secular instruction only; both sides also appreciated the fact that if this concession could not be won further strife would be useless.

[1] *Liverpool Mercury*, 11 March 1842.
[2] *Ibid.*, 3 June 1842.
[3] *Ibid.*, 7 October 1842.

Those who shared the opinions of the Rev. H. M'Neile were well aware that the issue to be debated was of more than local interest and importance. It remained as obvious as ever that if some means could be found of including the Roman Catholics within some acceptable system of education—even if this were confined to areas in which they were especially numerous—one of the great obstacles in the way of setting up a national system of education would have been removed. Only five months earlier Mr Protheroe, member of Parliament for Halifax, had proposed the establishment of a national system of education which should include special arrangements for such places as Liverpool and Manchester, where Roman Catholics were chiefly to be found.[1] Lord Eliot and even Viscount Sandon were expressing extremely unsatisfactory opinions about the 'Irish System' of education, as we have seen; and, nearer home, at the very meeting at which M'Neile's clerk had denounced the rebellious John Smith, the Conservative G. H. Lawrence had boldly justified his own advocacy of some compromise acceptable to local Roman Catholics by saying:

If this were a question of Liverpool alone, he would say nothing about it, but it was a question that would have to be met by the nation, and while differing from him they would differ from Sir R. Peel and Lord Stanley. . . . If they could get a better man [than himself] he was willing to retire on a moment's notice; but if they wished one who would oppose Sir R. Peel— one who would wish to impose fresh disabilities on the Roman Catholics— he was not the man.[2]

And now here was Robertson Gladstone, whose brother was on the verge of entering the Conservative Cabinet, supporting those who asked that Roman Catholics should be exempted from reading the Authorized Version in the Corporation Schools! David Hodgson revealed the uneasiness felt by those who held extreme opinions on the 'Religious Problem' when, reproaching Robertson Gladstone, who had recently become Mayor, he 'declared with great respect . . . his belief that the subject of education would not have been approached at all at present, but for a very prevalent opinion that the Mayor himself had taken doubtful views on the subject, and from a rumour that Lord Eliot had been put forth in Ireland, as a feeler from the Government, and that the Mayor of Liverpool was to be put forth as a feeler from the Government here'.[3] Clearly it behoved those who saw the

[1] Hansard, Third Series, Vol. LXV, Col. 187 (15 July 1842).

[2] Liverpool Mercury, 21 October 1842.

[3] Ibid., 9 December 1842. Robertson Gladstone's only allusion to this remark was his statement at the end of the debate: 'My own vote, which I beg to say is my own vote, although an allusion was made . . . to the contrary, is for the amendment' (i.e. in favour of admitting the Roman Catholic children for secular instruction).

danger approaching to make it known to the government and to all England that the Liverpool Education Committee had resolved 'to maintain inviolably the system of education now pursued' in the Corporation Schools.

Naturally enough, little was said on this occasion which had not been said during the earlier debates. Gladstone, as Mayor, took no part in the discussions but supported the 'moderate' Conservatives with his vote. There were some manifestations of independence from Christopher Bushell, whose conduct had earlier angered the Rev. H. M'Neile until a satisfactory explanation had been given: Bushell now asked whether 'they could not consistently, without any sacrifice of principle, do something for those children who were unfortunately shut out. He believed that they could, and he believed, further, that they ought.' He suggested that Roman Catholics might be given secular instruction in a separate school; if this could not be permitted, the schools should be sold. Bushell declared that he would not consent to be 'a mere puppet . . . nodding and bowing as the string might be pulled by some dictator from without'; but, fearing that Protestant children would suffer harm from seeing Roman Catholic children exempted from reading the Bible, he voted against the proposal of the 'moderate' Conservatives. Henry Lawrence, another Conservative, spoke in favour of allowing Roman Catholic children to attend the town's schools for secular education only; and he gave the only hint available of what the more responsible Church of England clergymen in the town may have been feeling about this way of dealing with the 'Religious Problem':

He did not believe that this view, out of doors, was so little extended as it seemed to be insinuated here. He had on many occasions discussed the subject with respectable persons, and with many clergymen of the highest standing, and he did not know whether any alteration had taken place in their views since, but he knew that this very course had been advocated by them.[1]

One or two other Conservatives showed that they shared the misgivings of Robertson Gladstone; and possibly more might have done so if the Town Clerk had not prevented the adoption of one method of overcoming the difficulty by ruling, a little earlier, that the Council had no power to set up separate schools for Roman Catholics.

The most impressive speech of the two-day debate was that of the Liberal, Thomas Blackburn; in the course of it he was able to satisfy those who doubted whether the Roman Catholic clergy would allow the children of their faith to attend the Corporation Schools to receive only secular instruction. Blackburn said:

[1] *Ibid.*

In anticipation of submitting this proposal to the Council, I judged it right to seek information on this point, and for that purpose I have had an interview with the Rev. Mr. Wilkinson, and am authorized by him to assure the Council, that if the plan be adopted, he and his brethren, the Roman Catholic clergy, will advise their congregations to send their children, assuming, of course, that good faith will be kept with them, that no insidious attempts will be made to tamper with their religion, or to treat them contemptuously or disparagingly on account of it. I learn from the same gentleman who officiates in Edmund-street chapel, that there are in his district, which borders on the North School, at least a thousand children, many of whose parents are anxious for their education, but have not the means of obtaining it. Numbers of these will immediately seek admission to our schools if they become accessible.[1]

Blackburn was able to show not only that the policy which he was now advocating had recently been adopted by the Irish Presbyterians, but that these had sought and obtained the full approval of three Church dignitaries who were scarcely anxious to encourage 'Popery': Dr Blomfield, Bishop of London; Dr Phillpotts, Bishop of Exeter; and the Primate of All Ireland. Blackburn also pointed out that both the former Liberal and the present Conservative governments, when they had planned to establish schools attached to Poor Law Unions, had made provision for the giving of doctrinal religious instruction in these schools by clergymen of the different denominations.

All the arguments were in vain. It was probably scarcely possible to influence the opinions of men who felt strongly that the proposed system would 'poison' the children of the poor, or who argued that, since God had prescribed the reading of the Authorized Version, the Education Committee 'did not violate the consciences of men any more than God himself did. If they violated the consciences of the Roman Catholics, then God himself violated them, and surely they could not be wrong in doing that which God had said to be right'. At all events the proposal that Roman Catholic children might be admitted to the Corporation Schools to receive secular instruction only was rejected by thirty-nine votes to twenty; five Conservatives, Messrs G. H. Lawrence, H. Lawrence and A. Lace, together with Alderman Turner and the Mayor, voted with the Liberals.

It must have been particularly galling to William Rathbone and to Thomas Blackburn that the message thus finally sent forth from the Liverpool Town Council should have been so very different from what,

[1] *On the Injustice and Impolicy of Excluding Roman Catholics from the Corporation Schools, a Speech Delivered at a Meeting of the Liverpool Town Council on . . . December 14th, 1842*, Second Edition, Liverpool, 1842, p. 9.

only a few years earlier, it had seemed certain to be. Blackburn ended his last speech on the subject with the words:

I sit down . . . with a confident persuasion that at no distant day, this plan or some other equivalent to it will be carried into effect. The children of the poorer classes will again meet together for education, without distinction of sect or party, in the public schools.[1]

But it is probably true to say that the animosity and suspicion engendered by the events which had taken place in Liverpool contributed not a little towards making it impossible that all the children of the poorer classes in England would 'again meet together . . . without distinction of sect . . . in the public schools'; for that animosity and suspicion lingered even where the events which had aroused them had long been forgotten.

[1] *Ibid.*, p. 16.

Chapter 12

CONCLUSION

I

IT was not to be expected that the decision to bring the Liverpool experiment to an end would give rise to a great deal of comment outside the town. Most of those who had once hoped that the experiment would succeed must have felt that the main battle had been lost when the Committee of Council had admitted defeat in 1839: a successful defensive action in such an important outpost as Liverpool represented would have been encouraging but was scarcely to be hoped for. On the other hand, the Conservative Cabinet could have derived little satisfaction from the intimation that their own attempts to find a solution to the 'Religious Problem' were likely to be thwarted by the uncompromising demands of some of their most intolerant supporters. *The Times*, as we have seen, was in no mood to congratulate the Liverpool Protestant Association on its contribution towards Conservative policy-making in Liverpool.

Nevertheless, the change of policy in the Liverpool Corporation Schools certainly did not pass unnoticed.[1] Lady Noel Byron, who had herself insisted on making her industrial school at Ealing Grove available to children of all denominations,[2] was shocked when she read in the *Scotsman* reports of what had taken place in Liverpool; and on 13 February 1842 she wrote to Mrs Rathbone:

> Do you not think that the proceedings of the Corporation should be mentioned in the House of Commons? and if so, it would be better that the Member who brought them forward should be a Protestant—It also seems to me desirable that a few facts should be stated with a brief comment, in some leading Journal, and I believe I could obtain the insertion in the Examiner, if I were furnished with precise information, which the Scotsman did not give.[3]

The proposal to have the matter raised in the House of Commons was evidently dropped; and on 12 March 1842 Lady Noel Byron had to inform Mrs Rathbone that 'the person through whom the notice about the Corporation Schools was to be inserted in the Examiner' was

[1] The *Chester Chronicle* published an article deploring the fact that Roman Catholic children had been 'excluded' from the Corporation Schools (7 January 1842).

[2] See B. F. Duppa, *Industrial Schools for the Peasantry*, pp. 188–9.

[3] *Rathbone Family Papers*.

'under great distress from her Father's imminent danger', so that the article would 'perhaps be delayed in consequence'.[1] However, an article duly appeared in *The Examiner* on 26 March 1842, recounting at some length the events which had led up to the withdrawal of the Roman Catholic children from the Corporation Schools and making scornful references to the new 'educators'.

Meanwhile the recently founded *Tablet*, the only Roman Catholic journal in England at that time, had been keeping its readers well informed about the discussions in the Liverpool Town Council concerning the Corporation Schools. The appointment of David Hodgson to the Education Committee was said on 27 November 1841 to have pronounced 'a sentence of expulsion against every poor Catholic child from the corporation schools'; a fortnight later, when it seemed that the moderate Conservatives might yet be able to restrain those holding more extreme views, *The Tablet* informed its readers that 'the bigots evidently wish to do what is wrong, but some are deficient in courage, and dare not act up to the purposes of their own proper malignity'. Finally, in an editorial published on 15 January 1842, *The Tablet* declared: 'The Tory blow against the poor Catholics of Liverpool, for which we have already prepared our readers, has been at length struck, and the Tory Town Council, acting under Mr M'Neile's instructions, have perpetrated their act of wholesale robbery.' Thus influential Roman Catholics in London and elsewhere were given to understand that, however sympathetic some of the Liberals might be to the establishment of schools available to all denominations, the last hope had gone that there might be established in England, even if only in particular localities, a publicly controlled system of education similar to that which had been set up in Ireland.

Perhaps almost as important, however, was the fact that the history of the Corporation Schools had not only indicated what concessions the Roman Catholics as a body were prepared to make in order to obtain education for their children in publicly owned schools, but had also shown what concessions they were *not* prepared to make for that purpose. In Liverpool, with the full consent of their priests, Roman Catholic children had attended schools controlled by a Protestant Committee, had received secular instruction from Protestant teachers and had received a non-denominational form of religious instruction in company with Protestant children.[2] But it had been frequently claimed and hoped

---

[1] *Ibid.*

[2] Curiously enough, they had continued to do so until they were withdrawn from the schools in January 1842, although the papal *Rescript* indicating that such instruction appeared 'very dangerous' had been published a year earlier (January 1841).

that Roman Catholic parents would go even further than this and, whether or not their priests gave permission, would readily send their children wherever a good education was available, especially if instruction in the Church Catechism were not insisted upon and nothing more were required than the reading of the Authorized Version of the Bible.

Reference has already been made in the second chapter of this book to evidence pointing towards a different conclusion, but it was by no means uncommon to find stated in the speeches and pamphlets of the day opinions similar to those expressed by the Rev. J. Jacob in his *Letter to the Marquess of Lansdowne on the Government Plan of Education*, which was published in 1839. After suggesting that a national system of education might be set up if the government were to establish schools in which the only compulsory religious exercise would be the reading of the Authorized Version, Jacob said:

> Some difficulty . . . presented itself respecting the version of the Scriptures to be used. But this difficulty may present itself to our fears in stronger colours than it will be found in reality to possess. . . . It will probably be in the Government Schools as in many private institutions, that the children of members of the Romish Church, . . . without offence or objection, will read the same Scriptures, in the same class with children of the Established Church.

Many Conservatives in Liverpool, as we have seen, had shared this belief and hope; and of course it was possible to show that some schools in which the Authorized Version was used were attended by some Roman Catholic children: the Archbishop of Canterbury himself had pointed out in July 1839 that in a single school established by the National Society in Westminster there were in attendance 'upwards of forty Roman Catholic children.'[1] The matter was clearly of the highest importance, since, if a considerable number of the Roman Catholics in Liverpool, when put to the test, had shown that, in order to obtain a satisfactory education for their children in publicly owned schools, they were prepared to accept conditions which some of their faith had evidently not found intolerable, then the government might have been encouraged to feel that the 'Religious Problem' was not so formidable as it appeared.

But the evidence provided by the events which followed the change of policy in the Liverpool Corporation Schools was incontrovertible and, recognizing its importance, one member of Parliament determined that the House of Commons should not be allowed to ignore it. In the course of the parliamentary discussions arising from the second reading

[1] Hansard, Third Series, Vol. XLVIII, Col. 1238.

of the Factory Bill in 1843, Mr Milner Gibson, member for Manchester, referred to the clauses concerned with the education of children working in factories and said:

With respect to the principle of liberty, as it was involved in the bill, he could not help saying that . . . when they passed an act of Parliament to the effect that the teachers of national schools should teach the Scripture only according to the authorised version—they did seem to him determined to impose terms of admission to these schools, which they knew beforehand that Roman Catholics could not agree to. Did they not know that Roman Catholics would not permit their children to be taught the authorised version of the Scriptures? When the system had been altered, and that version introduced into the Liverpool Corporation Schools, the effect had been to reduce the number attending them from 800 to 300. The immediate effect had been the withdrawal of Roman Catholic children; yet with full knowledge of this fact, they still persisted in enacting that all children should be taught the scriptures according to the legalized version. In no district was there a greater number of Catholics, compared with the entire population, than in Lancashire. A large portion of the people there were Irish and Catholics, and the ministers seemed to be trying, by the bill before the House, to make schools as little advantageous to the bulk of the population there as they could.[1]

When the government came to revise the educational clauses of the Bill in order to take into account the criticisms which some of them had aroused, it proposed that in factory schools Roman Catholic children should not be required to be present when 'teaching or reading of the Holy Scriptures' was going on, but should at such times 'be employed in any manner of instruction not religious in a room apart'.[2] As is well known, however, the controversial provisions relating to education had to be withdrawn, chiefly because Dissenters would not agree that the masters of the proposed schools should be members of the Church of England. When the government announced this decision to abandon yet another attempt to deal with the 'Religious Problem', a member who had known the Liverpool Corporation Schools in the days when there was reason to hope that ways of solving that problem might soon be found did not hesitate to say a word in praise of the schools. After Joseph Hume had proposed the establishment of schools in which all religious instruction would be left 'to religious teachers distinct from the school', William Ewart said:

He did not see why those beautiful precepts of Christian morality contained in the Sermon on the Mount, and other elementary parts of scripture, might not be points of union for different sects, instead of points of separation,

[1] *Ibid.*, Vol. LXVII, Cols. 1461–2.
[2] *Ibid.*, Vol. LXVIII, Col. 1113.

while distinctions of creed might be taught separately by the clergy of different denominations. This principle was not founded in theory alone; its truth had been proved in practice. In the corporation schools at Liverpool it had been tried with success, and in Ireland the combined system now united nearly 300,000 scholars.[1]

It was at least a gracious epitaph.

2

After Sir James Graham had announced to the House of Commons in 1843 the government's decision not to proceed with the controversial educational clauses of the Factory Bill, Lord Ashley wrote: 'Let this last trial be taken as sufficient proof that "United education" is an impossibility. It ought never again to be attempted.'[2] But those who hitherto had favoured 'united education' had, of course, done so for very good reasons, and some of those reasons—such as the expense involved in setting up separate schools for the various denominations in all areas—did not cease to be valid in 1843. It is not, of course, within the scope of this book to consider all of the plans subsequently put forward which included provisions for the establishment of elementary schools available for children of all sects: it may be of interest to note, however, that some of the best known of such plans were drawn up by men who must have been well aware of what had taken place in the Liverpool Corporation Schools during the years 1836–42.

It is curious that educational historians, whilst ignoring the practical experiment carried on in the Liverpool Corporation Schools, have devoted so much attention to what was, after all, the mere plea for 'united education' contained in the Rev. W. F. Hook's famous pamphlet: *On the Means of Rendering More Efficient the Education of the People. A Letter to the Lord Bishop of St. David's* (London, 1846). Hook proposed that a national system of education should be established which would include provision for the giving of religious instruction by the clergy of the Church of England and by 'dissenting ministers' who would visit the state schools for the purpose. As Adams rather curtly remarked in 1882: 'The scheme has been described as bold and original. Bold it was and generous in principle as proceeding from a Church clergyman, but it had no title to originality. It was merely an adaptation of the Irish system'.[3] Hook could scarcely have been ignor-

---

[1] *Ibid.*, Vol. LXX, Col. 1349.
[2] C. S. Parker, *Life and Letters of Sir James Graham, 1792–1861*, London, 1907, Vol. I, p. 345.
[3] *History of the Elementary School Contest in England*, p. 150.

ant of the attempt which had been made in Liverpool to introduce a version of the 'Irish System' into England, for even if he had not learnt of it earlier he must surely have been told of it when he visited Liverpool in June 1839; especially as he went to Liverpool at the invitation of the Liverpool Church of England clergy and for the purpose of preaching a sermon 'on the occasion of the Anniversary of the National Schools' in the town.[1]

It may well have been at least partly because of what he heard on this visit to Liverpool that Hook advised against the use of books of extracts from the Bible—this of course being an allusion to such books as those recommended, but not prescribed, for use in the schools aided by the Irish Board of Education. Hook wrote:

. . . above all things, selections from the Bible, as mere moral lessons, should be avoided; for such selections would lead to some of those consequences, from the dread of which . . . the opposition to a Government system of education is raised.[2]

If Hook had not already heard of the Liverpool experiment he would not have remained long in ignorance, for he was quickly informed that his 'Scheme' had been tried in Liverpool and had failed.[3] It is interesting to see, in the many pamphlets written to oppose Hook's proposals, how frequently the writers pointed to difficulties which experience in the Liverpool schools had shown to be much less formidable than they appeared; for instance, it was claimed that English people would not send their children to such schools as Hook described,[4] or that insuperable difficulties would arise concerning the religion of the masters.[5]

There were no doubt many who accepted without question the unqualified contention of such men as Watson that the experiment carried on in the Liverpool Corporation Schools during the years 1836–42 had ended in failure; and probably some who had earlier been inclined to support such a policy as the Liverpool Liberals had pursued now felt that the solution to the 'Religious Problem' would have to be sought elsewhere. Yet a number of those who formulated and sup-

[1] *Liverpool Standard*, 21 June 1839.

[2] Hook, *op. cit.*, Sixth Edition, 1846, p. 69.

[3] A. Watson, *The People, Education, & the Church. A Letter to the . . . Lord Bishop of Exeter, Occasioned by a Letter from the Rev. W. F. Hook to the . . . Lord Bishop of St. David's*, London, 1846, p. 26 n.

[4] See, e.g., the Rev. W. Harness, *Letter to James Phillips Kay-Shuttleworth, Esq., Considering Dr Hook's Plan for Educating the People, and Suggesting Another*. 'Not Published.' Westminster [?1846].

[5] See, e.g., Arthur Viscount Dungannon's *A Few Remarks Addressed to the Rev. W. F. Hook . . . on his Letter to the Lord Bishop of St. David's*, Oswestry, 1847.

ported some of the plans subsequently drawn up in Manchester for the establishment of local and national systems of education were well aware that the policy pursued in the Liverpool Corporation Schools, once it had been clearly understood, had come very near to winning at least tacit acceptance, in spite of the attitude adopted towards it by almost all of the Church of England clergy in the town. Among those who were closely connected with the various schemes put forward in Manchester for the promotion of popular education and who were particularly well acquainted with what had been achieved in the Liverpool Corporation Schools were, of course, Richard Cobden, William Ewart and W. B. Hodgson. In view of this, it is interesting that at one time the plan agreed upon permitted the giving of doctrinal religious instruction during stated school hours to those who wished to receive it,[1] and that earlier, in *A Plan for the Establishment of a General System of Secular Education in the County of Lancaster* (London, Manchester, 1847), it had been proposed that a book of selections from the Scriptures should be prepared, consisting of 'such portions as can be introduced without offence to any'.[2]

3

The Roman Catholics of Liverpool and, indeed, almost everyone else in the town, seem to have accepted as final the Town Council's decision of December 1842 that Roman Catholic children should not be permitted to attend the Corporation Schools except on terms which Roman Catholics felt unable to accept. A few days after the decision was announced a meeting was held of the 'Catholics of the District of St Mary's Chapel, Edmund Street', at which it was declared that the decision of the Town Council had 'virtually annihilated' all hope of 'the poor Catholic children of the town being educated at the expense of the Common Fund of the Borough'. Those present agreed that it was their duty 'as Catholics and as men, to make a vigorous struggle to educate the Catholic children of the town', who had 'been abandoned to ignorance and crime by the guardians of the public purse'; they decided to appeal to 'the friends of education, of all religious denominations, in the town, entreating them to aid us by their contributions in providing that education for our children which has been refused by

---

[1] Maltby, *op. cit.*, p. 145.

[2] Tenth edition, p. 15. According to Maltby the 'Lancashire Public School Association' modified its 'proposals relating to the religious question' in 1850 by declaring itself 'favourable to the adoption of the Scripture Extracts of the Irish National Schools as a general school book' (*op. cit.*, p. 77).

those whose bounden duty it was to have provided it'.[1] Numbers of the Protestant Liberals, including William Rathbone, responded to this appeal, and the Rev. Mr Parker thanked those who had 'struggled in the Town Council to obtain for the catholic community their share of education and now again came forward with their money'. The Earl of Sefton donated £25 'to express [his] abhorrence of the Liverpool Town Council in driving the catholic children from the schools'.[2]

As the Roman Catholic population of the town increased, largely because of the immigration of great numbers of Irish poor, the task of providing schools for Roman Catholic children became more and more formidable; and although great efforts were made it was, of course, impossible to provide anything approaching a satisfactory system of elementary education for the Roman Catholic children of the town. Nevertheless, it seems true to say that those who, at this period, opposed measures which would have made it possible for Roman Catholics to attend publicly owned schools along with children of other denominations, actually strengthened the position of the English Roman Catholics, since these were eventually able to point to the schools which they had built as evidence of their determination to maintain a great deal of control over the education of their children, whatever degree of financial assistance the state might, as times and ideas changed, feel bound, or be persuaded, to give towards the education of children of all sects. And it appears likely, incidentally, that when the Roman Catholic bishops of Ireland expressed disapproval of the 'Irish System' of education in 1850, and formally 'condemned the whole mixed system of education' in 1869,[3] they were to some extent encouraged to do so by contrasting the restraints to which they were subject in the 'National Schools' of 'Roman Catholic Ireland' with the freedom of control exercised by their fellow-bishops over the exclusively Roman Catholic schools of 'Protestant England'.

To return, however, to the situation in Liverpool. The controversy over the Corporation Schools had aroused so much passion that both Conservatives and Liberals appear to have decided, as time went on, to allow the subject of Corporation Schools—almost, one might say, of education in general—to be forgotten. When, in 1850, George Holt, one of the Liberals who had taken part in the conflict over the schools, once more proposed that Roman Catholic children might be allowed to attend the schools for secular instruction only, he was rebuked even

[1] *Liverpool Journal*, 24 December 1842.
[2] *Ibid.*, 30 April 1842.
[3] N. Costello, *John MacHale, Archbishop of Tuam*. Both Archbishop MacHale and the Rev. H. M'Neile lived to see this consummation of their wishes.

by members of his own party: Mr Picton observed that 'All who recollected the agitation which pervaded the town a few years ago on this subject, and the lamentable injury which this town sustained in consequence, must deprecate the revival of that unpleasant feeling . . . unless something of a very important character was to arise, it would be extremely injudicious to attempt to disturb the arrangements come to after the agitation was at an end'.

Hornby, a stalwart supporter of the Liberal policy in the schools during the stormy years, thought that Holt's motion came at a 'very inopportune moment', and he observed that 'it was only when questions of this sort could be carried in conformity with the general views of society, that they could be beneficially adopted'. Another of the older Liberals was 'afraid of introducing politics into the Council Chamber', and felt that 'it would be a pity if they should by any means revive within that chamber those national questions which did not come within their province'. The Conservatives manifested no great interest in the proposal, clearly recognizing that its rejection was beyond all doubt; but Mr Parker pointed out that 'the town at large was perfectly satisfied', that Holt had not produced any evidence of strong support for his proposal even from the Roman Catholics, and that 'Protestant principles were like the lion dormant, but if once aroused the people of Liverpool would support their principles, and that constitution on which these principles were based'.[1] Holt's motion was lost by twenty-six votes to five, almost all of those who voted for it explaining that they did so purely as a matter of principle.

Clearly this was an atmosphere very different from that which had existed in those earlier years when the Liberals had wished to set up Corporation Schools in every ward of the town: it was also very different from the atmosphere of Manchester at this time; and those Liverpool Liberals, including William Rathbone and James Aikin, who wished to support proposals for the establishment of a national system of education now looked to Manchester for initiative and enthusiasm on this subject.[2] No more Corporation Schools were built in Liverpool, in spite of the crying need for schools to accommodate Protestants and Roman Catholics alike; whilst the councillors carefully, and very understandably, sought to preserve peace in the Council Chamber, the Rev. Dr Hume was pointing out that in the one district of Vauxhall 'containing 13,000 inhabitants there [were] . . . upwards of 9,000 persons who attend neither church nor chapel, 932 heads of families who

[1] *Liverpool Mercury*, 8 October 1850.
[2] See reports of meetings in support of proposals drawn up in Manchester in *Liverpool Mercury*, 1 June, 1 November, 5 November 1850.

cannot read, and above 2,000 children of a suitable age who are receiving no education'; and one commentator remarked that 'from 20,000 to 30,000 of the juvenile population' of Liverpool were 'growing up in a state of comparative barbarism, and worse than barbarism, inasmuch as they inherit vices from which the barbarian savage is free'.[1]

Twenty years later, Dr Hume was still calling attention to the great need for schools; and to the discussions which led to the Act of 1870 he contributed the opinion that what was wanted, at least in Liverpool, was little more than an increase in the number of Corporation Schools. But the model provided by the Liverpool Corporation Schools in 1870 was certainly not generally acceptable to those who wished to establish a national system of education, and it would seem that at this time little interest was evinced in the curious status of the schools,[2] both of which were eventually taken over by the Liverpool School Board.

By this time Thomas Blackburn was dead. After the Liverpool experiment had come to an end, William Rathbone and his wife devoted a great deal of attention for many years to the non-denominational Hibernian School in Pleasant Street; Rathbone[3] died in 1868, but Mrs Rathbone not only lived to see the passing of the Education Act of 1870, but was able to draw on her long experience of organizing elementary schools to provide W. E. Forster with 'memoranda suggesting some practical alterations' in his Bill; Forster later described her proposals as 'the most valuable suggestions I received during the passage of the Bill'.[4] The Rev. Hugh M'Neile became Dean of Ripon in 1868, and died, apparently somewhat mellowed, in 1879; but his influence continued to be felt in Liverpool long after his death.

4

It is perhaps not difficult to understand why it is that very little has been remembered, or even recorded, of the history of the Liverpool Corporation Schools, beyond the bare fact that they gave rise to a local dispute. Various factors have helped to bring this about, some of them not very significant: there is, for example, the fact that local historians

[1] 'Statistics of the District of Vauxhall, by Dr. Hume,' review in *Roscoe Magazine*, 1 March 1849, p. 37.

[2] In November 1869 George Melly, M.P., nephew of William Rathbone, claimed that parents readily sent their children to the Corporation Schools because these were 'their own, supported by their own rates' (*The Children of Liverpool and the Rival Schemes of National Education*, Liverpool, 1869, p. 16).

[3] The late Miss Eleanor Rathbone, M.P., was one of his granddaughters.

[4] *A Sketch of Family History* . . . , by William Rathbone (6th), p. 57.

in Liverpool, as so often elsewhere, have tended, if they have been interested in education at all, to devote their attention to the history of institutions other than elementary schools. Probably more fundamentally important, however, has been the desire to forget, so far as that was possible, a quarrel which gave rise to so much enduring bitterness and mistrust even among sincerely religious men; a quarrel, moreover, of which it might be said that not all of the victors were proud of their success, whilst many of the vanquished—the Roman Catholics—soon ceased to regret that they had been defeated.

Only one of the schools—the North Corporation School—is still in existence; and now, as when it was first established, it is under the control of the Liverpool Council. Curiously enough, however, although the school is a 'county school' officially available to the children of all denominations, it is now attended only by Roman Catholic children, who are given secular and denominational religious instruction by Roman Catholic teachers appointed by the Liverpool Education Committee; this has been the state of affairs since 1945, when the premises began to be used for the instruction of Roman Catholic children after a neighbouring Roman Catholic school had been destroyed by enemy action during the Second World War. The present arrangement, although, of course, a temporary one, would probably surprise, if they could hear of it, the leading figures in the history we have been recording; but undoubtedly what would astonish them still more would be the fact that since the arrangement was made not a word suggesting criticism, or even interest, has been heard throughout the city.

SELECT BIBLIOGRAPHY

I. MANUSCRIPTS

Binns Collection of Maps, Plans . . . and MSS. and Printed Documents Serving to Illustrate the History of Lancashire. (L.R.O.)

Committee Book on Town Dues, Leasing, Premises to Sell . . . Free Schools. (L.R.O.)

Gladstone MSS. (British Museum.)

Holt and Gregson Papers. A Collection of MSS. and Printed Materials for a History of Liverpool, Made by John Holt of Walton and Matthew Gregson of Liverpool. (L.R.O.)

Minutes of a Select Committee of the Liverpool Town Council. (L.R.O.)

Minutes of the Select Finance Committee of the Liverpool Town Council. (L.R.O.)

Proceedings of the Education Committee of the Liverpool Town Council. (L.R.O.)

Proceedings of the Liverpool Town Council. (L.R.O.)

Rathbone Family Papers.

Records in the Possession of the Liverpool Preparative Meeting of the Society of Friends.

Wyse MSS. (National Library of Ireland.)

Note.—L.R.O. = Liverpool Record Office.

II. JOURNALS REFERRED TO IN THE TEXT

A. *Those published in Liverpool*

Albion (L)

Gore's General Advertiser

Liverpool Chronicle (L)

Liverpool Courier (C)

Liverpool Journal (L)

Liverpool Mail (C)

Liverpool Mercury (L)

Liverpool Standard (C)

Liverpool Telegraph (L)

Liverpool Times (L)

Note.—L = Liberal; C = Conservative.

(For most of the period covered, only *Liverpool Mercury* and *Liverpool Courier* are available outside the British Museum Newspaper Library; these are in L.R.O.)

B. *Those published outside Liverpool*

(Published in London unless otherwise indicated in the titles)

Athenæum

British and Foreign Review

Cheltenham Chronicle

Cheltenham Free Press

Chester Chronicle

Courier

Dublin Evening Post

Dublin Record

Edinburgh Evening Post	*Scotsman*
Examiner	*Scottish Guardian*
Globe	*Spectator*
Manchester Guardian	*Standard*
Morning Advertiser	*Sun*
Morning Chronicle	*Tablet*
Morning Herald	*Times*
Morning Post	*Watchman*

III. WORKS IN WHICH DIRECT REFERENCE IS MADE TO THE LIVERPOOL CORPORATION SCHOOLS

Anon., *Auxiliary 'Explanatory Notes' for the Use of the 'Children of All Sects', 'Who are to be Instructed at the Two Corporation Schools, Liverpool, from the Irish Bible Selections, with Notes!!'* Liverpool, 1836.

Anon. [Dr Sleigh], *A Visit to the Corporation Schools in Liverpool (April 1839).* 'By the Late Editor of the (Resuscitated) Liverpool Standard'. Liverpool, 1839.

Barrow, J. H. (ed.), *The Mirror of Parliament.* London.

'A Bible Christian', *A Letter to Mr. Councillor Blackburn, Containing a few Friendly Observations on his Speech at the Meeting of the Municipal Council on the 6th July, 1836 on the Subject of the Corporation Schools.* Liverpool, MDCCCXXXVI.

—— *A Second Letter to Mr. Councillor Blackburn Containing a Scriptural Refutation of his 'Defence of the System Adopted in the Corporation Schools of Liverpool'.* Liverpool, 1836.

Blackburn, T., *A Defence of the System Adopted in the Corporation Schools of Liverpool.* Liverpool [1836].

—— *On the Injustice and Impolicy of Excluding Roman Catholics from the Corporation Schools, a Speech Delivered at a Meeting of the Liverpool Town Council on Wednesday, Dec. 14, 1842.* Liverpool, Second edition, 1842.

Burke, T., *Catholic History of Liverpool.* Liverpool, 1910.

Campbell, Rev. A., *Address . . . at the Opening of the South Church of England School, Cornwallis-Street, December 5th, 1837.* Liverpool [n.d.].

Close, Rev. F., *National Education and Lord Brougham's Bill Considered; in a Series of Nine Letters . . . .* Cheltenham, 1838.

Cresswell, C., *To the Electors of Liverpool.* [Election Address dated London, 5 June 1841].

Dicky Sam [pseud.], *A Corn Jew's History Done into Heroics.* [A Squib on Joshua Walmsley.] Liverpool [n.d.].

Farrer, W., and Brownbill, J. (ed.), *Victoria History of the County of Lancaster.* Vol. III. London, 1907.

Farrill, A., *The Schoolmaster's Appeal to Public Candour: Being a Statement of Facts Explanatory of the Reasons which Have Occasioned the Removal of the Author from the Corporation Schools. With Observations on the General*

Management of these Institutions, as Conducted under the Direction of the Present Town Council of Liverpool. Liverpool, 1837.

Finch, J., Jnr. (comp. and ed.), *Statistics of Vauxhall Ward, Liverpool, Showing the Actual Condition of more than Five Thousand Families, Being the Result of an Inquiry Recently Instituted at the Request of the Liverpool Anti-Monopoly Association, with Observations and Explanatory Letters.* Liverpool, 1842.

Harwood, P., *National Education; Ought it to be Based upon Religion? A Sermon Preached at Bridport, February 24th, 1839.* London, 1839.

Hayden, Rev. J., *Observations Addressed to the Lord Bishop of Norwich on His Lordship's Speech and Pamphlet on the National System of Education in Ireland.* Dublin, 1838.

Hume, Rev. A., *Condition of Liverpool Religious and Social; Including Notices of the State of Education, Morals, Pauperism, and Crime.* Second Edition, 1858.

—— *Facts and Suggestions Connected with Primary Education, with Illustrations from the Borough of Liverpool.* Liverpool, 1870.

M'Ghee, Rev. R. J., and M'Neill [sic], Rev. H., *The Substance of Two Speeches Delivered at the General Meeting of the Sheffield Reformation and Protestant Association, at the Music Hall, Nov. 13th, 1839, by the Rev. Robert J. M'Ghee and the Rev. Hugh M'Neill.* Sheffield [n.d.].

M'Neile, Rev. H., *Letters on National Education, Addressed to the Town Council of Liverpool. To which are added a Correspondence Hitherto Unpublished with Two Members of the Council.* London, 1837.

—— *The Rev. Hugh M'Neile on the Irish System of Education, More Particularly as Regards the System Now in Operation in Liverpool; Being a Speech Delivered by him at the Assembly Rooms, Cheltenham, November 10th, 1837.* Cheltenham [?1837].

—— *Speech of the Rev. Hugh M'Neile, at the Church of England School Meeting Held in the Amphitheatre, Liverpool on Tuesday the 11th July 1837.* Liverpool [?1837].

Marsden, Rev. J. B., *Memoirs of the Life and Labours of the Rev. Hugh Stowell, M.A.* London, 1868.

Meiklejohn, J. M. D., *Life and Letters of William Ballantyne Hodgson.* Edinburgh, 1883.

Melly, G., *'The Age We Live In', A Collection of Pamphlets, Speeches & Essays, on Political and Social Subjects.* Liverpool, 1874.

—— *The Children of Liverpool and the Rival Schemes of National Education.* Liverpool, 1869.

Muir, J. R., *A History of Liverpool.* Liverpool, 1907.

Muir, J. R., and Platt, E. M., *History of Municipal Government in Liverpool . . . to the Municipal Reform Act of 1835.* Liverpool, 1906.

Ould, Rev. F., *An Exposure of the Means Employed to Prop up the Modern Scheme of Liberal Education at Present in Operation in Ireland and in the Schools of Liverpool Corporation.* Liverpool, 1839.

Peet, H. (ed.), *Liverpool Vestry Books 1681–1834.* Two vols. Liverpool, London, 1912.

Philalethes [Trevelyan, C. E.], *The No-Popery Agitation*. Liverpool, 1840.

Picton, Sir J. A., *City of Liverpool. Selections from the Municipal Archives and Records, From A.D. 1700 to the Passing of the Municipal Reform Act, 1835*. Liverpool, 1886.

—— *Memorials of Liverpool* . . . . Second Edition, Revised with Additions. Two vols. Liverpool, 1875.

Powell, Rev. B., *State Education Considered with Reference to Prevalent Misconceptions on Religious Grounds*. London, Oxford, 1840.

Rathbone, E. A., *Records of the Rathbone Family*. [Private Circulation.] Edinburgh, 1913.

Rathbone, E. F., *William Rathbone: a Memoir*. London, 1908.

Rathbone, W., *A Sketch of Family History During Four Generations Compiled from Old Letters and Papers and Rough Notes. Written by William Rathbone for the Use of his Children*. [Private Circulation.] 1894.

Rathbone, W. R., *The Life of Kitty Wilkinson*. Liverpool, 1910.

Stanley, E. [Bishop of Norwich], *Speech of the Lord Bishop of Norwich, Delivered in the House of Lords, May 21st, 1838, on the National System of Education in Ireland; with an Appendix of Letters on the Causes of the Opposition Made to the System in Ireland, and on the State of the National Schools in Liverpool*. London, 1838.

Stowell, Rev. H., *A Second Letter to the Inhabitants of Manchester on the Proposed System of National Education, Containing Strictures on Mr. Cobden's Letter, and on the Recent Meeting in the Theatre Royal, Manchester*. Manchester [?1837].

Thady Brady [pseud.], *The Happy Effects of Reading the New Scripture Lessons in the National Schools of Ireland*. Liverpool [n.d.].

Touzeau, J., *The Rise and Progress of Liverpool from 1551 to 1835*. Two vols. Liverpool, 1910.

Trevelyan, C. E., *The Liverpool Corporation Schools*. Liverpool, 1840.

Walmsley, H. M., *The Life of Sir Joshua Walmsley*. London, 1879.

Watson, A., *Examination of and Observations upon Mr. Blackburn's Defence of the Conduct of the New Town Council of Liverpool in Connexion with Their Recent Efforts to Deprive the Children of the Poor of Instruction from the Unmutilated Bible*. Liverpool, 1836.

Watson, Rev. A., *The People, Education, & the Church. A Letter to . . . Henry, Lord Bishop of Exeter, Occasioned by a Letter from the Rev. W. F. Hook to the . . . Lord Bishop of St. David's*. London, MDCCCXLVI.

White, B. D., *History of the Corporation of Liverpool (1835–1914)*. Liverpool, 1951.

Whittingham-Jones, B., *The Pedigree of Liverpool Politics: White, Orange and Green*. [Printed Manchester]. Third Edition, 1936.

Wilderspin, S., *A Reply to the Various Speeches Delivered at a Meeting Held at the Assembly Rooms, Cheltenham, . . . on the Subject of National Education*. London, Cheltenham, 1837.

Wray, Rev. C., *The Suppression of any Part of the Truth in the Work of Education, Unjustifiable*. London, Liverpool, 1843.

Youens, Rev. T., *Remarks on a Speech Delivered by the Rev. Hugh M'Neile at the Anniversary Meeting of the Protestant Operative Association*. Liverpool, 1842.

The Account of the Corporation of Liverpool with their Treasurer. [1825–26 onwards.] Liverpool.

Appendix to the Reports of the Select Committee of the House of Commons on Public Petitions. Session 1839.

Church of England Education Society. Proceedings of a Public Meeting Held in the Royal Amphitheatre, Liverpool, on Thursday, June 23, 1853. Liverpool [?1853].

Conservative Triumph or The Three Glorious Days! A Full and Corrected Report of the Speeches Delivered at the Meetings Held in the Amphitheatre on the 16th, 18th and 20th October, 1837, to Celebrate the Return of Lord Sandon and Cresswell Cresswell, Esq., as the Representatives of the Borough of Liverpool in Parliament. Liverpool [?1837].

Copious Report of the Inquiry into the Affairs of the Corporation of Liverpool, before His Majesty's Commissioners, 4th–30th Nov. 1833. Liverpool, 1833.

The Corporation Schools [Statement of the Committee of the Church of England School Society, signed by Rev. Augustus Campbell, Chairman]. Liverpool, 2 October, 1837.

A Full Report of the Proceedings at the Great Meeting on National Education, Held in the Theatre Royal, Manchester, Oct. 26, 1837. London, Manchester, 1837.

A Full Report of the Speeches & Proceedings at the Meeting Held at the Amphitheatre on Wednesday, July 13, 1836, for the Promotion of Scriptural Education in Liverpool. Liverpool [?1836].

A Full Report of the Speeches Delivered at the Great Protestant Meeting at the Royal Amphitheatre Liverpool on Wednesday, the 13th of July, 1836. Liverpool [1836].

Further Report of the Commissioners for Inquiring Concerning Charities. Vol. 20. London, 1830.

Gore's Directory of Liverpool and its Environs. Liverpool, 1829, *etc.*

Hansard's Parliamentary Debates.

'The Rev. Hugh M'Neile' in *Dublin University Magazine*, No. CLXXII, Vol. XXIX. April 1847. Dublin.

Report of a Committee of the Manchester Statistical Society on the State of Education in the Borough of Liverpool in 1835–1836. London, 1836.

A Report of the Proceedings of a Court of Inquiry into the Existing State of the Corporation of Liverpool . . . before . . . two of His Majesty's Commissioners appointed to inquire into Municipal Corporations in England and Wales, in the Month of November, 1833. Liverpool [n.d.].

A Verbatim Report of the Great Diocesan Meeting at Warrington for the Purpose of Organizing a System of National Education in Connexion with the Established Church. Second Edition. Warrington, 1839.

INDEX

Note.—LCS = Liverpool Corporation Schools